GRE®

Verbal Strategies

GRE Verbal Strategies

Retail ISBN: 978-1-5062-3823-4
Course ISBN: 978-1-5062-4850-9
Retail eISBN: 978-1-5062-3824-1
Course eISBN: 978-1-5062-4853-0

GRE STRATEGY GUIDES

1 GRE Math Strategies   **2** GRE Verbal Strategies

SUPPLEMENTAL MATERIALS

500 Essential Words:
GRE® Vocabulary Flash Cards

500 Advanced Words:
GRE® Vocabulary Flash Cards

5lb. Book of GRE® Practice Problems

September 4, 2018

Dear Student,

Thank you for picking up a copy of *GRE Verbal Strategies*. I hope this book provides the guidance you need to get the most out of your GRE studies.

At Manhattan Prep, we continually aspire to provide the best instructors and resources possible. We hope that you will find our commitment manifest in this book.

If you have any questions or comments in general, please email our Student Services team at toefl@manhattanprep.com.

Or give us a shout at 212-721-7400 (or 800-576-4628 in the United States or Canada).

We try to keep all our books free of errors. But if you think we've goofed, please visit manhattanprep.com/GRE/errata.

I look forward to hearing from you. Thanks again, and best of luck preparing for the GRE!

Sincerely,

Chris Ryan
Executive Director, Product Strategy
Manhattan Prep

HOW TO ACCESS YOUR ONLINE RESOURCES

If you…

⊙ are a registered Manhattan Prep GRE® student

and have received this book as part of your course materials, you have AUTOMATIC access to ALL of our online resources. This includes all practice exams, question banks, and online updates to this book. To access these resources, follow the instructions in the Welcome Guide provided to you at the start of your program. Do NOT follow the instructions below.

⊙ purchased this book from the Manhattan Prep online store or at one of our centers

1. Go to: www.manhattanprep.com/gre/studentcenter.

2. Log in using the username and password used when your account was set up.

⊙ purchased this book at a retail location

1. Create an account with Manhattan Prep at the website: www.manhattanprep.com/gre/createaccount.

2. Go to: www.manhattanprep.com/gre/access.

3. Follow the instructions on the screen.

Your online access begins on the day that you register your book at the above URL.

You only need to register your product ONCE at the above URL. To use your online resources any time AFTER you have completed the registration process, log in to the following URL: www.manhattanprep.com/gre/studentcenter.

Please note that online access is nontransferable. This means that only NEW and UNREGISTERED copies of the book will grant you online access. Previously used books will NOT provide any online resources.

⊙ purchased an eBook version of this book

1. Create an account with Manhattan Prep at the website: www.manhattanprep.com/gre/createaccount.

2. Email a copy of your purchase receipt to gre@manhattanprep.com to activate your resources. Please be sure to use the same email address to create an account that you used to purchase the eBook.

For any technical issues, email techsupport@manhattanprep.com or call 800-576-4628.

TABLE OF
CONTENTS

xi

Introduction

In This Chapter . . .

- The GRE Exam

- Verbal Question Formats in Detail

Introduction

We know that you're looking to succeed on the GRE so that you can go to graduate school and do the things you want to do in life.

We also know that you may not have read random Reading Comprehension passages and answered multiple-choice questions on them since high school. It's going to take hard work on your part to get a top GRE score. That's why we've put together the only set of books that will take you from the basics all the way up to the material you need to master for a near-perfect score—or whatever your goal score may be. You've taken the first step. Now it's time to get to work!

How to Use These Materials

Manhattan Prep's GRE materials are comprehensive. But keep in mind that, depending on your score goal, it may not be necessary to get absolutely everything. Grad schools only see your overall Quantitative, Verbal, and Writing scores—they don't see exactly which strengths and weaknesses went into creating those scores.

You may be enrolled in one of our courses, in which case you already have a syllabus telling you the order in which you should approach this book. But if you bought this book online or at a bookstore, feel free to approach the units—and even the chapters within the units—in whatever order works best for you. For the most part, the units, and the chapters within them, are independent; you don't have to master one section before moving on to the next. So if you're having a hard time with something in particular, you can make a note to come back to it later and move on to another section. Similarly, it may not be necessary to solve every single practice problem for every section. As you go through the material, continually assess whether you understand and can apply the principles in each individual section and chapter. The best way to do this is to solve the Check Your Skills and Problem Sets throughout. If you're confident you have a concept or method down, feel free to move on. If you struggle with something, make a note of it for further review. Stay active in your learning, and stay oriented toward the test—it's easy to read something and think you understand it, only to have trouble applying it in the 1–2 minutes you have to solve a problem.

Study Skills

As you're studying for the GRE, try to integrate your learning into your everyday life. For example, vocabulary is a real part of the GRE, and it's not something you can just cram for—you're going to want to do at least a little bit of vocab every day. So try to learn and internalize a small amount at a time, switching up topics often to help keep things interesting.

Keep in mind that, while many of your study materials are on paper (including Education Testing Service's most recent source of official GRE questions, *The Official Guide to the GRE General Test*), your exam will be administered on a computer. Because this is a computer-based test, you will *not* be able to underline portions of reading passages or otherwise physically mark up problems. So get used to this now. Solve the problems in these books on scratch paper. (Each of our books talks specifically about what to write down for different problem types.)

Again, as you study, stay focused on the test-day experience. As you progress, work on timed drills and sets of questions. Eventually, you should be taking full practice tests (available at www.manhattanprep.com/gre) under actual timed conditions.

The GRE Exam

Exam Structure

The GRE has six sections. You will get a 10-minute break between the third and fourth sections and a 1-minute break between the others. The Analytical Writing section, also known as the Essay, is always first. The other five sections can be seen in any order and will include:

- Two Verbal Reasoning sections (20 questions each in 30 minutes per section). We'll call these sections Verbal for short.

- Two Quantitative Reasoning sections (20 questions each in 35 minutes per section). We'll call these sections Math for short.

- Either an unscored section or a research section.

An unscored section will look just like a third Verbal or Math section. You will not be told which of the three sections doesn't count. If you get a research section, it will be identified as such, and it will be the last section you get.

Section #	Section Type	# Questions	Time	Scored?
1	Essay	2 essays	30 minutes each	Yes
2	Verbal #1	Approx. 20	30 minutes	Yes
3	Math #1 *(order can vary)*	Approx. 20	35 minutes	Yes
10-Minute Break				
4	Verbal #2	Approx. 20	30 minutes	Yes
5	Math #2 *(order can vary)*	Approx. 20	35 minutes	Yes
?	Unscored Section *(Verbal or Math, order can vary)*	Approx. 20	30 or 35 minutes	No
Last	Research Section	Varies	Varies	No

Navigating the Questions in a Section

The GRE offers you the ability to move freely around the questions in a section. You can go forward and backward one by one and can even jump directly to any question from the review list. The review list provides a snapshot of which questions you have answered, which ones you have tagged for "mark and review," and which ones are incomplete.

You should double-check the review list for completion if you finish the section early. Using the review list feature will take some practice as well, which is why we've built it into our online practice exams.

The majority of test-takers will be pressed for time. Some people won't be able to go back to multiple problems at the end of the section. Generally, if you can't get a question the first time, you won't be able to get it the second time around either. With these points in mind, here's what we recommend:

1. Do the questions in the order in which they appear.

2. When you encounter a difficult question, do your best to eliminate answer choices that you know are wrong.

3. If you're not sure of an answer, take an educated guess from the choices remaining. Do NOT skip it and hope to return to it later.

4. Using the "mark" button at the top of the screen, mark up to three questions per section that you think you might be able to solve with more time. Mark a question only after you have taken an educated guess.

5. Always click on the review list at the end of a section. This way, you can quickly make sure you have neither skipped nor incompletely answered any questions.

6. If you have time, identify any questions that you marked for review and return to them. If you do not have any time remaining, you will have already taken good guesses at the tough ones.

What you want to avoid is surfing—clicking forward and backward through the questions searching for "easy" ones. This will eat up valuable time. Of course, you'll want to move through the tough ones quickly if you can't get them, but try to avoid skipping around.

Following this guidance will take practice. Use our practice exams to fine-tune your approach.

Verbal Question Formats in Detail

The 20 questions in each Verbal section can be broken down by format as follows:

- 10 Reading Comprehension questions

  These will be associated with five or so passages. Most of these passages are just one paragraph long, but one or two are much longer. A passage typically has between one and four questions associated with it. As for the questions themselves, most are standard multiple-choice (pick one of A, B, C, D, or E). Some ask you to pick one or more choices from a list or to select a sentence within the passage.

- 6 Text Completion questions

  You are given a text of one to five sentences. There are one, two, or three blanks in that text. Your task is to select the best word or short phrase for each blank from a small set of choices.

- 4 Sentence Equivalence questions

  You are given a single sentence with one blank and six choices. Your task is to choose *two* words or short phrases that]produce "equivalent sentences"—that is, they means essentially the same thing. These sentences must also be sensible and coherent.

Before going into these Verbal question types further, let's go back to the beginning of the exam: the Analytical Writing section, also known as the Essay (although it's really two essays).

Essay Questions

The Analytical Writing section consists of two separately timed 30-minute writing tasks: Analyze an Issue and Analyze an Argument. As you can imagine, the 30-minute time limit implies that you aren't aiming to write an essay that would garner a Pulitzer Prize nomination, but rather to complete the tasks adequately and according to the directions. Each essay is scored separately, but your reported essay score is the average of the two, rounded up to the next half-point increment on a 0–6 scale.

Issue Task: This essay prompt will present a claim, generally one that is vague enough to be interpreted in various ways and discussed from numerous perspectives. Your job as a test-taker is to write a response discussing the extent to which you agree or disagree and support your position. Don't sit on the fence—pick a side!

For some examples of Issue Task prompts, visit the GRE website here:

www.ets.org/gre/revised_general/prepare/analytical_writing/issue/pool

Argument Task: This essay prompt will be an argument comprised of both a claim (or claims) and evidence. Your job is to dispassionately discuss the argument's structural flaws and merits (well, mostly the flaws). Don't agree or disagree with the argument—simply evaluate its logic.

For some examples of Argument Task prompts, visit the GRE website here:

www.ets.org/gre/revised_general/prepare/analytical_writing/argument/pool

Reading Comprehension Questions

You are probably already familiar with the format of the most common Reading Comprehension question: pick one of five answer choices. However, you may be less familiar with the other two Reading Comprehension formats.

Select One or More Answer Choices and Select-in-Passage

For the question type "Select One or More Answer Choices," you are given three statements about a passage and asked to "indicate all that apply." Either one, two, or all three can be correct (there is no "none of the above" option). There is no partial credit. You must indicate all of the correct choices and none of the incorrect choices.

On your screen, the answer choices for "Select One or More" will be *boxes*, not circles (as with standard "pick just one" multiple-choice questions). The boxes are a good visual reminder that you should be ready to pick more than one choice on these questions, just as you might check more than one box on a checklist.

> ### *Strategy Tip:*
>
> On "Select One or More Answer Choices," don't let your brain be tricked into telling you, "Well, if two of them have been right so far, the other one must be wrong," or any other arbitrary idea about how many of the choices *should* be correct (except for the fact that at least one choice must be correct). Make sure to consider each choice independently! You cannot use "process of elimination" in the same way as you do on normal multiple-choice questions.

For the question type "Select-in-Passage," you are given an assignment such as "Select the sentence in the passage that explains why the experiment's results were discovered to be invalid." Clicking anywhere on the sentence in the passage will highlight it. As with any GRE question, you will have to click "Confirm" to submit your answer, so don't worry about accidentally selecting the wrong sentence due to a slip of the mouse.

> **Strategy Tip:**
>
> On "Select-in-Passage," if the passage is short, consider numbering each sentence (i.e., writing 1 2 3 4 on your paper) and crossing off each choice as you determine that it isn't the answer. If the passage is long, you might write a number for each paragraph (I, II, III), and tick off each number as you determine that the correct sentence is not located in that paragraph.

Now give these unusual question types a try. You can find answers and explanations after this section.

The sample questions below are based on this passage:

Physicist Robert Oppenheimer, director of the fateful Manhattan Project, said, "It is a profound and necessary truth that the deep things in science are not found because they are useful; they are found because it was possible to find them." In a later address at MIT, Oppenheimer presented the thesis that scientists could be held only very nominally responsible for the consequences of their research and discovery. Oppenheimer asserted that ethics, philosophy, and politics have very little to do with the day-to-day work of the scientist, and that scientists could not rationally be expected to predict all the effects of their work. Yet, in a talk in 1945 to the Association of Los Alamos Scientists, Oppenheimer offered some reasons why the Manhattan Project scientists built the atomic bomb; the justifications included "fear that Nazi Germany would build it first" and "hope that it would shorten the war."

> For question #1, consider each of the three choices separately and indicate all that apply.

1. The passage implies that Robert Oppenheimer would most likely have agreed with which of the following views:

    (A) Some scientists take military goals into account in their work.

    (B) Deep things in science are not useful.

    (C) The everyday work of a scientist is only minimally involved with ethics.

2. Select the sentence in which the writer implies that Oppenheimer has not been consistent in his view that scientists have little consideration for the effects of their work.

    (Here, you would highlight the appropriate sentence with your mouse. Note that there are only four options.)

1. Oppenheimer says in the last sentence that one of the reasons the bomb was built was scientists' *hope that it would shorten the war*. Thus, Oppenheimer would likely agree with the view that *Some scientists take military goals into account in their work*. (B) is a trap answer using familiar language from the passage. Oppenheimer says that scientific discoveries' possible usefulness is not why scientists make discoveries; he does not say that the discoveries aren't useful. Oppenheimer specifically says that ethics has *very little to do with the day-to-day work of the scientist*, which is a good match for *only minimally involved with ethics*.

The correct answer choices are **(A)** and **(C)**.

Strategy Tip:

On "Select One or More Answer Choices," write A B C on your paper and mark each choice with a check, an *X*, or a symbol such as ~ if you're not sure. This should keep you from crossing out all three choices and having to go back (at least one of the choices must be correct). For example, say that on a *different* question you had marked

A   *X*

B   ~

C   *X*

The answer choice you weren't sure about, (B), is likely to be correct, since there must be at least one correct answer.

---

2. The correct sentence is this: **Yet, in a talk in 1945 to the Association of Los Alamos Scientists, Oppenheimer offered some reasons why the Manhattan Project scientists built the atomic bomb; the justifications included "fear that Nazi Germany would build it first" and "hope that it would shorten the war."** The word "yet" is a good clue that this sentence is about to express a view contrary to the views expressed in the rest of the passage.

Text Completion Questions

Text Completions can consist of 1–5 sentences with 1–3 blanks. When Text Completions have two or three blanks, you select words or short phrases for those blanks independently. There is no partial credit; you must make every selection correctly.

1.   Leaders are not always expected to (i) _____ the same rules as are those they lead; leaders are often looked up to for a surety and presumption that would be viewed as (ii) _____ in most others.

Blank (i)		Blank (ii)	
A	decree	**D**	hubris
B	proscribe	**E**	avarice
C	conform to	**F**	anachronism

Select your two choices by actually clicking and highlighting the words you want.

In the first blank, you need a word similar to "follow." In the second blank, you need a word similar to "arrogance." The correct answers are *conform to* and *hubris*.

Strategy Tip:

Do NOT look at the answer choices until you've decided for yourself, based on textual clues actually written in the sentence, what kind of word needs to go in each blank. Only then should you look at the choices and eliminate those that are not matches.

---

2. Now try an example with three blanks:

For Kant, the fact of having a right and having the (i) _____ to enforce it via coercion cannot be separated, and he asserts that this marriage of rights and coercion is compatible with the freedom of everyone. This is not at all peculiar from the standpoint of modern political thought—what good is a right if its violation triggers no enforcement (be it punishment or (ii) _____)? The necessity of coercion is not at all in conflict with the freedom of everyone, because this coercion only comes into play when someone has (iii) _____ someone else.

Blank (i)	
A	technique
B	license
C	prohibition

Blank (ii)	
D	amortization
E	reward
F	restitution

Blank (iii)	
G	questioned the hypothesis of
H	violated the rights of
I	granted civil liberties to

In the first sentence, use the clue "he asserts that this marriage of rights and coercion is compatible with the freedom of everyone" to help fill in the first blank. Kant believes that "coercion" is "married to" rights and is compatible with freedom for all. So you want something in the first blank like "right" or "power." Kant believes that rights are meaningless without enforcement. Only the choice *license* can work (while a *license* can be physical, like a driver's license, *license* can also mean "right").

The second blank is part of the phrase "punishment or _____," which you are told is the "enforcement" resulting from the violation of a right. So the blank should be something, other than punishment, that constitutes enforcement against someone who violates a right. (More simply, it should be something bad.) Only *restitution* works. Restitution is compensating the victim in some way (perhaps monetarily or by returning stolen goods).

In the final sentence, "coercion only comes into play when someone has _____ someone else." Throughout the text, "coercion" means enforcement against someone who has violated the rights of someone else. The meaning is the same here. The answer is *violated the rights of*.

The complete and correct answer is this combination:

Blank (i)	Blank (ii)	Blank (iii)
license	restitution	violated the rights of

In theory, there are 3 × 3 × 3, or 27 possible ways to answer a three-blank Text Completion—and only one of those 27 ways is correct. In theory, these are bad odds. In practice, you will often have certainty about some of the blanks, so your guessing odds are almost never this bad.

> *Strategy Tip:*
>
> Do not write your own story. The GRE cannot give you a blank without also giving you a clue, physically written down in the passage, telling you what kind of word or phrase must go in that blank. Find that clue. You should be able to give textual evidence for each answer choice you select.

Sentence Equivalence Questions

For this question type, you are given one sentence with a single blank. There are six answer choices, and you are asked to pick two choices that fit the blank and are alike in meaning.

Of the Verbal question types, this one depends the most on vocabulary and also yields the most to strategy.

No partial credit is given on Sentence Equivalence. Both correct answers must be selected, and no incorrect answers may be selected. When you pick 2 of 6 choices, there are 15 possible combinations of choices, and only one is correct. However, this is not nearly as daunting as it sounds.

Think of it this way: if you have six choices, but the two correct ones must be similar in meaning, then you have, at most, three possible *pairs* of choices, maybe fewer, since not all choices are guaranteed to have a partner. If you can match up the pairs, you can seriously narrow down your options.

Here is a sample set of answer choices:

- (A) tractable
- (B) taciturn
- (C) arbitrary
- (D) tantamount
- (E) reticent
- (F) amenable

The question is deliberately omitted here in order to illustrate how much you can do with the choices alone, if you have studied vocabulary sufficiently.

Tractable and *amenable* are synonyms (tractable, amenable people will do whatever you want them to do). *Taciturn* and *reticent* are synonyms (both mean "not talkative").

Arbitrary (based on one's own will) and *tantamount* (equivalent) are not similar in meaning and therefore cannot be a pair. Therefore, the *only* possible correct answer pairs are (A) and (F), and (B) and (E). You have improved your chances from 1 in 15 to a 50/50 shot without even reading the question!

Of course, in approaching a Sentence Equivalence, you do want to analyze the sentence in the same way you would a Text Completion—read for a textual clue that tells you what type of word *must* go in the blank. Then look for a matching pair.

> ### Strategy Tip:
>
> If you're sure that a word in the choices does *not* have a partner, cross it out! For instance, if (A) and (F) are partners and (B) and (E) are partners, and you're sure neither (C) nor (D) pair with any other answer, cross out (C) and (D) completely. They cannot be the answer together, nor can either one be part of the answer.

The sentence for the previous answer choice could read as follows:

Though the dinner guests were quite _____, the hostess did her best to keep the conversation active and engaging.

Thus, **(B)** and **(E)** are the best choices.

Try another example:

While athletes usually expect to achieve their greatest feats in their teens or twenties, opera singers don't reach the _____ of their vocal powers until middle age.

- (A) harmony
- (B) zenith
- (C) acme
- (D) terminus
- (E) nadir
- (F) cessation

Okay. Now that you've seen the structure and the verbal question formats of the GRE, it's time to begin fine-tuning your verbal skills.

Those with strong vocabularies might go straight to the choices to make pairs. *Zenith* and *acme* are synonyms, meaning "high point, peak." *Terminus* and *cessation* are synonyms meaning "end." *Nadir* is a low point and *harmony* is present here as a trap answer reminding you of opera singers. Cross off (A) and (E), since they do not have partners. Then, go back to the sentence, knowing that your only options are a pair meaning "peak" and a pair meaning "end."

The correct answer choices are **(B)** and **(C)**.

Reading Comprehension

This unit provides students with a comprehensive approach to the Reading Comprehension passages and questions on the GRE. Included are practical techniques for grasping difficult content and rapidly perceiving passage structure.

In This Unit ...

How to Read on the GRE

In This Chapter ...

- Logistics of Reading Comprehension
- Challenges of Reading Comprehension
- Two Extremes and a Balanced Approach
- Engage with the Passage
- Recruiting for Your Working Memory, Inc.
- Look for the Simple Story
- Link to What You Already Know
- Unpack the Beginning
- Link to What You Have Just Read
- Pay Attention to Signals
- Pick Up the Pace
- Practice on Non-GRE Material

CHAPTER 1 How to Read on the GRE

Logistics of Reading Comprehension

You are probably already familiar with Reading Comprehension (RC) from other standardized tests. You are given a passage to read, and you are asked questions about the substance and structure of the passage.

About half of the GRE Verbal Reasoning questions will be RC questions. You can expect about five passages per section. Each passage will be accompanied by 1–4 questions, for a total of about 10 RC questions per section.

Reading Comprehension Practice Formats

Long passages, which consist of about 460 words in three to five paragraphs, take up about 75–85 lines on the computer screen (or 25–30 printed lines in *The Official Guide to the GRE General Test*). Since only about 25 lines fit on the screen, you will have to scroll three to four times just to read the passage. Each long passage will have about four questions associated with it (while *The Official Guide to the GRE General Test* states that long passages can have up to six associated questions, official tests released by Educational Testing Service (ETS) always present long passages with only four associated questions). You can expect to see one long passage on your exam. There are only two examples of long passages in *The Official Guide to the GRE General Test*.

Short passages, which consist of about 160 words in one or two paragraphs, take up about 25–33 lines on the computer screen (or 8–15 printed lines in *The Official Guide to the GRE General Test*). Usually, you will have to scroll once to reveal the very bottom of a short passage. Most short passages will have one to three associated questions on the GRE, though it is possible to have as many as four questions. You can expect to see five to six short passages on your exam. Two examples of short passages appear in *The Official Guide to the GRE General Test*.

Argument Structure Passages (ASPs) consist of 25–75 words in one paragraph, take up between five and eight lines on the computer screen (or two to five lines in *The Official Guide to the GRE General Test*), and are sometimes no longer than a single sentence. You won't need to scroll to see the entire passage, and there will *always* be only one associated question. You can expect to see about three of these passages per exam. While the GRE still considers ASPs part of Reading Comprehension, they are significantly different from short and long passages. Short and long passages give you information about a topic, with associated questions relevant either to the structure of the passage or its content. Argument Structure Passages feature a short argument about which you will be asked the only salient question that the passage allows. In other words, the passage has been written with only *one* question in mind. Because of this disparity, the recommended approach for ASPs is quite different from that for long and short passages.

All RC questions appear one at a time on the right side of the computer screen. The passage will always be visible on the left side of the screen while you answer the questions associated with that passage. You are able to click through and preview all the questions associated with a given passage. This kind of previewing can be helpful, but make sure you give the passage a start-to-finish read before attempting to answer any individual question. This is critical for your overall comprehension.

Reading Comprehension Question Formats

There are three question formats associated with RC passages:

1. **Multiple choice, Select One:** This is a traditional multiple-choice format, in which you must select *only one* of five possible answer choices (labeled A–E, with circular buttons). Read all of the answer choices before making a decision. All questions associated with argument structure passages will be in this format.

2. **Multiple choice, Select All That Apply:** This format is also multiple-choice, only now there are just three possible answer choices (labeled A–C, with square-shaped buttons), and you must pick *all of them* that apply. At least one must be correct, and it is just as likely that all three will be correct as that any one or two of them will be. This type of question makes guessing more difficult, as there are technically seven different combinations of answers (A, B, C, A–B, A–C, B–C, and A–B–C), and there is no partial credit given for half-right answers. Make sure to evaluate each answer choice on its own; this question format should almost feel like three different questions in one.

3. **Select-in-Passage:** This question format asks you to click on the sentence in the passage that correctly answers a given question. For longer passages, the question will specify only one or two paragraphs with an arrow, and you will be unable to highlight anything in the rest of the passage. From a guessing perspective, the larger the specified area, the harder this type of question becomes.

Challenges of Reading Comprehension

The GRE makes Reading Comprehension difficult in several ways:

- The content is demanding. Passages focus on specific and often unfamiliar topics in physical science (physics, astronomy, geology, chemistry), biological science (biology, ecology), social science, history, and other humanities (literature, art, music). No specialized knowledge beyond high school is assumed, but the passages are written for an educated post-college audience. In fact, at least some of the passages seem to be adapted from journals published in particular fields for educated laypeople. You might be neither knowledgeable nor enthusiastic about these fields.

- You have to read on the screen. You cannot print the passage out and mark it up. Instead, you have to scroll a window up and down to see all of a long passage. Furthermore, reading on a computer screen is difficult on the eyes.

- You have to read quickly. You should only take at most three minutes to read a passage and understand it (about one and a half minutes for a short passage or Argument Structure Passage (ASP), about three minutes for a long passage). You may find RC frustrating for precisely this reason. If you had enough time, you could master almost any passage and answer almost any question correctly. But you do not have that luxury.

- You have to stay with it. RC demands that you answer multiple questions about the same block of content. With other question types, if you get completely stuck on the content of a particular question, you can always take a guess and move on to another question about something completely different. This will not incur too drastic a penalty. But you cannot afford to give up so easily on passages that have multiple associated questions.

Two Extremes and a Balanced Approach

One response to the challenges of Reading Comprehension is to become a **Hunter**. Hunters avoid the first read-through altogether, reasoning that most questions require some kind of detailed lookup anyway—so why not just skip the initial reading and go right to the questions? As their name implies, Hunters simply go hunting for the answer in a passage they have never read.

This strategy seems to save time up front, but you have to spend a lot more time per question. More importantly, this approach leads to many wrong answers. Without a good general understanding of the passage, Hunters can fall prey to trap answers.

At the other extreme, some GRE test-takers become **Scholars**. Scholars do a very careful first read-through, paying attention to details. "After all," Scholars worry, "I could be asked about any aspect of the passage—and if I skim over anything, how can I be sure that that one clause was not important—even critical—to my overall understanding?"

One obvious problem with this method is that it takes far too much time. More importantly, if you read *too* slowly and pay *too* much attention to all the details, you can easily lose sight of the big picture: the gist and structure of the whole passage. And the big picture is what you absolutely need to take away from the first read.

The middle ground between Hunters and Scholars is occupied by **Big-Picture Readers**, who take a balanced approach. Before trying to answer the questions, they read the passage with an eye toward structure. At the beginning of the passage, Big-Picture Readers go slowly, ensuring a solid grasp of the basics. But they go quickly at the end, keeping minor details at arm's length. They read *actively* but *efficiently*.

The goal of big-picture reading is to avoid finishing a passage and feeling that you just wasted your time—either because you got lost in the weeds or because you skimmed over the passage at too removed a level to grasp any content.

How do you become a Big-Picture Reader on the GRE? Here are **several techniques** to guide you. Keep in mind that these rules apply more directly to long and short passages than to Argument Structure Passages, which do not feature nearly as much content, in terms of either length or detail.

Engage with the Passage

The first technique has to do with your **emotional attitude** toward the passage. The maxim *engage with the passage* is not as warm and fuzzy as it seems. It is based on a simple truth about your brain: you simply cannot learn something that you actively loathe or viscerally reject. So getting over your dread of the passage is not just a feel-good exercise. It is a prerequisite. You do not have to fall madly in love with medieval Flemish poetry or the chemistry of zinc, but you do have to stop keeping the topic at arm's length.

One quick and effective method is to **pretend that you really like this stuff**. Say to yourself, "This is great! I get to spend the next six minutes thinking about *sea urchins*!" Who knows—you might actually like them, learn something along the way, and do well on the questions (the most important thing).

Another way to help yourself get into the passage psychologically is to **identify good guys and bad guys**. If the sea urchins are threatened by environmental damage, get a little angry on their behalf. If you engage your emotions, you will both enjoy the passage more and recall it better.

If you cannot stomach these steps, **simply acknowledge that you do not find the passage thrilling**. Allow yourself a moment of disappointment. Then hunker down and get back into it. Whatever you do, do not let yourself be pushed around by the passage. Love it or hate it, you have to own it.

The next several principles have to do with your **cognitive processes**: what you do with your brain as you do a Big-Picture Read. To illustrate these processes, here is an analogy: imagine, if you will, that your brain is a *company's headquarters*.

Recruiting for Your Working Memory, Inc.

More precisely, a *part* of your brain is like a company's headquarters: your **working memory**, where you store active thoughts. Your attention lives here. When you are thinking about sea urchins, your ideas about sea urchins live in your working memory. Only a few items fit at a time. Your working memory is the most valuable real estate in your brain.

Your job is to be the recruiter for the headquarters in your brain. A recruiter has two tasks: (1) to let *in* all the talented, important people and (2) to keep *out* all the people who will not contribute.

As you read the passage, you have to act like a selective recruiter. You have to let the important parts into your working memory, but you also have to skim over the unimportant parts so that you do not distract yourself with every last detail.

The following techniques explain how to be a good recruiter for your brain.

Look for the Simple Story

Every GRE passage has a **simple story—the gist or core meaning of the passage**. You must find this simple story on the first read-through.

How do you identify this simple story? For now, do not worry about whether, or how, you write down the simple story as you read a passage. Just focus on finding that story. Here are three different methods:

1. **Text it to me.** As you read, ask yourself this question: how would you retell all this stuff to an intelligent but bored teenager in just a couple of sentences? Can you give him or her just 5–10 words to describe a paragraph? You will find yourself cutting out the trivia.

    Simplifying does not contradict the principle of being engaged with the content of the passage. You should be extremely interested in the passage so you know what is important.

2. **Make a table of contents.** Alternatively, you can create a short table of contents. Use five words or fewer for the headline of each paragraph. As written, these headlines may not sound exactly like a story, but they outline the same narrative.

3. **Look for content and judgment.** The parts of a simple story can generally be classified as Content or Judgment, as follows:

    Content: the scientific, historical, or artistic subject matter of the passage

    a. Causes (effects, evidence, logical results)

    b. Processes (steps, means, ends)

    c. Categories (examples, generalities)

Judgment: what the author and any other people believe about the Content

a. Theories and hypotheses

b. Evaluations and opinions

c. Comparisons and contrasts

d. Advantages and disadvantages

Reminder: Don't forget the twist. Even as you look for the simple story, realize that, on the GRE, there will often be some important *qualification* or *contrast*—a **key twist** or two in the road. A qualification is a restriction or a limiting factor. After all, such twists help the GRE ask difficult questions. Be ready to incorporate a key twist or even two in your simple story.

For example, a passage might be about the worldwide decline in the population of bees. In describing various theories, the passage might emphasize a distinction between the pessimistic theories shared by most scientists and the optimistic theory of one, Scientist X, who believes that the decline is taking place within a natural oscillation.

The simple story might go like this:

> The number of bees in the world is falling fast. There are a few possible explanations, including pollution, climate change, and loss of habitat. Most scientists think this decline is a serious problem caused by human activity, but Scientist X thinks it's part of a natural cycle and the bees will come back soon on their own.

Here, the contrast is between what most scientists believe about the bee decline and what Scientist X believes.

Link to What You Already Know

When you read words on a page, they typically activate preexisting knowledge in your head. This is a crucial part of comprehending what you are reading. Every word that you know in the English language is naturally tied to a web of memories and ideas. But if a word does *not* activate ideas when you read it, it might as well be *zzyrglbzrch*!

Normally, your brain wakes up these ideas and memories as a natural part of reading. However, under stress, your eyes can pass over words and even recognize them, but no ideas come to life in your brain. You are too distracted and overwhelmed, and the words on the page remain "just words."

In this case, try making the story real. That is, **actively *imagine* what the words are referring to**. Re-explain the original text to yourself. Visualize what it represents. Indulge in simplifications, even stereotypes. Make up examples, and use any other mental handles that you can.

Of course, there is a danger in actively imagining part of a GRE passage—you might introduce outside ideas. However, that danger is small in comparison to the worse problem of *not understanding at all* what you are reading, especially at the start of a passage.

Consider the following sentence, which could be the opening of a passage:

> Most exobiologists—scientists who search for life on other planets or moons—agree that carbon probably provides the backbone of any extraterrestrial biological molecules, just as it does of terrestrial ones, since carbon is unique among the elements in its ability to form long, stable chains of atoms.

Ideally, you can read this sentence and grasp it without any problems. Under exam pressure, however, you might need some help understanding the sentence.

In your mind, you might imagine this sentence in the following manner:

Words	Real Ideas
. . . exobiologists—scientists . . .	smart folks in white coats
. . . who search for life on other planets or moons . . .	who peer through telescopes looking for little green men
. . . carbon probably provides the backbone of extraterrestrial biological molecules . . .	carbon: charcoal, key element in living things
	backbone: like a spine to a little molecule
. . . its ability to form long, stable chains of atoms.	carbon can make *long, stable chains* like bones in a backbone or links in a physical chain

You should *not* write the real ideas down (except as an exercise during your preparation). The process should happen quickly in your head. Moreover, as you read further into the passage, the need to do this should diminish. In fact, if you do it too much along the way, you might introduce too many outside ideas and lose track of what is actually written in the passage. However, making the story real can help you make sense of a difficult opening paragraph, so you should practice this technique.

For certain types of passages, especially science passages or any passage describing a multistep process, a T-chart, diagram, or picture can be an effective note-taking method.

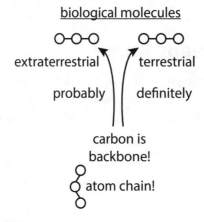

Unpack the Beginning

You must understand the first few sentences of every passage, because they supply critical context for the entire passage. If you do not grasp these sentences at first, you have two choices. Either you can take more time with them right away, or you can read a little further and gather more context. In the latter case, you *must* go back and reacquire those initial sentences later.

All too often, GRE students satisfy themselves with an impressionistic sense of the beginning of a passage. However, **forming an impression is not the same as comprehending the passage**. Given the importance of the initial sentences, try to grasp 100 percent of the beginning of any passage (even if you only grasp 40 percent of the end). That is far better than comprehending 70 percent of the text throughout.

Complicating matters, the GRE often opens passages with long, opaque sentences. How do you make sure you understand them, either now or later? The process of making the story real can help. You can also use the **unpacking** technique. Academic language is often dense, with long noun phrases formed out of simple sentences. **To unpack an academic-style sentence, turn it into a few simple sentences** that express essentially the same meaning.

In general, you should *not* write this unpacking out (except as an exercise) or apply it throughout the passage. Like making the story real, unpacking is a powerful tool to smash open resistant language, especially at the start of the passage. Use this technique judiciously.

Consider this example opening of a passage:

> In a diachronic investigation of possible behavioral changes resulting from accidental exposure in early childhood to environmental lead dust, two sample groups were tracked over decades.

The steps to unpacking a complex sentence are as follows:

1. **Grab a concrete noun first.** Pick something that you can touch and that causes other things to happen. Do not necessarily pick something at the start of the sentence. A good candidate is *lead dust*. The first sentence could simply be this: *There was lead dust in various environments*.

2. **Turn actions back into verbs.** In academic language, verbs are often made into noun or adjective phrases. Re-create the verbs. For instance, change *exposure* to *were exposed* and *behavioral* to *behaved*. Also, feel free to start with *There is* or *There was*.

3. **Put only *one* simple thought in a sentence.** An example is *There was lead dust in various environments*.

4. **Link each subsequent sentence to the previous one, using *this* or *these*.** For instance, *This resulted in …* This process mimics speech, which is usually easy to understand. So the second sentence could read, *Young children in these environments were exposed to this dust by accident*.

5. **Simplify or "quote off" details.** If a jargon word is used in an important way, put quotes around it. Think to yourself, "*Whatever that means …*" and keep going. If the term is necessary, you will figure it out from context later. For instance, the term *"diachronic"* needs a pair of quotes so that you do not focus on it. You might even think of it just as "*d*-something."

The final list of a few simple sentences could come out this way:

1. There was lead dust in various environments.

2. Young children in these environments were exposed to this dust by accident.

3. This exposure may have changed how the children behaved.

4. This whole matter was investigated.

5. In this investigation, two sample groups were tracked over time.

This unpacked "story" is easier to dive into and understand than the original sentence—even though the story contains nearly twice as many words! Also, note that the subject and verb of the original sentence do not appear until the end. This phenomenon is very common. Often, it is easiest to understand the outer "frame" of the original sentence *last*.

1

Again, it is often not practical to employ such an elaborate process in real time on the GRE. However, knowing how to break down a complex sentence into its component ideas can help you read more efficiently in general. In addition, you can use this technique if you are stuck on one of the early sentences, although it will require some effort.

Incidentally, the 10-dollar word *diachronic* means "happening over time" in certain technical settings. If you needed to know that word, you would be able to infer its meaning from context. For instance, the passage might contrast this decades-long *diachronic* investigation with a *synchronic* study of a cross-section of people all examined at one time. For GRE passages, you need to have an educated adult's working vocabulary, but you will not need knowledge of truly specialized jargon. For more on this issue, see the Vocabulary and Idioms chapter in the *Text Completion & Sentence Equivalence* book.

Link to What You Have Just Read

As you read further, continue to ask yourself about the **meaning** and **purpose** of what you are reading. What does this sentence mean *in relation to everything else I have read*? Why is this sentence here? What function does it serve in relation to the previous text?

In the unpacking technique, you saw the power of linking. Complicated ideas can be made digestible by breaking them into pieces and hooking them together. In writing, you do not always use *this* and *these*, but you often put references to *old* information at the beginnings of sentences, even complex ones, to hook them to previous material. Likewise, you tend to save *new* information for the ends of sentences.

What kinds of relationships can a sentence have to the previous text? In general, you should think about these possibilities:

1. Is the new sentence **expected or surprising**?

2. Does it **support or oppose** earlier material?

3. Does it **answer or ask** a question?

More specifically, the **Content/Judgment** framework that you encountered before can guide you. Do *not* use this framework as a checklist. Rather, simply be aware of the various possible relationships.

Content: the scientific or historical subject matter of the passage

a. Causes (effects, evidence, logical results)

b. Processes (steps, means, ends)

c. Categories (examples, generalities)

Judgment: what the author and any other people believe about the Content

a. Theories and hypotheses

b. Evaluations and opinions

c. Comparisons and contrasts

d. Advantages and disadvantages

Do not overanalyze as you read. You have been linking sentences together and making sense of them as a whole for many years; in fact, you are doing so now, as you read this chapter. The preceding is just a description of the process.

Pay Attention to Signals

Various language signals can help you link new material to text you have already read.

First of all, **paragraph breaks** are important. They indicate something new. The sentences in the simple story often correspond to different paragraphs in the passage. If you take a "Table of Contents" approach to the simple story, your headlines correspond to the different paragraphs.

This does not mean that paragraphs cannot shift direction; they occasionally do. But paragraph breaks are not random. Each one marks a new beginning of some kind.

Second, **signal words** indicate relationships to previous text. Here are a number of such relationships, together with their common signals:

Relationship	Signal
Focus attention	As for; Regarding; In reference to
Add to previous point	Furthermore; Moreover; In addition; As well as; Also; Likewise; Too
Provide contrast	On one hand/on the other hand; While; Rather; Instead; In contrast; Alternatively
Provide conceding contrast (author unwillingly agrees)	Granted; It is true that; Certainly; Admittedly; Despite; Although
Provide emphatic contrast (author asserts own position)	But; However; Even so; All the same; Still; That said; Nevertheless; Nonetheless; Yet; Otherwise; Despite
Dismiss previous point	In any event; In any case
Point out similarity	Likewise; In the same way
Structure the discussion	First, Second, etc.; To begin with; Next; Finally; Again
Give example	For example; In particular; For instance
Generalize	In general; To a great extent; Broadly speaking
Sum up, perhaps with exception	In conclusion; In brief; Overall; Except for; Besides
Indicate logical result	Therefore; Thus; As a result; So; Accordingly; Hence
Indicate logical cause	Because; Since; As; Resulting from
Restate for clarity	In other words; That is; Namely; So to speak
Hedge or soften position	Apparently; At least; Can, Could, May, Might, Should; Possibly; Likely
Strengthen position	After all; Must, Have to; Always, Never, etc.
Introduce surprise	Actually; In fact; Indeed; Yet; Surprisingly
Reveal author's attitude	Fortunately; Unfortunately; Luckily; So-called

Pick Up the Pace

As you read the passage, go faster after the first few sentences. In your working memory, hold the growing jigsaw puzzle that is the big picture of the passage. As you read text later in the passage, ask whether what you are reading adds anything truly significant to that jigsaw puzzle. Toward the end, only dive into information that is clearly part of the big picture.

1

Do *not* get lost in details later on in the passage. Do *not* try to master every bit of content. You must read the whole passage—but keep later parts at arm's length.

Only pay close attention to the following elements later on in a long passage:

1. **Beginnings of paragraphs.** The first or second sentence often functions as a topic sentence, indicating the content and/or purpose of the paragraph.

2. **Big surprises** or changes in direction.

3. **Big results,** answers, or payoffs.

Everything else is just detail. Do not skip the later text entirely. You must pass your eyes over it and extract *some* meaning so that if you are asked a specific question, you remember that you saw something about that particular point, and you know (sort of) where to look. Moreover, those big surprises and results can be buried in the middle of paragraphs.

Nevertheless, do not try to grasp the whole passage deeply the first time through. Your attention and your working memory are the most valuable assets you have on the GRE in general and on Reading Comprehension in particular. Allocate these assets carefully.

Practice on Non-GRE Material

Reading Comprehension may seem difficult to improve, especially in a short period of time. However, you can accelerate your progress by applying these principles to what you read *outside* of the GRE, as part of your daily life. Actively engage with the material, especially if you are not initially attracted to it. Look for the simple story. Link what you read to what you already know and to what you have just read. Unpack and/or make the story real if necessary. Pay attention to signals. And pick up the pace as you read, in order to avoid getting lost in details.

These principles work on a wide range of expository writing—a company's annual report, a book review in the newspaper, an article in your college alumni magazine. By applying these principles outside of a testing or test-prep environment, you will become much more comfortable with them.

Granted, some outside material is more GRE-like than other material. You should read major journals and newspapers, such as *The New Yorker, The Economist, The Wall Street Journal, The Atlantic,* and *The New York Times,* to become better informed about the world in general. However, these publications are somewhat *too* digestible. The paragraphs are too short, and neither the topics nor the writing itself is quite as boring as what you find on the GRE.

In this regard, **university alumni magazines** are good sources of articles that resemble Reading Comprehension passages in style and substance. (No offense to your alma maters!) Also, if you are not naturally attracted to science topics, then you should consider reading a few articles in *Scientific American* or similar publications that popularize the latest advances in science and technology. In this way, you can gain familiarity with science writing aimed at an educated but nonspecialized audience.

You might also find appropriate online resources. For instance, the website www.aldaily.com (Arts and Letters Daily) is an excellent source of articles with high intellectual content. Reading Arts and Letters Daily is an excellent way to prepare for the Reading Comprehension portion of the exam while also filling your brain full of information that might come in handy for the GRE Issue Essay. Make sure to look up any words you don't know, and practice reading with an eye for the main idea, tone, and structure of an argument or article.

Problem Set

In problems 1–4, make each excerpt real. Start with one specific term that you can visualize, and pair it with other words or actions. Associate these terms with your real-world knowledge. If possible, do the exercise in your head, but don't hesitate to jot down notes if needed. Check the answer after trying each problem.

1. Computer models of potential terrestrial climate change over the next century

2. Various popular works of art have been influenced by syncretic religious traditions such as candomblé, santeria, and voodoo, but few such works treat these traditions with appropriate intelligence or sensitivity.

3. Given the complexity of the brain's perceptual and cognitive processes

4. The rise of Athenian democracy in ancient times can be considered a reaction to class conflict.

In problems 5–8, **unpack** each complex sentence. Find a noun to start and form a sentence with just a portion of the information in the sentence. Then create a second sentence that adds some additional information to the first. Keep going until you have unpacked all of the detail in the sentence (this might take five or so sentences). Write the sentences down as you work.

5. The simplistic classification of living things as plant, animal, or "other" has been drastically revised by biologists in reaction to the discovery of microorganisms that do not fit previous taxonomic schemes.

6. Despite assurances to the contrary by governments around the world, the development of space as an arena of warfare is nearly certain, as military success often depends on not ceding the "high ground," of which outer space might be considered the supreme example.

7. Since the success of modern digital surveillance does not obviate the need for intelligence gathered via old-fashioned human interaction, agencies charged with counterterrorism responsibilities must devote significant effort to planting and/or cultivating "assets"—that is, spies—within terrorist organizations that threaten the country.

8. Students learning to fly fixed-wing aircraft are taught to use memory devices, such as the landing checklist GUMPS (gas, undercarriage, mixture, propeller, switches), that remain constant even when not every element of the device is relevant, as in the case of planes with nonretractable landing gear.

1

> Read the following passage, and then complete the exercises on the next page.

Passage: Pro-Drop Languages

In some "pro-drop" or pronoun-drop languages, verbs inflect for subject number and person. That is, by adding a prefix or suffix or by changing in some other way, the verb itself indicates whether the subject is singular or plural, as well as whether the subject is first person (*I* or *we*), second person (*you*), or third person (*he*, *she*, *it*, or *they*). For example, in Portuguese, at least partially a pro-drop language, the verb *falo* means "I speak": the *-o* at the end of the word indicates first person, singular subject (as well as present tense). As a result, the subject pronoun *eu*, which means "I" in Portuguese, does not need to be used with *falo* except to emphasize who is doing the speaking. In this regard, Portuguese can also be called a null-subject language, since no word in the sentence *falo português* ("I speak Portuguese") plays the precise role of subject. Some pro-drop languages omit object pronouns as well.

It should be noted that not every language that drops its pronouns inflects its verbs for subject characteristics. Neither Chinese nor Japanese verbs, for instance, change form at all to indicate the number or person of the subject; however, personal pronouns in both subject and object roles are regularly omitted in both speech and writing, leaving the meaning to be inferred from contextual clues. Despite these similarities, Chinese and Japanese verbs are extremely different in other respects. Chinese is an analytic language, in which words typically carry only one morpheme, or unit of meaning, whereas Japanese is an agglutinative language, in which individual words are often composed of many glued-together morphemes.

It should also be noted that not every language that inflects its verbs for subject person and number drops subject pronouns in all nonemphatic contexts. Linguists argue about the pro-drop status of the Russian language, but there is no doubt that, although the Russian present-tense verb *govoryu* ("I speak") unambiguously indicates a first person, singular subject, it is common for Russian speakers to express "I speak" as *ya govoryu*, in which *ya* means "I," without indicating either emphasis or contrast.

Nevertheless, Russian speakers do frequently drop subject and object pronouns; one study of adult and child speech indicated a pro-drop rate of 40–80 percent. Moreover, personal pronouns must in fact be dropped in some Russian sentences in order to convey particular meanings. It seems safe to conjecture that languages with verbs that inflect unambiguously for the person and number of the subject permit the subject pronoun to be dropped, if only under certain circumstances, in order to accelerate communication without loss of meaning. After all, in these languages, both the subject pronoun and the verb inflection convey the same information, so there is no real need both to include the subject pronoun and to inflect the verb.

9. Unpack the first two sentences of the first paragraph; that is, break them down into a series of simple linked sentences.

10. How does the second sentence of the first paragraph relate to the first sentence? What words indicate this relationship? Use the Content/Judgment framework, if it is helpful:

    Content: a. Causes (effects; evidence; logical result)

                 b. Processes (steps; means; end)

                 c. Categories (example; generality)

    Judgment: d. Theories/hypotheses

                 e. Evaluations/opinions

                 f. Comparisons/contrasts

                 g. Advantages/disadvantages

                 h. General judgments (support/oppose; expected/surprising; answer/ask questions)

11. How do the third and fourth sentences of the first paragraph relate to what came before? Use the Content/Judgment framework.

12. Analyze the second paragraph using the Content/Judgment framework. What does this paragraph say, in brief? How does this paragraph relate to the first paragraph? Where are the big surprises and big results, if any? Perform the same analysis on the third paragraph.

13. Perform the same analysis on the fourth paragraph.

14. What is the simple story of this passage? Try one or more of these different styles:

    (A) Full Sentences

        Summarize each paragraph in just a couple of sentences.

    (B) Text It to Me

        Summarize each paragraph in 5–10 words or abbreviations.

        Use symbols (such as = to equate two things).

        Still try to express full thoughts.

    (C) Table of Contents

        Give each paragraph a title or headline of no more than five words.

        Do not try to express full thoughts.

Answers and Explanations

Make Ideas Real

These specific examples will likely be different from your own. On the GRE, you will never write down full examples such as these. Rather, practice the process so that you can carry it out quickly in your head.

1.

Words	Real Ideas
Computer models of potential terrestrial climate change over the next century . . .	Big computers in some laboratory running programs about *potential terrestrial climate change* (how the Earth's weather might change) over the next 100 years . . .

2.

Words	Real Ideas
Various popular works of art	*Make up actual examples:* The latest Dan Brown book and James Bond movie
. . . have been influenced by syncretic religious traditions such as candomblé, santeria, and voodoo . . .	These books and movies show a voodoo ritual or something. (Ignore the world *syncretic*.)
. . . but few such works treat these traditions with appropriate intelligence or sensitivity.	These books and movies disrespect real voodoo and related religions. (If you've seen *Live and Let Die*, you get the picture!)

3.

Words	Real Ideas
Given the complexity of the brain's perceptual and cognitive processes . . .	The brain is complex. It does complex things, like a computer in your skull.
	perceptual: how we see and hear
	cognitive: how we think and reason
	Given all that . . .

4.

Words	Real Ideas
The rise of Athenian democracy in ancient times . . .	Athenian democracy in ancient times: People in togas voting in a public square; marble statues and pillars everywhere
. . . can be considered a reaction to class conflict . . .	You can think of all that as the result of class conflict: different economic and social groups struggling with each other; the workers versus the nobles

Unpacking

These unpacked sentences are examples of the process. Your versions will likely differ. Again, don't write down unpacked sentences during the GRE. This exercise is meant to develop your mental muscles so you can take apart complex academic language.

5. The simplistic classification of living things as plant, animal, or "other" has been drastically revised by biologists in reaction to the discovery of microorganisms that do not fit previous taxonomic schemes.

> Living things can be classified as plant, animal, or "other."
> This classification is simplistic.
> In fact, it has been drastically revised by biologists.
> Why? Because certain m's have been discovered.
> These m's do not fit previous taxonomic schemes (i.e., classifications).

6. Despite assurances to the contrary by governments around the world, the development of space as an arena of warfare is nearly certain, as military success often depends on not ceding the "high ground," of which outer space might be considered the supreme example.

> Space could be developed as an arena of warfare.
> In fact, that's nearly certain to happen.
> (Even though governments say otherwise.)
> That's because to win wars, you often have to hold the "high ground."
> And outer space may be the best "high ground" around.

7. Since the success of modern digital surveillance does not obviate the need for intelligence gathered via old-fashioned human interaction, agencies charged with counterterrorism responsibilities must devote significant effort to planting and/or cultivating "assets"—that is, spies—within terrorist organizations that threaten the country.

> There is something called "modern digital surveillance" (say, spy bugs in cell phones).
> This kind of surveillance has been successful.
> But you still need people to gather intelligence by talking to other people.
> So the CIA, etc. has to work hard to put "assets" (spies) inside Al Qaeda, etc.

8. Students learning to fly fixed-wing aircraft are taught to use memory devices, such as the landing checklist GUMPS (gas, undercarriage, mixture, propeller, switches), that remain constant even when not every element of the device is relevant, as in the case of planes with nonretractable landing gear.

> There are people who learn to fly "fixed-wing aircraft."
> These students learn memory devices.
> An example of a memory device is GUMPS, which is a landing checklist.
> These memory devices stay the same no matter what.
> In fact, they stay the same even when part of the memory device does not apply.
> An example is planes with nonretractable landing gear.

Passage: "Pro-Drop Languages"

9. The first two sentences could be unpacked in the following way:

> There are languages called "pro-drop" languages.
> In many of these languages, verbs "inflect" for number and person.
> That is, you change the verb itself somehow.
> This change shows who is doing the action (I, you, or someone else).
> The verb tells you whether that subject is singular or plural.
> The verb also tells you whether that subject is first, second, or third person.

10. The second sentence restates and **explains** the first sentence. A clear clue is given by the first two words: *That is.* The second sentence provides **specific examples** to help the reader understand a general assertion in the first sentence: *verbs inflect for subject number and person.* Also, the second sentence is **neutral in tone** and attitude.

11. The third and fourth sentences provide an **even more specific example** of the phenomenon described in the first two sentences ("verbs inflect for number and person"). A clear clue is given at the start of the third sentence: "For example." In the third sentence, you read about how the Portuguese verb *falo* is inflected. In the fourth sentence, you are told that the pronoun *eu* does not need to be used with *falo.* Again, the third and fourth sentences are **neutral in tone** and attitude.

12. The second paragraph provides **qualification and contrast** to the first paragraph. The second paragraph also provides **specific examples** to support this contrast.

In brief, the second paragraph indicates that some pro-drop languages do *not* have verb inflections. For example, Chinese and Japanese are pro-drop but not inflected.

The third paragraph indicates that an inflected-verb language might *not* drop its pronouns. For example, Russian is inflected but not pro-drop.

Logically, the categories of (A) pro-drop and (B) inflected verbs can be seen as overlapping circles on a Venn diagram. The assertion in the first paragraph is that these two circles overlap. In other words, *some A = B.* The second and third paragraphs counter that these circles do not completely overlap, nor does one circle completely contain the other. That is, *not all A = B,* and *not all B = A.* (For some passages, creating a T-chart, picture, or Venn diagram can be an excellent and appropriate note-taking method.)

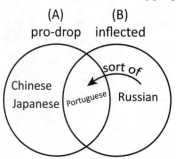

The big surprises and results are these two qualifications. You do not have to master the examples, although you should read them and make some sense of them. Moreover, at this stage, you might not grasp the nuances of the complicated Russian example. This is okay, as long as you understand the big picture of this paragraph.

13. In the first two sentences, the fourth paragraph provides a **contrast to the contrast** by continuing with the example of Russian, which turns out to be at least somewhat pro-drop.

Then the fourth paragraph proposes a **hypothesis** (inflected-verb languages are at least partially pro-drop) that follows from the Russian example. Finally, the paragraph offers a **rationale** for that hypothesis.

In brief, the third paragraph makes these points:

- Actually, Russian *is* sometimes pro-drop.
- Hypothesis: Inflected-verb languages are at least partially pro-drop.
- Why? The inflection and the subject pronoun are redundant.

The author is qualifying the example of the Russian language. Fortunately, you are given a clue in the very first word of the sentence, *Nevertheless*, which highlights a contrast to what came immediately prior. What follows *Nevertheless* is a position that the author wants to espouse.

The big result is the hypothesis in the third sentence. Note that this is the first time that the author goes beyond straight reporting and makes a claim: he or she states that *it is safe to conjecture* something.

14. The simple story of the passage can be expressed in at least three different styles.

Full Sentences

1. Many "pro-drop" languages have verbs that "inflect," or change.

   The inflected verb tells you something about the subject.

   So you can drop the subject pronoun.

   Portuguese is an example.

2. *Not* every pro-drop language has verb inflections.

   Chinese & Japanese are examples.

3. Likewise, *not* every inflected-verb language is pro-drop!

   Russian is an example.

4. *But* Russian is actually sort of pro-drop.

   So I think inflected-verb languages are all sort of pro-drop.

   Why? The inflected verb and the pronoun tell you the same thing.

Text It to Me

1. Pro-drop = inflect verbs. No subj.

2. Not all pro-drop = inflect.

3. Not all inflect = pro-drop, either.

4. But actually, inflect = sort of pro-drop. Why repeat urself?

Table of Contents

1. "Pro-Drop" Languages & Inflected Verbs

2. One Exception

3. Another Exception

4. Inflected Verbs = Pro-Drop Anyway

Introduction to Short & Long Passages

In This Chapter ...

- Short vs. Long

- Components of Passages

- Foreshadowing

CHAPTER 2 Introduction to Short & Long Passages

Short vs. Long

The next four chapters look at short and long passages. Any general rules laid out in these chapters should be taken to apply *only* to short and long passages. Argument Structure Passages will be discussed later in this book.

Short and long passages are quite similar in both their overall content and their associated question types. However, there are four important differences between the two:

1. **Length.** Long passages aren't just slightly longer than short passages. They're *significantly* longer. A long passage can be as much as three times as long as a short passage. This means you'll need to take far more time not only to read and outline the passage, but also to answer specific questions that require you to search through the passage for an answer. Keep this in mind when you're pacing yourself on the test. Only one of your Verbal sections should have a long passage. If you struggle to finish your Verbal sections in the time allotted, you might consider searching out and dealing with the long passage *first*. Just remember, long passages generally have four associated questions, and the last thing you want to do is miss all of them because you didn't pace yourself well.

2. **Number of questions.** Again, long passages will generally, but not always, have four associated questions. Short passages will usually have between one and three. Obviously, the more questions associated with a passage, the more essential it is that you grasp the passage.

3. **Complexity of detail.** Because of the length disparity between short and long passages, you should expect far more detail in a long passage. Generally, the first paragraph will be some kind of introduction, and the next two to three paragraphs will be full of dense details requiring significant unpacking. It may take multiple reads to fully understand these details, or you may skip some complex detail entirely.

4. **Complexity of argument.** Because long passages tend to be three to four paragraphs, it's possible to create complex arguments. They may begin by positing an old theory, then twisting to reveal a new theory, then twisting *again* to present problems with the new theory. Your outline for long passages should reflect this increased complexity. In a one to two paragraph short passage, there is usually only room for one twist.

Components of Passages

Reading Comprehension passages cover a wide range of topics and are structured in many different ways. However, all passages are made up of certain components. By understanding and looking for these components, you can more easily grasp the meaning and structure of the passage.

Any Reading Comprehension passage has four possible components:

1. The Point
2. Background
3. Support
4. Implications

Here, these components are considered in turn.

The Point

The Point is **the most important message of the passage**. In other words, the author has written the passage in order to convey the Point, even if nothing else gets through to the reader. The Point explains why the passage is interesting, at least in the author's opinion.

Every passage, long or short, contains a Point. Perhaps surprisingly, the Point is sometimes made explicit in a single sentence. In the "Pro-Drop Languages" passage from last chapter, the Point is the hypothesis put forward in the fourth paragraph:

> It seems safe to conjecture that **languages with verbs that inflect unambiguously for person and number permit pronoun dropping**, if only under certain circumstances, **in order to accelerate communication without loss of meaning**.

The author wants you to remember this Point. Of course, the author also wants you to understand how pro-drop languages work in general, how some pro-drop languages do not inflect their verbs, and so forth. But the most important message is this hypothesis, which is also the most important claim that the author puts forward.

How does the Point relate to the simple story of the passage, as discussed in Chapter 1? Very simply, **the Point is the crux of the simple story**. After all, the Point is the most important message that the author wants to convey. You can also relate the Point to the Content/Judgment framework. The Point contains the most important Judgment made by the author about the central Content of the passage.

Thus, a crucial task for you as a reader is to **find the Point**!

Where is the Point in the passage? It can be almost anywhere. The way to find the Point is to ask, "What is the most important message that the author is trying to convey in this passage?" Occasionally, the Point is at the very beginning of the passage; often, the first paragraph sets up a situation and the *second* paragraph contains a twist that constitutes the Point.

The Point may be any kind of important message, but across sample passages, there are a few common varieties that sometimes overlap:

- **Resolution:** resolves an issue or a problem
- **Answer:** answers a question (similar to Resolution)

- **New Idea:** describes a surprising new idea, theory, or research result
- **Reason:** explains an observation

During the GRE, you will *not* have to classify the Point as one of the preceding types. Rather, this list is meant to help you identify and understand the Point as you read a variety of passages.

Notice that **the Point is related to a passage's purpose**. The point is what the author wants to *convey*. The purpose of a passage is generally to convey that Point. However, the purpose can often be described more broadly or abstractly as well. For instance, the purpose of the "Pro-Drop Languages" passage is to describe how languages may be categorized as pro-drop and as verb-inflecting and to discuss the complex relationship between these two types of languages.

Also note that the Point may not make a lot of sense on its own. For instance, in order to understand and be convinced that "languages with verbs that inflect unambiguously for person and number permit pronoun dropping," you need to understand the rest of the "Pro-Drop Languages" passage.

Occasionally, the Point is spread across two sentences, or it may be less than explicit. However, most passages have a clear Point within a single sentence.

Note that passages do not always make impassioned arguments or take strong positions, so the Point of a passage might be less of a claim and more of a main message about the topic. The author may simply wish to inform the reader of this fact, rather than convince the reader of a debatable position.

Simply looking for the Point as you read will make you a more active reader. You will find that your comprehension of each passage will improve as a result.

Background, Support, and Implications

The other components all relate to the Point in some way:

1. **The Background is information you need to understand the Point.** The context and the basic facts about the topic are given in the Background. This component may be brief.

2. **The Support consists of assertions and opinions *for* the Point.** The Support might include concessions to the other side of the argument. This component is always present and often constitutes a substantial portion of the passage.

   The Background and the Support may be intertwined. It is never important to determine whether a particular sentence is Background or Support. A sentence can provide background information and support the Point at the same time.

3. **The Implications result from the Point**. In other words, the author now assumes that you are convinced of the Point and so begins to enumerate the consequences. Implications are not always present, but when they are, they tend to be important.

   Although you do not have to separate Background and Support in every case, you should understand what you are reading in terms of the four components:

   1. Is this the main message? If so, this is the Point.

   2. Is this just background information? If so, this is Background.

   3. Is this supporting evidence for the main message? If so, this is Support.

   4. Is this an implication of the main message? If so, this is an Implication.

Foreshadowing

Some part of the Background or the Support may also function as foreshadowing. **Foreshadowing sets up the Point.** It often does so by standing in contrast to the Point:

Foreshadowing		**Point**
Problem............	leads to............	Resolution
Question............	leads to............	Answer
Old Idea............	leads to............	New Idea
Observation............	leads to............	Reason or New Idea

Note that just as you will never have to classify the Point on the GRE, you will not have to classify the foreshadowing. This is only meant to help you identify and understand the relationships between any foreshadowing and the Point.

Foreshadowing is not always present. Do not rely on foreshadowing to identify the Point. However, if foreshadowing is present, it can help you to find the Point more quickly and easily.

Problem Set

Answer the questions below by referring to the following passage.

Passage: Rock Flour

Although organic agriculture may seem to be the wave of the future, some experts believe that the next stage in agricultural development requires the widespread adoption of something very inorganic: fertilizer made from powdered rocks, also known as rock flour. The biochemical processes of life depend not only on elements commonly associated with living organisms, such as oxygen, hydrogen, and carbon (the fundamental element of organic chemistry), but also on many other elements in the periodic table. Specifically, plants need the so-called big six nutrients: nitrogen, phosphorus, potassium, calcium, sulfur, and magnesium. In modern industrial agriculture, these nutrients are commonly supplied by traditional chemical fertilizers. However, these fertilizers omit trace elements, such as iron, molybdenum, and manganese, that are components of essential plant enzymes and pigments. For instance, the green pigment chlorophyll, which turns sunlight into energy that plants can use, requires iron. As crops are harvested, the necessary trace elements are not replaced and become depleted in the soil. Eventually, crop yields diminish, despite the application or even overapplication of traditional fertilizers. Rock flour, produced in abundance by quarry and mining operations, may be able to replenish trace elements cheaply and increase crop yields dramatically.

It may also be possible to restore forest health through the application of rock flour. Near Asheville, North Carolina, as part of a greenhouse study, hundreds of red spruce and Fraser fir trees were planted in depleted mountain soils that were remineralized with rock flour to varying degrees. Rock-dusted trees not only grew significantly faster than controls, at rates correlating with the application amount, but also manifested improved resistance to disease, demonstrated by increased survival rates. Preliminary field trials have also indicated that remineralization helps alleviate the deleterious effects of acid rain, which drains key nutrients from forest soils.

Not all rock flour would be suitable for use as fertilizer. Certain chemical elements, such as lead and cadmium, are poisonous to humans; thus, applying rock flour containing significant amounts of such elements to farmland would be inappropriate, even if the crops themselves do not accumulate the poisons, because human contact could result directly or indirectly (e.g., via soil runoff into water supplies). However, most rock flour produced by quarries seems safe for use. After all, glaciers have been creating natural rock flour for thousands of years as they advance and retreat, grinding up the ground underneath. Glacial runoff carries this rock flour into rivers; downstream, the resulting alluvial deposits are extremely fertile. If the use of man-made rock flour is incorporated into agricultural practices, it may be possible to make open plains as rich as alluvial soils. Such increases in agricultural productivity will be necessary to feed an ever more crowded world.

1. What is the Point of this passage? Justify your choice. Categorize the Point: (a) Resolution, (b) Answer, (c) New Idea, or (d) Reason. (The Point may fall into more than one category.)

2. Identify the other components of the passage, if present: Background, Support, and Implications. Again, justify your assignments.

3. If there is foreshadowing, categorize it: (a) Problem, (b) Question, (d) Old Idea, or (d) Observation. (Like the Point, foreshadowing may fall into more than one category.)

4. What is the simple story of this passage?

Answers and Explanations

Problem Set

1. The Point of this passage is contained in the first sentence of the first paragraph: "Some experts believe that the next stage in agricultural development requires the widespread adoption of something very inorganic: fertilizer made from powdered rocks, also known as "rock flour."" This is the most important message that the author intends to convey.

Two other candidates for the Point say nearly the same thing, as they extol the potential benefits of rock flour. In fact, these other sentences are perhaps even more emphatic than the Point itself, but they are slightly narrower in scope.

> a. Last sentence, first paragraph: "Rock flour ... may be able to replenish trace elements cheaply and increase crop yields dramatically." This sentence explains *how* rock flour may be able to help you achieve *the next stage in agricultural development*. Thus, this sentence is Support for the Point.

> b. Second to last sentence, third paragraph: "If the use of man-made rock flour is incorporated into agricultural practices, it may be possible to make open plains as rich as alluvial soils." This sentence practically restates the Point in concrete terms. However, those concrete terms (*open plains, alluvial soils*) are more specific than the Point. Thus, this sentence should also be classified as Support for the Point.

Categorization of the Point

The Point is a New Idea: a new type of fertilizer that may seem surprising initially. Alternatively, the Point can be considered the Resolution to a Problem (the depletion of trace elements essential for plant growth). As was mentioned in the text, it is not important for you to determine whether the Point is a New Idea or a Resolution; it could be both. These categories are only there to help you recognize and understand the Point.

2. The other parts of the passage can be labeled thus:

Background: First paragraph

First clause, first sentence:	*Although organic agriculture ... future ...*
Second sentence:	*The biochemical processes ... periodic table.*
Third sentence:	*Specifically ... magnesium.*
Fourth sentence:	*In modern ... traditional chemical fertilizers.*

These sentences give information, but they do not delineate the problem that must be solved.

Support: First paragraph

Fifth sentence:	*However, these fertilizers omit ... pigments.*
all the way through to	
Third paragraph	
Second to last sentence:	*If the use ... alluvial soils.*

This Support begins from the "However," which introduces the problem. The rest of that paragraph explains the problem that rock flour solves.

Note that the Support includes the qualifications and concessions in the first half of the second paragraph.

Implications: <u>Second paragraph</u>
                        Last sentence: *Such increases . . . more crowded world.*

This sentence tells you the result of the Point. That is, if you accept the Point, then with the *resulting increases in agricultural productivity*, you may able to *feed the world*!

3. The first clause of the first sentence ("Although organic agriculture may seem to be the wave of the future") is foreshadowing. This foreshadowing sets up the Point by telling you what may *seem* to be the solution (implying that something else *is* the solution). Note that this foreshadowing is immediately followed by the Point itself. This juxtaposition is not unusual.

The category of foreshadowing is Old Idea (the old "new idea" of organic agriculture, as the author implies). Thus, you can now see that the Point is really a New Idea: an idea that may solve a problem, of course, but you do not learn about that problem in the foreshadowing.

That is not the only foreshadowing in this passage. For example, the middle of the first paragraph contains foreshadowing: "In modern industrial agriculture, these nutrients are commonly supplied by traditional chemical fertilizers. However . . ." The word *However* foreshadows the idea that some nutrients are *not* commonly supplied by traditional fertilizers.

4. As you saw in the last chapter, the simple story of the passage can be expressed in at least three different styles:

Full Sentences

1. Some think the future of agriculture depends on rock flour (which is powdered rock).

   - Plants require certain elements.
   - Normal fertilizers do not give you the *trace* elements such as iron.
   - Rock flour might fill the gap.

2. Rock flour might also help forests.

3. Some rock flour is bad, even poisonous.
   But most would be fine.
   Glaciers make natural rock flour, which is good for the soil.
   If you use rock flour, maybe you can feed the world.

Text It to Me

1. Agricult. future = rock flour (= powder). Gives plants missing trace elems.

2. Rock flour = good for forests.

3. Some flour = bad. But glaciers make it & it's good. Might feed the world.

Table of Contents

1. Rock Flour as Future of Agriculture

2. Rock Flour Helps Forests

3. Concerns; Reassuring Glaciers

CHAPTER 3

Short Passages

In This Chapter ...

CHAPTER 3 Short Passages

As noted in Chapter 1, short passages consist of about 160 words in one to two short paragraphs, usually with one to three associated questions. If you struggle with pacing on the GRE, you might want to do a quick preview of the number of questions associated with a given passage. If it's only one, you might be able to afford skipping or skimming that passage. Previewing also helps you to know what to pay special attention to while reading the passage.

To approach short passages, recall the seven principles of active, efficient reading:

1. Engage with the passage.

2. Look for the simple story.

3. Link to what you already know.

4. Unpack the beginning.

5. Link to what you have just read.

6. Pay attention to signals.

7. Pick up the pace.

Imagine that you are taking the GRE and a new RC passage pops up. How do you apply these reading principles? Let us imagine two scenarios:

Positive scenario: You are feeling good about your performance on the GRE overall and on the Verbal section in particular. You are on pace or even ahead of pace. You are focused and energetic. Even better, the passage is about killer whales—and you happen to have majored in marine biology, a subject close to your heart.

Negative scenario: You are feeling anxious about your performance on the GRE overall and on the Verbal section in particular. You are short on time. You are tired and scatterbrained. Making matters even worse, the passage is about killer whales—and you happen to hate biology. You even dislike the ocean.

In the positive scenario, it will be easy for you to apply the seven principles. You love the subject, you already know something about it, and you are in good shape on the exam. In this case, what you should do is **simply read the passage**. Enjoy it as you quickly digest it; simply be sure not to bring in outside knowledge. In the positive scenario, you can read the passage rapidly, easily, and effectively, and you can then move to answering the questions, a subject that will be covered later in this book.

The negative scenario might happen to you during the GRE. In fact, it is likely that you will be stressed at least some of the time during the exam. Moreover, even in the best of circumstances, you *might* find that only one or two passages fall on your home turf of topics. The others will probably be unfamiliar territory. In addition, the GRE makes otherwise interesting passages as boring and tedious as possible by using dry, clinical language and overloading the passages with details.

So how do you apply the seven principles in the negative scenario, that is, when the passage is unfriendly and you are stressed out?

Don't Just Read, Do Something!

The temptation will be simply to read the passage and then jump into the questions. The problem with this approach is that your grasp of the passage will be superficial. Moderately difficult questions will trick or stump you. You will have to reread the passage nonsystematically. In fact, you might even answer every question without feeling that you *ever* understood this passage!

When the passage is unfriendly, you should NOT *just* read it!

There is a better way. Students use three general methods to learn something new:

1. They read, as when they read a college textbook (or this guide).

2. They write, as when they take notes during a college lecture.

3. They listen, as during a lecture in a college course.

You can build your comprehension more quickly and effectively—*especially* when the passage is unfriendly— by using more than one learning method. Under normal circumstances, you cannot have someone read the passage aloud to you, nor can you read the passage aloud to yourself (although you might benefit from mouthing it or *quietly* mumbling to yourself). Thus, **you should make use of *writing***, which activates a second learning process that facilitates comprehension.

Identifying and writing down key elements of the passage will force you to read *actively* as opposed to passively. If you write in the right way, your comprehension of unfriendly passages will improve dramatically. Indeed, you should develop a writing strategy for *every* passage during practice, because you need that strategy to be robust under all circumstances.

Of course, it is not possible to rewrite an entire passage in the time allocated for Reading Comprehension questions. But even writing and summarizing key elements will help you understand the structure and content of a passage while saving you time for questions.

Now, what you write during the GRE must be different from other kinds of notes you have taken (e.g., during a college lecture). In college, you take notes in order to study from them later. In contrast, **you take notes during the GRE in order to create comprehension right there and then**. This is a very different goal. In fact, you should take notes that, in theory, you could *crumple up and throw away* before answering any questions, if you were forced to. Why take notes, then? To force your mind to carry out the Seven Principles of Active, Effective Reading—*not* to study for some later test. So you must fundamentally change your approach to taking notes.

You are looking for the **simple story** of the passage. You do *not* want much detail! Imagine that you have limited ink and need to create an outline of the story. What is so important that you're willing to spare some precious ink to jot it down?

When you encounter a short passage, create a Headline List of the passage during your first reading.

A Headline List serves two main purposes:

1. It provides a general structure and overall understanding without getting you bogged down in details.

2. It promotes a fast first reading of a passage that still gives you enough time to answer questions.

The Headline List

To create a Headline List, follow these steps:

1. A headline summarizes the main idea of a newspaper article. Likewise, **your Headline List should summarize or indicate the main idea of each paragraph.**

Most paragraphs have one topic sentence. Generally, the topic sentence is the first or second sentence, although it can also be a combination of the two.

Read the first sentence or two of the first paragraph. Identify the topic sentence and summarize it concisely on your scratch paper in the form of a headline. Use either the Text It to Me style or the Table of Contents style (a headline of five words or fewer). If you cannot identify a topic sentence, then your headline should summarize the main idea or purpose of the paragraph in your own words.

2. Read the rest of the paragraph with an eye for big surprises and results.

As you read the rest of the paragraph, briefly summarize anything else that is very important or surprising in the paragraph. Often, this will consist of jotting down just a word or two. You may not add anything to the original topic sentence if the paragraph fits neatly within the scope of that sentence.

3. If there is a second paragraph, follow the same process.

Each paragraph may introduce a whole new idea. Therefore, your approach to any second paragraph should be the same as with the first paragraph. As you create your Headline List, relate the headlines to each other.

How much you read before stopping to take notes depends. If the passage is really tough, slow down and go sentence by sentence. If the passage is easier and you think you are getting it, read more (even a whole paragraph) before taking notes on that chunk. Stopping to take notes can take you out of the flow. At the same time, you should force yourself to stop periodically and consider adding to your Headline List.

4. Once you have finished the passage, **identify the passage's Point**.

After you have finished reading the passage and creating the Headline List, make sure you know what the Point of the passage is. If it is not in your Headline List already, be sure to add it. Then label or mark the Point so that you articulate it to yourself. Now proceed to the first question.

Common Notations

To create your Headline List as quickly as possible, consider the following notations:

- Abbreviate long terms, particularly proper nouns.
- Use arrows (e.g., →) to indicate cause-effect relationships or changes over time.
- If a passage contains speakers, writers, points of view, arguments, and so on, keep them organized by placing the person with the opinion before a given opinion with a colon. For example, if a passage says that historians believe that economic interests led to the outbreak of war, you might write: **H: econ int → war**.
- If you write down examples, mark them with parentheses or "Ex." For example: **Ex: Insects = inflexible (wasp)**.
- Number each paragraph. Paragraph breaks are important to remember.

You will have your own note-taking style. For instance, if you are a visual thinker, you may draw pictures or use graphs to show relationships. Regardless of the notations you use, practice them and keep them *consistent.*

Using Your Headline List

How do you use your Headline List to answer questions about the passage?

- You should be able to answer all *General* questions without referring either to your notes or to the passage. General questions pertain to the passage's main idea, its purpose, or its structure overall.

- As for *Specific* questions, you will have to return to the passage to find particular details. Do not depend on your memory, as the GRE knows how to take advantage of this. *Prove* your answer in the text. In many cases, you will be able to find the relevant details on your own. But you can also use your Headline List as a search tool to help you know which paragraph to check.

Timing for Short Passages

To determine how much time to spend on a passage, use this as a rule: **you have about one and one-half minutes per Reading Comprehension question, total**. The total number of minutes includes time for reading the passage, creating a Headline List, and answering all the questions. So, if a short passage has two questions associated with it, you would have roughly *Three minutes* to read and sketch the short passage and then answer the two associated questions.

Out of this three-minute period, you should spend approximately one and one-half minutes reading the passage and generating your Headline List. Then you should spend an average of 45 seconds actually answering each question. You should try to answer General questions in about 30 seconds. Specific questions will be more time-consuming, because they demand that you review the text of the passage. You should allocate up to 60 seconds for any Specific question.

You can best learn to create Headline Lists with repeated practice. Study the following model, then do the Problem Set exercises. Later, for more practice, create Headline Lists for passages from the ETS Guide.

Model Short Passage:

Insect Behavior

Insect behavior generally appears to be explicable in terms of unconscious, inflexible stimulus-response mechanisms. For instance, a female sphex wasp leaves her egg sealed in a burrow alongside a paralyzed grasshopper, which her larvae can eat upon hatching. Before she deposits the grasshopper in the burrow, she inspects the burrow; if the inspection reveals no problems, she drags the grasshopper inside by its antennae. As thoughtful as this behavior appears, it reveals its mechanistic character upon interference. Darwin discovered that prior removal of the grasshopper's antennae prevents the wasp from depositing the grasshopper, even though the legs or ovipositor could also serve as handles. Likewise, Fabre moved the grasshopper a few centimeters away from the burrow's mouth while the wasp was inside inspecting. The wasp returned the grasshopper to the edge of the burrow and then began a new inspection. Fabre performed this disruptive maneuver 40 times; the wasp's response never changed.

Model Headline List:

Insect Behavior

Insect behav = unconsc stim/resp = inflexible ← Point

    Ex: wasp

    D: w won't drag g w/o ant

    F: endless cycle

The Headline List summarizes the topic sentence of the paragraph, and the example is briefly listed. Likewise, the two experiments are simply bullet points. Note that single letters can stand for whole words (w = wasp, g = grasshopper). Remember that you are not taking notes that you need to study from later!

In this example, the Point of the passage is the first sentence of the paragraph. The rest of the passage is Support for the Point.

Problem Set

1. Read the following passage and create a Headline List within 2.5–3 minutes (note that this is a bit more time than you'll want to spend on the actual exam). After answering the questions below the passage, compare your Headline List to the sample in the answer key. How well did your Headline List succeed in pushing you to read actively? How well did it capture the simple story of the passage without getting bloated with details?

Passage: Arousal and Attraction

In 1974, psychologists Dutton and Aron discovered that male subjects who had just crossed a precarious wire-suspension bridge reacted to an attractive female interviewer differently than subjects who had instead crossed a low, solid bridge. Specifically, in response to a questionnaire that secretly measured sexual arousal, subjects from the wire-suspension bridge revealed significantly more sexual imagery than the others; moreover, a far greater fraction of wire-suspension subjects than of solid-bridge subjects contacted the interviewer afterward. Dutton and Aron explained their results in terms of misattribution. In their view, subjects crossing the wobbly bridge experienced physiological fear reactions, such as increased heart rate. Such reactions with ambiguous or suppressed causes are easily reinterpreted, in the presence of a potential partner, as sexual attraction. However, Foster and others later found that an unattractive interviewer is actually perceived as much less attractive by subjects physiologically aroused by fearful situations. Thus, the arousal is reinterpreted either as attraction or as repulsion, but in either case, the true cause is masked.

2. What is the Point of this passage? Justify your choice.

3. Identify the other components of the passage, if present: Background, Support, and Implications. Again, justify your assignments.

4. Based on the passage, which of the following could be reasonably assumed about passengers of a particularly turbulent flight? Select all that apply.

    [A] They would be likely to misattribute the cause of a sexual attraction they felt to a fellow passenger during a lull in turbulence.

    [B] They would be likely to misattribute the cause of a sexual attraction they felt to a fellow passenger a few days after the flight.

    [C] They would be more likely to find themselves viscerally disgusted by a baggage handler at their arrival gate whom they typically would have found merely unappealing.

5. Read the following passage and create a Headline List in 1.5 minutes. After answering the questions below the passage, compare your Headline List to the sample in the answer key and provide critiques.

Passage: Animal Treatment

In the early nineteenth century, educated Britons came to accept the then-novel notion that animals must be treated humanely, as evidenced by the outlawing of certain forms of domestic animal abuse, as well as the founding of the Society for the Prevention of Cruelty to Animals in 1824. This trend may be regarded as part of a broader embrace of compassionate ideals, such as abolitionism and alleviation of poverty. For instance, in 1785 the Society for the Relief of Persons Imprisoned for Small Sums persuaded Parliament to restrict that archaic punishment, and similar societies focused on various issues of humane treatment emerged around this time. However, a deeper explanation should be traced to socioeconomic conditions related to ongoing industrialization. Those protesting cruelty to animals were city dwellers who viewed animals as pets rather than as livestock, despite the ubiquity of horse transport. In fact, nature was no longer considered menacing, since society's victory over wilderness was conspicuous. Animals were to some extent romanticized as emblems of a bucolic, pre-industrial age.

6. What is the Point of this passage? Justify your choice.

7. Identify the other components of the passage, if present: Background, Support, and Implications. Again, justify your assignments.

8. Based on the passage, which of the following is true about the first few decades of the nineteenth century? Select all that apply.

   [A] English society was becoming more compassionate toward some oppressed animals and humans.

   [B] England was entering a more bucolic age of industry.

   [C] Some viewed industrialization as a victory over wilderness.

9. Select the sentence that, according to the author, would best explain the early nineteenth-century trends toward more humane treatment of animals.

Answers and Explanations

Problem Set

1. Arousal and Attraction—Headline List

> Psychs D+A:
>
> Wire bridge: aroused → attr
>
> Expl: misattrib physiol fear AS attractn
>
> BUT actually: attr OR repuls masks the cause ← Point

2. The Point of the passage is in the last sentence: "Thus, the arousal is reinterpreted either as attraction or as repulsion, but in either case, the true cause is masked." The author is taking a little stand here. Everything in the passage leads up to this Point.

3. The paragraph is all Background and Support, leading up to the Point at the end.

4. A, C

This is a Select-One-or-More question that asks you to extrapolate from the bridge example to an example involving an airplane. This isn't nearly as complicated as it sounds, as a turbulent flight would be almost exactly like crossing a wobbly bridge.

- (A) **CORRECT.** This example is analogous to the one given in the passage. A passenger on a turbulent flight would still likely be experiencing "physiological fear reactions" even during a lull in the turbulence. This physiological arousal can be "reinterpreted either as attraction or repulsion," so any feeling of attraction is likely to be caused by the fear reaction.

- (B) The passage stresses the manner in which the researchers interviewed subjects *immediately* after crossing the bridge, when the "physiological fear reactions" were still fresh. A few days after a turbulent flight, passengers would be unlikely to continue to experience those reactions.

- (C) **CORRECT.** This example is analagous to the one given in the passage. A passenger coming off of a turbulent flight would likely still be experiencing "physiological fear reactions," which you are told can cause repulsion as easily as attraction. The passage states that an "unattractive interviewer is actually perceived as much less attractive by subjects physiologically aroused by fearful situations."

5. Animal Treatment—Headline List

> 19th c: Educ B's: animal cruelty = bad
>
> Why: Part of broader embrace of compassn. Ex's ← Point
>
> Deeper Why: Industzn → city dwellers ← Point
>
> Nature romantic

6. The Point here is complicated; it needs to be synthesized from key ideas spread throughout the paragraph. The main message of the author can be written like this:

> *19th c. British rejection of cruelty to animals was part of a broader embrace of compassion, but actually stemmed from a romanticization of nature by city dwellers.*

7. The paragraph begins with Background (rejection of animal cruelty), then moves to Support (causes of this rejection).

8. A, C

This is a Select-One-or-More question asking about the beginning of the nineteenth century. The passage mentions a few dates, all of which will be useful in determining what was true at the dawn of the nineteenth century.

(A) **CORRECT.** The passage states that, in the early nineteenth century, some "forms of domestic animal abuse" were outlawed and society was also embracing "abolitionism and alleviation of poverty" (both of which are aimed at humans).

(B) The last sentence says that in the nineteenth century, animals became emblems of a "bucolic, pre-industrial age." The point is that that bucolic age was coming to an end at this time. England was not "entering" that age.

(C) **CORRECT.** The author's "deeper explanation" relates the trends to "ongoing industrialization," as city dwellers came to view animals more as pets. The passage then states that "nature was no longer menacing, since society's victory over wilderness was conspicuous." Society, in this context, is the city dwellers who are living a more industrialized life.

9. This is another Select-in-Passage question asking for examples. The second sentence states, "This trend may be regarded as part of a broader embrace of compassionate ideals, such as abolitionism and alleviation of poverty." This sentence provides one possible explanation, but the author presents a "deeper explanation" later on. "However, a deeper explanation should be traced to socioeconomic conditions related to ongoing industrialization" is the correct sentence.

Long Passages

In This Chapter ...

- Headline Notes

- Using Your Notes

- Timing for Long Passages

- Common Structures of Long Passages

- Model Long Passage: Electroconvulsive Therapy

- Model Headline Notes: Electroconvulsive Therapy

CHAPTER 4 Long Passages

Long passages consist of approximately 450–475 words spread over three to five paragraphs and 75 to 85 lines on the computer screen. Most likely, you will see one long passage per GRE exam (one Verbal section will have a long passage, and one will not). Each long passage will likely have four questions.

Long passages present much the same challenge as short passages, but with increased length and complexity. Further, because there are multiple associated questions, it is not typically advisable to guess on the entire passage. However, the individual questions associated with long passages will not be any harder, on average, than questions for shorter passages.

As discussed in the case of short passages, what really makes the difference between an easy, or "friendly," passage and a difficult, or "unfriendly," one is your background (*How much do you like this topic? What do you already know about this topic?*). It also depends on your status on the exam at that moment (*Are you ahead of pace or lagging behind? How are you feeling about how you are doing? How is your energy level, your focus, your processing speed?*).

If the long passage turns out to be friendly, then simply read it and take any notes you like (indeed, it is a good habit to take light notes every time).

On the other hand, when the passage is unfriendly (as, in fact, the majority of long passages are likely to be), you need to **know what to read and what not to read**, and you need a **robust note-taking process**, in order to get through the passage actively, rapidly, and effectively. Also, remember that a passage that looks friendly at first glance may turn ugly in the middle. Concentrate on the main ideas, and continue to take light notes.

The note-taking process is largely the same for long passages as for short ones, except that you will pay a bit more attention to the first paragraph of a long passage. As with short passages, the note-taking process serves two main purposes:

1. It provides a general structure and overall understanding without getting you bogged down in details.

2. It promotes an efficient first reading that still gives you enough time to answer questions.

Headline Notes

The creation of your notes has three key elements:

1. The first paragraph of a long passage sets the basic context and gives shape to the text. As such, you'll start out reading more slowly and carefully.

Unlike most short passages, long passages often have a first paragraph that is substantially more important than the other paragraphs, setting the tone and (typically) describing what the rest of the passage will be about. As a result, take a little more time to summarize the first paragraph, making sure that you thoroughly understand the main idea as well as any big surprises or contrasting ideas.

As with short passages, you must decide how frequently you stop to take notes: after each sentence, after a couple of sentences, or after the entire paragraph. Base your decision on how well you are grasping the content and purpose of the text, as well as the length of the paragraph at issue. The more difficult the passage, the more frequently you should stop to process what you have read. (Note: If something is too detailed, however, don't get bogged down; start skimming and looking only for big ideas.)

2. Note the main point of each remaining paragraph. As you get further into a long passage, you will be able to pick up speed and pay less attention to detail. Continue to read for main ideas and contrasts or surprises; save the detail for later.

Pay special attention to the first one or two sentences of the paragraph; this is where you'll discover the purpose of the paragraph. Once you've grasped that purpose, read the remaining sentences quickly. If you see any other big ideas, or any significant contrasts (*However . . .*), pay attention and jot down a note. You can mostly ignore any details or examples that go along with the main idea. If you are asked a question about this detail, you will come back to reread these sentences at that point.

In fact, it is actually *counterproductive* to try to absorb many details during your initial read-through, since doing so takes you away from the main goal of grasping the overall point and the major ideas presented in the passage. You wouldn't want to depend on your memory when answering detail questions anyway; check for proof in the passage.

Be on the lookout for big surprises or important results. Sometimes the GRE buries such surprises or results within the body of a later paragraph, and you don't want to miss these!

Focus on constructing the simple story and you will read with the appropriate level of attention: not too close, not too far away, but just right.

3. Once you have finished the passage, identify the Point. In a long passage, you will most likely encounter the point during the first paragraph, as the vast majority of long passages reference the main idea right at the beginning. You can't be 100 percent sure, though, until you have finished reading the passage. When you're at the end, make sure that you've noted the point before you start looking at any answer choices. A solid understanding of the main idea is crucial to your success on RC.

Using Your Notes

The purpose of your notes is twofold: to help you grasp the main ideas and to know where to look for certain details. If you've done your job well, you'll be able to answer all *General* questions without referring to the passage and you may not even need to refer to your notes.

As for *Specific* questions, you will need to reread the details in the passage. If you don't happen to remember where something was mentioned, use your notes as a guide—this is precisely why you created them! Also, note that if you can answer a detailed question using just your notes, then you wrote too much down. You will never be asked about every aspect of the passage, so don't waste time taking notes on every last detail when you'll never need most of the information.

Timing for Long Passages

As with short passages, **you have 1.5 minutes per question, total**, including time to read the passage, take notes, and answer all of the questions. Typically, each long passage has four questions associated with it, so you'll have **roughly six minutes** to do everything.

Out of this six-minute period, spend approximately 2–3 minutes reading and generating your Skeletal Sketch. Then spend about 45 seconds per General question and between 45–60 seconds per Specific question.

Repeated practice will be key, as will analyzing your process. Study the model given at the end of this chapter, and do the Problem Sets. After finishing a particular passage-and-questions set, ask yourself:

- Did I miss any major messages on my initial read-through? Why? How can I avoid repeating that mistake in future?

- Did I get too bogged down in any detail on my initial read-through? Were there any indications not to pay so much attention to that detail?

- How could my notes be better? (Consider rewriting them to match your ideal.)

- How could I answer the questions more effectively? What kind of wrong answers was I drawn to and why? If I guessed, was the basis for my guess optimal or at least reasonable?

- How could I answer the questions more efficiently? Could I have found the relevant detail more quickly? Could I have eliminated some of the answers more quickly?

Common Structures of Long Passages

Long passages often have more of a narrative, or sequence of events, to their simple story than short passages do. As a result, it's useful to create an executive summary of the story.

Here are a couple of **executive summaries** of some long passages on the GRE. (Of course, there can be many others. These are only two examples.)

1. A Theory

    Introduction: an area of scientific or historical **research**.

    A **theory** about that area of research exists.

    Here is **support** for that theory.

    (Possibly) Here are **implications** of that theory.

    Point: The theory itself exists/is valid OR an assertion about the theory is made, e.g., **Theory X can now be tested**. In the latter case, support for the assertion is given.

2. A Couple of Theories

    Introduction: a **phenomenon** in some area of scientific or historical research.

    Here are a couple of **theories** about that phenomenon.

    Here is **support** (possibly positive and negative) for each of those theories.

    Point: **Theory X is best** *or* **they all fall short** *or* **more research is needed**.

Model Long Passage:

Electroconvulsive Therapy

Electroconvulsive therapy (ECT) is a controversial psychiatric treatment involving the induction of a seizure in a patient via the passage of electricity through the brain. While beneficial effects of electrically induced seizures are evident and predictable in most patients, a unified mechanism of action has not yet been established and remains the subject of numerous investigations. According to most, though not all, published studies, ECT has been shown to be effective against several conditions, such as severe depression, mania, and some acute psychotic states, that are resistant to other treatments. However, like many other medical procedures, ECT has its risks.

Since the inception of ECT in 1938, the public has held a strongly negative conception of the procedure. Initially, doctors employed unmodified ECT. Patients were rendered instantly unconscious by the electrical current, but the strength of the muscle contractions from induced, uncontrolled motor seizures often led to compression fractures of the spine or damage to the teeth. In addition to the effect this physical trauma had on public sentiment, graphic examples of abuse were documented in nonfiction or loosely fictional books and movies, such as Ken Kesey's *One Flew Over the Cuckoo's Nest*, which portrayed ECT as punitive, cruel, overused, and violative of patients' legal rights. Indeed, the alternative term *electroshock* has a negative connotation, tainted by these depictions in the media.

In comparison with its earlier incarnation, modern ECT is virtually unrecognizable. The treatment is modified by the muscle relaxant succinylcholine, which renders muscle contractions virtually nonexistent. Additionally, patients are given a general anesthetic. Thus, the patient is asleep and fully unaware during the procedure, and the only outward sign of a seizure may be the rhythmic movement of the patient's hand or foot. ECT is generally used in severely depressed patients for whom psychotherapy and medication prove ineffective. It may also be considered when there is an imminent risk of suicide, since antidepressants often require several weeks to show results. Exactly how ECT exerts its influence on behavior is not known, but repeated applications affect several important neurotransmitters in the brain, including serotonin, norepinephrine, and dopamine.

The consensus view of the scientific and medical community is that ECT has been proven effective, but the procedure remains controversial. Though decades-old studies showing brain cell death have been refuted in recent research, many patients do report retrograde amnesia (of events prior to treatment) and/or anterograde amnesia (of events during or shortly after treatment). Patients have also reported that their short-term memories continue to be affected for months after ECT, though some doctors argue that this memory malfunction may reflect the type of amnesia sometimes associated with severe depression. A recent neuropsychological study at Duke University documents a significant decline in performance on memory tests, ironically accompanied at times by self-reports of improved memory function; however, the researchers recommended only that these potential detriments be weighed against the potential benefits of ECT in any particular case.

4

Model Headline Notes:

Electroconvulsive Therapy

1. ECT controv psych treat.: Electr into brain → seizure
   —Beneficial, but mech not understood
   **Effective for some conditions; has risks

2. Since 1938, public dislikes ECT

3. Modern ECT totally diff

4. <u>ECT effective but still controv</u> ← Point

Notice that the first paragraph includes the most detail, as this sets the context for everything to come.

The remaining notes are much more concise, consisting only of a brief summary of the main idea of each body paragraph. Note that for each of the body paragraphs, the main idea is found in the first one or two sentences of the paragraph. This is often the case.

The Point of the passage is contained in the first sentence of the last paragraph: ECT has proven effective, but it remains controversial. This is the most important message that the author wants to convey. Of course, you need the rest of the passage to supply context (e.g., to explain what ECT is in the first place). In fact, the last sentence of the first paragraph is very similar to the Point and nicely foreshadows the overall message.

Notice that the summary here does *not* exactly fit one of the patterns mentioned earlier. The summary here might best be expressed as a judgment about a method: *Here is a method. It is effective but controversial.*

Problem Set

1. Read the following passage, and take notes in 2–3 minutes. Afterward, using the sample given, critique your notes by identifying ways in which they succeed, as well as ways in which they could be improved.

Passage: Ether's Existence

In 1887, an ingenious experiment performed by Albert Michelson and Edward Morley severely undermined classical physics by failing to confirm the existence of ether, a ghostly massless medium that was thought to permeate the universe. Although the implications of this experimental failure were not completely evident for many years, they ultimately paved the way for Einstein's special theory of relativity.

Prior to the Michelson–Morley experiment, nineteenth-century physics conceived of light as a wave of electric and magnetic fields. These fields were governed by Maxwell's equations, which predicted that these waves would propagate at a particular speed c. The existence of ether was hypothesized in part to explain the propagation of light waves, which was believed to be impossible through empty space. Moreover, the ether provided the theoretical baseline for the speed of light predicted by Maxwell's equations: light was to travel at speed c relative to the ether. Physical objects, such as planets, were also thought to glide frictionlessly through the unmoving ether.

The Michelson–Morley experiment relied on the concept that the Earth, which orbits the Sun, would be in motion relative to the fixed ether. Just as a person on a motorcycle experiences a "wind" caused by the cycle's motion relative to the air, the Earth would experience an "ethereal wind" caused by its motion through the ether. Such a wind would affect our measurements of the speed of light. If the speed of light is fixed with respect to the ether, but the Earth is moving through the ether, then to an observer on Earth light must appear to move faster in a downwind direction than in an upwind direction.

In 1887, there were no clocks sufficiently precise to detect the speed differences that would result from an ethereal wind. Michelson and Morley surmounted this problem by using the wavelike properties of light itself to test for such speed differences. In their apparatus, known as an interferometer, a single beam of light is split in half. Mirrors guide each half of the beam along a separate trajectory before ultimately reuniting the two half-beams into a single beam. If one half-beam has moved more slowly than the other, the reunited beams will be out of phase with each other. In other words, peaks of the slower half-beam will not coincide exactly with peaks of the faster half-beam, resulting in an interference pattern in the reunited beam. However, this interference pattern failed to appear. No matter how they positioned the arms of the interferometer in relation to the theoretical ethereal wind, Michelson and Morley detected only a tiny degree of interference in the reunited light beam—far less than what was expected based on the motion of the Earth. This null result helped demolish the ether construct and replace it, in the end, with a far stranger view of time and space.

2. What is the Point of this passage? Justify your choice.

3. Identify the other components of the passage, if present: Background, Support, and Implications. Again, justify your assignments.

4. What is the executive summary of this passage?

5. Select the sentence in the final two paragraphs that explains why Michelson and Morley had to depend on interference patterns to test their theory.

6. Which of the following would the author of the passage be likely to agree with? Indicate all that apply.

   [A] Michelson and Morley's experiment failed to produce meaningful results.

   [B] The lack of precise stopwatches did not significantly impact Michelson and Morley's eventual results.

   [C] Twentieth-century physics would not necessarily have progressed as quickly as it did without Michelson and Morley's experiment.

7. Read the following passage, and take notes in 2–3 minutes. Afterward, using the sample given, critique your notes by identifying ways in which they succeed, as well as ways in which they could be improved.

Passage: Prescription Errors

In Europe, medical prescriptions were historically written in Latin, for many centuries the universal medium of communication among the educated. A prescription for eye drops written in Amsterdam could be filled in Paris, because the abbreviation *OS* meant "left eye" in both places. With the disappearance of Latin as a lingua franca, however, abbreviations such as *OS* can easily be confused with *AS* (left ear) or *per os* (by mouth), even by trained professionals. Such misinterpretations of medical instructions can be fatal. In the early 1990s, two infants died in separate but identical tragedies: they were each administered 5 milligrams of morphine, rather than 0.5 milligrams, as the dosage was written without an initial zero. The naked decimal (.5) was subsequently misread.

The personal and economic costs of misinterpreted medical prescriptions and instructions are hard to quantify. However, anecdotal evidence suggests that misinterpretations are prevalent. While mistakes will always happen in any human endeavor, medical professionals, hospital administrators, and policymakers should continually work to drive the prescription error rate to zero, taking simple corrective steps and also pushing for additional investments.

Certain measures are widely agreed upon, even if some are difficult to enforce, given the decentralization of the country's healthcare system. For instance, the American Medical Association and other professional organizations have publicly advocated against the use of Latin abbreviations and other relics of historical pharmacology. As a result, incidents in which *qd* (every day), *qid* (four times a day), and *qod* (every other day) have been mixed up seem to be on the decline. Other measures have been taken by regulators who oversee potential areas of confusion, such as drug names. For instance, the FDA asked a manufacturer to change the name of Levoxine, a thyroid medication, to Levoxyl so that confusion with Lanoxin, a heart failure drug, would be reduced. Likewise, in 1990 the antacid Losec was renamed Prilosec at the FDA's behest to differentiate it from Lasix, a diuretic. Unfortunately, since 1992 there have been at least a dozen reports of accidental switches between Prilosec and Prozac, an antidepressant. As more drugs reach the market, drug name "traffic control" will only become more complicated.

Other measures are controversial or require significant investment and consensus-building. For instance, putting the patient's condition on the prescription would allow double-checking but also reduce patient privacy; thus, this step continues to be debated. Computerized prescriber order entry (CPOE) systems seem to fix the infamous problem of illegible handwriting, but many CPOE systems permit naked decimals and other dangerous practices. Moreover, since fallible humans must still enter and retrieve the data, any technological fixes must be accompanied by substantial training. Ultimately, a multi-pronged approach is needed to address the issue.

8. What is the Point of this passage? Justify your choice.

9. Identify the other components of the passage, if present: Background, Support, and Implications. Again, justify your assignments. What is the executive summary of this passage?

10. Select the sentence in the middle two paragraphs that provides a reason why prescription errors could become more common in the future.

11. According to the passage, which of the following measures have not already been implemented to prevent prescription errors? Indicate all that apply.

    A   A reduction in the use of anachronistic terminology

    B   A law requiring drug companies to name new products in ways that make confusion with preexisting drugs less likely

    C   Including a patient's condition on the prescription

4

Answers and Explanations

Problem Set

1. Ether's Existence—Notes
1. 1887, <u>M+M experim undermined class. physics</u> ← Point
   → No ether (ghostly medium thru-out univ)
   —not apparent right away, but led to Einstein's rel
2. Before: light = wave of fields
3. M+M used Earth's motion in ether (like wind)
4. → looked for speed diffs, found ∼0

Notice that you have to delve more deeply into the last paragraph than just the first sentence. You do not have to master how an interferometer works (thankfully!), but you have to have read through nearly everything in that last paragraph to understand the main idea, which is distributed throughout.

2. The Point of the passage is contained in the first sentence of the passage: "In 1887, an ingenious experiment performed by Albert Michelson and Edward Morley severely undermined classical physics by failing to confirm the existence of ether . . ." (Of course, don't copy this word for word into your notes, but instead abbreviate it dramatically, as shown.) Everything else in this passage is secondary to this assertion.

3. The first paragraph gives Background on the ether ("a ghostly massless medium that was thought to permeate the universe") and also gives an Implication ("Although the implications . . . theory of relativity"). The rest of the passage is a combination of Background knowledge and Support for the assertion made in the Point.

4. The summary might be called "An Experiment": *M+M shook physics, paved the way for Einstein. Here is what people used to think existed. Here is what M+M did to look. Here is what they found: nothing!*

5. This is a Select-in-Passage question asking for a particular detail. You can look to where *interference* is mentioned, and then try to work backward to figure out why Michelson and Morley needed it. The first sentence of the final paragraph states: "In 1887, there were no clocks sufficiently precise to detect the speed differences that would result from an ethereal wind." Because they couldn't simply time the light, Michelson and Morley had to depend on the interference patterns of split light beams.

6. B, C

This is a very general Select-One-or-More question, which could draw from information provided anywhere in the passage.

(A) The passage indicates that the experiment "failed to confirm the existence of ether," but this does not mean that the experiment failed to produce any usable or meaningful results. In fact, the results of the experiment were far-reaching; the end of the first paragraph says that the implications "ultimately paved the way for Einstein's special theory of relativity."

(B) **CORRECT.** You are told in the final paragraph that Michelson and Morley *surmounted* the problem of not having precise enough clocks. That means that the lack of such clocks did not significantly impact their results.

(C) **CORRECT.** The second sentence of the first paragraph tells you that the results of the experiment "paved the way for Einstein's special theory of relativity." In other words, without the experiment, it is *possible* that physics would not have progressed as quickly.

7. <u>Prescription Errors</u>—Notes

1. Eur: Rx in Latin hist
   BUT now → mistakes
   —Can be fatal. Ex: 2 babies
2. Cost Rx mistakes = hard to quant, but lots
   All should elim errors ← Point
3. Some steps = agreed
4. Other steps harder, need multi-prong

Incidentally, *Rx* is an abbreviation for *prescription*, probably originating from Latin. If you happen to encounter a passage on prescription drugs, feel free to use this abbreviation; otherwise, use it to locate a pharmacy when traveling abroad!

8. The Point combines the last sentence of the second paragraph with the end of the fourth paragraph: "While mistakes will always happen in any human endeavor, medical professionals, hospital administrators, and policymakers should continually work to drive the prescription error rate to zero, taking simple corrective steps and also pushing for additional investments." This is the strongest and most general claim made by the author. The author finishes the point via the end of the fourth paragraph: "Ultimately, a multi-pronged approach is needed to address the issue."

9. What comes before the Point is a mixture of Background (e.g., the use of Latin on medieval prescriptions) and Support (e.g., the explanation of the fatal tragedies). After the Point is mostly Implications (various potential steps with pros and cons). The last two paragraphs could be interpreted as Judgments on specific tactics, *given* that everyone would like to drive the error rate down to zero.

10. This Select-in-Passage question is quite specific. Notice that it doesn't ask for problems with the prescription-writing process, but a reason why the problem could get worse. The final sentence of the third paragraph states: "As more drugs reach the market, drug name "traffic control" will only become more complicated." While other sentences mention other *current* problems with drug name confusion, this is the only sentence giving a reason why things might get *worse* in the future.

11. B, C

This Select-One-or-More question asks about measures that have *not* yet been taken to reduce prescription errors.

(A) The third paragraph describes the confusion caused by the use of the terms *qd*, *qid*, and *qod*. The reduction in the use of these abbreviations is "widely agreed upon, even if ... difficult to enforce." This measure has already been implemented, at least partially, as such terminology mix-ups "seem to be on the decline."

(B) **CORRECT.** The third paragraph describes instances of the FDA asking manufacturers to change drug names to make confusion with other drugs less likely. However, the passage does not say that any law was passed to require drug companies to name new products in a certain way.

(C) **CORRECT.** The fourth paragraph discusses other measures, some of which are controversial or otherwise difficult to implement. These include "putting a patient's condition on the prescription," which "would allow double-checking but also reduce patient privacy." The passage states that "this step continues to be debated," so it has not already been implemented.

Strategies for RC Questions

In This Chapter ...

- Question Types

- General Questions

- Specific Questions

- Strategies for All Reading Comprehension Questions

- Seven Strategies for Reading Comprehension

CHAPTER 5 Strategies for RC Questions

Question Types

As discussed earlier, GRE Reading Comprehension questions come in a variety of forms, but they can be placed into two major categories:

1. *General* questions

2. *Specific* questions

In this chapter, you will learn seven strategies for answering Reading Comprehension questions. The first of these strategies will help you answer General questions. The second and third strategies will help you answer Specific questions. The last four strategies are applicable to both General and Specific questions.

General Questions

General questions deal with the main idea, purpose, or structure of a passage. Typical General questions are phrased as follows:

> The primary purpose of the passage is …
> The author is chiefly concerned with …
> A good title for the passage would be …
>
> The passage as a whole can best be characterized as which of the following?

The correct answer to General questions such as *What is the primary purpose of this passage?* should relate to as much of the passage as possible.

Your understanding of the passage gained through your initial read-through provides the key to answering General questions. You should be able to answer General questions without having to reread the entire passage. In fact, rereading the entire passage can actually be distracting. An incorrect answer choice may pertain only to a detail in a body paragraph. As you reread, you might spot that attractive detail and choose the wrong answer.

So, instead of rereading, first articulate the point to yourself in your own words. Then **dive right into the answer choices and start eliminating**. If you need to, **review your notes** so that you are confident in your knowledge of the author's main message. Armed with the Point, you should be able to eliminate two or three choices quickly.

The last four strategies described in this chapter will help you get to the final answer. Occasionally, though, you may still find yourself stuck between two answer choices on a General question. If this is the case, use a scoring system to determine which answer choice relates to more paragraphs in the passage. Assign the answer choice two points if it relates to the first paragraph. Give one more point for each additional related paragraph. The answer choice with more points is usually the correct one. In the event of a tie, select the answer choice that pertains to the first paragraph over any choices that do not.

Don't spend too much time deciding. If you're not sure whether to assign a point, don't. If two choices tie exactly, just pick one and move on.

> **(1) Strategy for General Q's: If you are stuck between two answer choices, use a scoring system to assign a value to each one.**

Specific Questions

Specific questions deal with details, inferences, assumptions, and arguments. Typical Specific questions are phrased as follows:

> According to the passage … ?
>
> It can be inferred from the passage that … ?
>
> All of the following statements are supported by the passage EXCEPT … ?
>
> Which of the following would weaken the assertion in the passage?

In contrast to your approach to General questions, you *will* need to reread and grasp details in the passage to answer Specific questions. First, read the question and focus on the key words you are most likely to find in the passage. Then, look back over the passage to find those key words. Use your notes as a search tool, if necessary. Do *not* look at the answer choices. Four out of five of them are meant to mislead you.

> **(2) Strategy for Specific Q's: Identify the key words in the question. Then, go back to the passage and find those key words.**

Consider the following sample notes:

1. Standardized tests = not valid predict.

2. Timing test implies → "fast = smart" BUT not true

3. Tests = also biased ag. non-native spkrs

Imagine that you are presented with this question: *Robinson raises the issue of cultural bias to do which of the following?* You would start scanning the passage looking for *cultural bias*. Since you just created the sketch, you would probably head toward the third paragraph anyway, but if necessary, the sketch would remind you to look there.

Sometimes you will need to find a synonym for the key words in the question. For example, if the question addresses *weapons of mass destruction*, you may need to find a paragraph that addresses *nuclear* or *chemical* or *biological weapons*.

Once you find the key words, reread the surrounding sentence or sentences to answer the question. You may have to do a little thinking or take a few notes to figure out what the sentences mean. That is expected: after all, you did not master those details the first time through. In fact, do not look at the answer choices until you **boil down the relevant sentence or sentences into a mantra**—five words of truth. Then you can bring back that mantra and hold it in your head as you scan the five answer choices, eliminating the four lies and matching your mantra to the truth.

If you can't develop a mantra, then you know the question is hard. There's a good chance that you'll need to guess; eliminate any answers you can, then pick one and move on.

> **(3) Strategy for Specific Q's: Find one or two *proof sentences* to defend the correct answer choice. Boil them down into your mantra.**

Only a handful of Specific questions require more than two proof sentences.

Strategies for All Reading Comprehension Questions

You can implement the following strategies for all Reading Comprehension questions.

> **(4) Strategy: Justify every word in the answer choice.**

In the correct answer choice, **every word must be completely true** and within the scope of the passage. If you cannot justify *every* word in the answer choice, eliminate it. For example, consider the following answer choices:

(A) The colonists resented the king for taxing them without representation.

(B) England's policy of taxation without representation caused resentment among the colonists.

The difference in these two answer choices lies in the word *king* versus the word *England*. Although this seems like a small difference, it is the key to eliminating one of these answer choices. If the passage does not mention the *king* when it discusses the colonists' resentment, then the word *king* cannot be justified, and the answer choice should be eliminated.

> **(5) Strategy: Justify extreme words.**

Extreme words, such as *all* and *never*, tend to broaden the scope of an answer choice too much or make it too extreme. **The GRE prefers moderate language and ideas.** Eliminate answer choices that go too far. Of course, occasionally you are justified in picking an extreme choice, but the passage must back you up 100 percent.

> **(6) Strategy: Infer as little as possible.**

Many Reading Comprehension questions ask you to infer something from the passage. An inference is an informed deduction. Reading Comprehension inferences rarely go far beyond what is stated in the passage. In general, you should infer so little that the inference seems obvious. It is often surprising how simplistic GRE inferences are. If an answer choice answers the question and can be confirmed by language in the passage, it will be the correct one. Conversely, you should eliminate answer choices that require any logical stretch or leap. When you read *The passage suggests . . .* or *The passage implies . . .*, you should rephrase that language: *The passage states just a little differently . . .* **You must be able to prove the answer, just as if the question asked you to look it up in the passage.**

---

(7) Strategy: Preview the question.

As stated earlier, you will always see one question on the screen next to the passage. Because you are able to skip questions on the GRE, you could theoretically preview all of the questions you'll be asked before you read the passage. However, previewing all of the questions is not a good use of time. Instead, quickly click through to see how many questions are associated with the passage, and then go back to the first question. Before reading the passage, read the first question. Previewing the first question will give you a good sense for what you can expect in the passage. To review: first check the number of questions associated with the passage, then preview the first question, then read the passage.

Seven Strategies for Reading Comprehension

You now have seven effective strategies to use on Reading Comprehension questions on the GRE. Practice them frequently.

For General questions:

    (1) Use a **scoring system** when stuck between two answer choices.

For Specific questions:

    (2) Match **key words** in specific questions to key words (or synonyms) in the passage.

    (3) Defend your answer choice with one or two **proof sentences**, and develop your mantra.

For all questions:

    (4) **Justify** every word in your answer choice.

    (5) **Justify extreme words** in answer choices.

    (6) Choose an answer choice that **infers** as *little* as possible.

And do not forget:

    (7) **Preview** the first question before reading the passage.

Question Type Analysis

In This Chapter...

- Types of Wrong Answer Choices

- Differences Among Question Formats

- Model Short Passage Revisited: Insect Behavior

- Model Long Passage Revisited: Electroconvulsive Therapy

CHAPTER 6 Question Type Analysis

As you begin a Reading Comprehension question, classify it right away as General or Specific. This distinction determines your fundamental approach to the question. With General questions, you dive right into eliminating answer choices, but with Specific questions, you go back to the passage and find proof sentences before looking at the answer choices.

You may be able to identify several common subtypes as described in this chapter. Whenever you are able to do so, you'll be in a better position to answer the question—though note that you shouldn't devote extra time simply to identifying the subtype. If it jumps out at you, great; if not, move forward anyway.

1. Main Idea

This asks you about the main idea of the passage. This question type is always General.

Typical wordings:

> The author is primarily concerned with … ?
> Which of the following best states the author's main point?
> Which of the following would be the most appropriate title for the passage?

Remember that you'll know the main idea from your initial read-through. Glance at your notes to find the Point if you need a reminder.

2. Lookup Detail

This asks you for a detail that you can look up right in the passage. This question type is always Specific.

Typical wordings:

> According to the passage, X resulted primarily from which of the following … ?
> According to the passage, as the process of X continues, all of the following may occur EXCEPT …
> According to the passage, person X indicates that all of the following were true of Y EXCEPT …
> The author provides information that would answer which of the following questions?

Notice that Lookup Detail questions can be made harder with EXCEPT. With an EXCEPT variation, you have to find the one answer that *isn't* true. The primary way to do so is by process of elimination: knock out the four answer choices that *are* true according to the passage.

3. Infer about Facts

This asks you to make a clear, unshakeable deduction about facts presented in the passage. This deduction should be almost mathematical or dictionary-like in nature. For instance, if the passage tells you that there is less calcium in water than in milk, then you can infer that there is more calcium in milk than in water. This question type is always Specific.

Typical wordings:

> It can be inferred from the passage that slower X than those discussed in the passage ...
> The author implies that a major element of X is ...
> Which of the following statements concerning X is most directly suggested in the passage?
> The quality of X described in lines 10–15 is most clearly an example of ...
> The passage supports which of the following statements about X?

Occasionally, you will need to make an inference connecting two parts of the passage. Regardless, you must not make any new assumptions or draw on knowledge from outside the passage.

4. Infer about Opinions

This asks you to make a clear, unshakeable deduction about an opinion or attitude. This opinion or attitude may be of someone referred to in the passage, or it may be of the author himself or herself. No matter what, you must find clear justification in the passage. This justification might come in the form of just one word, such as *regrettably* or *understandably*. This question type is usually Specific, but occasionally it might be General.

Typical wordings:

> The author's attitude toward X, as discussed in the passage, is best described as ... [answer choices are adjectives]
> In the first paragraph of the passage, the author's attitude toward X can best be described as ...
> It can be inferred from the passage that person X chose Y because X believed that ...
> It can be inferred from the passage that the author believes which of the following about X?

5. Author's Purpose

This asks you *why* or *for what purpose* the author has written something or constructed the passage in a certain way. These questions address the role, structure, and function of particular words, phrases, sentences, paragraphs, and even the passage as a whole. In the last case, the question would be General, but usually this question type is Specific.

Typical wordings:

> The author refers to X (line 45) primarily in order to ...
> Which of the following phrases best expresses the sense of word X as it is used in lines 20–21 of the passage?

6. Minor Types

You may be asked to extrapolate the content of the passage (e.g., What would be the best sentence to add onto the end of the passage?) or to evaluate what would strengthen or weaken a claim (e.g., Which of the following pieces of evidence would most strengthen the claim made in lines 13–15?). These questions are almost always Specific.

Types of Wrong Answer Choices

Wrong answers on Reading Comprehension questions tend to fall into one of five broad categories. Caution: On the real test, do not waste precious time or attention classifying an answer choice that is obviously wrong. Rather, use this classification in the last stage of elimination if you are stuck deciding among answer choices that all seem attractive. However, while practicing Reading Comprehension, you should attempt to categorize all the wrong answers after you have completed the section (during your review).

1. **Out of Scope**

    *   **Introduces an unwarranted assertion** supported nowhere in the passage.
    *   Might be "real-world plausible." That is, the answer might be true or seem to be true in the real world. However, if the answer is not supported in the passage, it is out of scope.

2. **Direct Contradiction**

    *   **States the exact opposite** of something asserted in the passage.
    *   Paradoxically attractive, because it relates to the passage closely. If you miss one contrast or switchback in the trail, you can easily think a direct contradiction is the right answer.

3. **Mix-Up**

    *   **Scrambles together different words or phrases** from the passage, but the meaning of the choice does not reflect what the passage said.
    *   Tries to trap the student who simply matches language, not meaning.

4. **One Word Wrong**

    *   **Just one word (or maybe two) is incorrect.** Includes extreme words.
    *   More prevalent in General questions.

5. **True but Irrelevant**

    *   **True according to the passage, but does not answer the given question.**
    *   May be too narrow or simply unrelated.

This framework can be particularly helpful as you analyze the patterns in wrong answers that you incorrectly choose during practice (whether under exam-like conditions or not). If you frequently choose Direct Contradiction answers, for instance, then you might incorporate one more double check into your process to look for that particular sort of error. Again, however, **you should not attempt to classify wrong answers as a first line of attack.** Rather, use this strategy as a tiebreak for the most tempting answer choices. If, while the clock is ticking, you're already confident that an answer is wrong, don't bother trying to classify it.

Differences Among Question Formats

Long and short passage questions can be presented in one of three formats: Select One, Select One or More, and Select in Passage. Select One is the standard, five-answer multiple choice question for which you pick one answer. The other two types have some intricacies to keep in mind:

1. **Select One or More**

    It is unlikely that you'll be asked structural questions (main idea, author's purpose), because questions like that could really only have one answer. Instead, expect to see mostly Inference questions, though they can be either Specific or General. Select-One-or-More questions are a bit like three Inference questions in one. Because each of the answer choices can be correct, all three have to be considered in isolation.

2. **Select in Passage**

These questions can only be Specific (as they must relate to only *one* sentence in the passage), and they can be deceptively difficult. Remember that the correct answer needs to be relevant to every aspect of the question, but that the correct sentence is allowed to do or say more than just what the question demands. Don't ignore a sentence if part of it seems out of scope. If it contains the details requested by the prompt, it doesn't matter what else is discussed within it.

The rest of this chapter will review two of the passages used as examples in the previous chapters covering short and long passages.

Note: For the purpose of practice and exposure to different question types, this chapter will review six questions on the short passage and seven questions on the long passage. However, on the GRE, a short passage will typically have only one to three questions associated with it, and a long passage will typically have only four questions associated with it.

Reread the first passage, reproduced on the following page for your convenience. As you read, take notes. Do not try to reproduce the earlier version; make new notes. On the pages that follow, try to answer each question in the appropriate amount of time (between 45–60 seconds) *before* you read the accompanying explanation.

6

Model Short Passage Revisited:

Insect Behavior

Insect behavior generally appears to be explicable in terms of unconscious, inflexible stimulus-response mechanisms. For instance, a female sphex wasp leaves her egg sealed in a burrow alongside a paralyzed grasshopper, which her larvae can eat upon hatching. Before she deposits the grasshopper in the burrow, she inspects the burrow; if the inspection reveals no problems, she drags the grasshopper inside by its antennae. As thoughtful as this behavior appears, it reveals its mechanistic character upon interference. Darwin discovered that prior removal of the grasshopper's antennae prevents the wasp from depositing the grasshopper, even though the legs or ovipositor could also serve as handles. Likewise, Fabre moved the grasshopper a few centimeters away from the burrow's mouth while the wasp was inside inspecting. The wasp returned the grasshopper to the edge of the burrow and then began a new inspection. Fabre performed this disruptive maneuver 40 times; the wasp's response never changed.

> Take notes on a separate piece of paper.

1.   The primary purpose of the passage is to _____.

   (A)   prove, based on examples, that insects lack consciousness

   (B)   argue that insects are unique in their dependence on rigid routines

   (C)   analyze the maternal behavior of wasps

   (D)   compare and contrast the work of Darwin and Fabre

   (E)   argue that insect behavior relies on rigid routines which appear to be unconscious

This is a General question (subtype: Main Idea), so answer the question using the understanding of the passage that you gained through creating your notes. In this case, the Point is contained in the first sentence: insect behavior is unconscious and inflexible. The remaining text gives examples of rigid insect behavior.

You can eliminate answer choice (A) based upon the topic sentence of the paragraph. The passage does not claim to prove that insects lack consciousness; it merely suggests, rather tentatively, that insect behavior *appears to be explicable* in terms of unconscious mechanisms. The word *prove* is too extreme in answer choice (A). [One Word Wrong]

Answer choice (B) reflects the language of the passage in that the passage does indicate that insects depend on rigid routines. However, it does not address the question of whether there are any other animals that depend on such routines, as is stated in answer choice (B). The passage makes no claim about whether or not insects are *unique* in this respect. Remember that every word in an answer choice must be justified from the text. [Out of Scope]

The sphex wasp's maternal behavior is used as an example to illustrate a more general idea; this behavior is not itself the Point of the passage. Eliminate answer (C). [True but Irrelevant]

Fabre and Darwin are simply mentioned as sources for some of the information on wasps. Moreover, their results are not contrasted; rather, their experiments are both cited as evidence to support the Point. Answer choice (D) is incorrect. [Out of Scope]

(E) CORRECT. The passage begins with a topic sentence that announces the author's Point. The Point has two parts, as this answer choice correctly indicates: (1) insect behavior relies on rigid routines, and (2) these routines appear to be unconscious. The topic sentence does not use the term *rigid routine*, but it conveys the idea of rigidity by describing insect behavior as *inflexible*. The concept of routine is introduced later in the passage.

As is typical on the GRE, the correct answer choice avoids restating the passage. Instead, this choice uses synonyms (e.g., *rigid* instead of *inflexible*).

---

2.   The author mentions the work of Darwin and Fabre in order to

  (A)   provide experimental evidence of the inflexibility of one kind of insect behavior

  (B)   contradict the conventional wisdom about "typical" wasp behavior

  (C)   illustrate the strength of the wasp's maternal affection

  (D)   explore the logical implications of the thesis articulated earlier

  (E)   highlight historical changes in the conduction of scientific research

Questions that ask about the purpose of a reference are Specific questions (subtype: Author's Purpose). Go back to the passage to determine why this work was included, although you may be able to use your notes. In fact, you may even have jotted down something like the following:

  D: wasp won't drag g. w/o anten.

  F: similar evid

The sentences on Darwin and Fabre describe experiments that are used as examples of inflexible insect behavior. This concept is mirrored closely in answer choice (A), the correct answer.

Review all answer choices, just in case.

The passage does not mention any challenge to a conventional view; for all you know, the passage simply states the mainstream scientific position on insect behavior. Eliminate answer (B). [Out of Scope]

For answer choice (C), it might be tempting to infer that the wasp's persistence is caused by maternal affection. This inference is questionable, however, because the passage states that insect behavior is determined by mechanistic routines that appear to be unemotional in nature. Always avoid picking an answer choice that depends on a debatable inference, because the correct answer should not stray far from what is directly stated in the text. [Out of Scope]

Choice (D) is incorrect because Darwin's and Fabre's experiments do not explore the logical *implications* of the idea that insect behavior is inflexible. Rather, the experiments are presented as *evidence* of inflexibility. [Direct Contradiction]

Answer choice (E) goes beyond the scope of the passage. The paragraph mentions work by two scientists, but it does not tell you whether any differences in their methods were part of a historical change in the conduction of scientific research. [Out of Scope]

3. Which of the following hypothetical variations in the experiments described in the passage would most weaken the primary claim of the passage?

    (A) Darwin removes the ovipositor, a small appendage, instead of the antennae; the wasp fails to deposit the grasshopper in the burrow.

    (B) Darwin restrains the grasshopper while the wasp attempts to drag it by its antennae, which subsequently break off; although Darwin then releases the grasshopper, the wasp ignores it.

    (C) Fabre moves the grasshopper several meters away during the wasp's inspection; the wasp takes significant time to retrieve the grasshopper, then re-inspects the burrow.

    (D) Fabre repeatedly varies the exact position near the burrow to which he moves the grasshopper, causing the wasp to adjust its retrieval path slightly before re-inspecting the burrow.

    (E) Fabre replaces the grasshopper with a paralyzed praying mantis, a rather different insect, that the wasp inspects and then deposits in the burrow.

This is a Specific question (subtype: Weaken) that requires you to interpret the hypothetical effect of variations in the experiments described in the passage.

Because the question asks *which variation would most weaken the primary claim,* review that primary claim: insect behavior can be explained by unconscious, inflexible behaviors. To weaken this claim, you would need evidence that the insect can act in a flexible way, adapting or changing its behavior in some way.

Further, the question talks about *variations in the experiments* (described in the passage), so review the two experiments. Darwin interrupts the wasp's standard behavior by removing the antennae, even though the wasp could have adapted by using something else to drag the grasshopper. Fabre interrupts the process by moving the grasshopper a short distance away; because the grasshopper is no longer in the "right" spot, the wasp begins the inspection process all over again.

Answer choice (A) depicts a situation in which Darwin removes the small ovipositor appendage instead of the antennae. This removal disturbs the wasp enough to prevent it from using the grasshopper, although the slightness of the change is implied by the term "small appendage," and thus you can assume that the grasshopper would still be appropriate for the wasp's purpose (feed the larvae). This result actually strengthens the primary claim. [Direct Contradiction]

In answer choice (B), the wasp and Darwin get into a tug of war, during which the wasp winds up breaking off the antennae and then abandoning the grasshopper, even though the latter became available once Darwin released it. In essence, this choice is similar to the real experiment Darwin conducted: in both cases, the wasp rejects a grasshopper lacking antennae; therefore, this choice also strengthens the primary claim. [Direct Contradiction]

In answer choice (C), the wasp re-inspects the burrow only after a long delay, because the grasshopper has been moved several meters away. Thus, the re-inspection might be seen as a result either of an inflexible behavior ("inspect after bringing the grasshopper to the burrow") or of a flexible, conscious decision process ("since I have been absent from the burrow for a while, I'd better check it again"). This choice is tricky, since flexibility now enters the picture. However, choice (C) does not rule out the inflexible mechanism or create any preference one way or the other, so it does not attack the primary claim itself, which is still permitted. At most, you can say that this choice provides ambiguous evidence, and so does not really strengthen or weaken the primary claim. As such, this choice is "Out of Scope," because it does not provide definitive evidence one way or the other. [Out of Scope]

Answer choice (D) is similar to (B) in that it describes a variation that isn't really a change. In the real experiment, Fabre moved the grasshopper 10 centimeters. In this choice, Fabre *varies the exact position,* causing the wasp to change its path *slightly.* In both cases, the wasp continues to be inflexible and re-inspect the burrow because the grasshopper is not where the wasp expected it to be.

In answer choice (E), the wasp is confronted with a significantly changed situation (praying mantis instead of grasshopper). The wasp inspects the new insect, which is described as rather different, and then deposits it in the burrow anyway. This indicates that the wasp is able to accept a significant difference and, after inspection, proceed with the original plan anyway; in other words, the wasp demonstrates substantial flexibility, especially in comparison to how it acts in the real experiments. The correct answer is (**E**).

4. The passage supports which of the following statements about insect behavior?

(A) Reptiles such as snakes behave more flexibly than do insects.

(B) Insects such as honeybees can always be expected to behave inflexibly.

(C) Many species of insects leave eggs alongside living but paralyzed food sources.

(D) Stimulus-response mechanisms in insects have evolved because, under ordinary circumstances, they help insects to survive.

(E) More than one species of insect displays inflexible, routine behaviors.

This is a difficult Specific question (subtype: Lookup Detail). The key words *insect behavior* indicate the topic of the passage; they could plausibly refer to almost anything mentioned. Change tactics and start with the answer choices. Each answer choice gives you additional key words; use these to look up the reference for each answer choice and determine whether the choice is justified.

The key to finding the correct answer is to focus on what is stated *explicitly* in the passage, and to examine whether each answer choice goes beyond what can be supported by the passage. Again, justify every word in the answer choice that you select.

Answer choice (A) mentions reptiles and snakes. Since the passage never mentions either of these, eliminate this choice. This is the case even though one could argue that the passage draws an implicit contrast between insect inflexibility and the more flexible behavior of some other creatures. Discard any answer choice that goes too far beyond the passage. [Out of Scope]

Answer choice (B) is a great example of a tempting GRE answer choice. Honeybees are insects, and the passage does claim that insect behavior tends to be inflexible. However, the passage does not say that every single species of insect behaves inflexibly; perhaps honeybees are an exception. Further, this answer choice states that honeybees *always* behave inflexibly, whereas the author states that insect behavior **generally appears to be** *inflexible.* The extreme word *always* cannot be justified in this answer choice. [One Word Wrong]

Answer choice (C) seems plausible. The sphex wasp is probably not the only species of insect that provides its young with paralyzed prey. However, the word *Many* is not justified in the passage. You do not know the behavior of any other insect in this regard. Through the use of the word *Many,* answer choice (C) goes too far beyond the passage. [One Word Wrong]

The passage never explicitly mentions evolution, nor does it make any statement about why insects have stimulus-response mechanisms. Answer choice (D) also requires drawing inferences from beyond the text of the passage. [Out of Scope]

The first sentence of the passage indicates that *Insect behavior generally appears to be explicable in terms of unconscious stimulus-response mechanisms.* The passage goes on to describe the case of sphex wasps as a *classic example.* Thus, the passage clearly indicates that the case of sphex wasps is not completely unique; that is, there must be more than one species of insect that exhibits inflexible behavior. Note that *more than one* can be justified by the passage in a way that a more extreme term such as *most* or *all* cannot be. Answer choice (E) is correct.

5. Based on the passage, which of the following would prove a similar point to that promoted by the author? Indicate all that apply.

    A   In a similar experiment, the paralyzed grasshopper was replaced with another equally nutritive insect, and the wasp did not drag it into the burrow.

    B   In a similar experiment with a bird, the bird was shown to act in the exact same manner as the wasp.

    C   In a similar experiment with a different wasp, the wasp dragged the grasshopper into the burrow by its ovipositor.

This is another difficult specific question, presented in a Select-One-or-More multiple-choice format. Consider each answer choice on its own. Start by reminding yourself of the main point: insects exhibit inflexible behaviors.

(A) CORRECT. In this case, the wasp would have access to an insect that could provide just as much nutrition for her larvae as the grasshopper. The rational, conscious response would be to drag the new insect into the burrow in place of the grasshopper. The decision not to drag the insect into the burrow would imply that the wasp is not being rational or logical, but obeying inflexible stimulus-response mechanisms, which require the insect to be a grasshopper.

(B) While at first glance this answer may seem tempting, as it describes an animal acting in the "exact same manner as the wasp," the passage is very specifically about *insect* behavior. Birds do not fit into that category. [One Word Wrong.]

(C) You've read that the wasp only drags the grasshopper in by its antennae, and if those antennae are removed, it will not drag it into the burrow at all. If a wasp were to deviate from her typical process, dragging the grasshopper in by something other than its antennae, she would be changing her response in reaction to circumstances, meaning her responses were *not* inflexible. This is actually the opposite of the point you want to make. [Direct Contradiction.]

The only correct answer is **(A)**.

6

6.   Select the sentence that names the mechanism by which a seemingly conscious behavior can be proven autonomic?

This is a Select-in-Passage question, which by definition has to be specific. Don't be afraid of complex language on the GRE. Often the meaning of difficult words can be inferred from the context. In this case, even if you didn't know what the word "autonomic" meant, you could use context. It is being contrasted with "conscious behavior," so it likely means the opposite of that (unconscious behavior). So now you're looking for the sentence that names the mechanism used to prove that a seemingly conscious behavior was actually unconscious.

The fourth sentence says: *As thoughtful as this behavior appears, it reveals its mechanistic character upon interference.* The mechanism at issue has been named: "interference." While many of the following sentences give examples of interference, the mechanism is only named in this sentence. Always be careful to read the question very carefully. It would be easy to pick one of the example sentences later in the paragraph if you didn't notice the use of the word "names" in the question.

Now reread the Model Long Passage and take your own notes. On the pages that follow, try to answer each question in the appropriate amount of time (between 45–60 seconds) before you read the accompanying explanation.

Model Long Passage Revisited:

Electroconvulsive Therapy

Electroconvulsive therapy (ECT) is a controversial psychiatric treatment involving the induction of a seizure in a patient via the passage of electricity through the brain. While beneficial effects of electrically induced seizures are evident and predictable in most patients, a unified mechanism of action has not yet been established and remains the subject of numerous investigations. According to most, though not all, published studies, ECT has been shown to be effective against several conditions, such as severe depression, mania, and some acute psychotic states, that are resistant to other treatments. However, like many other medical procedures, ECT has its risks.

Since the inception of ECT in 1938, the public has held a strongly negative conception of the procedure. Initially, doctors employed unmodified ECT. Patients were rendered instantly unconscious by the electrical current, but the strength of the muscle contractions from induced, uncontrolled motor seizures often led to compression fractures of the spine or damage to the teeth. In addition to the effect this physical trauma had on public sentiment, graphic examples of abuse were documented in nonfiction or loosely fictional books and movies, such as Ken Kesey's *One Flew Over the Cuckoo's Nest*, which portrayed ECT as punitive, cruel, overused, and violative of patients' legal rights. Indeed, the alternative term *electroshock* has a negative connotation, tainted by these depictions in the media.

In comparison with its earlier incarnation, modern ECT is virtually unrecognizable. The treatment is modified by the muscle relaxant succinylcholine, which renders muscle contractions virtually nonexistent. Additionally, patients are given a general anesthetic. Thus, the patient is asleep and fully unaware during the procedure, and the only outward sign of a seizure may be the rhythmic movement of the patient's hand or foot. ECT is generally used in severely depressed patients for whom psychotherapy and medication prove ineffective. It may also be considered when there is an imminent risk of suicide, since antidepressants often require several weeks to show results. Exactly how ECT exerts its influence on behavior is not known, but repeated applications affect several important neurotransmitters in the brain, including serotonin, norepinephrine, and dopamine.

The consensus view of the scientific and medical community is that ECT has been proven effective, but the procedure remains controversial. Though decades-old studies showing brain cell death have been refuted in recent research, many patients do report retrograde amnesia (of events prior to treatment) and/or anterograde amnesia (of events during or shortly after treatment). Patients have also reported that their short-term memories continue to be affected for months after ECT, though some doctors argue that this memory malfunction may reflect the type of amnesia sometimes associated with severe depression. A recent neuropsychological study at Duke University documents a significant decline in performance on memory tests, ironically accompanied at times by self-reports of improved memory function; however, the researchers recommended only that these potential detriments be weighed against the potential benefits of ECT in any particular case.

> Take notes on a separate piece of paper.

1. The passage is primarily concerned with

    (A) recommending a provocative medical practice

    (B) explaining a controversial medical treatment

    (C) arguing for further testing of a certain medical approach

    (D) summarizing recent research concerning a particular medical procedure

    (E) relating the public concern toward a particular medical therapy

This is a General question (subtype: Main Idea). It asks for the primary purpose of the passage, although the question is worded slightly differently.

The answer should reflect your understanding of the Point. As you noted before, the Point of this passage is the topic sentence of the fourth paragraph: *The consensus view ... is that ECT has been proven effective, but it is not without controversy.* This Point is neutral and balanced; it is not advocating either the adoption of or the elimination of ECT.

Answer choice (A) states that the author recommends ECT. The passage addresses ECT in an objective manner; the author does not attempt to say that ECT should be used. Answer choice (A) is incorrect. [One Word Wrong]

Answer choice (**B**) is correct. The primary purpose of the passage is to explain ECT. This includes briefly discussing both its purpose and the reasons why it has generated such controversy.

Continue to rule out other answer choices, just to be safe.

Answer choice (C) describes a need for further testing; this need is never mentioned in the passage. You might think that the passage implies this need, since you do not know *exactly how ECT exerts its effects,* for instance. However, the primary concern of the passage will not be implied; it will be asserted. Answer choice (C) is incorrect. [Out of Scope]

Although recent research concerning a particular side effect of ECT is mentioned in the final paragraph, this is not the primary purpose of the passage. This answer choice is too specific; it does not relate to the content of the passage as a whole. Using the scoring system strategy, you would give this answer choice only one point, since it relates to the final paragraph. In contrast, correct answer choice (B) would be assigned 5 points since it relates to the first paragraph (2 points) and each of the subsequent 3 paragraphs (1 point each). Answer choice (D) is incorrect. [True but Irrelevant]

The passage does state that ECT is a controversial procedure that the public views in a negative manner; however, the passage only focuses on public concern over the procedure in the second paragraph. This answer choice does not encompass the majority of the passage. Thus, answer choice (E) is also incorrect. [True but Irrelevant]

2.   Which of the following is NOT cited in the passage as a current or historical criticism of ECT?

    (A)   ECT causes the death of brain cells.

    (B)   ECT has been used to punish certain individuals.

    (C)   Seizures during ECT can cause bodily harm.

    (D)   Short-term memory loss results from ECT.

    (E)   Repeated applications of ECT affect several neurotransmitters in the brain.

This Specific question (subtype: Lookup Detail) asks you which criticism of ECT is *not* cited in the passage. A methodical process of elimination is the best approach to answer a NOT or EXCEPT question. Use your notes to help determine which paragraphs are likely to contain the necessary details. Because the question asks about criticisms of ECT, concentrate on the second and fourth paragraphs, which discuss, respectively, historical and current criticisms. Then eliminate each answer choice as soon as you prove that it *is* cited as a criticism of ECT.

The second sentence of the last paragraph indicates that the death of brain cells was the basis for a historical criticism of ECT. Although the research was recently refuted, brain cell death was once a criticism of the procedure. Answer choice (A) can be ruled out.

According to the second-to-last sentence of the second paragraph, ECT has been *documented in nonfiction or loosely fictional books and movies.* In other words, these abuses actually happened. Moreover, these abuses have been documented as *punitive*; that is, ECT has been used to punish people. Thus, answer choice (B) can be eliminated.

The second and third sentences of the second paragraph explicitly and prominently mentions the bodily harm caused by seizures during unmodified ECT. Answer choice (C) is clearly incorrect.

The final paragraph also cites short-term memory loss as a major reason that ECT, in its current modified form, still generates controversy. Thus, answer choice (D) is incorrect.

The end of the third paragraph specifically states that *repeated applications [of ECT] affect several neurotransmitters in the brain.* However, this statement is offered in a neutral way, not as a criticism of ECT, but simply as additional information about the procedure. You might suppose that this effect is negative, but the text itself does not apply a judgment one way or the other. If anything, paragraph three is generally positive. Answer choice (E) is the only answer choice that is not cited as a past or current criticism of ECT. Therefore, answer choice (**E**) is the correct answer.

With a NOT or EXCEPT question, it is often easier to eliminate incorrect answer choices than to identify the correct answer choice directly. Also, the GRE has a slight but significant tendency to make the correct answer (D) or (E) on EXCEPT questions, to force you to read all of the answer choices. Thus, for this sort of question, you may want to start with the last answer choice and work your way up.

6

3.   The passage suggests that the author regards ECT with

   (A)   conditional support

   (B)   academic objectivity

   (C)   mild advocacy

   (D)   unreserved criticism

   (E)   increasing acceptance

This is a General question (subtype: Infer about Opinions). Although you can often answer an Attitude question using only your general understanding of the passage, you should still closely examine the specific words the author uses to convey information. Here, the author presents evidence both for and against the efficacy and safety of ECT; he or she does not clearly lean toward or against more widespread adoption of the treatment. When presenting criticisms of ECT, the author does so in a manner that does not indicate a clear bias. The correct answer will reflect this balance.

Also, note that when answer choices are only two words long, the wrong answers will be wrong by just one or two words. Thus, all the incorrect answers below are One Word Wrong.

Answer choice (A) is incorrect, as the author's attitude does not indicate support for ECT. Moreover, there are no clear conditions placed upon any support by the author.

Answer choice (**B**) is the correct answer. The attitude of the author as expressed in the passage is impartial and objective. The passage explains and discusses ECT in an unbiased, academic manner. Continue to examine the remaining answer choices.

Answer choice (C) is incorrect, as the tone of the passage does not suggest even mild advocacy on the part of the author. Though the author admits the *proven* efficacy of ECT, this admission is counterbalanced by accounts of criticisms and controversy surrounding the treatment. The tone of the passage is neither for nor against ECT.

Answer choice (D) is incorrect, as the language is too extreme. The tone of the passage is not unreserved, and the author is not clearly critical in his or her stance toward ECT.

Answer choice (E) is also not an accurate representation of the attitude of the author. It may be the case that ECT has achieved growing acceptance since its inception, but this reflects the popular or medical perception, not that of the author.

4. Which of the following statements can be inferred from the third paragraph?

   (A) Greater amounts of the neurotransmitters serotonin, norepinephrine, and dopamine seem to reduce symptoms of depression.

   (B) ECT is never used prior to attempting psychotherapy or medication.

   (C) Succinylcholine completely immobilizes the patient's body.

   (D) ECT often works faster than antidepressants.

   (E) One ECT treatment is often sufficient to reduce symptoms of depression significantly.

This is a Specific question (subtype: Infer about Facts). The answer to an Inference question must be directly supported by evidence from the text. As always, be sure to pay particular attention to the precise words used in the answer choices and how they relate to the information presented in the passage.

For answer choice (A), the third paragraph specifically states that ECT *affects* these particular neurotransmitters. However, no information is provided to suggest how these neurotransmitters are affected. Since the passage does not indicate an increase in these neurotransmitters, this cannot be the best answer. [Out of Scope]

The third paragraph states: *ECT is generally used in severely depressed patients for whom psychotherapy and medication prove ineffective.* This does not mean that ECT is *never* used before these other therapies. Answer choice (B) is too extreme to be the correct answer. [One Word Wrong]

According to the third paragraph, succinylcholine renders muscle contractions *virtually nonexistent*, rather than *completely* nonexistent. Moreover, the passage states that a patient's hand or foot may rhythmically move during ECT. Thus, the patient's body is not *completely* immobilized. Eliminate answer choice (C). [Direct Contradiction]

The paragraph also states that ECT may be used *when there is an imminent risk of suicide, since antidepressants often take several weeks to work effectively.* The conjunction *since* indicates that the length of time ECT takes to work is being contrasted with that of antidepressants. That is, it is implied that ECT often works faster than antidepressants. Answer choice **(D)** is correct.

The final sentence of the third paragraph states that *repeated applications* of ECT affect several neurotransmitters. However, you are told nothing about how many treatments are needed to achieve results of any kind. Answer choice (E) is incorrect. [Out of Scope]

5.   According to the passage, which of the following statements is true?

(A)   Most severely depressed individuals have suicidal thoughts.

(B)   The general public was unaware of the bodily harm caused by unmodified ECT.

(C)   Research into the side effects of ECT has only recently begun.

(D)   ECT does not benefit individuals with anxiety disorders.

(E)   Patients undergoing ECT today are unconscious throughout the procedure.

This is a difficult Specific question (subtype: Lookup Detail) that does not indicate a particular part of the passage in the question stem. Thus, you have to use key words from the answer choices, look up proof sentences, and eliminate choices one by one. Use your notes to locate the important information in the passage, and then eliminate an answer choice as soon as you prove that it is not cited in the passage as true.

Answer choice (A) includes the key words *severely depressed* and *suicidal*, which lead you to the third paragraph of the passage. This paragraph indicates that ECT is considered as a treatment option *when there is an imminent risk of suicide*. However, nothing in the passage indicates the percentage (or number) of severely depressed individuals who have suicidal thoughts. The use of the word *Most* is unjustified. Answer choice (A) can be eliminated. [One Word Wrong]

Answer choice (B) includes the key words *bodily harm* and *unmodified ECT*, which lead you to the second paragraph (which gives examples of the *bodily harm* caused by ECT in some cases). This paragraph describes ways in which the public was aware of the bodily harm caused by unmodified ECT. This knowledge influenced the general public's strongly negative conception of the procedure. Answer choice (B) is incorrect. [Direct Contradiction]

In answer choice (C), the key words *only recently* prompt you to look for time references. The second sentence of the final paragraph cites *decades-old studies* of ECT. Thus, research has not begun only recently. Answer choice (C) should be ruled out. [Direct Contradiction]

The first paragraph states that *ECT is effective against severe depression, some acute psychotic states, and mania*. This does *not* necessarily mean that ECT is ineffective for *anxiety disorders*. With an "According to the passage" question, the correct answer must be provable by the passage text. Answer choice (D) is not shown by the passage to be true. [Out of Scope]

The third paragraph explains that, for modern ECT, *patients are given a general anesthetic* and *the patient is asleep and fully unaware during the procedure*. Thus, ECT patients today are unconscious while undergoing the procedure. Answer choice (**E**) is correct.

6

6. According to the passage, which of the following is true of the general population's opinion of ECT? Indicate all that apply.

- [A] It has improved in the years since the treatment was first introduced.
- [B] It has been affected by artistic representations of the treatment.
- [C] It has likely had an effect on the terminology that proponents of ECT might use to describe the treatment.

This is a difficult Specific question presented in a Select-One-or-More format. The question is about the general population's opinion of ECT, which is discussed primarily in the second paragraph.

(A) While the fourth paragraph states: *the consensus view of the scientific and medical community is that ECT has been proven effective*, you are never told that the general public has come to the same conclusion. The first sentence of the critical second paragraph states: *since the inception of ECT in 1938, the public has held a strongly negative conception of the procedure*. Nowhere does the passage state that this general opinion has improved, in spite of the fact that the process has grown far less violent and traumatic over the years. [Direct Contradiction]

(B) CORRECT. In the second paragraph, you are told that Ken Kesey's *One Flew Over the Cuckoo's Nest* affected public sentiment by providing *graphic examples of abuse*. This film can be described as an "artistic representation" of ECT, and so this answer is correct.

(C) CORRECT. The final sentence of the second paragraph says: *the alternative term "electroshock" has a negative connotation*. This means that proponents of ECT would be unlikely to use the term, because it would summon up the negative feelings people have about the term. They would be more likely to call it ECT.

7. In the final two paragraphs, select a sentence that describes two possible causes of a given phenomenon.

This Specific question of the Select-in-Passage variety is very difficult because it fails to reference any individual detail of the passage. It does indicate that you need to look in the final two paragraphs, at the least. The third paragraph explains the factual science behind the current state of ECT, so start with the fourth paragraph (but be prepared to go to the third if you don't find anything in the fourth).

The third sentence of the final paragraph says: *Patients have also reported that their short-term memories continue to be affected for months after ECT, though some doctors argue that this memory malfunction may reflect the type of amnesia sometimes associated with severe depression*. This sentence gives two possible explanations for the phenomenon of short-term amnesia: either ECT or the depression that the ECT was intended to cure.

CHAPTER 7

Reading Comprehension Problem Set

Problem Set

The following problem set consists of reading passages followed by a series of questions on each passage. Use the following guidelines as you complete this problem set:

1. Preview the first question before reading, but do not attempt to answer any of the questions before you have read the whole passage.

2. As you read the passage, apply the seven principles of active, efficient reading. Create a Headline List. Then use your notes to assist you in answering all the questions that accompany the passage.

3. When first reading a question, identify it as either a General or a Specific question. Use the seven strategies for Reading Comprehension to assist you in answering the questions.

4. On the GRE, you will typically see one to three questions with short passages and about four questions with long passages. However, in this problem set, you will see six or seven questions associated with each passage. As such, use the following modified timing guidelines:

    *   **When reading passages**, spend approximately 1.5 minutes for shorter passages and 2–3 minutes for longer passages. If a topic is more complex or detailed, spend less time on the details; just get the main ideas and major twists!

    *   **When answering questions**, spend approximately 30 to 45 seconds on General questions and approximately 45 to 60 seconds on Specific questions. Expect to spend the full time on Select-One-or-More and EXCEPT questions; these will almost always take longer.

Finally, if you'd like, answer only three or four of the questions the first time you do these passages. You can then save the passage for a second pass (with the remaining three or four questions) later on in your study.

7

Passage A: Japanese Swords

Historians have long recognized the traditional Japanese sword, or *nihonto*, as one of the finest cutting weapons ever produced, but it has even been considered a spiritual entity. The adage "the sword is the soul of the samurai" reflects the sword's psychic importance, not only to its wielder, but also to its creator, the master smith. Not classically regarded as artists, master smiths nevertheless exerted great care in the process of creating swords, no two of which were ever forged exactly the same way. Over hundreds of hours, two types of steel were repeatedly heated, hammered, and folded together into thousands of imperceptible layers, yielding both a razor-sharp, durable edge and a flexible, shock-absorbing blade. Commonly, though optionally, the smith physically signed the blade; moreover, each smith's secret forging techniques left an idiosyncratic structural signature. Each unique finished product reflected the smith's personal honor and devotion to the craft, and today, the Japanese sword is valued as much for its artistic merit as for its historical significance.

1. The primary purpose of the passage is to

   (A) challenge the observation that the Japanese sword is highly admired by historians

   (B) introduce new information about the forging of Japanese swords

   (C) identify the Japanese sword as an ephemeral work of art

   (D) argue that Japanese sword makers were motivated by honor

   (E) explain the value attributed to the Japanese sword

2. Each of the following is mentioned in the passage EXCEPT

   (A) every Japanese sword has a unique structure that can be traced back to a special forging process

   (B) master smiths kept their forging methodologies secret

   (C) the Japanese sword was considered by some to have a spiritual quality

   (D) master smiths are now considered artists by major historians

   (E) the Japanese sword is considered both a work of art and a historical artifact

3. The author is most likely to agree with which of the following observations?

   (A) The Japanese sword is the most important handheld weapon in history.

   (B) The skill of the samurai is what made the Japanese sword so special.

   (C) If a sword had a physical signature, other swords could be attributed to that sword's creator.

   (D) Master smiths were more concerned about the artistic merit of their blades than about the blades' practical qualities.

   (E) The Japanese sword has more historical importance than artistic importance.

4. Which of the following can be inferred about the words "structural signature" in this passage?

   (A) They indicate the inscription that the smith places on the blade during the forging process.

   (B) They imply the particular characteristics of a blade created by a smith's unique forging process.

   (C) They suggest that each blade can be traced back to a known master smith.

   (D) They reflect the soul of the samurai who wielded the sword.

   (E) They refer to the unique curved shape of the blade.

7

5. The author most likely describes the forging process in order to

   (A) present an explanation for a change in perception

   (B) determine the historical significance of Japanese swords

   (C) explain why each Japanese sword is unique

   (D) compare Japanese master smiths to classical artists

   (E) review the complete process of making a Japanese sword

6. Select the sentence in the passage that best indicates that the author believes traditional Japanese swords are works of art.

7. Which of the following statements about Japanese swords is supported by the passage? Indicate all that apply.

   [A] There is a way to determine the creator of a given sword other than his signature on the blade.

   [B] They have been viewed in terms other than the purely material.

   [C] They have not always received the artistic recognition that they deserve.

Passage B: Television's Invention

In the early years of television, Vladimir Zworykin was considered the device's inventor, at least publicly. His loudest champion was his boss David Sarnoff, the president of RCA and the "father of television," as he was and is widely regarded. Modern historians agree that Philo Farnsworth, a self-educated prodigy who was the first to transmit live images, was television's technical inventor. But Farnsworth's contributions have gone relatively unnoticed, since it was Sarnoff, not Farnsworth, who put televisions into living rooms. More importantly, it was Sarnoff who successfully borrowed from the radio industry the paradigm of advertiser-funded programming, a paradigm still dominant today. In contrast, Farnsworth lacked business savvy and was unable to realize his dream of television as an educational tool.

Perhaps Sarnoff simply adapted his business ideas from other industries such as newspapers, replacing the revenue from subscriptions and newsstand purchases with that of television set sales, but Sarnoff promoted himself as a visionary. Some critics argue that Sarnoff's construct has damaged programming content. Others contend that it merely created a democratic platform allowing audiences to choose the programming they desire.

1. The primary purpose of the passage is to

    (A) correct public misconception about Farnsworth's role in developing early television programs

    (B) debate the influence of television on popular culture

    (C) challenge the current public perception of Vladimir Zworykin

    (D) chronicle the events that led from the development of radio to the invention of the television

    (E) describe and debate Sarnoff's influence on the public perception of television's inception

2. It can be inferred from the second paragraph of the passage that

    (A) television shows produced by David Sarnoff and Vladimir Zworykin tended to earn negative reviews

    (B) educational programs cannot draw as large an audience as sports programs

    (C) a number of critics feel that Sarnoff's initial decision to earn television revenue through advertising has had a positive or neutral impact on content

    (D) educational programs that are aired in prime time, the hours during which the greatest number of viewers are watching television, are less likely to earn a profit than those that are aired during the daytime hours

    (E) in matters of programming, the audience's preferences should be more influential than those of the advertisers

3. According to the passage, the television industry earned revenue from

    (A) advertising only

    (B) advertising and the sale of television sets

    (C) advertising and subscriptions

    (D) subscriptions and the sale of television sets

    (E) advertising, subscriptions, and the sale of television sets

4. Select the sentence that provides factual evidence that Sarnoff's talents were more imitative than innovative.

5. Which of the following statements is supported by the passage? Indicate all that apply.

    A The advertising-funded model of television has damaged programming content.

    B The contributions of television's technical inventor were overshadowed by the actions of those who popularized the medium.

    C There is no way to definitively prove who invented the first television.

Passage C: Life on Mars

Because of the proximity and likeness of Mars to Earth, scientists have long speculated about the possibility of life on Mars. Roughly three centuries ago, astronomers observed Martian polar ice caps, and later scientists discovered other similarities to Earth, including length of day and axial tilt. But in 1965, photos taken by the *Mariner 4* probe revealed a Mars without rivers, oceans, or signs of life. Moreover, in the 1990s, it was discovered that unlike Earth, Mars no longer possessed a substantial global magnetic field, allowing celestial radiation to reach the planet's surface and solar wind to eliminate much of Mars's atmosphere over the course of several billion years.

More recent probes have investigated whether there was once liquid water on Mars. Some scientists believe that the presence of certain geological landforms definitively resolves this question. Others posit that wind erosion or carbon dioxide oceans may be responsible for these formations. Mars rovers *Opportunity* and *Spirit*, which landed on Mars in 2004, have both discovered geological evidence of past water activity. These findings substantially bolster claims that there was once life on Mars.

1. The author's stance on the possibility of life on Mars can best be described as

   (A) optimistic

   (B) disinterested

   (C) skeptical

   (D) simplistic

   (E) cynical

2. The passage is primarily concerned with which of the following?

   (A) Disproving a widely accepted theory

   (B) Initiating a debate about the possibility of life on Mars

   (C) Presenting evidence in support of a controversial claim

   (D) Describing the various discoveries made concerning the possibility of life on Mars

   (E) Detailing the findings of the Mars rovers *Opportunity* and *Spirit*

3. Each of the following discoveries is mentioned in the passage EXCEPT

   (A) wind erosion and carbon dioxide oceans are responsible for certain geological landforms on Mars

   (B) Mars does not have a substantial global magnetic field

   (C) Some water activity existed on Mars at some point in the past

   (D) the length of day on Mars is similar to that on Earth

   (E) the axial tilt of Mars is similar to that of Earth

4. In the first paragraph, the author most likely mentions the discovery of polar ice caps to suggest that

   (A) until recently Mars's polar ice caps were thought to consist largely of carbon dioxide

   (B) Martian polar ice caps are made almost entirely of water ice

   (C) Mars has multiple similarities to Earth, including the existence of polar ice caps

   (D) Mars has only a small fraction of the carbon dioxide found on Earth and Venus

   (E) conditions on the planet Mars were once very different than they are at present

5.   Each of the following can be inferred from the passage EXCEPT

   (A)   the presence of certain geological landforms is not definitive proof that there was once life on Mars

   (B)   similarities to Earth bolster the idea that a planet might be or have been capable of supporting life

   (C)   the absence of a substantial global magnetic field on Mars suggests that it would be difficult to sustain life on Mars

   (D)   the presence of water activity on Mars is related to the possibility of life on Mars

   (E)   the claim that there was once water on Mars has only marginal support from recent discoveries

6.   It can be inferred from the passage that which of the following characteristics of a planet would imply that it might support life? Indicate all that apply.

   A   A significant global magnetic field

   B   Evidence of liquid carbon dioxide on the planet's surface

   C   The average daily level of sunlight reaching the planet's surface

7.   Select the sentence in the passage that provides the best evidence that, at the given time, life did not exist on Mars.

Passage D: Fossils

Archaeological discoveries frequently undermine accepted ideas, giving rise to new theories. Recently, a set of 3.3-million-year-old fossils, the remains of the earliest well-preserved child ever found, were discovered in Ethiopia. Estimated to be 3 years old at death, the female child was of the *Australopithecus afarensis* species, a human ancestor that lived in Africa over 3 million years ago. "Her completeness, antiquity, and age at death make this find of unprecedented importance in the history of paleo-anthropology," said Zeresenay Alemseged, a noted paleo-anthropologist, opining that the discovery could reconfigure conceptions about early humans' capacities.

Previously, *afarensis* was believed to have abandoned arboreal habitats. However, while the new fossil's lower limbs support the view of an upright stance, its gorilla-like arms suggest that *afarensis* was still able to swing through trees, initiating a reexamination of long-held theories of early human development. Also, the presence of a hyoid bone, a rarely preserved larynx bone that supports throat muscles, has dramatically affected concepts of the origin of speech. Although primitive and more ape-like than human-like, this fossil hyoid is the first found in such an early human-related species.

1. The organization of the passage could best be described as

   (A) discussing a controversial scientific discovery

   (B) contrasting previous theories of development with current theories

   (C) illustrating a general contention with a specific example

   (D) arguing for the importance of a particular field of study

   (E) refuting a popular misconception

2. The passage quotes Zeresenay Alemseged in order to

   (A) provide evidence to qualify the main idea of the first paragraph

   (B) question the claims of other scientists

   (C) provide evidence to support the linguistic abilities of the *afarensis* species

   (D) provide corroboration for the significance of the find

   (E) provide a subjective opinion that is refuted in the second paragraph

3. Each of the following is cited as a factor in the importance of the discovery of the fossils EXCEPT

   (A) the fact that the remains were those of a child

   (B) the age of the fossils

   (C) the location of the discovery

   (D) the species of the fossils

   (E) the intact nature of the fossils

4. It can be inferred from the passage's description of the discovered fossil hyoid bone that

   (A) *Australopithecus afarensis* was capable of speech

   (B) the discovered hyoid bone is less primitive than the hyoid bone of apes

   (C) the hyoid bone is necessary for speech

   (D) the discovery of the hyoid bone necessitated the reexamination of prior theories

   (E) the hyoid bone was the most important fossil found at the site

5. The impact of the discovery of the hyoid bone in the field of archaeology could best be compared to which one of the following examples in another field?

    (A) The discovery and analysis of cosmic rays lend support to a widely accepted theory of the origin of the universe.

    (B) The original manuscript of a deceased nineteenth-century author confirms ideas of the development of an important work of literature.

    (C) The continued prosperity of a state-run economy stirs debate in the discipline of macroeconomics.

    (D) Newly revealed journal entries by a prominent Civil War–era politician lead to a questioning of certain accepted historical interpretations about the conflict.

    (E) Research into the mapping of the human genome gives rise to nascent applications of individually tailored medicines.

6. Select the sentence that most distinctly undermines an accepted paleo-anthropological theory.

7

Passage E: Polygamy

Polygamy in Africa has been a popular topic for social research over the past half-century; it has been analyzed by many distinguished minds and in various well-publicized works. In 1961, when Remi Clignet published his book *Many Wives, Many Powers*, he was not alone in sharing the view that in Africa co-wives may be perceived as direct and indirect sources of increased income and prestige. For instance, some observers argued that polygamous marriages are more able than monogamous marriages to produce many children, who can legitimately be seen as a form of wealth as well as of "this-world" immortality connected to the transmission of family names (as opposed to "other-world" immortality in an afterlife). Moreover, polygamy is rooted in and sanctioned by many ancient traditions, both cultural and religious; therefore, some assert that polygamy can provide a stabilizing function within societies frequently under stress from both internal and external forces.

By the 1970s, such arguments had become crystallized and popular. Many other African scholars who wrote on the subject became the new champions of this philosophy. For example, in 1983, John Mbiti proclaimed that polygamy is an accepted and respectable institution serving many useful social purposes. Similarly, G.K. Nukunya, in his paper "Polygamy as a Symbol of Status," reiterated Mbiti's idea that a plurality of wives is a legitimate sign of affluence and power in African society.

However, the colonial missionary voice provided consistent opposition to polygamy by viewing the practice as unethical and destructive of family life. While the missionaries propagated this view citing the authority of the Bible, they were convinced that Africans had to be coerced into partaking in the vision of monogamy understood by the Western culture. The missionary viewpoint even included, in some instances, dictating immediate divorce in the case of newly converted men who had already contracted polygamous marriages. Unfortunately, both the missionary voice and the scholarly voice did not consider the views of African women important. Although there was some awareness that women regarded polygamy as both a curse and a blessing, the distanced, albeit scientific, perspective of an outside observer predominated both on the pulpit and in scholarly writings.

Contemporary research in the social sciences has begun to focus on the protagonist's voice in the study of culture, recognizing that the views and experiences of those who take part in a given reality ought to receive close examination. This privileging of the protagonist seems appropriate, particularly given that women in Africa have often used literary productions, which feature protagonists and other "actors" undergoing ordeals and otherwise taking active part in real life, to comment on marriage, family, and gender relations.

7

1. Which of the following best describes the main purpose of the passage above?

    (A) To discuss scholarly works that view polygamy as a sign of prestige, respect, and affluence in the African society

    (B) To trace the origins of the missionary opposition to African polygamy

    (C) To argue for imposing restrictions on polygamy in the African society

    (D) To explore the reasons for women's acceptance of polygamy

    (E) To discuss multiple perspectives on African polygamy and contrast them with contemporary research

2. The third paragraph of the passage plays which of the following roles?

    (A) It discusses the rationales for viewing polygamy as an indication of prestige and affluence in the African society.

    (B) It supports the author's view that polygamy is unethical and destructive of family life.

    (C) It contrasts the views of the colonial missionary with the position of the most recent contemporary research.

    (D) It describes the views on polygamy held by the colonial missionary and indicates a flaw in this vision.

    (E) It demonstrates that the colonial missionary was ignorant of the scholarly research on monogamy.

3. The passage provides each of the following EXCEPT

    (A) the year of publication of Remi Clignet's book *Many Wives, Many Powers*

    (B) the year in which John Mbiti made a claim that polygamy is an accepted institution

    (C) examples of African women's literary productions devoted to family relations

    (D) reasons for missionary opposition to polygamy

    (E) current research perspectives on polygamy

4. According to the passage, the colonial missionary and the early scholarly researchers shared which of the following views on polygamy?

    (A) Both considered polygamy a sign of social status and success.

    (B) Neither accounted for the views of local women.

    (C) Both attempted to limit the prevalence of polygamy.

    (D) Both pointed out polygamy's destructive effects on family life.

    (E) Both exhibited a somewhat negative attitude toward polygamy.

5. Which of the following statements can most properly be inferred from the passage?

    (A) Nukunya's paper "Polygamy as a Symbol of Status" was not written in 1981.

    (B) John Mbiti adjusted his initial view on polygamy, recognizing that the experiences of African women should receive closer attention.

    (C) Remi Clignet's book *Many Wives, Many Powers* was the first well-known scholarly work to proclaim that polygamy can be viewed as a symbol of prestige and wealth.

    (D) Under the influence of the missionary opposition, polygamy was proclaimed illegal in Africa as a practice "unethical and destructive of family life."

    (E) A large proportion of the scholars writing on polygamy in the 1970s and 1980s were of African descent.

7

6.   Which of the following examples fit the model of cultural studies cited in the final paragraph of the passage? Indicate all that apply.

A   A documentary about the modern-day slave trade that relied on interviews with those who had been enslaved

B   A study of relationship changes caused by long-term separation, using letters exchanged between prisoners and their loved ones

C   An experimental theater piece about blindness in which audience members were required to wear a blindfold

7.   Select the sentence in the first two paragraphs that cites a specific benefit of polygamy without mentioning the economic ramifications.

Passage F: Sweet Spot

Though most tennis players generally strive to strike the ball on the racket's vibration node, more commonly known as the "sweet spot," many players are unaware of the existence of a second, lesser-known location on the racket face, the center of percussion, that will also greatly diminish the strain on a player's arm when the ball is struck.

In order to understand the physics of this second sweet spot, it is helpful to consider what would happen to a tennis racket in the moments after impact with the ball if the player's hand were to vanish at the moment of impact. The impact of the ball would cause the racket to bounce backward, experiencing a translational motion away from the ball. The tendency of this motion would be to jerk all parts of the racket, including the end of its handle, backward, or away from the ball. Unless the ball happened to hit the racket precisely at the racket's center of mass, the racket would additionally experience a rotational motion around its center of mass—much as a penny that has been struck near its edge will start to spin. Whenever the ball hits the racket face, the effect of this rotational motion will be to jerk the end of the handle forward, toward the ball. Depending on where the ball strikes the racket face, one or the other of these motions will predominate.

However, there is one point of impact, known as the center of percussion, which causes neither motion to predominate; if a ball were to strike this point, the impact would not impart any motion to the end of the handle. The reason for this lack of motion is that the force on the upper part of the hand would be equal and opposite to the force on the lower part of the hand, resulting in no net force on the tennis player's hand or forearm. The center of percussion constitutes a second sweet spot because a tennis player's wrist typically is placed next to the end of the racket's handle. When the player strikes the ball at the center of percussion, her wrist is jerked neither forward nor backward, and she experiences a relatively smooth, comfortable tennis stroke.

The manner in which a tennis player can detect the center of percussion on a given tennis racket follows from the nature of this second sweet spot. The center of percussion can be located via simple trial and error by holding the end of a tennis racket between your finger and thumb and throwing a ball onto the strings. If the handle jumps out of your hand, then the ball has missed the center of percussion.

1. What is the primary message the author is trying to convey?

    (A) A proposal for an improvement to the design of tennis rackets

    (B) An examination of the differences between the two types of sweet spots

    (C) A definition of the translational and rotational forces acting on a tennis racket

    (D) A description of the ideal area in which to strike every ball

    (E) An explanation of a lesser-known area on a tennis racket that dampens unwanted vibration

2. According to the passage, all of the following are true of the forces acting upon a tennis racket striking a ball EXCEPT

    (A) the only way to eliminate the jolt that accompanies most strokes is to hit the ball on the center of percussion

    (B) the impact of the ball striking the racket can strain a tennis player's arm

    (C) there are at least two different forces acting upon the racket

    (D) the end of the handle of the racket will jerk forward after striking the ball unless the ball strikes the racket's center of mass

    (E) the racket will rebound after it strikes the ball

3.   What is the primary function served by paragraph 2 in the context of the entire passage?

   (A)   To establish the main idea of the passage

   (B)   To provide an explanation of the mechanics of the phenomenon discussed in the passage

   (C)   To introduce a counterargument that elucidates the main idea of the passage

   (D)   To provide an example of the primary subject described in the passage

   (E)   To explain why the main idea of the passage would be useful for tennis players

4.   The author mentions "a penny that has been struck near its edge" in order to

   (A)   show how the center of mass causes the racket to spin

   (B)   argue that a penny spins in the exact way that a tennis racket spins

   (C)   explain how translational motion works

   (D)   provide an illustration of a concept

   (E)   demonstrate that pennies and tennis rackets do not spin in the same way

5.   Which of the following can be inferred from the passage?

   (A)   If a player holds the tennis racket anywhere other than the end of the handle, the player will experience a jolting sensation.

   (B)   The primary sweet spot is more effective at damping vibration than is the secondary sweet spot.

   (C)   Striking a tennis ball at a spot other than the center of percussion can result in a jarring feeling.

   (D)   Striking a tennis ball repeatedly at spots other than a sweet spot leads to "tennis elbow."

   (E)   If a player lets go of the racket at the moment of impact, the simultaneous forward and backward impetus causes the racket to drop straight to the ground.

6.   Select the sentence in the second or third paragraph that describes the physics of the center of percussion's perceived sweetness.

7.   It can be inferred that a tennis ball that strikes a racket's center of percussion will do which of the following? Indicate all that apply.

   [A]   Cause the racket to bounce backward

   [B]   Not cause the wrist to jerk

   [C]   Allow for a cleaner stroke than a ball striking a racket's primary sweet spot

Passage G: Chaos Theory

Around 1960, mathematician Edward Lorenz found unexpected behavior in apparently simple equations representing atmospheric air flows. Whenever he reran his model with the same inputs, different outputs resulted—although the model lacked any random elements. Lorenz realized that tiny rounding errors in his analog computer mushroomed over time, leading to erratic results. His findings marked a seminal moment in the development of chaos theory, which, despite its name, has little to do with randomness.

To understand how unpredictability can arise from deterministic equations, which do not involve chance outcomes, consider the non-chaotic system of two poppy seeds placed in a round bowl. As the seeds roll to the bowl's center, a position known as a point attractor, the distance between the seeds shrinks. If, instead, the bowl is flipped over, two seeds placed on top will roll away from each other. Such a system, while still not technically chaotic, enlarges initial differences in position.

Chaotic systems, such as a machine mixing bread dough, are characterized by both attraction and repulsion. As the dough is stretched, folded, and pressed back together, any poppy seeds sprinkled in are intermixed seemingly at random. But this randomness is illusory. In fact, the poppy seeds are captured by "strange attractors," staggeringly complex pathways whose tangles appear accidental but are in fact determined by the system's fundamental equations.

During the dough-kneading process, two poppy seeds positioned next to each other eventually go their separate ways. Any early divergence or measurement error is repeatedly amplified by the mixing until the position of any seed becomes effectively unpredictable. It is this "sensitive dependence on initial conditions" and not true randomness that generates unpredictability in chaotic systems, of which one example may be the Earth's weather. According to the popular interpretation of the "Butterfly Effect," a butterfly flapping its wings causes hurricanes. A better understanding is that the butterfly causes uncertainty about the precise state of the air. This microscopic uncertainty grows until it encompasses even hurricanes. Few meteorologists believe that we will ever be able to predict rain or shine for a particular day years in the future.

1.   The main purpose of this passage is to

   (A) explore a common misconception about a complex physical system

   (B) trace the historical development of a scientific theory

   (C) distinguish a mathematical pattern from its opposite

   (D) describe the spread of a technical model from one field of study to others

   (E) contrast possible causes of weather phenomena

2.   In the example discussed in the passage, what is true about poppy seeds in bread dough, once the dough has been thoroughly mixed?

   (A) They have been individually stretched and folded over, like miniature versions of the entire dough.

   (B) They are scattered in random clumps throughout the dough.

   (C) They are accidentally caught in tangled objects called "strange attractors."

   (D) They are bound to regularly dispersed patterns of point attractors.

   (E) They are in positions dictated by the underlying equations that govern the mixing process.

3.   According to the passage, the rounding errors in Lorenz's model

    (A)   indicated that the model was programmed in a fundamentally faulty way

    (B)   were deliberately included to represent tiny fluctuations in atmospheric air currents

    (C)   were imperceptibly small at first, but tended to grow

    (D)   were at least partially expected, given the complexity of the actual atmosphere

    (E)   shrank to insignificant levels during each trial of the model

4.   The passage mentions each of the following as an example or potential example of a chaotic or non-chaotic system EXCEPT

    (A)   a dough-mixing machine

    (B)   atmospheric weather patterns

    (C)   poppy seeds placed on top of an upside-down bowl

    (D)   poppy seeds placed in a right-side-up bowl

    (E)   fluctuating butterfly flight patterns

5.   It can be inferred from the passage that which of the following pairs of items would most likely follow typical pathways within a chaotic system?

    (A)   Two particles ejected in random directions from the same decaying atomic nucleus

    (B)   Two stickers affixed to a balloon that expands and contracts over and over again

    (C)   Two avalanches sliding down opposite sides of the same mountain

    (D)   Two baseballs placed into a device designed to mix paint

    (E)   Two coins flipped into a large bowl

6.   The author implies which of the following about weather systems? Indicate all that apply.

    [A]   They illustrate the same fundamental phenomenon as Lorenz's rounding errors.

    [B]   Experts agree unanimously that weather will never be predictable years in advance.

    [C]   They are governed mostly by seemingly trivial events, such as the flapping of a butterfly's wings.

7.   Select the sentence in the second or third paragraph that illustrates why "chaos theory" might be called a misnomer.

Answers and Explanations

Answers to Passage A: Japanese Swords

Historians have long recognized the traditional Japanese sword, or *nihonto*, as one of the finest cutting weapons ever produced, but it has even been considered a spiritual entity. The adage "the sword is the soul of the samurai" reflects the sword's psychic importance, not only to its wielder, but also to its creator, the master smith. Not classically regarded as artists, master smiths nevertheless exerted great care in the process of creating swords, no two of which were ever forged exactly the same way. Over hundreds of hours, two types of steel were repeatedly heated, hammered, and folded together into thousands of subtle layers, yielding both a razor-sharp, durable edge and a flexible, shock-absorbing blade. Commonly, though optionally, the smith physically signed the blade; moreover, each smith's secret forging techniques left an idiosyncratic structural signature. Each unique finished product reflected the smith's personal honor and devotion to the craft, and today, the Japanese sword is valued as much for its artistic merit as for its historical significance.

Here is one example of a possible set of notes for this passage:

1. H: J sword = 1 of best cutting weapons, but even spiritual ← Point

   —Soul of Samurai

   —Impt to smith too

2. —Smiths careful, swords unique

   —Forging = complex

   —Physical + structural signat

1. **The primary purpose of the passage is to**

   (A) challenge the observation that the Japanese sword is highly admired by historians

   (B) introduce new information about the forging of Japanese swords

   (C) identify the Japanese sword as an ephemeral work of art

   (D) argue that Japanese sword makers were motivated by honor

   (E) explain the value attributed to the Japanese sword

To identify the primary purpose of the passage, examine the passage as a whole. Avoid answer choices that address only limited sections of the passage. The Point of the passage (*the Japanese sword has been considered not just a fine weapon but a spiritual entity*) is clearly established in the first two sentences; the purpose of the passage is to explain and support that Point.

(A) The passage does not call into question the admiration that historians have for the Japanese sword.

(B) The middle of the passage discusses forging techniques, but none of the information is presented as new. Moreover, these forging techniques are not the overall focus of the passage.

(C) The Japanese sword is not identified as an ephemeral (passing) work of art in the passage.

(D) Japanese sword makers were indeed motivated by honor, at least in part, according to the last sentence, but this is not the overall purpose of the passage, much of which describes the Japanese sword's physical properties and reasons for its importance.

(E) **CORRECT.** The passage as a whole describes the immense value of the Japanese sword to both the samurai (the sword's owner) and the smith (its maker). The saying "the sword is the soul of the samurai" is referenced early to indicate this importance. Later portions of the passage detail the tremendous effort that is put into each sword, reflecting the importance of each one.

2. **Each of the following is mentioned in the passage EXCEPT**

(A) every Japanese sword has a unique structure that can be traced back to a special forging process

(B) master smiths kept their forging methodologies secret

(C) the Japanese sword was considered by some to have a spiritual quality

(D) master smiths are now considered artists by major historians

(E) the Japanese sword is considered both a work of art and a historical artifact

For an EXCEPT question (almost always a Specific question), use the process of elimination to cross out those details mentioned in the passage.

(A) In the passage, this *unique signature* is referred to as a "structural signature" in the fifth sentence.

(B) The fifth sentence mentions the "secret forging techniques" used by each smith.

(C) The first sentence indicates that "the traditional Japanese sword . . . has even been considered a spiritual entity."

(D) **CORRECT.** The time and effort master smiths devote to making a sword is discussed, and the passage does indicate that the Japanese sword is valued for its artistic merit. However, the passage does not state that major historians consider master smiths themselves to be artists. *Major* historians are not referenced in the passage. Moreover, who values the Japanese sword for its artistic merit is not mentioned.

(E) In the last sentence, the passage indicates that "the Japanese sword is valued as much for its artistic merit as for its historical significance."

3. **The author is most likely to agree with which of the following observations?**

    (A) The Japanese sword is the most important handheld weapon in history.

    (B) The skill of the samurai is what made the Japanese sword so special.

    (C) If a sword had a physical signature, other swords could likely be attributed to that sword's creator.

    (D) Master smiths were more concerned about the artistic merit of their blades than about the blades' practical qualities.

    (E) The Japanese sword has more historical importance than artistic importance.

When looking for statements with which the author could agree, be sure to avoid extreme words and positions that go beyond the author's statements in the passage. This question requires attention to both the general Point of the passage and specific details throughout.

(A) The opening sentence says: "Historians have long recognized the traditional Japanese sword . . . as one of the finest cutting weapons ever produced"; however, there is no indication that the Japanese sword is the *most* important handheld weapon in history.

(B) This passage does not discuss the skill of the samurai warrior.

(C) **CORRECT.** According to the passage, every master smith had a "structural signature" due to his own secret forging process. Therefore, if a physical signature is present on a blade, that blade's structural signature could then be associated with a master smith, whose *master* status implies the creation of numerous swords.

(D) The passage mentions that each sword "reflected the smith's personal honor and devotion to craft"; however, there is no claim that master smiths emphasized their swords' artistic merit at the expense of practical qualities.

(E) The final sentence indicates that the sword "is valued as much for it artistic merit as for its historical significance." According to the passage, the two attributes are essentially equally valued; the Japanese sword is not more valued for the historical aspect.

4. **Which of the following can be inferred about the term "structural signature" in this passage?**

    (A) They indicate the inscription that the smith places on the blade during the forging process.

    (B) They imply the particular characteristics of a blade created by a smith's unique forging process.

    (C) They suggest that each blade can be traced back to a known master smith.

    (D) They reflect the soul of the samurai who wielded the swords.

    (E) They refer to the unique curved shape of the blade.

7

The author states that "each smith's secret forging techniques left an idiosyncratic structural signature." The words *idiosyncratic* and *signature* imply the uniqueness of the smith's process. Be careful not to infer any additional information, particularly when the question refers to a specific sentence or phrase.

(A) In the passage, such an inscription is referred to as a "physical signature," not a "structural signature."

(B) **CORRECT.** Note that the proof sentence indicates that each smith had his own process, and so the "structural signature" was unique to each smith (not necessarily to each individual blade).

(C) This statement seems reasonable. However, the passage does not say whether all master smiths are currently "known." Certain swords with a "structural signature" may be of unknown origin.

(D) The second sentence mentions the saying "the sword is the soul of the samurai," but you are not told that the "structural signature" was the aspect of the sword reflecting the soul of the samurai who wielded it. The second paragraph explains that the sword "reflected the **smith's** personal honor and devotion to craft." This statement, however, does not justify the claim that the structural signature itself reflects the soul of the samurai who wielded it.

(E) The passage does not discuss the shape of any Japanese blade.

5. **The author most likely describes the forging process in order to**

(A) present an explanation for a change in perception

(B) determine the historical significance of Japanese swords

(C) explain why each Japanese sword is unique

(D) compare Japanese master smiths to classical artists

(E) review the complete process of making a Japanese sword

To determine the function(s) of any part of a passage, pay attention to the emphasized content of that part, in particular any reiterated points, and to the relationship that part has to other portions of the passage. In this case, the description of the forging process extends the idea introduced earlier that the Japanese sword is revered.

(A) The final sentence mentions that Japanese swords are now appreciated more for their artistic merit, but no explanation as to why is provided.

(B) The words "historical significance" close the passage, but the description of the forging process fails to explain or outline that significance.

(C) **CORRECT.** The description of the forging process underscores the uniqueness of individual Japanese swords. One sentence mentions that "no two [swords] were ever forged in exactly the same way." Later, "structural signature" and "unique finished product" reinforce this point.

(D) The passage explains that master smiths were not considered artists in the classical sense, and then goes on to point out the painstaking creation of each sword. This implicitly draws a parallel between the creation of the sword and classical artistry. However, the passage does not actually describe or discuss classical artists, nor does it set forth criteria for classical artists. There is no actual comparison to classical artists, despite the mention of "artistic merit." This answer choice goes too far beyond the passage.

(E) Elements of the forging process are discussed, but the "complete" process of making a Japanese sword, such as making the handle, polishing the blade, etc., is not discussed in the paragraph.

6. **Select the sentence in the passage that best indicates that the author believes traditional Japanese swords are works of art.**

The passage first mentions the idea of art in the third sentence, but indicates that master smiths were *not* regarded as artists. After describing the meticulous forging process, the last sentence indicates that each sword is "unique" and is valued for its "artistic merit." The last sentence, then, best indicates that the author would consider these swords works of art.

7. **Which of the following statements about Japanese swords is supported by the passage? Select all that apply.**

   A There is a way to determine the creator of a given sword other than his signature on the blade.

   B They have been viewed in terms other than the purely material.

   C They have not always received the artistic recognition that they deserve.

(A), (B), and **(C):** This is a General question of the Select-One-or-More variety. Tackle each answer choice as its own question.

   A **CORRECT.** The second-to-last sentence says that "each smith's secret forging techniques left an idiosyncratic structural signature." This structural signature, then, could possibly be used to determine the creator of a given sword, even in the absence of a physical signature.

   B **CORRECT.** The first sentence tells you that the Japanese sword "has even been considered a spiritual entity." In other words, it has been viewed in terms other than the strictly material.

   C **CORRECT.** The last sentence tells you that "today, the Japanese sword is valued as much for its artistic merit as for its historical significance." Earlier in the passage, however, you were told that master smiths were "not classically regarded as artists." This means that those smiths viewed as artists today did not always receive the same recognition and neither did the swords they made.

Answers to Passage B: Television's Invention

In the early years of television, Vladimir Zworykin was considered its inventor, at least publicly. His loudest champion was his boss David Sarnoff, the president of RCA and the "father of television," as he was and is widely regarded. Modern historians agree that Philo Farnsworth, a self-educated prodigy who was the first to transmit live images, was television's technical inventor. But Farnsworth's contributions have gone relatively unnoticed, since it was Sarnoff, not Farnsworth, who put televisions into living rooms. More importantly, it was Sarnoff who successfully borrowed from the radio industry the paradigm of advertiser-funded programming, a paradigm still dominant today. In contrast, Farnsworth lacked business savvy and was unable to realize his dream of television as an educational tool.

Perhaps Sarnoff simply adapted his business ideas from other industries such as newspapers, replacing the revenue from subscriptions and newsstand purchases with that of television set sales, but Sarnoff promoted himself as a visionary. Some critics argue that Sarnoff's construct has damaged programming content. Others contend that it merely created a democratic platform allowing audiences to choose the programming they desire.

Here is one example of a possible set of notes for this passage:

---

1. Early TV, Z seen as invntr

    —Champ by Sarn (father of TV!)

    BUT now hist agree: F = TRUE invntr

    —S: launched: advrs pay ← Point

    —F: not biz savvy, wanted TV = educ

2. S: visionary or adopter?

    + or − effect?

---

1. **The primary purpose of the passage is to**

    (A) correct public misconception about Farnsworth's role in developing early television programs

    (B) debate the influence of television on popular culture

    (C) challenge the current public perception of Vladimir Zworykin

    (D) chronicle the events that led from the development of radio to the invention of the television

    (E) describe and debate Sarnoff's influence on the public perception of television's inception

The answer to a primary purpose question should incorporate elements of the entire passage. Avoid answer choices that address limited sections of the passage. The Point: Sarnoff was responsible for introducing television to the public and establishing a dominant paradigm. This is foreshadowed when Sarnoff is called "the father of television."

(A) Farnsworth's influence on the development of the television itself is only mentioned in the first paragraph; Farnsworth's role in developing programs is never mentioned.

(B) The impact of television is not discussed until the second paragraph. Although this paragraph debates whether or not Sarnoff's influence was a positive one, it does not address the influence of television on popular culture.

(C) Vladimir Zworykin is only mentioned briefly in the first paragraph, so he is clearly not the primary subject of the passage. Furthermore, even though the passage mentions the initial public perception, it says nothing about the current public perception of Zworykin.

(D) The passage discusses events that occurred after the invention; there is no mention of the events that led up to the invention of the television.

(E) **CORRECT.** This answer includes the main elements of both paragraphs; it functions as a good summary of the entire passage.

2. **It can be inferred from the second paragraph of the passage that**

(A) television shows produced by David Sarnoff and Vladimir Zworykin tended to earn negative reviews

(B) educational programs cannot draw as large an audience as sports programs

(C) a number of critics feel that Sarnoff's initial decision to earn television revenue through advertising has had a positive or neutral impact on content

(D) educational programs that are aired in prime time, the hours during which the greatest number of viewers are watching television, are less likely to earn a profit than those that are aired during the daytime hours

(E) in matters of programming, the audience's preferences should be more influential than those of the advertisers

The second paragraph states that some critics viewed Sarnoff's approach negatively and others thought his approach embodied a democratic concept. The correct answer must follow from at least one of those statements.

(A) You have been given no information about the television programs Sarnoff and Zworykin produced; in fact, you have not been told that they produced television shows. The paragraph is about the advertising revenue construct Sarnoff implemented, not about the television shows he produced.

(B) It is implied that ratings for educational programs are, in general, not strong, but that does not mean that any one particular educational program cannot have higher ratings than one particular sports program. Beware of answer choices that contain absolutes such as *cannot*.

(C) **CORRECT.** You are told that "some critics argue that Sarnoff's paradigm has damaged programming content." Since the word is *some*, it must be true that others feel it has played either a positive role or a neutral role. A group of these critics is mentioned in the last sentence of the paragraph.

(D) The passage does not differentiate programming based on what time television shows air, nor does it mention profitability.

(E) The word "should" implies a moral judgment, and the answer is therefore out of the scope of the passage. The second paragraph does not indicate a belief as to who should influence programming choices.

3. **According to the passage, the television industry earned revenue from**

(A) advertising only

(B) advertising and the sale of television sets

(C) advertising and subscriptions

(D) subscriptions and the sale of television sets

(E) advertising, subscriptions, and the sale of television sets

In an attempt to trick you on a Specific question such as this, the GRE will offer incomplete answers that incorporate language from throughout the passage but do not directly bear on the question at hand. Two sections in the passage discuss ways in which the television industry brought in revenue. The first paragraph mentions "advertiser-funded programming." The second paragraph states that Sarnoff borrowed from other business models by "replacing the revenue from subscriptions and newsstand purchases with that of television set sales."

(A) This answer choice does not account for the revenue generated from selling television sets.

(B) **CORRECT.** Advertising and the sale of television sets are the two ways mentioned through which the industry could generate revenue.

(C) Subscriptions are mentioned as a method for newspapers to earn revenue; the last paragraph clearly states that television replaced this revenue with that earned by selling the sets themselves.

(D) This choice does not mention advertising revenue; moreover, it incorrectly mentions subscription revenue.

(E) This answer choice incorrectly mentions subscription revenue.

4.   **Select the sentence that provides factual evidence that Sarnoff's talents were more imitative than innovative.**

This is a Select-in-Passage question relating to Sarnoff's legacy as an imitator versus his legacy as an innovator. There are two plausible candidates. First, the second-to-last sentence of the first paragraph says that Sarnoff "successfully borrowed from the radio industry the paradigm of advertiser-funded programming." This sentence states a fact indicating that Sarnoff took a business model from another medium, which would be imitative rather than innovative.

The second possible answer is the first sentence of the second paragraph, which says: "Perhaps Sarnoff simply adapted his business ideas from other industries such as newspapers." However, the use of the word *perhaps* means that this is an idea of the author's, rather than a statement of fact. For this reason, this cannot be the answer.

The correct answer is the second-to-last sentence of the first paragraph.

5.   **Which of the following statements is supported by the passage? Indicate all that apply.**

[A] The advertising-funded model of television has damaged programming content.

[B] The contributions of television's technical inventor were overshadowed by the actions of those who popularized the medium.

[C] There is no way to definitively prove who invented the first television.

Expect to need extra time on Select-One-or-More questions. This one, annoyingly, does not provide any clues about where to look in the passage. Use the key words in each statement to determine where to examine the passage.

[A] While the last sentence says that some critics "argue that Sarnoff's construct has damaged pro-gramming content," this is not stated as a fact, only a possible opinion. Always be careful to differ-entiate between opinions and facts on RC passages.

[B] **CORRECT.** The first paragraph indicates that Farnsworth was the technical inventor of television. That paragraph also says that "Farnsworth's contributions have gone relatively unnoticed, since it was Sarnoff who put televisions into living rooms."

[C] Though the passage describes the ways in which both Zworykin and Farnsworth have been described as the progenitors of television, and though it makes a case that there remains a lively debate over who deserves the credit, this does not mean that there is "no way" of determining who invented the first television. Always be wary of **extreme** language like this when dealing with RC questions.

Answers to Passage C: Life on Mars

Because of the proximity and likeness of Mars to Earth, scientists have long speculated about the possibility of life on Mars. Roughly three centuries ago, astronomers observed Martian polar ice caps, and later scientists discovered other similarities to Earth, including length of day and axial tilt. But in 1965, photos taken by the *Mariner 4* probe revealed a Mars without rivers, oceans, or signs of life. Moreover, in the 1990s, it was discovered that unlike Earth, Mars no longer possessed a substantial global magnetic field, allowing celestial radiation to reach the planet's surface and solar wind to eliminate much of Mars's atmosphere over the course of several billion years.

More recent probes have investigated whether there was once liquid water on Mars. Some scientists believe that the presence of certain geological landforms definitively resolves this question. Others posit that wind erosion or carbon dioxide oceans may be responsible for these formations. Mars rovers *Opportunity* and *Spirit*, which landed on Mars in 2004, have both discovered geological evidence of past water activity. These findings substantially bolster claims that there was once life on Mars.

Here is one example of a possible set of notes for this passage:

> 1. S: Mars close, simil to Earth → poss life on M!
>
>   —Sims (polar ice, day, tilt)
>
>   —Diffs (no water, no more mag field)
>
> 2. Rec. focus: was there water?
>
>   —Evid: yes/no, now <u>more</u> support for life on M ← Point

1. **The author's stance on the possibility of life on Mars can best be described as**

    (A) optimistic

    (B) disinterested

    (C) skeptical

    (D) simplistic

    (E) cynical

This passage is concerned with the possibility of life on Mars. It details the various discoveries that have been made over centuries. The passage can best be described as factual and unbiased. When considering a tone question such as this, look for instances in which the author's opinion is revealed. You should also remember to be wary of extreme words in the answer choices.

(A) The author is neither optimistic nor pessimistic about the possibility of life on Mars.

(B) **CORRECT.** Note that the primary meaning of *disinterested* is "impartial" or "neutral," which accurately describes the tone of the argument.

(C) There is no indication that the author of the passage is skeptical. The passage simply puts forth facts and does not offer an opinion one way or the other.

(D) The author considers several different factors in the determination of life on Mars. The author's stance could not appropriately be described as simplistic.

(E) Again, the author is objective in tone and could not accurately be characterized as cynical.

2. **The passage is primarily concerned with which of the following?**

   (A) Disproving a widely accepted theory

   (B) Initiating a debate about the possibility of life on Mars

   (C) Presenting evidence in support of a controversial claim

   (D) Describing the various discoveries made concerning the possibility of life on Mars

   (E) Detailing the findings of the Mars rovers *Opportunity* and *Spirit*

This passage is primarily concerned with the possibility of life on Mars. The two paragraphs discuss various discoveries that have been made over the past few centuries. The passage concludes that recent findings substantiate claims that there was once life on Mars. However, scientists are still not certain. In determining the purpose or main idea of the passage, you should avoid extreme words and be able to defend every word.

   (A) This passage does not set out to *disprove* the theory that there is life on Mars. It is also too extreme to suggest that this is a "widely accepted theory."

   (B) This answer choice is tempting because it is relatively neutral. However, the passage does not seek to initiate a debate; it is more concerned with documenting findings that pertain to life on Mars. In other words, the passage presents the findings that frame a debate; it doesn't initiate the debate itself.

   (C) The passage presents evidence in support of and against the possibility of life on Mars. It is too limited to suggest that the passage is primarily concerned with presenting evidence "in support of" life on Mars.

   (D) **CORRECT.** This answer choice avoids extreme words and best summarizes the purpose of the passage.

   (E) This answer choice is too specific. The passage does mention the Mars rovers *Opportunity* and *Spirit*, but it is inaccurate to suggest that the passage is primarily concerned with these two rovers.

3. **Each of the following discoveries is mentioned in the passage EXCEPT**

   (A) wind erosion and carbon dioxide oceans are responsible for certain geological landforms on Mars

   (B) Mars does not have a substantial global magnetic field

   (C) some water activity existed on Mars at some point in the past

   (D) the length of day on Mars is similar to that on Earth

   (E) the axial tilt of Mars is similar to that of Earth

To address this Specific question, point out specific evidence in the text to defend your answer choice. The passage discusses several discoveries; to answer this question, find which of the answer choices is *not* a discovery specifically mentioned in the passage.

(A) **CORRECT.** The passage does make mention of wind erosion and carbon dioxide oceans, but the author states that these are other possible explanations for certain geological landforms on Mars. Wind erosion and carbon dioxide oceans are *possible causes* of the geological landforms rather than "discoveries."

(B) At the end of the first paragraph, the passage states that "in the 1990s, it was discovered that, unlike Earth, Mars no longer possessed a substantial global magnetic field."

(C) In the second paragraph, the author indicates that two rovers "both discovered geological evidence of past water activity."

(D) Certain similarities Mars has to Earth were discovered sometime between three centuries ago and 1965, including the length of day, as noted in the second sentence of the first paragraph.

(E) Certain similarities Mars has to Earth were discovered sometime between three centuries ago and 1965, including the axial tilt of Mars being similar to that of the Earth, as noted in the second sentence of the first paragraph.

4. **In the first paragraph, the author most likely mentions the discovery of polar ice caps to suggest that**

(A) until recently Mars's polar ice caps were thought to consist largely of carbon dioxide

(B) Martian polar ice caps are made almost entirely of water ice

(C) Mars has many similarities to Earth, including the existence of polar ice caps

(D) Mars has only a small fraction of the carbon dioxide found on Earth and Venus

(E) conditions on the planet Mars were once very different than they are at present

This is a Specific question that refers back to the second sentence in the first paragraph. The best approach is to reread this sentence and determine, using surrounding sentences, what the author's purpose is in mentioning Mars's polar ice caps. If you read the second part of the sentence, "later scientists discovered other similarities to Earth, including length of day and axial tilt," you notice that polar ice caps are introduced as an example of the similarity of Mars to Earth (note the use of the word *other*).

(A) The passage does not mention the content of the polar ice caps, just that they were observed.

(B) Again, you do not know, from the passage, the composition of Mars's polar ice caps.

(C) **CORRECT.** As stated above, polar ice caps are introduced as one of several similarities of Mars to Earth.

(D) The passage does not indicate the carbon dioxide content of Mars or Earth. It also does not mention Venus.

(E) While you know from the rest of the passage that conditions on Mars were probably different from what they are now, the author does not mention polar ice caps in order to indicate this.

5. **Each of the following can be inferred from the passage EXCEPT**

(A) the presence of certain geological landforms is not definitive proof that there was once life on Mars

(B) similarities to Earth bolster the idea that a planet might be or have been capable of supporting life

(C) the absence of a substantial global magnetic field on Mars suggests that it would be difficult to sustain life on Mars

(D) the presence of water activity on Mars is related to the possibility of life on Mars

(E) the claim that there was once water on Mars has only limited and indirect support from recent discoveries

A question that asks for an inference from the passage is a Specific question; it is helpful to find evidence for any inference in the text. Make sure each inference can be defended by going back to the text and does not go far beyond the language in the passage.

(A) In the second paragraph, the author states that while the presence of geological landforms may indicate the presence of water, it is also possible that these landforms were caused by wind erosion or carbon dioxide oceans.

(B) The first paragraph describes three similarities between Mars and Earth (polar ice caps, length of day, and axial tilt). The passage then contrasts that evidence: "But" later photos showed a planet "without rivers, oceans, or signs of life." If this later evidence showed no signs of life, in contrast to earlier evidence showing similarities with Earth, then the similarities must support the possibility of life on Mars.

(C) In the second paragraph, the absence of a substantial global magnetic field is presented as evidence of the lack of life on Mars. Again, note that this answer choice avoids extreme words by using the word *suggests*.

(D) The first sentence in the second paragraph states that "more recent probes have investigated whether there was once liquid water on Mars." Given this purpose, it is clear that the existence of water is important in order to establish whether or not there was life on Mars.

(E) **CORRECT.** According to the second paragraph, the "Mars rovers *Opportunity* and *Spirit* . . . have both discovered geological evidence of past water activity." As made clear by the subsequent sentence that "these findings substantially bolster claims," the evidence supporting the claim that there was once water on Mars is substantial. Thus, the passage contradicts the statement that this claim is supported by only marginal evidence.

6. **It can be inferred from the passage that which of the following characteristics of a planet would imply that it might support life? Indicate all that apply.**

[A] A significant global magnetic field

[B] Evidence of liquid carbon dioxide on the planet's surface

[C] The average daily level of sunlight reaching the planet's surface

Most of the passage is about what aspects of Mars might or might not imply that it once supported life. Seek out direct language in the passage to prove or disprove each possible answer choice.

[A] **CORRECT.** The passage says that "Mars no longer possessed a substantial global magnetic field," which led to the disappearance of Mars's atmosphere. This dissimilarity with Earth is used in the passage as evidence against life on Mars.

[B] The passage mentions "carbon dioxide oceans" as a possible cause for certain geological formations. Another possible (and contrasting) cause is liquid water. Since water activity is associated with possible life, and carbon dioxide oceans are mentioned in contrast, carbon dioxide is probably not evidence of life.

[C] While your general knowledge of the importance of the sun might make it reasonable to assume that the sun would be important on other planets as well, the passage does not discuss this particular issue. The passage does mention "length of day" as a similarity between Mars and the Earth, but length of day does not necessarily mean hours of daylight. A day can also refer to the length of time it takes a planet to rotate on its own axis.

7. **Select the sentence in the passage that provides the best evidence that, at the given time, life did not exist on Mars.**

This Select-in-Passage question asks for evidence that there was not life on Mars at the time that evidence was collected.

The correct answer probably will not be found in the second paragraph, which mostly provides evidence that there *was* life on Mars at one point. In the first paragraph, the third sentence says that in 1965, photos "revealed a Mars without rivers, oceans, or signs of life," providing evidence that life did not exist at that time. The next sentence indicates that the lack of a magnetic field caused some negative consequences incompatible with life. However, this sentence says that there is no longer such a magnetic field, indicating that the field did once exist.

The correct sentence is "But in 1965, photos taken by the *Mariner 4* probe revealed a Mars without rivers, oceans, or signs of life."

Answers to Passage D: Fossils

Archaeological discoveries frequently undermine accepted ideas, giving rise to new theories. Recently, a set of 3.3-million-year-old fossils, the remains of the earliest well-preserved child ever found, were discovered in Ethiopia. Estimated to be 3 years old at death, the female child was of the *Australopithecus afarensis* species, a human ancestor that lived in Africa over 3 million years ago. "Her completeness, antiquity, and age at death make this find of unprecedented importance in the history of paleo-anthropology," said Zeresenay Alemseged, a noted paleo-anthropologist, opining that the discovery could reconfigure conceptions about early humans' capacities.

Previously, *afarensis* was believed to have abandoned arboreal habitats. However, while the new fossil's lower limbs support the view of an upright stance, its gorilla-like arms suggest that *afarensis* was still able to swing through trees, initiating a reexamination of long-held theories of early human development. Also, the presence of a hyoid bone, a rarely preserved larynx bone that supports throat muscles, has dramatically affected concepts of the origin of speech. Although primitive and more ape-like than human-like, this fossil hyoid is the first found in such an early human-related species.

Here is one example of a possible set of notes for this passage:

1. Arch: disc → undermine old, lead to new thry ← Point

   —e.g., child foss Eth

2. Before: thought af no longer in trees

   BUT disc → reexam old thry

   Also hy bone → Δ thry

1. **The organization of the passage could best be described as**

   (A) discussing a controversial scientific discovery

   (B) contrasting previous theories of human development with current theories

   (C) illustrating a general contention with a specific example

   (D) arguing for the importance of a particular field of study

   (E) refuting a popular misconception

When assessing a passage's organization, consider the main idea of each paragraph. This passage begins by noting that "archaeological discoveries frequently undermine accepted ideas, giving rise to new theories." It supports this statement by relating the impact of one discovery in the field. Thus, the best answer will reference both the overall contention and the use of the example.

(A) This choice omits the phenomenon that the discovery is meant to illustrate: discoveries often give rise to new theories. Also, there is nothing controversial about the described discovery.

(B) The passage does not focus on the contrast between previous theories of human development and current theories. Rather, it discusses a singular discovery that affects previous theories. The passage would need to outline both previous and current theories of development and then contrast them. Instead, the passage focuses on how one example illustrates a way in which the field of archaeology evolves.

(C) **CORRECT.** The passage makes a general claim and uses a specific example to support that claim, just as this choice states.

(D) One might feel that the evolution of theories of human development is a worthwhile object of contemplation, but the *passage* does not argue for the importance of archaeology as a field of study. This answer choice misstates the organization of the passage.

(E) The passage does not indicate how popular the earlier theories of human development were. Also, the passage provides only one example of a single discovery and its importance. The language employed in the passage does not warrant describing the passage as a refutation of past theories.

2. **The passage quotes Zeresenay Alemseged in order to**

(A) provide evidence to qualify the main idea of the first paragraph

(B) question the claims of other scientists

(C) provide evidence to support the linguistic abilities of the *afarensis* species

(D) provide corroboration for the significance of the find

(E) provide a subjective opinion that is refuted in the second paragraph

This quotation in the first paragraph highlights the importance of the discovery and is followed by another similar reference. The quotation is used to emphasize the exceptional importance of this find; the correct answer for this Inference question will reflect this emphasis.

(A) The main idea of the first paragraph is that a new finding can call accepted archaeological theories into question. The rest of the paragraph provides an example of this phenomenon. The quotation emphasizes the importance of the discovery itself, not the example, nor does the quotation qualify or limit the main idea of the first paragraph.

(B) The passage does not discuss claims of other scientists. Thus, this answer choice is incorrect.

(C) The discussion of the linguistic ability of the *afarensis* species is in the second paragraph and is unrelated to this quotation.

(D) **CORRECT.** The point of this paragraph is to illustrate that in archaeology, important factual discoveries lead to theoretical changes. The quotation corroborates the idea that this discovery is in fact a significant one.

(E) The quotation is offered as corroboration of the importance of the discovery and is not refuted at any point in the passage.

3. **Each of the following is cited as a factor in the importance of the discovery of the fossils EXCEPT**

   (A) the fact that the remains were those of a child

   (B) the age of the fossils

   (C) the location of the discovery

   (D) the species of the fossils

   (E) the intact nature of the fossils

On Except questions, it is often easier to eliminate incorrect answer choices until only one is left.

   (A) The fourth sentence of the first paragraph cites a quotation from a noted paleo-anthropologist that the find of the child fossils was of unprecedented importance due to the child's "age at death." Therefore, the fact that the remains were those of a child was of substantial significance.

   (B) The "antiquity" (a synonym for *age*) of the fossils is mentioned in the fourth sentence of the first paragraph as a reason why the fossils were an important discovery.

   (C) **CORRECT.** The location of the fossil discovery is mentioned in the first paragraph of the passage. However, the location is not provided as a reason why the fossils are significant.

   (D) This choice is tricky. The second paragraph describes what was previously "believed" about *afarensis* and that this evidence "dramatically affected" certain theories about the development of speech in humans. The fossils were of a "human-related species," so the species itself was significant in influencing the theories about human speech.

   (E) The fourth sentence of the first paragraph notes that the find was important due its "completeness." The intact nature of the fossils is another way of saying that the fossils are complete.

4. **It can be inferred from the passage's description of the discovered fossil hyoid bone that**

   (A) *Australopithecus afarensis* was capable of speech

   (B) the discovered hyoid bone is less primitive than the hyoid bone of apes

   (C) the hyoid bone is necessary for speech

   (D) the discovery of the hyoid bone necessitated the reexamination of prior theories

   (E) the hyoid bone was the most important fossil found at the site

The passage provides the following information about the discovered hyoid bone: it is the oldest ever found, since this type of bone is rarely preserved, and it is "primitive and more ape-like than human-like." The passage also states that the discovery will impact theories about speech.

   (A) The passage gives no information about the linguistic capacities of *Australopithecus afarensis*. The passage does not give enough information to infer that the species was capable of speech.

   (B) The passage indicates that the discovered hyoid bone more closely resembles those of apes than humans. However, while the passage does generally relate to evolution, the discovered bone is not necessarily less primitive than that of an ape. It could be slightly different in an equally primitive way; not all differences in structure would make a bone more advanced.

   (C) While it can be inferred that this bone has some effect on speech, the passage does not indicate that it is "necessary for speech." It is possible that a species could be capable of speech without a hyoid bone.

   (D) **CORRECT.** The passage states that the discovery of the hyoid bone "has dramatically affected concepts of the origin of speech." Thus, it can be inferred that the discovery made the reexamination of prior theories necessary.

   (E) The passage does not rank the importance of the fossils found; as a result, this choice is not necessarily true. It is possible that other fossils were of equal or greater importance.

5. **The impact of the discovery of the hyoid bone in the field of archaeology could best be compared to which one of the following examples in another field?**

   (A) The discovery and analysis of cosmic rays lend support to a widely accepted theory of the origin of the universe.

   (B) The original manuscript of a deceased nineteenth-century author confirms ideas of the development of an important work of literature.

   (C) The continued prosperity of a state-run economy stirs debate in the discipline of macroeconomics.

   (D) Newly revealed journal entries by a prominent Civil War–era politician lead to a questioning of certain accepted historical interpretations about the conflict.

   (E) Research into the mapping of the human genome gives rise to nascent applications of individually tailored medicines.

When you are asked to choose which answer best parallels a part of a passage, be sure that you grasp the nature of the example in the passage before considering the answer choices.

The passage indicates that the discovery of the hyoid bone "has dramatically affected concepts of the origin of speech." This evidence supports the passage's main point: new discoveries can undermine or call into question existing theories and give rise to new ones.

The correct answer will reflect this sort of impact in another field.

   (A) In this example, the discovery serves to support a widely accepted theory, as opposed to causing a reexamination of that theory.

   (B) In this answer choice, the discovery serves to confirm earlier held ideas, as opposed to causing a reexamination of those ideas.

   (C) There is no indication that an accepted theory is applicable and being called into question. Further, the "continued prosperity" is not a new discovery or change in the way that things used to be done or viewed.

   (D) **CORRECT.** This answer choice correctly describes a discovery that causes a reexamination of earlier ideas. In this case, newly uncovered journal entries spur a reevaluation of certain historical ideas regarding an important conflict.

   (E) In this answer, scientific advances in the field of biology give rise to new applications. It does not discuss a discovery that calls accepted ideas into question.

6. **Select the sentence that most distinctly undermines an accepted paleo-anthropological theory.**

This Select-in-Passage question asks for a specific example of the main point: a new discovery that undermines or calls into question an accepted theory or idea.

The first sentence of the second paragraph describes a previously accepted theory about *afarensis*. The next sentence describes how this theory was undermined, and it is the correct answer: "its gorilla-like arms suggest that *afarensis* was still able to swing through trees, initiating a reexamination of long-held theories of human development." The example of the hyoid bone mentioned later never describes exactly what theory was undermined by its discovery.

Answers to Passage E: Polygamy

Polygamy in Africa has been a popular topic for social research over the past half-century; it has been analyzed by many distinguished minds and in various well-publicized works. In 1961, when Remi Clignet published his book *Many Wives, Many Powers*, he was not alone in sharing the view that in Africa co-wives may be perceived as direct and indirect sources of increased income and prestige. For instance, some observers argued that polygamous marriages are more able than monogamous marriages to produce many children, who can legitimately be seen as a form of wealth as well as of "this-world" immortality connected to the transmission of family names (as opposed to "other-world" immortality in an afterlife). Moreover, polygamy is rooted in and sanctioned by many ancient traditions, both cultural and religious; therefore, some assert that polygamy can provide a stabilizing function within societies frequently under stress from both internal and external forces.

By the 1970s, such arguments had become crystallized and popular. Many other African scholars who wrote on the subject became the new champions of this philosophy. For example, in 1983, John Mbiti proclaimed that polygamy is an accepted and respectable institution serving many useful social purposes. Similarly, G.K. Nukunya, in his paper "Polygamy as a Symbol of Status," reiterated Mbiti's idea that a plurality of wives is a legitimate sign of affluence and power in African society.

However, the colonial missionary voice provided consistent opposition to polygamy by viewing the practice as unethical and destructive of family life. While the missionaries propagated this view citing the authority of the Bible, they were convinced that Africans had to be coerced into partaking in the vision of monogamy understood by the Western culture. The missionary viewpoint even included, in some instances, dictating immediate divorce in the case of newly converted men who had already contracted polygamous marriages. Unfortunately, both the missionary voice and the scholarly voice did not consider the views of African women important. Although there was some awareness that women regarded polygamy as both a curse and a blessing, the distanced, albeit scientific, perspective of an outside observer predominated both on the pulpit and in scholarly writings.

Contemporary research in the social sciences has begun to focus on the protagonist's voice in the study of culture, recognizing that the views and experiences of those who take part in a given reality ought to receive close examination. This privileging of the protagonist seems appropriate, particularly given that women in Africa have often used literary productions, which feature protagonists and other "actors" undergoing ordeals and otherwise taking active part in real life, to comment on marriage, family, and gender relations.

Here is one example of a possible set of notes for this passage:

1. <u>Past 50 yrs: Polyg in Afr = pop topic soc rsch</u>

   — '61 Clig: co-wives = $, prestige

   — Kids = wealth, immort

   — polyg = tradition, stable

2. By 70s many Afr scholars agree

3. BUT missnry opp polyg

   —Unfortly miss + scholars: ignore Afr wmn views ← Point (part)

4. Now: focus on protag (Afr wmn) ← Point (part)

1.   **Which of the following best describes the main purpose of the passage above?**

   (A)   To discuss scholarly works that view polygamy as a sign of prestige, respect, and affluence in the African society

   (B)   To trace the origins of the missionary opposition to African polygamy

   (C)   To argue for imposing restrictions on polygamy in the African society

   (D)   To explore the reasons for women's acceptance of polygamy

   (E)   To discuss multiple perspectives on African polygamy and contrast them with contemporary research

On Main Idea questions, be sure to avoid extreme answer choices and those answers that refer to only a part of the passage rather than the whole text. Typically, test writers will include incorrect answers that will be factually true but will describe the purpose of just one paragraph. The Point of this passage is arguably split in at least two pieces. The author wants to convey not only that two views of polygamy in Africa (those of the early scholars and of the missionaries) were *unfortunately* limited, but also that current research is addressing this limitation by examining the perspectives of the women protagonists.

   (A)   Scholarly works that view polygamy positively are discussed only in the first two paragraphs of the passage. This answer is too narrow to capture the purpose of the entire text.

   (B)   While the third paragraph discusses the missionary opposition and traces its sources to the Bible, this analysis is not central to the entire passage.

   (C)   While the text discusses multiple perspectives on polygamy, it does not argue in favor of or against restricting polygamy.

   (D)   The passage provides no information about the reasons that women accept polygamy, other than mentioning that they view it "as both a curse and a blessing."

   (E)   **CORRECT.** The entire passage is devoted to the discussion of multiple perspectives on polygamy. The first two paragraphs review scholarly works that view polygamy as a sign of prestige and respect, while the third paragraph offers an opposing view. Finally, the concluding paragraph contrasts both of these perspectives with contemporary research.

2.   **The third paragraph of the passage plays which of the following roles?**

   (A)   It discusses the rationales for viewing polygamy as an indication of prestige and affluence in the African society.

   (B)   It supports the author's view that polygamy is unethical and destructive of family life.

   (C)   It contrasts the views of the colonial missionary with the position of the most recent contemporary research.

   (D)   It describes the views on polygamy held by the colonial missionary and indicates a flaw in this vision.

   (E)   It demonstrates that the colonial missionary was ignorant of the scholarly research on monogamy.

On this type of question, it is helpful to reread the topic sentence of the paragraph at issue. The topic sentence is typically in the first or second sentence of the paragraph. Furthermore, look for the answer that effectively captures the entire paragraph and avoids making unjustified statements.

(A) These rationales are discussed in the first and second rather than the third paragraph.

(B) While the third paragraph discusses the views of the colonial missionary, nothing in the passage suggests that the author shares this vision.

(C) While the third paragraph presents the position of the colonial missionary, the most recent contemporary research is discussed only in the fourth paragraph of the passage.

(D) **CORRECT.** The third paragraph describes the position of the colonial missionary and indicates a flaw in this perspective. The missionary's position is described in the opening sentence of the paragraph: "However, the colonial missionary voice provided consistent opposition to polygamy by viewing the practice as unethical and destructive of family life." Furthermore, after discussing this position, the author goes on to identify a deficiency in this reasoning: "Unfortunately, both the missionary voice and the scholarly voice did not consider the views of African women important."

(E) While the third paragraph discusses the perspective of the colonial missionary, nothing is mentioned in the passage about the attitude of the missionary toward scholarly research on monogamy.

3. **The passage provides each of the following EXCEPT**

(A) the year of publication of Remi Clignet's book *Many Wives, Many Powers*

(B) the year in which John Mbiti made a claim that polygamy is an accepted institution

(C) examples of African women's literary productions devoted to family relations

(D) reasons for missionary opposition to polygamy

(E) current research perspectives on polygamy

On Detail questions, look for signal words. Since this is an EXCEPT question, find the statements that were mentioned in the passage and eliminate them from consideration. Make sure to use proper nouns (such as Remi Clignet) and dates (such as 1983) as your signals. Since dates and capitalized nouns stand out in the text, they can speed up the process of verifying the answer choices. (Of course, be aware that a wrong answer choice might include words from the passage but fail to include the idea behind the words.)

(A) The second sentence of the opening paragraph states that Remi Clignet published his book *Many Wives, Many Powers* in 1961.

(B) According to the second sentence of the second paragraph, John Mbiti proclaimed that polygamy is an accepted and respectable institution in 1983.

(C) **CORRECT.** The concluding paragraph mentions that "women in Africa have often used literary productions . . . to comment on marriage" but provides no specific examples of such works.

(D) According to the third paragraph of the passage, the colonial missionary opposed polygamy because it considered this practice "unethical and destructive of family life."

(E) The last paragraph indicates that contemporary research is focused on examining the voice of women.

4. **According to the passage, the colonial missionary and the early scholarly research shared which of the following views on polygamy?**

(A) Both considered polygamy a sign of social status and success.

(B) Neither accounted for the views of local women.

(C) Both attempted to limit the prevalence of polygamy.

(D) Both pointed out polygamy's destructive effects on family life.

(E) Both exhibited a somewhat negative attitude toward polygamy.

Glance at your notes: paragraph 3 offers a comparison of the views of the colonial missionary and those of early scholars. Note that the correct answer will outline the trait that was shared by both groups, while incorrect answers will typically restate characteristics that were true of only one rather than both groups.

(A) While the early scholarly researchers indeed viewed polygamy as a sign of prestige, this perspective was not shared by the colonial missionary, who declared it "unethical and destructive of family life."

(B) **CORRECT.** This statement is explicitly supported by the penultimate sentence of the third paragraph: "Unfortunately, both the missionary voice and the scholarly voice did not consider the views of African women important."

(C) While the passage suggests that the colonial missionary may have attempted to limit the prevalence of polygamy by coercing Africans "into partaking in the vision of monogamy," nothing in the passage suggests that the scholarly research shared this perspective.

(D) This view was characteristic of the colonial missionary, as discussed in the third paragraph, but not of the early scholarly research.

(E) According to the third paragraph, the colonial missionary certainly maintained a negative attitude toward polygamy, considering this practice "unethical and destructive of family life." By contrast, early scholarly research considered this phenomenon "a sign of affluence and power." Nothing in the passage suggests that the early scholars had a negative attitude toward polygamy.

5. **Which of the following statements can most properly be inferred from the passage?**

(A) Nukunya's paper "Polygamy as a Symbol of Status" was not written in 1981.

(B) John Mbiti adjusted his initial view on polygamy, recognizing that the experiences of African women should receive closer attention.

(C) Remi Clignet's book *Many Wives, Many Powers* was the first well-known scholarly work to proclaim that polygamy can be viewed as a symbol of prestige and wealth.

(D) Under the influence of the missionary opposition, polygamy was proclaimed illegal in Africa as a practice "unethical and destructive of family life."

(E) A large proportion of the scholars writing on polygamy in the 1970s and 1980s were of African descent.

Look for an answer that can be inferred strictly based on the information given in the passage, without making any additional assumptions. Typically, the correct answer must be very closely connected to the actual text of the passage and directly supported by one or two sentences. Avoid answers that may be seen as plausible but would require information not provided in the passage.

(A) **CORRECT.** The second paragraph states that Nukunya's work "Polygamy as a Symbol of Status" "reiterated Mbiti's idea that a plurality of wives is a legitimate sign of affluence and power." Since Nukunya's work reiterated the views of Mbiti, "Polygamy as a Symbol of Status" must have been written *after* Mbiti expressed his perspective on polygamy. According to the text, it was not until 1983 that "John Mbiti proclaimed that polygamy is an accepted and respectable institution." Therefore, Nukunya's "Polygamy as a Symbol of Status" must have been written in 1983 or later; you can conclude that it was not written in 1981.

(B) While the text mentions that contemporary research acknowledges that the perspective of African women should receive closer attention, nothing in the passage suggests that Mbiti subsequently embraced this view and changed his initial stance.

(C) In the second sentence of the opening paragraph, the author states that "when Remi Clignet published his book *Many Wives, Many Powers*, he was not alone in sharing the view. . ." suggesting that at the time of publication, other scholars viewed polygamy as a symbol of prestige and wealth. Therefore, Clignet's book may not have been the first to give this perspective.

(D) While the passage mentions that the colonial missionary opposed polygamy, viewing it as "unethical and destructive," nothing in the passage suggests that polygamy was declared illegal in Africa.

(E) The passage does say that many African scholars in this era championed polygamy, but the passage does not indicate whether these scholars represented "a large proportion" of all of the "scholars writing on polygamy."

6. **Which of the following examples fit the model of cultural studies cited in the final paragraph of the passage? Indicate all that apply.**

[A] A documentary about the modern-day slave trade that relied on interviews with those who had been enslaved

[B] A study of relationship changes caused by long-term separation, using letters exchanged between prisoners and their loved ones

[C] An experimental theater piece about blindness in which audience members were required to wear a blindfold

It might be helpful to reread the final paragraph before attempting to answer the question. The first sentence indicates that "contemporary research . . . has begun to focus on the protagonist's voice . . . recognizing that the views and experiences of those who take part in a given reality ought to receive close examination."

[A] **CORRECT.** In this example, those actually involved in the slave trade are being interviewed about it. This is a prime example of protagonist-centric research.

[B] **CORRECT.** In this example, the researchers are studying letters written by the very people who are experiencing the separation.

[C] In this example, audience members are being asked to step into the shoes of the blind. However, this does not represent a privileging of the protagonists (in this case, blind people), because no time is given to actual blind people describing their personal experience.

7. **Select the sentence in the first two paragraphs that cites a specific benefit of polygamy without mentioning the economic ramifications.**

A number of sentences can be eliminated, including the third sentence of the first paragraph ("a form of wealth") and the last sentence of the second paragraph ("a legitimate sign of affluence").

The second sentence of the second paragraph fails to cite a specific benefit; "many useful social purposes" is very general. A better answer (*and the correct one*) is the final sentence of the first paragraph, which says that "polygamy can provide a stabilizing function within societies frequently under stress from both internal and external forces." This describes a specific benefit without mentioning any economic factors.

Answers to Passage F: Sweet Spot

Though most tennis players generally strive to strike the ball on the racket's vibration node, more commonly known as the "sweet spot," many players are unaware of the existence of a second, lesser-known location on the racket face, the center of percussion, that will also greatly diminish the strain on a player's arm when the ball is struck.

In order to understand the physics of this second sweet spot, it is helpful to consider what would happen to a tennis racket in the moments after impact with the ball if the player's hand were to vanish at the moment of impact. The impact of the ball would cause the racket to bounce backward, experiencing a translational motion away from the ball. The tendency of this motion would be to jerk all parts of the racket, including the end of its handle, backward, or away from the ball. Unless the ball happened to hit the racket precisely at the racket's center of mass, the racket would additionally experience a rotational motion around its center of mass—much as a penny that has been struck near its edge will start to spin. Whenever the ball hits the racket face, the effect of this rotational motion will be to jerk the end of the handle forward, toward the ball. Depending on where the ball strikes the racket face, one or the other of these motions will predominate.

However, there is one point of impact, known as the center of percussion, which causes neither motion to predominate; if a ball were to strike this point, the impact would not impart any motion to the end of the handle. The reason for this lack of motion is that the force on the upper part of the hand would be equal and opposite to the force on the lower part of the hand, resulting in no net force on the tennis player's hand or forearm. The center of percussion constitutes a second sweet spot because a tennis player's wrist typically is placed next to the end of the racket's handle. When the player strikes the ball at the center of percussion, her wrist is jerked neither forward nor backward, and she experiences a relatively smooth, comfortable tennis stroke.

The manner in which a tennis player can detect the center of percussion on a given tennis racket follows from the nature of this second sweet spot. The center of percussion can be located via simple trial and error by holding the end of a tennis racket between your finger and thumb and throwing a ball onto the strings. If the handle jumps out of your hand, then the ball has missed the center of percussion.

Here is one example of a possible set of notes for this passage:

1. Tennis: hit ball on "sweet spot"

   <u>Many unaware: 2nd spot, CP, also ↓ arm strain ← Point</u>

2. Motion without hand

   —Jerk handle back or fwd

3. If ball hits CP, no jerk—doesn't jerk wrist either

4. Find CP w/trial & error

1. **What is the primary message the author is trying to convey?**

   (A) A proposal for an improvement to the design of tennis rackets

   (B) An examination of the differences between the two types of sweet spots

   (C) A definition of the translational and rotational forces acting on a tennis racket

   (D) A description of the ideal area in which to strike every ball

   (E) An explanation of a lesser-known area on a tennis racket that dampens unwanted vibration

The first paragraph introduces the idea that there are two sweet spots on the face of a tennis racket: one well-known spot and another "lesser-known" spot. The second and third paragraphs detail how the mechanism of the second sweet spot, the center of percussion, works. The fourth paragraph describes a way to find the center of percussion.

   (A) Nothing in the passage suggests that the author is trying to propose an improvement to the design of tennis rackets.

   (B) The passage does mention both types of sweet spots in the first paragraph, but it does not focus on the differences between the two.

   (C) Paragraph 2 explains the types of forces acting on the racket, but this topic is too narrow to be the primary message of the overall passage. The passage as a whole focuses on the idea of sweet spots in general.

   (D) While the passage does mention one benefit of hitting the ball on a sweet spot, it does not claim that this is the "ideal area" to hit "every" ball. There may be other areas that convey other benefits. The word *every* is too extreme.

   (E) **CORRECT.** The passage introduces the notion of a "second, lesser-known" sweet spot and explains how it works.

2. **According to the passage, all of the following are true of the forces acting upon a tennis racket striking a ball EXCEPT**

   (A) the only way to eliminate the jolt that accompanies most strokes is to hit the ball on the center of percussion

   (B) the impact of the ball striking the racket can strain a tennis player's arm

   (C) there are at least two different forces acting upon the racket

   (D) the end of the handle of the racket will jerk forward after striking the ball unless the ball strikes the racket's center of mass

   (E) the racket will rebound after it strikes the ball

EXCEPT questions require you to validate the answer choices. Go through the choices one by one, labeling true answers with a T and the one false answer with an F.

(A) **CORRECT.** False. This choice contradicts information given in the first paragraph: the center of percussion is only one of two sweet spots that minimize vibration. The vibration node is the other sweet spot.

(B) True. The first paragraph introduces the concept that the impact can "strain" the player's arm.

(C) True. The second paragraph describes at least two different forces that act upon a tennis racket striking the ball: "translational," as described in the second and third sentences, and "rotational," as described in the fourth and fifth sentences.

(D) True. The fourth sentence of the second paragraph states that "unless the ball happened to hit the racket precisely at the racket's center of mass, the racket would additionally experience a rotational motion." The fifth sentence then reads: "Whenever the ball hits the racket face, the effect of this rotational motion will be to jerk the end of the handle forward, toward the ball."

(E) True. The second sentence of the second paragraph states that a racket will "bounce backward" after striking the ball; these words are synonyms for *rebound*.

3. **What is the primary function served by paragraph 2 in the context of the entire passage?**

(A) To establish the main idea of the passage

(B) To provide an explanation of the mechanics of the phenomenon discussed in the passage

(C) To introduce a counterargument that elucidates the main idea of the passage

(D) To provide an example of the primary subject described in the passage

(E) To explain why the main idea of the passage would be useful for tennis players

Paragraph 2 introduces and explains, in great detail, the forces that act on a racket when striking a ball.

(A) The main idea is established in the first paragraph: there is a second sweet spot that results in minimal vibration when a tennis racket strikes a ball.

(B) **CORRECT.** This matches the function of the second paragraph, which explains the forces that occur when a racket strikes a ball.

(C) The second paragraph introduces the forces that act on a racket when striking a ball. This follows from the main idea; it is not a counterargument.

(D) While the second paragraph does provide an example, this is not an example of the center of percussion, which is the primary subject described in the passage. The example helps to explain the forces behind the center of percussion, but is not itself an example of a center of percussion.

(E) The first and third paragraphs, not the second paragraph, make reference to why tennis players would want to know about the sweet spot: to minimize strain on the arm.

4. **The author mentions "a penny that has been struck near its edge" in order to**

(A) show how the center of mass causes the racket to spin

(B) argue that a penny spins in the exact way that a tennis racket spins

(C) explain how translational motion works

(D) provide an illustration of a concept

(E) demonstrate that pennies and tennis rackets do not spin in the same way

The passage says that "the racket would additionally experience a rotational motion around its center of mass—much as a penny that has been struck near its edge will start to spin." In other words, the motion of the penny is an example that closely mimics the situation with the tennis racket. The correct answer should match this characterization.

(A) The center of mass does not cause the racket to spin; rather, a ball striking the racket causes it to spin.

(B) The author does not present the information about the penny as an argument; rather, it is an example. In addition, the author implies, via the words "much as," that the penny and the racket spin in similar ways; this is not the same as saying that they spin in the "exact" same way.

(C) This sentence is about rotational motion, not translational motion.

(D) **CORRECT.** The example of the penny is an analogy for the rotational motion experienced by the tennis racket.

(E) The example is intended to demonstrate a situation in which tennis rackets and pennies do spin in similar ways.

5. **Which of the following can be inferred from the passage?**

(A) If a player holds the tennis racket anywhere other than the end of the handle, the player will experience a jolting sensation.

(B) The primary sweet spot is more effective at damping vibration than is the secondary sweet spot.

(C) Striking a tennis ball at a spot other than the center of percussion can result in a jarring feeling.

(D) Striking a tennis ball repeatedly at spots other than a sweet spot leads to "tennis elbow."

(E) If a player lets go of the racket at the moment of impact, the simultaneous forward and backward impetus causes the racket to drop straight to the ground.

Because the question applies to the whole passage, examine the answer choices first. It is useful to remember that when the GRE asks you to *infer*, you need to base the inference only on information presented in the passage.

(A) The passage does explain that holding the racket at the end of the handle and hitting the ball at a particular spot results in a comfortable stroke that reduces the strain on a player's arm. It does not address, however, what would happen if the player grasped the racket at a different point. It is possible that grasping the racket at another point would simply result in a different center of percussion.

(B) The passage states that there is one commonly known sweet spot and a second, lesser-known sweet spot. However, the passage says nothing about the relative efficacy of these two sweet spots.

(C) **CORRECT.** You are told that playing tennis can result in strain on a player's arm. You are also told that striking the ball at the center of percussion leads to a "smooth, comfortable stroke," or one which does not cause the same kind of damage as a regular stroke. Striking the ball at a spot other than the center of percussion, then, could lead to a jarring stroke, or one that could cause damage to a player's arm.

(D) The passage mentions nothing about "tennis elbow" or what behavior can result in this injury; it merely talks about "strain." Be careful not to add additional information beyond what is presented in the passage.

(E) The second paragraph obliquely addresses a situation in which a tennis player lets go of the racket at the moment of impact. However, this question does not specify the point at which the tennis ball struck the racket. If the ball did not strike a sweet spot, the racket may have some translational or rotational force transferred from the ball and so might not drop straight to the ground.

6.   **Select the sentence in the second or third paragraph that describes the physics of the center of percussion's perceived sweetness.**

This is a very specific Select-in-Passage question, asking you to find something in the highly complex second and third paragraphs. The second paragraph of the passage explores what happens when a ball strikes a racket in general, but doesn't go into any detail about the sweet spot itself. The sentence you want will be in the third paragraph.

The correct sentence is the second sentence of the third paragraph: "The reason for this lack of motion is that the force on the upper part of the hand would be equal and opposite to the force on the lower part of the hand, resulting in no net force on the tennis player's hand or forearm." The final sentence of this paragraph describes the effects of hitting this second sweet spot, but it does not describe the actual physics of the sweetness.

7.   **It can be inferred that a tennis ball that strikes a racket's center of percussion will do which of the following? Indicate all that apply.**

[A]   Cause the racket to bounce backward

[B]   Not cause the wrist to jerk

[C]   Allow for a cleaner stroke than a ball striking a racket's primary sweet spot

This is a Select-One-or-More question. The answers are likely to be found in the first or third paragraphs, as the second explores a hypothetical situation and the fourth describes how to find the center of percussion.

[A]   The passage states that the ball would cause the racket to bounce backward in a hypothetical situation: if the player's hand were to vanish at the moment of impact. This part of the passage is not discussing what happens with a real stroke at the center of percussion.

[B]   **CORRECT.** The last sentence of the third paragraph says that a player who strikes the center of percussion will not have his or her wrist jerked "forward or backward."

[C]   The passage does state that when someone hits the center of percussion, the player will experience "a relatively smooth, comfortable tennis stroke." The passage never compares this situation, however, to what happens when the player hits the primary sweet spot. The passage doesn't indicate whether one is cleaner than the other or whether they're both the same.

Answers to Passage G: Chaos Theory

Around 1960, mathematician Edward Lorenz found unexpected behavior in apparently simple equations representing atmospheric air flows. Whenever he reran his model with the same inputs, different outputs resulted—although the model lacked any random elements. Lorenz realized that tiny rounding errors in his analog computer mushroomed over time, leading to erratic results. His findings marked a seminal moment in the development of chaos theory, which, despite its name, has little to do with randomness.

To understand how unpredictability can arise from deterministic equations, which do not involve chance outcomes, consider the non-chaotic system of two poppy seeds placed in a round bowl. As the seeds roll to the bowl's center, a position known as a point attractor, the distance between the seeds shrinks. If, instead, the bowl is flipped over, two seeds placed on top will roll away from each other. Such a system, while still not technically chaotic, enlarges initial differences in position.

Chaotic systems, such as a machine mixing bread dough, are characterized by both attraction and repulsion. As the dough is stretched, folded, and pressed back together, any poppy seeds sprinkled in are intermixed seemingly at random. But this randomness is illusory. In fact, the poppy seeds are captured by "strange attractors," staggeringly complex pathways whose tangles appear accidental but are in fact determined by the system's fundamental equations.

During the dough-kneading process, two poppy seeds positioned next to each other eventually go their separate ways. Any early divergence or measurement error is repeatedly amplified by the mixing until the position of any seed becomes effectively unpredictable. It is this "sensitive dependence on initial conditions" and not true randomness that generates unpredictability in chaotic systems, of which one example may be the Earth's weather. According to the popular interpretation of the "Butterfly Effect," a butterfly flapping its wings causes hurricanes. A better understanding is that the butterfly causes uncertainty about the precise state of the air. This microscopic uncertainty grows until it encompasses even hurricanes. Few meteorologists believe that we will ever be able to predict rain or shine for a particular day years in the future.

Here is one example of a possible set of notes for this passage:

> 1. 1960 L: unexp behav in air flow eqs
>
>   Reran model, diff results
>
>   tiny rounding errors blew up
>
>   help dev <u>chaos thry</u>—<u>little to do with randomness</u> ← Point
>
> 2. Unpredict can come fr determ eqs
>
>   —non-chaotic: 2 poppy seeds in or on bowl
>
> 3. Dough mixing (chaos): seed movmnt <u>seems</u> random but is NOT
>
> 4. Seeds go sep ways → unpredict, not truly random
>
>   —weather, butterfly eff

1.   **The main purpose of this passage is to**

   (A) explore a common misconception about a complex physical system

   (B) trace the historical development of a scientific theory

   (C) distinguish a mathematical pattern from its opposite

   (D) describe the spread of a technical model from one field of study to others

   (E) contrast possible causes of weather phenomena

The first paragraph introduces chaos theory by describing a historical moment in its development. The Point comes at the end of the first paragraph: "chaos theory ... has little to do with randomness." The next three paragraphs focus on further explaining this mystery with analogies involving poppy seeds and bread dough to illustrate the explanations. Finally, as a minor addendum, the last paragraph mentions how this understanding of chaos theory might be applied to the weather, as a possible specific case of a chaotic system.

Taking all of these roles together, the main purpose of the passage is to introduce chaos theory and explain how chaotic systems *seem* to be random (a common misconception) but actually are governed by very complex equations.

   (A) **CORRECT.** The complicated aspects are the characteristic features of chaotic systems, such as "sensitive dependence on initial conditions and staggeringly complex pathways." The Point of the passage is to explain such features.

   (B) The first paragraph, as an introduction, describes a particular milestone in the historical development of chaos theory. However, the passage does not go on to describe other developments of this theory over time.

   (C) Perhaps the behavior of chaotic systems could arguably be described as a "mathematical pattern." However, the passage does not discuss any category of systems that is categorized clearly as the *opposite* of chaotic systems. Certain non-chaotic systems are described in the second paragraph, but it is not clear whether these systems would be the opposite of chaotic systems, or whether *random* systems would be the opposite.

   (D) If chaos theory is the technical model mentioned in the answer choice, the passage never describes how that model spreads from one field of study to any other.

   (E) In the fourth paragraph, the "Butterfly Effect" is mentioned as a popular explanation for at least some hurricanes. However, no other causes of weather phenomena are ever discussed.

2.   **In the example discussed in the passage, what is true about poppy seeds in bread dough, once the dough has been thoroughly mixed?**

   (A) They have been individually stretched and folded over, like miniature versions of the entire dough.

   (B) They are scattered in random clumps throughout the dough.

   (C) They are accidentally caught in tangled objects called "strange attractors."

   (D) They are bound to regularly dispersed patterns of point attractors.

   (E) They are in positions dictated by the underlying equations that govern the mixing process.

The third paragraph describes what happens to these poppy seeds: they "are intermixed seemingly at random." But the positions of the seeds are not random, as the next sentences emphasize. Rather, the seeds "are captured by "strange attractors," staggeringly complex pathways whose tangles . . . are in fact totally determined by the system's fundamental equations." Thus, the positions of the seeds are themselves "determined by the system's fundamental equations."

(A) The passage mentions nothing about any stretching or folding of the poppy seeds themselves; rather, the dough is stretched and folded.

(B) The poppy seeds are scattered throughout the dough, but not in random clumps.

(C) The poppy seeds are caught in strange attractors, but there is nothing *accidental* about their capture. Moreover, the strange attractors described in the passage are not physical objects but rather mathematical pathways.

(D) Point attractors are not mentioned in relation to the dough-mixing process. Also, the poppy seeds, which have been "intermixed seemingly at random," are not placed at regular intervals.

(E) **CORRECT.** The poppy seeds may seem to be scattered at random, but they follow the pathways of the strange attractors. These pathways, and thus the seeds' positions, have been "determined by the system's fundamental equations."

3.   **According to the passage, the rounding errors in Lorenz's model**

(A) indicated that the model was programmed in a fundamentally faulty way

(B) were deliberately included to represent tiny fluctuations in atmospheric air currents

(C) were imperceptibly small at first, but tended to grow

(D) were at least partially expected, given the complexity of the actual atmosphere

(E) shrank to insignificant levels during each trial of the model

Use the key words "rounding errors" and "Lorenz's model" to find the relevant text. The reference to Lorenz leads to the first paragraph: "Lorenz realized that tiny rounding errors in his analog computer mushroomed over time, leading to erratic results." In other words, the rounding errors started out small but became larger.

(A) Although these rounding errors are in fact *errors*, nothing in the passage indicates or implies that the model overall was built incorrectly.

(B) The errors were not deliberately included in the model. The passage's first sentence states that Lorenz found "unexpected behavior" in his model. It may be argued that the role of these errors is similar to the role of "tiny fluctuations in atmospheric air currents"—that is, they both introduce uncertainty that grows over time. However, this answer choice claims incorrectly that the errors were inserted on purpose.

(C) **CORRECT.** This answer choice corresponds very closely to the statement in the passage. Some synonyms have been used, but the meaning is the same: "were imperceptibly small at first" substitutes for "tiny," and "tended to grow" substitutes for "mushroomed over time."

(D) The passage indicates that the behavior of the model was *unexpected*. Nothing in the passage indicates that Lorenz expected the errors at all.

(E) The errors did not shrink, but rather "mushroomed over time."

4.   **The passage mentions each of the following as an example or potential example of a chaotic or non-chaotic system EXCEPT**

(A) a dough-mixing machine

(B) atmospheric weather patterns

(C) poppy seeds placed on top of an upside-down bowl

(D) poppy seeds placed in a right-side-up bowl

(E) fluctuating butterfly flight patterns

The passage mentions several examples of systems, both chaotic and non-chaotic, to illustrate the special characteristics of chaos. This question is an exercise in finding the references to the four wrong answers quickly.

(A) A dough-mixing machine is first mentioned at the beginning of the third paragraph as an example of chaos in action: "Chaotic systems, such as a machine mixing bread dough . . ."

(B) Atmospheric weather patterns as a system to be studied are mentioned in both the first and the last paragraphs. In the last paragraph, the passage states that the Earth's weather may be an example of a chaotic system.

(C) Poppy seeds placed on an upside-down bowl are described in the second paragraph as an example of a non-chaotic system that creates divergence.

(D) Poppy seeds placed in a bowl that is right-side-up are described in the second paragraph as an example of a non-chaotic system that creates convergence.

(E) **CORRECT.** Butterfly flight patterns are not discussed as examples of systems themselves. According to the last paragraph, the "Butterfly Effect" is caused by the flapping of a single butterfly's wings, and this effect can potentially affect atmospheric systems.

5.   **It can be inferred from the passage that which of the following pairs of items would most likely follow typical pathways within a chaotic system?**

(A) Two particles ejected in random directions from the same decaying atomic nucleus

(B) Two stickers affixed to a balloon that expands and contracts over and over again

(C) Two avalanches sliding down opposite sides of the same mountain

(D) Two baseballs placed into a device designed to mix paint

(E) Two coins flipped into a large bowl

Stripped down to its essence, the question asks you to infer which of the five choices describes a system that is the most *chaotic,* according to the characteristics of chaos outlined in the passage. The most important proof sentence is at the beginning of the third paragraph: "Chaotic systems, such as a machine mixing bread dough, are characterized by both attraction and repulsion." Thus, you should look for the system that is the most analogous to the dough-mixing machine. Moreover, the system should contain both attractive and repulsive elements: in other words, the two items embedded within the system should sometimes come near each other and then separate again.

At the beginning of the fourth paragraph, there is a "red herring" sentence: "During the dough-kneading process, two poppy seeds positioned next to each other eventually go their separate ways." This sentence could lead you to think that the defining characteristic of chaotic systems is simply that two embedded items move away from each other. The question is asked in such a way as to focus your attention on the two items, so that you might then use this proof sentence alone and choose an incorrect answer.

(A) The two particles ejected from a nucleus do diverge, but they do not approach each other again. Moreover, there is no implication of any activity analogous to mixing bread dough.

(B) The stickers on the balloon separate and come together repeatedly. This behavior meets the criterion of "both attraction and repulsion." However, there is no mixing, and as a result, the system cannot be said to be analogous to a machine mixing dough.

(C) As in answer choice (A), the two items in question (avalanches) separate but never draw near each other again. Likewise, there is no mixing in the system.

(D) **CORRECT.** Two baseballs placed into a device designed to mix paint is analogous to two poppy seeds placed in bread dough being mixed by a machine: parts of the system are separated, intermingled, and brought back together again in regular, though complex, ways, as determined by the laws of physics. The pathways of the two baseballs will diverge and converge repeatedly, as in any other chaotic system.

(E) The two coins flipped into a bowl are closely analogous to the example in the second paragraph of the passage of two poppy seeds placed in a bowl and allowed to fall; this system is presented as non-chaotic.

6. **The author implies which of the following about weather systems? Indicate all that apply.**

[A] They illustrate the same fundamental phenomenon as Lorenz's rounding errors.

[B] Experts agree unanimously that weather will never be predictable years in advance.

[C] They are governed mostly by seemingly trivial events, such as the flapping of a butterfly's wings.

This is a Select-One-or-More question of a very specific variety. It is mostly relevant to the last paragraph of the passage, so you should make sure you have a solid understanding of the few sentences devoted to weather systems.

[A] **CORRECT.** Lorenz's rounding errors are actually found in the first paragraph, where you read that "Lorenz realized that tiny rounding errors . . . mushroomed over time." Similarly, in the final paragraph, you read: "this microscopic uncertainty grows until it encompasses even hurricanes." These are both examples of chaotic systems.

[B] The last sentence of the passage says: "few metereologists believe that we will ever be able to predict rain or shine for a particular day years in the future." The sentence does not indicate that meteorologists are unanimous; in fact, "few meteorologists" indicates that at least one actually believes that such predictions might be able to be made in the future.

[C] While you are told that the wings of a butterfly can affect weather systems, you are never told that this is the most important contributing factor. Likely, major climatic events are more important than seemingly trivial events, such as a butterfly taking flight.

7. **Select the sentence in the second or third paragraph that illustrates why "chaos theory" might be called a misnomer.**

Misnomer means that something has been given an incorrect or misleading name. You learned in the first paragraph that chaos theory, despite its name, "has little to do with randomness." So you want to find a sentence in the second or third paragraph that illustrates this point.

The final sentence of the third paragraph uses poppy seeds to show that even the bread-mixing machine, which appears to be mixing things at random (in a "chaotic" manner), is actually moving the seeds through "staggeringly complex pathways whose tangles appear accidental but are in fact determined by the system's fundamental equations." In other words, there's nothing chaotic at all, only a very complex organization. This is a perfect example of why "chaos theory" is a kind of misnomer.

Note that the second-to-last sentence of the third paragraph, "But this randomness is illusory," does indicate that chaos theory might be called a misnomer. This sentence, though, does not illustrate *why* this is so.

Argument Structure Passages

In This Chapter ...

- Identifying the Parts of an Argument

- Recognizing Argument Structure Passages

- Four-Step Process

- Taking Notes

- Strategies for All Question Types

- Question Types

CHAPTER 8 Argument Structure Passages

Reading Comprehension also contains another type of passage: Argument Structure Passages (ASPs).

Expect to see about one to three ASPs per section; each passage will be accompanied by a single question. These individual questions shouldn't take any longer than a similar question on a short or long passage. Though there aren't multiple questions to preview, you absolutely must read the question before you read the passage, as it will tell you exactly what kind of ASP you're dealing with.

ASPs consist of brief arguments (each argument is generally one to three sentences long) and questions relating to those arguments. These arguments are made up of premises, counter premises, assumptions, and conclusions. Some arguments will also contain background information or context; this information helps you to understand the topic under discussion but is not actually part of the argument itself.

The main point of the argument is the **conclusion**, which is logically supported by the premises (and assumptions). Conclusions are in the form of an opinion or a claim; they are not pure facts. Most arguments contain conclusions, but not all of them do.

Premises provide support for the argument's conclusion. They may be facts, opinions, or claims. If they are opinions or claims, they will not be the overall claim the author is making; rather, they will be some intermediate claim the author is using to support the overall claim (conclusion).

Counter premises undermine or go against the conclusion. Occasionally, an argument will present both sides of an argument, with evidence to support both. The passage will still come down one way or the other in terms of an overall conclusion, but some of the provided evidence will be used as premises and some as counter premises (supporting a kind of counter conclusion).

Assumptions are unstated pieces of information that the argument requires to function.

Here's a simple example to illustrate:

> While the plot of the movie was compelling, the acting was atrocious. Thus, the movie will not win an Oscar.
> Conclusion: Thus, the movie will not win an Oscar.
> Supporting premise: The acting was atrocious.
> Counter premise: The plot of the movie was compelling.
> Assumption: Atrocious acting prevents a movie from winning an Oscar (any kind of Oscar).

Identifying the Parts of an Argument

In order to do well on Argument Structure Passage questions, you must be able to identify the parts of an argument as described in the previous section. Consider the following argument and try to find the different pieces. Don't read on until you've tried it!

> Studying regularly is one factor that has been shown to improve one's performance on the GRE. Melissa took the GRE and scored a 150. If she studies several times a week, Melissa can expect to improve her score.

In analyzing an argument, **look first for the conclusion**, which is the main point of the argument. The conclusion can be the last sentence of an argument, but not always. Sometimes the conclusion is the first sentence or in the middle of the paragraph.

Where is the conclusion? The main claim of this argument is the last sentence:

> If she studies several times a week, Melissa can expect to improve her score.

Note that the conclusion is not just that she'll improve her score. The conclusion does cover the full If–Then statement: if she does X, she can expect Y to happen. After finding the conclusion, look for the premises that support or lead to the conclusion.

Where are the premises? Each of the first two sentences is a premise:

> Premise: Studying regularly is one factor that has been shown to improve one's performance on the GRE.
> Premise: Melissa took the GRE and scored a 150.

Finally, what does this conclusion assume? It assumes that studying "several times a week" is the same as studying "regularly." Maybe "regularly" means every day! In that case, studying several times a week may not be enough.

Recognizing Argument Structure Passages

The Official Guide to the GRE General Test does not differentiate between regular Reading Comprehension passages and Argument Structure Passages, but the difference is critical to your process. Your first job on any passage will be to categorize it.

How? You'll use the question stem! Before you dive into the argument itself, you're going to read the question stem to determine what you've got.

You can distinguish between RC questions and ASP questions. The following question types appear only on ASPs:

- Analyze Argument Structure: These questions will highlight a sentence or two in the passage, and then ask you what purpose they're serving in the argument. Generally, when you see the word *argument*, you should think ASP.

- Strengthen/Weaken: If a passage asks you to strengthen (support) or weaken (undermine) the argument, it's an ASP.

- Resolve a Paradox/Explain a Discrepancy: If the question asks you to resolve or explain something puzzling, then you've got an ASP.

These question types appear only on RC passages:

- Main Idea, Tone, and Attitude: ASPs are generally too short to get across any kind of overall main point or tone.
- Look-Up Detail: Any question that begins "According to the passage" or asks what the author talked about in detail signals a regular RC passage.
- Author's Purpose: Some questions ask why the author mentioned a particular detail. If you see the language "in order to" in the question stem, then you know you've got a regular RC passage.
- Select-in-Passage or Select-One-or-More questions always signal a regular RC passage. ASP questions always ask you to choose exactly one answer choice from a listed set of five answers.

This question type can appear on both RC passages and ASPs:

- Inference: When the question asks what is inferred, implied, or suggested, there's no good way to know whether you're dealing with a regular RC or an ASP. Here's the good news: it doesn't matter! The solution process for Inference is the same regardless of the type of passage.

You don't need to memorize any of this right now—you will see plenty of examples in the pages to come.

Four-Step Process

You'll use a four-step process for every ASP you encounter:

Step 1: Identify the question type.
Step 2: Deconstruct the argument.
Step 3: State the goal.
Step 4: Work from wrong to right.

An overview follows; later, you'll go through the process in detail for each question type.

Step 1: Identify the Question Type

The vast majority of question stems will allow you to categorize a question, which will direct everything else you do. However, if the question stem is not immediately helpful or the question type is difficult to identify, do not dwell on the issue. Go ahead to the next step; afterward, you can reexamine the question.

Step 2: Deconstruct the Argument

The question type will help you anticipate what to expect from the argument. For example, some types do have conclusions and others don't; after you've identified the question type, you'll know whether to look for a conclusion when reading the argument. You'll also take light notes during this stage.

Step 3: State the Goal

You'll have a particular goal that you're trying to accomplish for each question type. For example, on Strengthen questions, the goal is to find the answer that makes the conclusion at least a little more likely to be true or valid. This step only takes about 3–5 seconds, but don't skip it! Make sure that you have a clear idea of your goal before you move to the final step.

Step 4: Work from Wrong to Right

As on any RC question, process of elimination rules the day. As a general rule, cross definite wrong answers off first and then compare any remaining tempting answers. Certain question types have common traps in the wrong answers; it's important to be familiar with those before test day.

Taking Notes

When dealing with Argument Structure Passages, you should take some light notes as you do for regular Reading Comprehension passages. These notes will be even more abbreviated, though, and they will focus on the flow of the information. What leads to what?

There are any number of ways to take notes; a few ideas are presented here, and you can choose what you think would work best for your brain. First, though, make sure you know what these notes are supposed to accomplish.

You already know that arguments contain different pieces of information: a conclusion, premises, and so on. Your two main goals are as follows:

1. To classify each piece of information

2. To understand how the different pieces of information fit together

Option 1: Stream-of-Consciousness Notes

This option tends to work for people who prefer to jot down notes as they read. Read the first sentence (or enough of the first sentence to come up with a big idea). Then, jot down a (heavily abbreviated!) note and move on to the next sentence. At times, you may decide not to jot down a particular detail (e.g., background information may not be necessary to write down). Each new idea gets its own line.

When you're done, determine the conclusion (if applicable—not all arguments have conclusions). Place a C next to it (it's also a good idea to put a circle around the C). Put + (plus) signs next to any premises that support that conclusion. Put − (minus) signs next to any counter premises that go against the conclusion.

Here's an example:

> Environmentalist: The national energy commission's current plan calls for the construction of six new nuclear power plants during the next decade. The commission argues that these plants are extremely safe and will have minimal environmental impact on their surrounding communities. However, all six nuclear power plants will be located far from densely populated areas. Clearly, the government is tacitly admitting that these plants do pose a serious health risk to humans.
>
> Which of the following, if true, most seriously weakens the environmentalist's claim of an unspoken government admission?

Sample Notes:

NEC plan: 6 NP next 10yr	*This is a fact, not a conclusion. I don't know yet whether it will support or go against the conclusion.*
NEC: v. safe, low enviro impact	*Okay, this group is claiming something.*
BUT NP not in pop areas	*Big contrast. Another fact.*
Gov admits NP = health risk	*Okay, this is the big claim.*

Now that you know what's going on, go back and add labels to each line:

NEC plan: 6 NP next 10yr
− NEC: v. safe, low enviro impact
+ BUT NP not in pop areas
C Gov admits NP = health risk

8

The first line represents context; these plants are going to be built. This information doesn't actually work for or against the argument. The second line represents information that goes against the conclusion. The author thinks these nuclear plants are bad, but the NEC thinks they will be safe. The third line represents the author's sole premise and helps to support the author's conclusion. Since the NEC isn't placing any of these nuclear power plants in populated areas, the author concludes that the nuclear power plants must represent a health risk.

What does the author assume when drawing this conclusion?

One thing the author assumes is that there is no other reason why the nuclear power plants might be located in less populated areas. Perhaps the power plants need a lot of land and there isn't enough room in populated areas. If you think of that when reading the argument, you can add it to your notes:

[no other reason NP not in pop areas?]

Note the brackets; these indicate that the argument itself doesn't mention this information. Rather, it's something you thought of yourself.

Option 2: The T-Diagram

This option tends to work for people who prefer to read the entire argument first and then jot down notes.

First, draw a large T on your scratch paper. Make it asymmetrical, leaving more room on the left side, which will be the "pro" side. In most arguments, you will have very little on the "con" side (to the right).

Step 1.

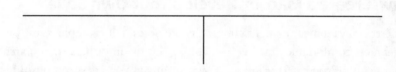

Second, read the argument and look for the conclusion. Once you find the conclusion, **write it above the top line of the T**, abbreviating heavily.

Step 2.

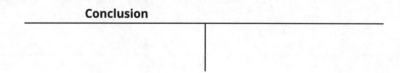

Third, add the rest of the argument information to the diagram. Write anything that supports the conclusion on the left side of the T ("pro" or "premise"), and write anything that goes against the conclusion on the right side of the T ("con" or "counter premise").

Step 3.

Conclusion	
– Pro	– Con
– Pro	
– [Assumption]	

 151

Finally, if you happened to think of any assumptions while reading, place them in brackets somewhere below the T. Make sure you can differentiate between information stated in the argument and your own thoughts when looking at your notes.

Here's how the original argument might look in T-diagram form:

Environmentalist: The national energy commission's current plan calls for the construction of six new nuclear power plants during the next decade. The commission argues that these plants are extremely safe and will have minimal environmental impact on their surrounding communities. However, all six nuclear power plants will be located far from densely populated areas. Clearly, the government is tacitly admitting that these plants do pose a serious health risk to humans.

Which of the following, if true, most seriously weakens the environmentalist's claim of an unspoken government admission?

plnts = ↑ hlth rsk	
plnts far frm pop areas	Comm: plnts safe, ↓ enviro impct
[No other reason for distance?]	

Note that this diagram contains different abbreviations from the first one. We did that on purpose to illustrate that everyone will take notes differently. There is more than one way to write something down; use what works best for you.

Option 3: Draw, Create a Map, or Develop Your Own Style

There are many different ways someone might choose to take notes. For example, some people are more visual and might feel most comfortable drawing or mapping out the information. You aren't obligated to follow one particular method; you can develop your own as long as you are accomplishing three goals:

1. If the argument does contain a conclusion, then you do need to find and note it. The conclusion (when present) is the most important part of the argument.

2. If the argument contains any kind of *flow* of information (e.g., one thing leads to another or one thing goes against another), then you definitely want to take note of how that information fits together.

3. You need simple and consistent ways to note important information. You don't need to designate the conclusion with a C, but you do need to designate the conclusion the same way every time. You don't want to spend time thinking about how to write something down or wondering what one of your abbreviations means.

If your note-taking style accomplishes those three goals at a minimum, then your process is good.

8

Strategies for All Question Types

You'll employ a few other strategies as you tackle the various question types.

Boundary Words in the Argument

For any question, it is helpful to focus your attention on the **boundary** words and phrases provided in the argument. These words and phrases narrow the scope of a premise. For example:

> Premise: The percentage of literate adults has increased.

The boundary word "percentage" limits the scope of the premise. It restricts the meaning to percentage only, as opposed to the actual number of literate adults. For all you know, the actual number went down. The boundary word "adults" also limits the scope of the premise. It restricts the meaning to adults only, as opposed to the total population or children.

Here is another example:

> Conclusion: Controversial speech should be allowed, provided it does not incite major violence.

The boundary phrase "provided it does not incite major violence" limits the scope of the conclusion. It restricts the meaning to some types of controversial speech, as opposed to all types of controversial speech. The boundary word "major" limits the exception—controversial speech should not be allowed when it incites major violence, as opposed to any violence. Note that the argument doesn't define what constitutes major versus minor violence.

Boundary words and phrases are vital because they provide nuances to the argument, and these nuances will often be major factors in the answer choices. These details can single-handedly make some answer choices correct or incorrect. Therefore, in your diagram, be sure to include boundary words and underline them or capitalize them for emphasis. This will help you identify answer choices that try to trick you on the argument boundaries.

Extreme Words in the Argument

Another general strategy for all ASP questions involves **extreme** words and phrases in the body of the argument. Extreme words, such as *always*, *never*, *all*, and *none*, are the opposite of boundary words—they make the argument very broad or far-reaching.

Using extreme words opens up an argument unreasonably, making it very susceptible to strengthening or weakening. For example:

> Conclusion: Sugar is never healthy for anyone trying to lose weight.

The extreme word "never" unreasonably opens up this argument, placing no limitation on the claim that sugar is unhealthy. A more moderate conclusion would argue that sugar is often unhealthy or that excessive sugar is unhealthy. The extreme word "anyone" further opens up this argument. A more moderate conclusion might be that this claim applies to most people trying to lose weight. Note any extreme language used in premises or conclusions; any such words will likely be very useful in responding to the question.

Boundary Words in the Answer Choices

Boundary words in the answers are just as important as boundary words in the body of the argument, though for a different reason. A correct answer choice must be 100 percent correct. As long as you interpret the words legitimately, such a choice must be valid no matter which way you interpret it. This principle provides an approach to evaluating answer choices. When you see boundary words in an answer choice, ask yourself, "What is the most extreme example I can think of that would still fit the wording of this answer choice?" Then, using the conclusion and the question asked, see whether your extreme example allows you to eliminate that answer choice.

For example, an answer choice might say:

(D) Some teachers leave the profession entirely within three years of beginning their teaching careers.

You might choose to address one of two different boundaries here. The word "Some" refers to some number of teachers but does not specify the size of the group. The phrase "within three years" refers to a period of time but does not specify the exact length of time.

If you choose to address the word "Some," you could say that 1 percent of teachers leave within three years or that 99 percent of teachers do so. Either way, the statistics still fit the criterion that some teachers do this. Suppose the conclusion asserted that new teacher turnover is having a major impact on the industry. If only 1 percent of new teachers leave within three years, then new teacher turnover will probably not have much of an impact.

Alternatively, you could interpret "within three years" to mean that many teachers in this category leave after one day of teaching. You could also imagine that many teachers in this category leave after two years and 364 days of teaching. Again, either way, the statistics still fit the criterion that new teachers leave the profession within three years of beginning their careers. Depending upon the conclusion and the question, you would then try to disprove answer choices by using these extreme interpretations.

Extreme words, such as *only* or *never*, can appear in correct answers as long as those same extreme words, or synonyms, appear in the original argument. If the answer choice uses an extreme word that is not explicitly supported by the text of the argument, eliminate that choice.

Process of Elimination

It is important to eliminate answer choices on your scratch paper. Do *not* eliminate answer choices in your head! As you go through many different questions during the test, it is very difficult to keep straight which answer choices you have ruled out. You do not want to find yourself reevaluating answers that you have already eliminated or—even worse—accidentally choosing an answer that you meant to eliminate! By the end of the Verbal section of the GRE, your scratch paper will be filled with columns or rows of "A–E" (and a bit of "A–C") with incorrect answer choices crossed out and correct answers circled. Study this way when practicing as well; don't write in your books, since you can't write on the problem itself during the real test.

Even if you believe you have found the correct answer, always check all of the answer choices on Verbal questions. You may find that another answer choice might be better, and you will have to rethink your initial choice.

Question Types

Argument Structure Passages come in five main categories:

Question Type	Example	How to Recognize
Strengthen the Conclusion	Which of the following, if true, most strongly supports the scientists' hypothesis?	In the question stem: *strengthen, support,* or similar Will often (but not always) include the words *"if true"*
Weaken the Conclusion	Which of the following, if true, most seriously undermines the mayor's claim?	In the question stem: *weaken, undermine,* or similar May ask what *supports* the idea that something will *not* be successful Will often (but not always) include the words *"if true"*
Analyze the Argument Structure	In the argument above, the two portions in boldface play which of the following roles?	In the question stem: *role* or similar In the argument: boldface font
Draw a Conclusion (Inference)	Which of the following conclusions can best be drawn from the information above?	In the question stem: *conclusion, assertion, infer,* or similar
Resolve a Paradox	Which of the following pieces of evidence, if true, would provide the best explanation for the discrepancy?	In the question stem: *paradox, discrepancy, resolve,* or similar

The GRE may make a question a bit more complex by structuring it as a "Fill-in-the-Blank" question. This is not a new type of question; rather, it is a disguised version of one of the question types listed previously. The Fill-in-the-Blank form is sometimes harder to categorize than the more typical ones; you'll see examples below. Once you recognize that a "Fill-in-the-Blank" question is of a certain type, you can use the standard strategies associated with that type.

Let's take a look at each question type in more detail.

Strengthen the Conclusion

On Strengthen questions, your goal is to find an answer that makes the conclusion a little more likely to be valid. The conclusion likely won't be made perfect—just somewhat better than it was before.

Step 1: Identify the Question Type

Strengthen the Conclusion questions ask you to provide additional support for a given conclusion. The question stem may appear in a number of forms:

- Which of the following, if true, most strengthens the argument above?
- Which of the following, if true, most strongly supports the scientists' hypothesis?
- Which of the following provides the strongest reason to expect that the plan will be successful?
- Shuai will win the tournament because _____.

Step 2: Deconstruct the Argument

Strengthen arguments will always contain conclusions; because your task is to strengthen the conclusion, your first task is to find that conclusion. Also take note of the premises offered to support the conclusion and think about the gaps in the argument. What is the author assuming must be true in order to draw that particular conclusion?

You may or may not be able to brainstorm any assumptions made by the author; it's worth spending about 15 to 20 seconds to try. For example, consider this short argument:

> Shuai is the number one tennis player in the country. She lost in the final match of last year's national tennis championship, but she will win the tournament this year because _____.

What is the author assuming in drawing this conclusion? Shuai is the number one player, which sounds great, but she did lose last year. The author is assuming that there is some reason that Shuai will have a better chance this year. Perhaps she wasn't the top-ranked player last year. Perhaps the player who beat her last year has retired. Perhaps Shuai has gotten better than the player who beat her last year. Who knows? The correct answer will provide some reason to support the idea that Shuai will win this year (though the answer won't absolutely guarantee that Shuai will win).

Step 3: State the Goal

For Strengthen questions, the correct answer will be a new piece of information that will make the conclusion at least a little more likely to be valid or true. It could be inserted into the argument as a new premise supporting the conclusion.

Step 4: Work from Wrong to Right

Use an S-W-Slash Chart to keep track of the answers. Each answer choice will either strengthen the conclusion (S), weaken it (W), or do nothing to it (∼). (Technically, that symbol is called a tilde, but "slash" is easier.) Label each letter on your scrap paper accordingly.

Cross off W and ∼ answers immediately. If you have more than one S, compare the answer choices. Only one choice will strengthen the conclusion in the end, so see whether you mistakenly labeled something an S when it should have been labeled something else. If they both still look good, then try to decide which one supports the conclusion more strongly. Pick and move on!

At times it may not be entirely clear whether an answer choice strengthens or weakens the conclusion. For example, an answer choice may serve to strengthen the conclusion, but only in an indirect or arguable way. If that is the case, write down S∼ in order to indicate that the answer choice is borderline. As you assess the other choices, determine whether you need to refine your categorization of that answer choice. Depending upon the other answer choices, it may be obvious that this answer choice is wrong or, alternatively, that it is the best answer.

> Here's an example (real test questions will have five answer choices):

1. At QuestCorp, many employees have quit recently and taken jobs with a competitor. Shortly before the employees quit, QuestCorp lost its largest client. Clearly, the employees were no longer confident in QuestCorp's long-term viability.

   Which of the following, if true, most strengthens the claim that concerns about QuestCorp's viability caused the employees to quit?

   (A) Employees at QuestCorp's main competitor recently received a large and well-publicized raise.

   (B) QuestCorp's largest client accounted for 40 percent of sales and nearly 60 percent of the company's profits.

   (C) Many prospective hires who have interviewed with QuestCorp ultimately accepted jobs with other companies.

Step 1: Identify the Question Type

The "most strengthens" and "if true" language indicate that this is a Strengthen the Conclusion question.

Step 2: Deconstruct the Argument

The question stem provides the conclusion: concerns about Q's viability caused employees to quit. One set of notes might look like this:

   + Q lost client, then E quit, went to compet

   (C) E lost conf in Q viab

Step 3: State the Goal

The author assumes that the employees weren't quitting for some other reason. One way to strengthen the argument would be to show that there was some significant negative consequence because the largest client left.

Step 4: Work from Wrong to Right

Use an S-W-slash chart to categorize and eliminate answer choices.

(A) Weaken or slash. If the competitor is offering more money, then perhaps that's why the employees switched companies; if so, this choice weakens the argument. Note that this choice doesn't actually say that the competitor is now paying more money than QuestCorp, so perhaps this information is irrelevant. Either way, this choice does not strengthen the argument.

(B) Strengthen. The largest client accounted for a very large percentage of both sales and profits. This piece of information does strengthen the idea that some employees may have lost confidence in QuestCorp's long-term viability.

(C) Slash. The argument concludes something about QuestCorp employees, not people who interviewed with QuestCorp but ultimately accepted a job elsewhere.

Answer choice **(B)** is correct.

Wrong Answer Choice Types

1. No Tie to the Conclusion

Many wrong answers will be tied to a premise but not to the conclusion. The answer choice could provide unnecessary information about that premise or talk about something tangential to the argument, such as answer (A) in the last example.

A few wrong answers with "No Tie to the Conclusion" do bring in language from the conclusion, but they do not meaningfully support the conclusion. Deceptive answers such as these seem relevant. Make sure that the answer you choose is not simply related to the conclusion, but in fact supports it.

Also, some wrong answers can be "Real-World Plausible". You are not assessing a choice's truth in the real world—only whether the choice strengthens the particular argument given.

2. Wrong Direction

Many wrong answers on Strengthen questions in fact weaken the argument. Make sure that you note whether a particular question is a Strengthen the Conclusion or a Weaken the Conclusion question so that you do not mistakenly pick the wrong answer. In the example provided above, answer choice (C) is an example of this deceptive answer type.

Weaken the Conclusion

Weaken the Conclusion questions are exactly like Strengthen the Conclusion questions in every way except the obvious (they want you to weaken instead of strengthen!).

Step 1: Identify the Question Type

The question stem may appear in a number of forms:

- Which of the following, if true, most seriously weakens the argument?
- Which of the following, if true, could present the most serious disadvantage of XYZ Corporation's new marketing initiative?
- Which of the following, if true, most strongly supports the view that the drug treatment program will *not* be successful?

Step 2: Deconstruct the Argument

Weaken arguments will always contain conclusions; because your task is to weaken the conclusion, your first task is to find that conclusion. Also take note of the premises offered to support the conclusion and think about the gaps in the argument. What is the author assuming must be true in order to draw that particular conclusion?

You may or may not be able to brainstorm any assumptions made by the author; it's worth spending about 15 to 20 seconds to try. For example, consider this short argument (the same one you saw in the Strengthen section):

> Shuai is the number one tennis player in the country. She lost in the final match of last year's national tennis championship, but she will win the tournament this year. Which of the following, if true, most undermines the author's claim?

What is the author assuming in drawing this conclusion? Shuai is the number one player, which sounds great, but she did lose last year. The author is assuming that there is some reason that Shuai will have a better chance this year.

The correct answer will provide some reason to weaken the idea that Shuai will win this year (though the answer won't absolutely guarantee that Shuai will lose). Perhaps the same player who beat her last year will be in the tournament again this year. Perhaps another player, who has beaten Shuai recently, will be playing in the tournament. Perhaps Shuai will be injured or sick.

Step 3: State the Goal

For Weaken questions, the correct answer will be a new piece of information that will make the conclusion at least a little less likely to be valid or true. If it were inserted into the argument, the conclusion would be doubtful.

Step 4: Work from Wrong to Right

Use an S-W-slash chart to keep track of the answers. Each answer choice will either strengthen the conclusion (S), weaken it (W), or do nothing to it (∼). (Technically, that symbol is called a tilde, but "slash" is easier.) Label each letter on your scrap paper accordingly.

Cross off S and ∼ answers immediately. If you have more than one W, compare the answer choices. Only one choice will weaken the conclusion in the end, so see whether you mistakenly labeled something a W when it should have been labeled something else. If they both still look good, then try to decide which one weakens the conclusion the most. Pick and move on!

At times it may not be entirely clear whether an answer choice strengthens or weakens the conclusion. For example, an answer choice may serve to weaken the conclusion, but only in an indirect or arguable way. If that is the case, write down W∼ in order to indicate that the answer choice is borderline. As you assess the other choices, determine whether you need to refine your categorization of that answer choice. Depending upon the other answer choices, it may be obvious that this answer choice is wrong or, alternatively, that it is the best answer.

> Here's an example:

1. The national infrastructure for airport runways and air traffic control requires immediate expansion to accommodate the increase in private, smaller planes. To help fund this expansion, the Federal Aviation Authority (the FAA) has proposed a fee for all air travelers. However, this fee would be unfair, as it would impose costs on all travelers to benefit only the few who utilize the new private planes.

   Which of the following, if true, would cast the most doubt on the claim that the proposed fee would be unfair?

   (A) The existing national airport infrastructure benefits all air travelers.

   (B) The fee, if imposed, will have a negligible effect on the overall volume of air travel.

   (C) The expansion would reduce the number of delayed flights resulting from small private planes congesting runways.

   (D) Travelers who use small private planes are almost uniformly wealthy or traveling on business.

   (E) A substantial fee would need to be imposed in order to pay for the expansion costs.

Step 1: Identify the Question Type

The "cast the most doubt" and "if true" language indicate that this is a Weaken the Conclusion question.

Step 2: Deconstruct the Argument

The question stem indicates the conclusion: the proposed fee would be unfair. One set of notes might look like this:

Fee unfair	
Cost for all, benefits only for priv planes	

Step 3: State the Goal

The author assumes that the benefits will apply only to those flying in the private plans. One way to weaken the argument would be to show that there was some benefit for a greater group, or perhaps for all of the people who would be paying the fee.

Step 4: Work from Wrong to Right

Use an S-W-slash chart to categorize and eliminate answer choices.

(A) Slash. The argument concerns a fee needed in order to expand the existing infrastructure. The status of the existing infrastructure is irrelevant to the argument.

(B) Slash. A negligible impact is a very small impact. The fee, though, is intended to be used for infrastructure expansion. The argument makes no claim about what will happen with the overall volume of air travel.

(C) Weaken. This choice offers a benefit for all air travelers: if the expansion can reduce congestion, and therefore the number of delayed flights in general, then others besides the private plane travelers will benefit from the fee.

(D) Slash. The wealth or employment status of the passengers does not address whether the fee benefits just these passengers versus all of the passengers.

(E) Strengthen or slash. The amount of the fee does not address whether the fee is unfair. If anything, you might argue that a very high fee is even more unfair, in which case this choice would strengthen the argument, not weaken it.

Answer choice (C) is the correct answer.

Wrong Answer Choice Types

The common categories of wrong answers for Weaken the Conclusion questions are essentially the same as those for Strengthen the Conclusion questions.

1. No Tie to the Conclusion

Many wrong answers are tied to a premise but not to the conclusion. Answer (A) in the previous problem is an example of a tempting wrong answer of the No Tie type.

8

2. Wrong Direction

Some wrong answers on Weaken questions in fact strengthen the argument. Make sure that you note whether a particular question is a Weaken the Conclusion or a Strengthen the Conclusion question so that you do not mistakenly pick the wrong answer. Answer (E) in the previous problem is a possible example of a Wrong Direction trap.

Analyze the Argument Structure

Analyze the Argument Structure questions ask you to describe the role of a part or parts of the argument; these portions will be shown in bold font. Annoyingly, the arguments tend to be complex, often with an argument/counterargument structure. Be prepared with guessing strategies (discussed next).

Step 1: Identify the Question Type

The question type will be immediately apparent because of the boldface font in portions of the argument. The question will typically ask what "role" the bold portions play in the overall argument.

Step 2: Deconstruct the Argument

The boldface portions can play one of three primary roles:

1. (C): The statement in boldface is the author's *conclusion*.

2. (S): The statement in boldface is a premise that *supports* the author's conclusion.

3. (W): The statement in boldface is *something else* (usually *weakens* the conclusion, but not always).

Find the author's conclusion, then classify each statement according to the categories C, S, or W. These arguments tend to be longer than average; note that you do not need to categorize the entire argument, just the two statements in bold font. Do not go to the answer choices until you have found the conclusion and categorized the statements!

Step 3: State the Goal

Your goal is to categorize the boldface statements and then to find an answer choice that matches your categorization. Note also whether the boldface statements are on the same side of the fence (categories 1 and 2) or on opposite sides of the fence (1 versus 3 or 2 versus 3).

Step 4: Work from Wrong to Right

The wrong answers will provide descriptions of the wrong combination of categories. For example, you might decide that the first boldface is a C while the second is an S. One wrong answer might describe the combination C, W (in that order). Another might describe the combination W, C. Both would be wrong if you are looking for the combination C, S.

8

Here's an example:

1. Mathematician: Recently, Zubin Ghosh made headlines when he was recognized to have solved the Hilbert Conjecture, postulated a hundred years ago. Ghosh posted his work on the Internet rather than submit it to established journals. In fact, **he has no job, let alone a university position**; he lives alone and has refused all acclaim. In reporting on Ghosh, the press unfortunately has reinforced the popular view that mathematicians are antisocial loners. **But mathematicians clearly form a tightly knit community**, frequently collaborating on important efforts; indeed, teams of researchers are working together to extend Ghosh's findings.

    In the argument above, the two portions in boldface play which of the following roles?

    (A) The first is an observation the author makes to illustrate a social pattern; the second is a generalization of that pattern.

    (B) The first is evidence in favor of the popular view expressed in the argument; the second is a brief restatement of that view.

    (C) The first is an example of a generalization that the author contradicts; the second is a reiteration of that generalization.

    (D) The first is a counterexample to a generalization that the author asserts; the second is that generalization.

    (E) The first is a judgment that counters the primary assertion expressed in the argument; the second is a circumstance on which that judgment is based.

Step 1: Identify the Question Type

The boldface font in the argument and the word "role" in the question stem indicate that this is an Analyze the Argument Structure question.

Step 2: Deconstruct the Argument

The author's conclusion is that mathematicians actually form a tightly knit community. The counterargument is that mathematicians are antisocial loners. Now, label each statement as either Conclusion (C), Support (S), or Weaken/Something Else (W).

The first boldface represents an example that supports the counterargument; label this statement W. The second boldface represents the author's conclusion, C.

Step 3: State the Goal

You're looking for an answer that describes the first statement as a W and the second statement as a C. Note that these two statements are on opposite sides of the fence (the first goes with the counterargument and the second goes with the author's argument).

Step 4: Work from Wrong to Right

(A) This answer says that the author uses the first statement to illustrate a pattern. On the contrary, the author believes that the pattern described by the counterargument is not valid. Eliminate answer (A).

(B) The first portion of this answer is accurate: the first statement does support the popular view, which goes against the view held by the author. The second half of this answer, though, is inaccurate. The second statement does not restate the popular view; rather, it provides the author's opposing view. Eliminate answer (B).

(C) The first portion of this answer is accurate: the first statement does support an idea that the author contradicts. The second statement, though, is not "that generalization," or the popular view. Rather, the second statement reflects the author's opposing point of view. Eliminate answer (C).

Note that answers (A), (B), and (C) all describe the two statements as being on the same side of the fence. That's not what you want! You're looking for the two statements to be on opposite sides of the fence.

(D) **CORRECT.** The author does assert something and the first statement does go against that assertion; the first half of this answer is accurate. The second half of this choice refers to "that generalization," or the generalization that the author asserts. The author asserts his own conclusion, so the second half of this answer is also accurate. Leave this answer in.

(E) The first does counter the author's assertion, or conclusion, though note that this answer choice describes the first statement as a "judgment." It is not a judgment; rather, it's a fact or example. The second half of the choice says that the second boldface statement is based on the first statement; in fact, the second statement goes against the first one. Eliminate answer (E).

The correct answer is **(D)**.

Alternative Approach

If you have trouble with the above approach, or you hit a very confusing or convoluted argument, you can try an alternative method for steps 2 through 4 that should help you to eliminate some answers (though you may not be able to eliminate all four wrong answers).

Step 2: Deconstruct the Argument

Read the passage and label each boldface statement as one of the following:

> (F) Fact   (a verifiable statement)
> (O) Opinion   (a minor claim, or an opinion of someone other than the author)
> (C) Conclusion   (the major claim of the author)

In the case of the previous problem, the first statement represents a Fact while the second statement represents the Conclusion.

Step 3: State the Goal

You're looking for F followed by C.

Step 4: Work from Wrong to Right

When working through the answers, look for words that can indicate the type of statement:

> (F) Fact   = "evidence" "circumstance" "finding"
> (O) Opinion   = "judgment" "claim" "position" (taken by someone else)
> (C) Conclusion   = "position" (taken by the argument) "assertion" (of the author)

Do *not* dive very deeply into the content of the answer choices; rather, focus on moving pretty quickly and eliminating answer choices that do not match the Fact/Opinion/Conclusion classification. In the case of the previous problem, you can confidently eliminate answer (E) because a judgment is not the same thing as a fact.

Answer (A) is questionable; an observation can be a fact, but facts are more often described as evidence or examples. If you had to guess, you probably would not guess (A) on this one.

With this alternate method, you can avoid getting bogged down in the messy details and make a good guess without spending too much time, but you might not be able to eliminate all of the wrong answers.

If you can figure out how to categorize only one of the two boldface statements, then assess the corresponding half of the answer choices. Eliminate whatever answer choices you can, choose immediately from among the remaining answer choices, and move on.

Draw a Conclusion (Inference)

Draw a Conclusion questions are very similar to Inference questions for regular Reading Comprehension passages. You need to find the answer that logically follows, or must be true, based upon the information given in the argument.

It's critical to make a distinction between conclusions given in an argument and conclusions (or inferences) given in answer choices. When an ASP provides a conclusion for you in the argument itself, that conclusion is pretty faulty. It's an arguable statement, or claim, that is only partially supported by the premises of the argument, and you can find lots of gaps in the argument.

By contrast, if you are asked to draw a conclusion or to infer something yourself, that conclusion must be able to be *proven* from the given premises. The conclusion should not require you to make any additional assumptions at all, even tiny ones. The correct answer to a Draw a Conclusion question is *not* a claim or an arguable statement. Rather, the correct answer *must* be true based directly and only upon the information given in the argument.

Step 1: Identify the Question Type

The question stem may appear in a number of forms:

- If the statements above are true, which of the following must be true?
- Which of the following conclusions can best be drawn from the information above?
- The statements above, if true, best support which of the following assertions?
- Which of the following can properly be inferred from the statement above?
- (A full argument) Students typically study five days a week. Therefore, _____.

The last is an example of a Fill-in-the-Blank format. The word "Therefore" signals that the correct answer is the conclusion of the argument.

Step 2: Deconstruct the Argument

Draw a Conclusion questions do not contain a conclusion in the argument. The argument will contain only premises and these premises will be primarily factual (though some might be more on the opinion or claim side). As with the other question types, jot down some light notes. If you can brainstorm any possible conclusions, do so—but remember that you might not think of actually what the correct answer will say.

Consider the following simplified example:

Samantha and Isabel are the only two people in the dining room. They are both women.

What can be safely inferred from these facts? That is, what absolutely *must* be true as a result?

Must be true: There are no men in the dining room.

8

This conclusion may not seem very meaningful or important in a real-world sense, but this is what the correct answer to a Draw a Conclusion question is like. Avoid grand conclusions in these problems. A correct answer might simply restate one or more of the premises, using synonyms. Alternatively, a correct answer might be a mathematical or logical deduction.

Step 3: State the Goal

You need to find the answer choice that must be true given some or all of the information found in the argument. (Note that the correct answer is not required to use *all* of the given information.)

Step 4: Work from Wrong to Right

Eliminate any answers that require additional assumptions or outside information in order to be true. The wrong answers will all include something that doesn't have to be true.

> Consider the following example:

1. In certain congested urban areas, commuters who use public transportation options, such as trains and subways, spend approximately 25 percent less time in transit, on average, to reach their destinations than commuters who travel by car. Even individuals who drive their entire commute in carpool lanes, which are typically the least congested sections of roadways, still spend more time, on average, than commuters who use trains and subways.

   The statements above, if true, best support which of the following assertions about commuting in the congested urban areas mentioned above?

   (A) Waiting in traffic accounts for approximately 25 percent of the commuting time for individuals who drive to their destinations.

   (B) Walking between a subway or train station and one's final destination does not, on average, take longer than walking between one's car and one's final destination.

   (C) Using carpool lanes does not, on average, reduce driving time by more than 25 percent.

   (D) Individuals who commute via public buses spend approximately 25 percent more time in transit than those who commute using public trains or subways.

   (E) Subways and trains are available in the majority of congested urban areas.

Step 1: Identify the Question Type

The word "assertion" coupled with the fact that the assertion is in the answer choices indicates that this is a Draw a Conclusion/Inference question.

Step 2: Deconstruct the Argument

One set of notes might look like this:

> Pub trans (trn, sub): ~25% < t than ppl using car
>
> Even true for carpool

Step 3: State the Goal

You're looking for something that must be true using at least some of the presented information. It might be tempting to conclude that people "should" use public transportation—but note that this doesn't have to be true. Don't introduce opinions or real-world logic.

Step 4: Work from Wrong to Right

(A) While waiting in traffic probably does account for *some* of the commuting time, there's no reason why it must account for approximately 25 percent of that time. This might be an appropriate answer for a Strengthen question, but not for an Inference question. Eliminate answer (A).

(B) Careful! This one is tempting initially because it might cause someone to think, "Oh, wait, did they account for the time it takes to get from the subway to work or your house? Maybe this is it!" The difficulty here is that this length of time does not have to be similar to the length of time it takes to walk from the car to the final destination. The argument compares the overall commute time, not the time for smaller pieces of the commute. Eliminate answer (B).

(C) The argument does mention that "even" when someone uses a carpool lane, which should save time, it's still faster to take public transportation. Given that info, if public transportation also takes about 25 percent less time than using a car, then it actually must be the case that using a carpool lane does not (on average) save more than 25 percent of car commuting time. If it did, then carpooling might actually be faster than taking public transportation. Leave this answer in.

(D) The argument does not make a comparison between different forms of public transportation. Rather, it compares all of public transportation to all commuting by car. Eliminate answer (D).

(E) Tricky! Again, this one might make someone think, "Oh, they're assuming that public transportation is actually available!" Note first that this argument is assuming nothing at all—it does not contain a conclusion and, by definition, only arguments containing conclusions also have assumptions. Next, the argument provides actual data for areas that do have public transportation, so that's the only concern. Finally, the argument never specifies that these areas must have subways and trains, specifically (buses are also public transportation), nor does it specify that a "majority" of these areas have public transportation. In fact, the argument refers only to "certain congested urban areas."

The correct answer is **(C)**. Note that the correct answer addressed only one narrow part of the situation. It did not assume anything or go at all beyond the scope of the information given in the argument.

Wrong Answer Choice Types

As with the earlier question types, knowing the common wrong answer types will help when you get stuck between two choices.

1. Out of Scope

For Draw a Conclusion questions, "Out of Scope" answers require you to assume at least one piece of information not explicitly presented in the argument. For example, answer choice (A) in the example goes beyond the scope of the argument by bringing in waiting time.

A subset of Out of Scope answers will contain information that seems "Real-World Plausible". In other words, this information is very plausible, or likely to be true in the real world. For example, in answer (D) above, it seems reasonable that buses would take longer than subways or trains—after all, buses share the road with cars.

A Real-World Plausible answer may even contain what people would reasonably surmise to be true in an article or conversation about the general topic. The Draw a Conclusion question type, however, requires you to find something that must be true according to the given premises, not something that could be true or merely sounds reasonable. If you cannot say that the premises prove an answer choice to be true, eliminate that answer choice. Do not bring external knowledge into the picture on Draw a Conclusion questions.

2. Wrong Direction

"Wrong Direction" answers might provide a conclusion that is the opposite of what the argument says. For example, a Wrong Direction answer choice for the argument above could just be the opposite of the correct answer:

> Using carpool lanes *does*, on average, reduce driving time by more than 25 percent.

This statement actually asserts the opposite of what the premises together imply, but because it brings up some of the issues one might expect to see, it would be easy to misread and then choose this choice.

Resolve a Paradox

This question type poses two seemingly contradictory premises and asks you to find the answer choice that best reconciles them.

Step 1: Identify the Question Type

The question will often, though not always, indicate what the discrepancy is or provide a keyword pointing to the discrepancy in the argument. For example:

> Which of the following statements, if true, would best explain the sudden drop in temperature?

> Which of the following, if true, most helps to resolve the paradox described above?

Step 2: Deconstruct the Argument

Like Draw a Conclusion passages, Paradox passages do not contain a conclusion in the argument. The argument will contain only premises and these premises will be primarily factual (though some might be more on the opinion or claim side). Jot down some light notes and articulate the paradox to yourself.

Consider the following simplified example:

> According to researchers, low dosages of aspirin taken daily can significantly reduce the risk of heart attack or stroke. Yet doctors have stopped recommending daily aspirin for most patients.

What? That doesn't make any sense! If aspirin is beneficial, why wouldn't doctors recommend it for patients?

There must be some other reason why they wouldn't want patients to take aspirin. Perhaps there are some other side effects that are worse than the possible benefits. The correct answer will contain some new information that helps to explain why the doctors no longer recommend daily aspirin. If you insert the correct answer into the argument, someone who reads it would then say, "Oh, I see! Now it makes sense why they've stopped recommending aspirin."

Step 3: State the Goal

Your goal is to find an answer that explains why the surprising facts given in the argument are not so paradoxical after all. The correct answer should resolve whatever paradox caused you to think, "Wait, that doesn't make sense!"

Step 4: Work from Wrong to Right

As with all ASPs, read through each answer. Eliminate choices that do not serve to explain or resolve the paradox presented in the argument.

Consider the following example:

1. In a recent poll, 71% of respondents reported that they cast votes in the most recent national election. Voting records show, however, that only 60% of eligible voters actually voted in that election.

    Which of the following pieces of evidence, if true, would provide the best explanation for the discrepancy?

    (A) The margin of error for the survey was plus or minus 5 percentage points.

    (B) Fifteen percent of the survey's respondents were living overseas at the time of the election.

    (C) Prior research has shown that people who actually do vote are also more likely to respond to polls than those who do not vote.

    (D) Some people who intend to vote are prevented from doing so by last-minute conflicts on election day or other complications.

    (E) Polls about voting behavior typically have margins of error within plus or minus 3 percentage points.

Step 1: Identify the Question Type

The word "discrepancy" in the question stem indicates that this is a Resolve the Paradox question.

Step 2: Deconstruct the Argument

> Poll: 71% of ppl said they voted
> Rec: 60% of eligible voters voted

Step 3: State the Goal

The goal is to find something that resolves the apparent discrepancy in these two numbers. First, the people who responded to the poll might not be the same group of people who were eligible to vote. Alternatively, there might be a reason why people said they voted when they actually didn't. Possibly there is some other reason to explain what happened.

Step 4: Work from Wrong to Right

(A) This choice begins promisingly by discussing a margin of error. However, a margin of error of 5 percentage points will not close the 11 percentage point gap between the two statistics in the argument. Eliminate answer (A).

(B) Fifteen percent is larger than the 11-point discrepancy in the argument. The percentage, however, applies to the percentage of respondents living overseas at the time of the election. If absentee ballots are allowed, then these people could still have voted. This choice doesn't definitively resolve the paradox. Eliminate (B).

(C) If people who do vote are also more likely to respond to polls, then those people are overrepresented in the polling results. That is, they represent a greater proportion of the people answering the poll than they do of the overall population; this explains why a greater percentage of poll respondents said they had voted. Keep this answer in.

8

(D) This is probably true, but it does not explain the discrepancy in the statistics presented in the argument. The 60 percent figure represents people who actually did vote, not those who intended to vote but didn't.

(E) This choice does not explain the discrepancy in the statistics presented in the argument; this poll might not have the same margin of error of "typical" polls. Even if you do adjust for a 3 percent margin of error, 11 percent still represents a substantial gap.

Wrong Answer Choice Types

1. Out of Scope

A common wrong answer type will discuss something that is not at issue in the paradox, such as answer (D) in the example. The people who intended to vote but didn't are not at issue in the argument.

Alternatively, this type might address one of the premises but not actually address the discrepancy itself between the two premises. Choices (A) and (B) fall into this category.

2. Wrong Direction

A choice of this type will support the fact that the discrepancy exists rather than explain why there is not actually a discrepancy after all. Choice (E) in the above example falls into this category: a 3-percentage-point margin of error supports the idea that an 11-percentage-point gap represents a discrepancy. Note that you are not supposed to explain why the apparent discrepancy exists. Rather, you must explain why the apparent discrepancy is not a real discrepancy after all.

Problem Set

> Use the four-step process taught for all ASPs, as well as any specific techniques recommended for that question type (e.g., the S-W-slash chart). Consider all five answer choices before you make your final decision!

1. John was flying from San Francisco to New York with a connecting flight in Chicago on the same airline. Chicago's airport is one of the largest in the world, consisting of several small stand-alone terminals connected by trams. John's plane arrived on time. John was positive he would make his connecting flight 30 minutes later because _____.

   Which of the following most logically completes the argument above?

   (A) John's airline is known for always being on time

   (B) a number of other passengers on John's first flight were also scheduled to take John's connecting flight

   (C) at the airport in Chicago, airlines always fly into and out of the same terminal

   (D) John knew there was another flight to New York scheduled for one hour after the connecting flight he was scheduled to take

   (E) the airline generally closes the doors of a particular flight 10 minutes before it is scheduled to take off

2. Media Critic: Network executives have alleged that television viewership is decreasing due to the availability of television programs on other platforms, such as the internet, video-on-demand, and mobile devices. These executives claim that **declining viewership will cause advertising revenue to fall so far that networks will be unable to spend the large sums necessary to produce programs of the quality now available**. That development, in turn, will lead to a dearth of programming for the very devices that cannibalized television's audience. However, technology executives point to research that indicates that **users of these platforms increase the number of hours per week that they watch television** because they are exposed to new programs and promotional spots through these alternate platforms. This analysis demonstrates that networks can actually increase their revenue through higher advertising rates, due to larger audiences lured to television through other media.

   The portions in boldface play which of the following roles in the media critic's argument?

   (A) The first is an inevitable trend that weighs against the critic's claim; the second is that claim.

   (B) The first is a prediction that is challenged by the argument; the second is a finding upon which the argument depends.

   (C) The first clarifies the reasoning behind the critic's claim; the second demonstrates why that claim is flawed.

   (D) The first acknowledges a position that the technology executives accept as true; the second is a consequence of that position.

   (E) The first opposes the critic's claim through an analogy; the second outlines a scenario in which that claim will not hold.

3. In the last year, real estate prices, such as those for houses and condominiums, have gone up an average of 7 percent in the city of Galway but only 2 percent in the town of Tuam. On the other hand, average rents for apartments have risen 8 percent in Tuam over the last year but only 4 percent in Galway.

    Which of the following is an inference that can be reasonably drawn from the premises given above?

    (A) In the last year, the ratio of average apartment rents to average real estate prices has increased in Tuam but fallen in Galway.

    (B) Tuam has experienced a greater shift in demand toward the rental market than Galway has.

    (C) It has become easier for Galway real estate to be bought and sold, whereas it has become easier for Tuam real estate to be rented.

    (D) The supply of rental apartment units has decreased more in Tuam than in Galway.

    (E) The average amount spent on housing is higher in Galway than it is in Tuam.

4. Due to the increase in traffic accidents caused by deer in the state, the governor last year reintroduced a longer deer hunting season to encourage recreational hunting of the animals. The governor expected the longer hunting season to decrease the number of deer and therefore decrease the number of accidents. However, this year the number of accidents caused by deer has increased substantially since the reintroduction of the longer deer hunting season.

    Which of the following, if true, would best explain the increase in traffic accidents caused by deer?

    (A) Many recreational hunters hunt only once or twice per hunting season, regardless of the length of the season.

    (B) The deer in the state have become accustomed to living in close proximity to humans and are often easy prey for hunters as a result.

    (C) Most automobile accidents involving deer result from cars swerving to avoid deer, and they leave the deer in question unharmed.

    (D) The number of drivers in the state has been gradually increasing over the past several years.

    (E) A heavily used new highway was recently built directly through the state's largest forest, which is the primary habitat of the state's deer population.

8

5. Political Analyst: After a coalition of states operating under a repressive regime collapsed, some hoped that freedom would bolster the population of the largest state, Algan, but as a result of dislocation and insecurity, the Algan population continues to dwindle at the rate of 700,000 a year. The government proposes to address the problem with a wide range of financial incentives, along with investments in improved healthcare, road safety, and the like. These are positive measures, but **they have been tried before, to little avail**. A better plan to reverse the population decline is to improve Algan's governance in both the public and the private sphere. **If a greater part of the population participated in important decisions and shared in Algan's wealth, then larger families would result.** In addition, if corruption and greed among the elite were curbed, public health would improve, and average life expectancy would increase.

The two boldfaced statements serve what function in the argument above?

(A) The first is the main point of the analyst's argument; the second is a premise that supports the first.

(B) The first is a premise that undermines an alternative to the analyst's proposal; the second is a premise that supports the analyst's main claim.

(C) The first is a premise that contradicts the main point made by the analyst; the second is the main point of the argument.

(D) The first is a premise that supports a proposal; the second is that proposal.

(E) The first is a conclusion that the argument endorses; the second is a premise that opposes that conclusion.

6. Displayco is marketing a holographic display to supermarkets that shows three-dimensional images of certain packaged goods in the aisles. Displayco's marketing literature states that patrons at supermarkets will be strongly attracted to goods that are promoted in this way, resulting in higher profits for the supermarkets that purchase the displays. Consumer advocates, however, feel that the displays will be intrusive to supermarket patrons and may even increase minor accidents involving shopping carts.

Which of the following, if true, most seriously weakens the position of the consumer advocates?

(A) The holographic displays are expensive to install and maintain.

(B) Many other venues, including shopping malls, are considering adopting holographic displays.

(C) Accidents in supermarkets that are serious enough to cause injury are rare.

(D) Supermarkets tend to be low-margin businesses that struggle to achieve profitability.

(E) Studies in test markets have shown that supermarket patrons quickly become accustomed to holographic displays.

8

7. Brand X designs and builds custom sneakers, one sneaker at a time. It recently announced plans to sell "The Gold Standard," a sneaker that will cost five times more to manufacture than any other sneaker that has ever been created.

   Which of the following, if true, most supports the prediction that The Gold Standard shoe line will be profitable?

   (A) Because of its reputation as an original and exclusive sneaker, The Gold Standard will be favored by urban hipsters willing to pay exceptionally high prices in order to stand out.

   (B) Of the last four new sneakers that Brand X has released, three have sold at a rate that was higher than projected.

   (C) A rival brand recently declared bankruptcy and ceased manufacturing shoes.

   (D) The market for The Gold Standard will not be more limited than the market for other Brand X shoes.

   (E) The Gold Standard is made using canvas that is more than five times the cost of the canvas used in most sneakers.

8. With information readily available on the internet, consumers now often enter the automobile retail environment with certain models and detailed specifications in mind. In response to this trend, CarStore has decided to move toward a less aggressive sales approach. Despite the fact that members of its sales personnel have an average of 10 years of experience each, CarStore has implemented a mandatory training program for all sales personnel, because _____.

   (A) the sales personnel in CarStore have historically specialized in aggressively selling automobiles and add-on features

   (B) the sales personnel in CarStore do not themselves use the internet often for their own purposes

   (C) CarStore has found that most consumers do not mind negotiating over price

   (D) information found on the internet often does not reflect sales promotions at individual retail locations

   (E) several retailers that compete directly with CarStore have adopted "customer-centered" sales approaches

9. Government restrictions have severely limited the amount of stem cell research that companies in the United States can conduct. Because of these restrictions, many U.S.-based scientists who specialize in the field of stem cell research have signed long-term contracts to work for foreign-based companies. Recently, the U.S. government has proposed lifting all restrictions on stem cell research.

Which of the following statements can most properly be inferred from the information above?

(A) Some foreign-based companies that conduct stem cell research work under fewer restrictions than some U.S.-based companies do.

(B) Because U.S.-based scientists are under long-term contracts to foreign-based companies, there will be a significant influx of foreign professionals into the United States.

(C) In all parts of the world, stem cell research is dependent on the financial backing of local government.

(D) In the near future, U.S.-based companies will no longer be at the forefront of stem cell research.

(E) If restrictions on stem cell research are lifted, many of the U.S.-based scientists will break their contracts and return to U.S.-based companies.

10. Traditionally, public school instructors have been compensated according to seniority. Recently, the existing salary system has been increasingly criticized as an approach to compensation that rewards lackadaisical teaching and punishes motivated, highly qualified instruction. Instead, educational experts argue that, to retain exceptional teachers and maintain quality instruction, teachers should receive salaries or bonuses based on performance rather than seniority.

Which of the following, if true, most weakens the conclusion of the educational experts?

(A) Some teachers express that financial compensation is not the only factor contributing to job satisfaction and teaching performance.

(B) School districts will develop their own unique compensation structures that may differ greatly from those of other school districts.

(C) Upon leaving the teaching profession, many young, effective teachers cite a lack of opportunity for more rapid financial advancement as a primary factor in the decision to change careers.

(D) A merit-based system that bases compensation on teacher performance reduces collaboration, which is an integral component of quality instruction.

(E) In school districts that have implemented pay for performance compensation structures, standardized test scores have dramatically increased.

8

Answers and Explanations

Problem Set

1. The solution key sometimes shows sample notes to illustrate how they might look and to help you brainstorm abbreviations and other note-taking methods.

John was flying from San Francisco to New York with a connecting flight in Chicago on the same airline. Chicago's airport is one of the largest in the world, consisting of several small stand-alone terminals connected by trams. John's plane arrived on time. John was positive he would make his connecting flight 30 minutes later, because _____.

Which of the following most logically completes the argument above?

(A) John's airline is known for always being on time

(B) a number of other passengers on John's first flight were also scheduled to take John's connecting flight

(C) at the airport in Chicago, airlines always fly into and out of the same terminal

(D) John knew there was another flight to New York scheduled for one hour after the connecting flight he was scheduled to take

(E) the airline generally closes the doors of a particular flight 10 minutes before it is scheduled to take off

Step 1: Identify the Question Type

The blank in this Fill-in-the-Blank question is preceded by the word "because," most commonly signaling a Strengthen question, but you'll need to read the argument to be sure. The beginning of that sentence contains the conclusion, so this is indeed a Strengthen question.

Step 2: Deconstruct the Argument

The Chicago airport is busy and very large, consisting of several small stand-alone terminals. Despite this, John thinks he will make his connecting flight.

Step 3: State the Goal

The correct answer choice will make it a little more likely that John's conclusion is valid. The information needs to support the idea that he'll make the connecting flight despite the size of the airport.

Step 4: Work from Wrong to Right

(A) Slash. This is a general observation about the timeliness of John's airline, but it does not provide any new information—the argument already states that John's particular flight arrived on time. The fact that his connecting flight will probably depart on time might even weaken the argument.

(B) Slash. Airlines have been known to delay flights in order to ensure that a large number of passengers can make the connection, but you should not have to make an additional assumption in order to say that this choice strengthens the given conclusion.

(C) **CORRECT.** Strengthen. John will not have to take a tram to another terminal in order to reach his connecting flight. The premises describe the individual terminals as "small." If he can walk to his next flight in a small terminal, then 30 minutes is likely enough time to make the connection.

(D) Slash. This choice is out of scope. The argument concludes that John will make his current flight; the following flight has no bearing on John's ability to catch the flight on which he is currently booked.

(E) Slash/Weaken. If anything, this choice weakens the idea that John will catch the connecting flight by shortening the length of time he has to get to the second flight's gate. He now has only 20 minutes, not 30.

2. Media Critic: Network executives have alleged that television viewership is decreasing due to the availability of television programs on other platforms, such as the internet, video-on-demand, and mobile devices. These executives claim that **declining viewership will cause advertising revenue to fall so far that networks will be unable to spend the large sums necessary to produce programs of the quality now available**. That development, in turn, will lead to a dearth of programming for the very devices that cannibalized television's audience. However, technology executives point to research that indicates that **users of these platforms increase the number of hours per week that they watch television** because they are exposed to new programs and promotional spots through these alternate platforms. This analysis demonstrates that networks can actually increase their revenue through higher advertising rates, due to larger audiences lured to television through other media.

The portions in boldface play which of the following roles in the media critic's argument?

(A) The first is an inevitable trend that weighs against the critic's claim; the second is that claim.

(B) The first is a prediction that is challenged by the argument; the second is a finding upon which the argument depends.

(C) The first clarifies the reasoning behind the critic's claim; the second demonstrates why that claim is flawed.

(D) The first acknowledges a position that the technology executives accept as true; the second is a consequence of that position.

(E) The first opposes the critic's claim through an analogy; the second outlines a scenario in which that claim will not hold.

Step 1: Identify the Question Type

The boldface font indicates that this is an Analyze the Argument question. Note that the question stem references the "media critic's argument"—this is the conclusion you want.

Step 2: Deconstruct the Argument

The first three sentences describe the network executives' argument: alternate viewing platforms will cause fewer people to watch TV, resulting in lower advertising revenues. The networks then won't have enough money to continue producing high-quality programming, so everyone will lose, even the people who are watching on alternate viewing platforms.

The fourth sentence begins with the word "However." The argument goes on to indicate that technology executives have research that contradicts the network executives' view. The media critic then concludes that the networks can actually *increase* their advertising revenues.

The first boldface portion opposes this position by predicting smaller audiences; label it W. The second boldface lends support to the critic's conclusion by citing evidence that alternate media platforms lead their users to watch more television; label this one S.

8

Step 3: State the Goal

The correct answer will first describe a W and then a S.

Step 4: Work from Wrong to Right

(A) The first boldface statement does weigh against the critic's claim, but it is a prediction, rather than an inevitable trend. The second boldface statement is a premise supporting the claim; it is not the conclusion itself.

(B) **CORRECT.** The critic's conclusion about a potential increase in network revenue is contrary to the first boldface statement's prediction about shrinking audiences and falling revenue. Also, the critic's argument does depend upon the second boldface statement's assertion that users of alternate devices will actually watch more hours of television.

(C) The first boldface statement opposes the critic's claim, rather than clarifies it. The second boldface statement is used to support the critic's claim; it does not indicate that the critic's claim is flawed.

(D) The argument does not indicate whether the technology executives accept or deny the prediction of the network executives. (Given, though, that the technology executives think that people will watch more television, not less, it doesn't seem likely that the technology executives will agree with the network executives.) The second boldface statement contradicts the first one; it does not follow as a consequence.

(E) The first boldface statement offers a prediction, not an analogy. The second boldface statement is in agreement with, not in opposition to, the critic's claim.

3. In the last year, real estate prices, such as those for houses and condominiums, have gone up an average of 7 percent in the city of Galway but only 2 percent in the town of Tuam. On the other hand, average rents for apartments have risen 8 percent in Tuam over the last year but only 4 percent in Galway.

Which of the following is an inference that can be reasonably drawn from the premises given above?

(A) In the last year, the ratio of average apartment rents to average real estate prices has increased in Tuam but fallen in Galway.

(B) Tuam has experienced a greater shift in demand toward the rental market than Galway has.

(C) It has become easier for Galway real estate to be bought and sold, whereas it has become easier for Tuam real estate to be rented.

(D) The supply of rental apartment units has decreased more in Tuam than in Galway.

(E) The average amount spent on housing is higher in Galway than it is in Tuam.

Step 1: Identify the Question Type

The word "inference" indicates that this is a Draw a Conclusion/Inference question. Expect to see only premises in the argument.

Step 2: Deconstruct the Argument

One set of notes might look like this:

Past yr: RE $ > 7% in G but 2% in T

Avg rent > 4% in G but 8% in T

Notice two things. First, the argument gives only percentages, not real numbers; you can't conclude anything that involves real numbers, including where rents or home prices are higher. Second, rents are increasing at a faster rate in Tuam but home prices are increasing at a faster rate in Galway.

Step 3: State the Goal

What must be true according to the given information?

Step 4: Work from Wrong to Right

(A) **CORRECT.** While it isn't possible to conclude anything about real numbers, you can use percentages to determine something about ratios. In Tuam, rents have gone up at a faster rate (8 percent) than have real estate prices (2 percent). Thus, the ratio of average rents to average real estate prices must have grown in that city—the numerator has grown faster than the denominator. In contrast, Galway rents have gone up at a slower rate (4 percent) than real estate prices (7 percent). Thus, the ratio of average rents to average real estate prices has actually decreased.

(B) It is not necessarily true that Tuam has experienced a greater shift in demand away from buying and toward the rental market; that is only one possible explanation. For instance, the larger increase in Tuam rents could be explained by a reduction in the supply of rental units in Tuam.

(C) This might be true but does not have to be. The premises do not indicate whether Galway real estate is easier or harder to be bought and sold or whether Tuam real estate is easier or harder to be rented. The premises simply indicate the growth in prices and rents.

(D) It is not necessarily true that the supply of rental units has decreased more in Tuam than in Galway. For instance, there could be a sudden growth in demand in Tuam for rental units (e.g., because of an influx of young singles who are eager to rent), causing rents to increase more rapidly.

(E) The premises indicate nothing about the actual amounts of money spent in the two towns. You are given only percentage growth rates.

4. Due to the increase in traffic accidents caused by deer in the state, the governor last year reintroduced a longer deer hunting season to encourage recreational hunting of the animals. The governor expected the longer hunting season to decrease the number of deer and therefore decrease the number of accidents. However, this year the number of accidents caused by deer has increased substantially since the reintroduction of the longer deer hunting season.

Which of the following, if true, would best explain the increase in traffic accidents caused by deer?

(A) Many recreational hunters hunt only once or twice per hunting season, regardless of the length of the season.

(B) The deer in the state have become accustomed to living in close proximity to humans and are often easy prey for hunters as a result.

(C) Most automobile accidents involving deer result from cars swerving to avoid deer, and they leave the deer in question unharmed.

(D) The number of drivers in the state has been gradually increasing over the past several years.

(E) A heavily used new highway was recently built directly through the state's largest forest, which is the primary habitat of the state's deer population.

Step 1: Identify the Question Type

The words "explain" and "if true" signal that this is a Resolve a Paradox question. Look for the paradox!

Step 2: Deconstruct the Argument

Attempting to decrease the number of deer in his state, a governor extended the recreational hunting season. However, since the reintroduction of the longer hunting season, the number of accidents caused by deer has not declined—instead, it has increased substantially.

Step 3: State the Goal

You need to find the answer choice that explains why the accidents have increased rather than decreased as expected. Perhaps the traffic accidents weren't caused by deer in the first place. Perhaps the accidents are caused by deer fleeing the hunters, in which case a longer hunting season would probably lead to more accidents.

Step 4: Work from Wrong to Right

- (A) If many hunters hunt once or twice per hunting season regardless of the length of the season, then a longer hunting season wouldn't make a difference to the situation. However, this would not explain the observed *increase* in accidents.

- (B) If the deer are "easy prey," then the governor's extension of the hunting season should be *effective* in reducing the deer overpopulation. This does not explain the increase in traffic accidents.

- (C) Careful! This does explain how accidents occur but does not explain why there are more accidents this year, after the governor put in place a plan designed to reduce accidents.

- (D) This answer choice would contribute to an explanation of a gradual increase in traffic accidents over the last several years. However, it does not explain a substantial increase in accidents from just last year to this year. Both the extent of the increase and the time frame serve to make this answer choice an unsatisfactory explanation of the observed rise in accidents.

- (E) **CORRECT.** A new highway system recently built directly through the primary habitat of the state's deer population provides a specific explanation as to why the number of accidents involving deer has increased: more people are driving in the area where deer live. It also explains the time frame of the increase.

5. Political Analyst: After a coalition of states operating under a repressive regime collapsed, some hoped that freedom would bolster the population of the largest state, Algan, but as a result of dislocation and insecurity, the Algan population continues to dwindle at the rate of 700,000 a year. The government proposes to address the problem with a wide range of financial incentives, along with investments in improved healthcare, road safety, and the like. These are positive measures, but **they have been tried before, to little avail**. A better plan to reverse the population decline is to improve Algan's governance in both the public and the private sphere. **If a greater part of the population participated in important decisions and shared in Algan's wealth, then larger families would result.** In addition, if corruption and greed among the elite were curbed, public health would improve, and average life expectancy would increase.

The two boldfaced statements serve what function in the argument above?

- (A) The first is the main point of the analyst's argument; the second is a premise that supports the first.

- (B) The first is a premise that undermines an alternative to the analyst's proposal; the second is a premise that supports the analyst's main claim.

(C) The first is a premise that contradicts the main point made by the analyst; the second is the main point of the argument.

(D) The first is a premise that supports a proposal; the second is that proposal.

(E) The first is a conclusion that the argument endorses; the second is a premise that opposes that conclusion.

Step 1: Identify the Question Type

The bold font indicates that this is an Analyze the Argument Structure question. Expect two opposing points of view in the argument. Use the CSW or FCO technique to label the two boldface statements.

Step 2: Deconstruct the Argument

The analyst recounts a proposal by the Algan government to increase the Algan population. The analyst acknowledges that the proposal contains good ideas but dismisses the plan with the implication that, because the measures have not worked in the past, they will not work now. The analyst then offers a "better plan" (the analyst's conclusion) and offers two premises (the two if-then statements) in support of this better plan.

Step 3: State the Goal

The first boldface statement dismisses the government's plan; as such, it is in support of the analyst's conclusion. Label it with an S. The second boldface directly supports the analyst's proposal; it is also an S.

Step 3: Work from Wrong to Right

(A) The first statement supports the analyst's proposal by undermining the government's plan; it is not the conclusion of the argument. The second statement is a premise in support of the argument's proposal, not in support of the first statement.

(B) **CORRECT.** The first statement does undermine the alternative proposal made by the government. The second statement does support the analyst's conclusion by showing one way in which better governance might lead to a population increase.

(C) The first statement does not contradict the analyst's conclusion; rather, it undermines the government proposal. The second statement is not the analyst's conclusion; rather, it supports the conclusion.

(D) The first statement only indirectly supports the analyst's proposal by showing that the government's plan is less likely to succeed. The second statement is not a proposal at all; rather, it is support for the analyst's proposal.

(E) The first statement is not a conclusion at all, but a premise in support of the analyst's conclusion. The second statement is a premise, but it does not oppose either the first statement or the analyst's conclusion; rather, it is in support of the conclusion.

6. Displayco is marketing a holographic display to supermarkets that shows three-dimensional images of certain packaged goods in the aisles. Displayco's marketing literature states that patrons at supermarkets will be strongly attracted to goods that are promoted in this way, resulting in higher profits for the supermarkets that purchase the displays. Consumer advocates, however, feel that the displays will be intrusive to supermarket patrons and may even increase minor accidents involving shopping carts.

8

Which of the following, if true, most seriously weakens the position of the consumer advocates?

(A) The holographic displays are expensive to install and maintain.

(B) Many other venues, including shopping malls, are considering adopting holographic displays.

(C) Accidents in supermarkets that are serious enough to cause injury are rare.

(D) Supermarkets tend to be low-margin businesses that struggle to achieve profitability.

(E) Studies in test markets have shown that supermarket patrons quickly become accustomed to holographic displays.

Step 1: Identify the Question Type

The words "weaken" and "if true" indicate that this is a Weaken the Conclusion question. Find the conclusion and look for an answer that makes this conclusion at least a little less likely to be valid. Note that the question stem specifically references the conclusion of the "consumer advocates."

Step 2: Deconstruct the Argument

One set of notes might look like this:

D: 3D goods → cust want → > profits
CA: bad, accident

The company, Displayco, points out the potential benefits of its new technology: increased profits for the stores. The advocates, though, point out a possible negative effect: shopping cart accidents. Note that the advocates don't deny that stores will increase their profits; rather, they offer other reasons for avoiding use of the technology. At the least, then, the advocates assume their concerns outweigh the possible benefits of increased profits.

Step 3: State the Goal

Find an answer that makes the advocates' conclusion at least a little less likely to be valid. Use the S-W-slash technique to eliminate answers.

Step 4: Work from Wrong to Right

(A) Slash/Strengthen. This answer choice may weaken Displayco's claim that the stores will have better profits; if anything, this would strengthen the advocates' argument. This choice does not influence whether patrons will find the displays intrusive and distracting.

(B) Slash. The potential adoption of holographic displays by other venues does not impact the concerns of consumer advocates that the displays will be intrusive and distracting. It could be the case that holographic displays will be intrusive and distracting in all of these other venues as well. Alternatively, the argument might not apply to other venues where there might not be potential for minor shopping cart accidents.

(C) Slash. One might think that this answer choice would weaken the consumer advocates' argument. However, the consumer advocates' argument did not claim that the minor accidents would result in injury. Minor accidents can be bothersome to patrons without causing injury.

(D) Slash. While this choice might help Displayco to convince supermarkets to use its product, you were asked to weaken the consumer advocates' concerns. The struggles of supermarkets to achieve profitability is not relevant to the consumer advocates' specific concerns.

(E) **CORRECT.** If studies in test markets have shown that patrons quickly become accustomed to holographic displays, then patrons are much less likely to find the displays intrusive after an initial adjustment period. Further, if patrons become used to the displays, the displays are less likely to increase the frequency of minor accidents involving shopping carts. Note that this choice does not completely dismiss the advocates' concerns; rather, the concerns are diminished just a little bit.

7. Brand X designs and builds custom sneakers, one sneaker at a time. It recently announced plans to sell "The Gold Standard," a sneaker that will cost five times more to manufacture than any other sneaker that has ever been created.

Which of the following, if true, most supports the prediction that The Gold Standard shoe line will be profitable?

(A) The Gold Standard will be favored by urban hipsters willing to pay exceptionally high prices for an exclusive product.

(B) Of the last four new sneakers that Brand X has released, three have sold at a rate that was higher than projected.

(C) A rival brand recently declared bankruptcy and ceased manufacturing shoes.

(D) The market for The Gold Standard will not be more limited than the market for other Brand X shoes.

(E) The Gold Standard is made using canvas that is more than five times the cost of the canvas used in most sneakers.

Step 1: Identify the Question Type

The question stem asks you to "support" a particular "prediction"; this is a Strengthen the Conclusion question type.

Step 2: Deconstruct the Argument

The conclusion is located in the question stem: The Gold Standard shoe line will be profitable. The passage states only that the costs of manufacturing this shoe are exceptionally high. Profit equals revenue minus cost. If costs are exceptionally high, the only way a profit can be made is if revenue is also exceptionally high.

Step 3: State the Goal

Find an answer that makes the conclusion at least a little more likely to be valid. Keep an eye out for information about revenue, as that may be the assumption that is addressed in the correct answer.

Step 4: Work from Wrong to Right

(A) **CORRECT.** Strengthen. If some potential customers are willing to pay exceptionally high prices, then the exceptionally high costs might be offset enough for the shoe line to be profitable. (Note that this answer doesn't indicate that the new shoe line definitely will be profitable, only that it is a little more likely to be.)

(B) Slash. A higher sales rate than projected does not actually give you any information about profitability. In any case, the results of past releases are not necessarily indicative of the case at hand.

(C) Slash. One can argue that this is good for Brand X, in that it will mean that there is one less competitor, or that this is bad for Brand X, in that it is indicative of a sagging sneaker market. In any case, there is no direct connection between this rival brand and the potential profitability of The Gold Standard.

(D) Slash. You have been told nothing that connects the market to profitability. The size of the market does not necessarily have any bearing on profitability.

(E) Slash/Weaken. This is perhaps one reason why manufacturing costs are so high, but you already knew the costs were high from the argument. If anything, this piece of information weakens the conclusion by providing more information about the high costs.

8. With information readily available on the internet, consumers now often enter the automobile retail environment with certain models and detailed specifications in mind. In response to this trend, CarStore has decided to move toward a less aggressive sales approach. Despite the fact that members of its sales personnel have an average of 10 years of experience each, CarStore has implemented a mandatory training program for all sales personnel, because _____.

(A) the sales personnel in CarStore have historically specialized in aggressively selling automobiles and add-on features

(B) the sales personnel in CarStore do not themselves use the internet when making their own purchase decisions

(C) CarStore has found that most consumers do not mind negotiating over price

(D) information found on the internet often does not reflect sales promotions at individual retail locations

(E) several retailers that compete directly with CarStore have adopted "customer-centered" sales approaches

Step 1: Identify the Question Type

The word "because" just before the blank signals a possible Strengthen question, but you'll have to read the argument to be sure. The "Despite X, CarStore has implemented Y, because [answer]" structure indicates that this is actually a somewhat less common type: Resolve a Paradox.

Step 2: Deconstruct the Argument

The argument describes CarStore's decision to move toward a less aggressive sales approach in response to consumers coming into the stores with all kinds of information they have already found on the internet. Surprisingly, despite the fact that its sales personnel are very experienced, CarStore is implementing a mandatory training program. Why?

Step 3: State the Goal

Find an answer that explains why CarStore would require its very experienced sales team to go through a mandatory training program.

Step 4: Work from Wrong to Right

(A) **CORRECT.** If the sales personnel at CarStore have historically specialized in aggressive sales tactics and promoting add-on features, but CarStore wants to move to a less aggressive approach, then the sales team will need to learn new sales tactics. This explains the need for a mandatory retraining program.

(B) Though it may be helpful for the sales personnel of CarStore to use the internet to research car details so that they can relate to many of their customers, this choice refers to the sales team using the internet to research their own purchases, not necessarily for cars. The mandatory training must have something to do with the job of selling cars, so this choice is irrelevant to the given situation.

(C) The fact that consumers do not mind negotiating over price, if true, suggests that a less aggressive sales approach may not be necessary. This does not fit logically with the overall argument about CarStore adopting a new, less aggressive sales approach.

(D) The fact that information gained from the internet may not be exhaustive or up-to-date is irrelevant to the argument, which centers on the need for training salespeople in a new sales approach. Also, experienced salespeople would presumably know about location-specific sales promotions.

(E) What is a "customer-centered" sales approach? Perhaps CarStore already does this. This choice seems to imply that competitors are already using the less-aggressive approach, in which case perhaps CarStore needs to retrain its employees in order to stay competitive. But there is really no way to tell what "customer-centered" actually means.

9. Government restrictions have severely limited the amount of stem cell research that companies in the United States can conduct. Because of these restrictions, many U.S.-based scientists who specialize in the field of stem cell research have signed long-term contracts to work for foreign-based companies. Recently, the U.S. government has proposed lifting all restrictions on stem cell research.

Which of the following statements can most properly be inferred from the information above?

(A) Some foreign-based companies that conduct stem cell research work under fewer restrictions than some U.S.-based companies do.

(B) Because U.S.-based scientists are under long-term contracts to foreign-based companies, there will be a significant influx of foreign professionals into the United States.

(C) In all parts of the world, stem cell research is dependent on the financial backing of local government.

(D) In the near future, U.S.-based companies will no longer be at the forefront of stem cell research.

(E) If restrictions on stem cell research are lifted, many of the U.S.-based scientists will break their contracts and return to U.S.-based companies.

Step 1: Identify the Question Type

The word "inferred" indicates that this is a Draw a Conclusion/Inference question type. There won't be a conclusion in the argument.

Step 2: Deconstruct the Argument

Two things have already occurred: the U.S. government has restricted stem cell research for companies in the United States. As a result, U.S.-based scientists in this field have chosen to work instead for foreign-based companies. One thing has been proposed: the U.S. government is considering lifting the restrictions on this type of research.

(A) **CORRECT.** If United States-based scientists signed contracts with foreign-based companies *specifically because* of government restrictions in the United States, then the new companies with which these scientists signed must operate under fewer restrictions. Therefore, at least some foreign companies must work under fewer restrictions than some American companies do.

(B) Under the current terms, stem cell research is restricted for everybody in the United States, so foreign professionals in this field would not necessarily want to come to the United States. While it is possible that once the restrictions are lifted, American companies will want to hire more scientists and will seek them overseas, the government has only proposed to lift the restrictions; it hasn't actually done so.

(C) This passage is about government restrictions in the United States; financial backing in particular is out of the scope of the argument.

(D) You are not given any information regarding America's current or future position in terms of stem cell research. Though government restrictions and scientists switching companies could be issues related to a company's prosperity, you are given no information about how these directly affect America's position.

(E) Though this could happen, it is impossible to conclude for certain that it will happen.

10. Traditionally, public school instructors have been compensated according to seniority. Recently, the existing salary system has been increasingly criticized as an approach to compensation that rewards lackadaisical teaching and punishes motivated, highly qualified instruction. Instead, educational experts argue that, to retain exceptional teachers and maintain quality instruction, teachers should receive salaries or bonuses based on performance rather than seniority.

Which of the following, if true, most weakens the conclusion of the educational experts?

(A) Some teachers express that financial compensation is not the only factor contributing to job satisfaction and teaching performance.

(B) School districts will develop their own unique compensation structures that may differ greatly from those of other school districts.

(C) Upon leaving the teaching profession, many young, effective teachers cite a lack of opportunity for more rapid financial advancement as a primary factor in the decision to change careers.

(D) A merit-based system that bases compensation on teacher performance reduces collaboration, which is an integral component of quality instruction.

(E) In school districts that have implemented pay for performance compensation structures, standardized test scores have dramatically increased.

Step 1: Identify the Question Type

The words "weaken" and "if true" indicate that this is a Weaken the Conclusion question. Look for the conclusion made by the "educational experts."

Step 2: Deconstruct the Argument

The argument is concerned with how public school teachers are compensated. According to the argument, educational experts claim that a system of teacher compensation based on performance rather than seniority would help to retain exceptional teachers and maintain quality instruction.

What are the experts assuming? Can "performance" actually be measured in a meaningful way? Should it be based on how much the students like the teacher? A fun but incompetent teacher might be beloved by students. A challenging teacher might receive lower teacher ratings even though his students learn more.

Step 3: State the Goal

The correct answer to this Weaken question will make the experts' conclusion at least a little less likely to be valid.

Step 4: Work from Wrong to Right

(A) Slash. The fact that other factors also contribute to job satisfaction and teaching performance neither weakens nor strengthens this argument. Either way, the teachers are getting paid; the issue is whether that pay should be based on performance or seniority.

(B) Slash. Nothing in the argument indicates that one universal system of compensation must be adopted in order to implement this plan. It is very possible that several effective models of performance-based pay could be developed and implemented successfully.

(C) Strengthen. This choice indicates that many young, effective teachers are extremely frustrated by the traditional pay structure, in which financial advancement is directly tied to seniority. This bolsters the experts' argument: these young but effective teachers who are leaving the profession might stay longer if they had better opportunity for advancement based on performance.

(D) **CORRECT.** Weaken. This choice indicates that collaboration among teachers is integral to high-quality instruction and that a system of compensation based on teacher performance reduces collaboration. Thus, the effect of a merit-based system of pay might undermine quality instruction, which is one of the two stated goals of the educational experts.

(E) Strengthen. The educational experts' argument in favor of performance-based compensation is bolstered if standardized test scores have dramatically risen in school districts that have instituted such pay structures.

Text Completion & Sentence Equivalence

This unit contains important strategies for tackling Text Completion & Sentence Equivalence questions, two question formats unique to the GRE. Also included are proven strategies for mastering vocabulary, which is key to excelling on these GRE questions.

In This Unit ...

Text Completion

In This Chapter . . .

CHAPTER 9 Text Completion

Text Completion questions on the GRE are sentences or paragraphs with one, two, or three blanks for which you must select the appropriate word or words.

Here's an example of the simplest variety of Text Completion, one with a single blank:

Despite his intense _____, he failed to secure the prestigious university's coveted diploma.

imbibition
lugubriousness
lucubration
magnanimity
character

All single-blank Text Completions have exactly five answer choices, of which exactly one is correct. The answer choices for a given blank will always be the same part of speech.

These questions are very much like some of the questions you probably saw on the SAT.

Your task is to find the choice that **best fits the meaning** of the sentence as a whole.

The best approach will be to **anticipate an answer** before looking at the choices. Many people don't do this. Rather, they just plug in the choices one-by-one, rereading the sentence and stopping when it sounds good.

Here's how you can tell that many people don't anticipate answers: based on empirical data about the GRE, you know that problems of this type with right answer (A) are, on average, significantly easier than problems with right answer (E). Twenty-seven percent of test-takers got (A) problems wrong, whereas 46 percent of test-takers got (E) problems wrong—almost twice as many!

Do you think the GRE deliberately creates (E) problems that are so much harder than (A) problems? That's very unlikely. What's probably happening is that people are lazy. If you don't predict the answer and just plug in the choices instead—and the correct answer is (A)—then you get lucky. The sentence probably makes sense, and you pick (A). On the other hand, if the right answer is (E), then your lack of good process punishes you. You waste a lot of time plugging in all five choices, then get confused and end up picking the wrong one.

By the way, the GRE doesn't actually label the choices (A), (B), (C), (D), and (E) anymore (as in the example, the choices appear in boxes). To answer a question, you simply click on your choice, and the entire box is highlighted. You get a chance to confirm before submitting that answer. (Also, you're allowed to go back and change answers anytime before the clock runs out.)

Although the real problems don't label the answers with letters, this book still uses that nomenclature, because it is easy to understand what is meant by "answer choice (D)," and because saying "the choice second from the bottom" sounds pretty silly. Try to write "A B C D E" on your paper for each question so that you have somewhere to keep track of which answers you think are wrong, which you think might be right, and which feature words you don't know. (We will revisit the previous example shortly.)

Three-Step Process for Text Completions

You can approach every Text Completion question with the same three-step process.

Take a look at the following example:

If the student had been less _____, he would not have been expelled from his grade school.

indefatigable
persevering
refractory
playful
indigent

1. Read only the sentence.

The answer choices will distract you if you read them before you've made sense of the sentence.

The sentence is the truth. Four of the five answer choices are lies.

Don't read the lies until you're solid on the truth.

2. Write down your own fill-in, using proof from the sentence.

Come up with your *own* word or words to go in the blank.

What guides you? The proof that you find in the rest of the sentence.

The proof is what forces the contents of the blank to be perfectly predictable. In other words, the proof solves the mystery of the blank. After all, the GRE is a standardized test, and every question has exactly one right answer. There's no fuzziness.

We sometimes use the term *clue* or *evidence* to talk about things in the sentence that point to the blank. That's all well and good. But the term *proof* really captures the idea that stuff elsewhere in the sentence *rigorously determines* the contents of the blank.

Okay, where's that proof? To begin with, look for dramatic action or emotion. The blank describes something: "the student." Did the student do or feel anything dramatic, or did anything dramatic happen to him?

Yes. He apparently was "expelled" from a school. So "expelled" is at least part of the proof.

Now think about how that idea of being expelled is related to the blank in this sentence. Will the blank *agree* with the word or words you've already found? Or will the blank actually *disagree* with the clue?

That all depends on little *signal words*. These signal words are also part of the proof. They provide logical connections between ideas. After you find dramatic actions or feelings, look for these little connectors in the sentence.

9

Pay special attention to words that signal *reversals*. Are there any in the sentence?

Yes. "Less," right before the blank. And "not," right before "expelled." So "less" and "not" are signals that each perform a reversal.

So now you've got the proof. The sentence reads "less _____ … not expelled." Those proof words force the blank to take on a very particular meaning.

Think about what these words mean. If the student were *less* <u>such-and-such</u>, then he would *not* have been expelled.

So being <u>such-and-such</u> actually got him expelled. In other words, the blank agrees with "expelled." "Less" and "not" cancel each other out as negatives.

Now you can fill in the blank. **The fill-in is what you predict the answer to be.** At this point, how would you use this blank to describe this student? Come up with your own word or phrase.

Write down this word or phrase, as well as your (A) through (E).

> badly behaved
>
> A
> B
> C
> D
> E

3. Compare to each answer choice.

Here are the choices again. One at a time, simplify the choices, then see how well your fill-in matches up. Mark down one of the following next to your "A B C D E": Good (✔), Bad (✗), Sort Of (~), or Unknown (?).

> indefatigable = tireless
> persevering = determined
> refractory = ?
> playful
> indigent = poor

So now your paper might look like this:

> badly behaved
>
> A ✗
> B ✗
> C ?
> D ~
> E ~

The correct answer is in fact **(C)**, since *refractory* means "rebellious." But even if you didn't know what *refractory* means, you would have a good shot at getting this problem right through process of elimination.

Also, notice that you can write a *plausible, interesting, but unproven* story around some of the wrong answer choices. For example, "If the student had been less *playful*, he wouldn't have been expelled." This could make sense if the student was playing games during a serious lesson.

Or maybe, "If the student had been less *indigent*, he wouldn't have been expelled." What an indictment of the school's administration!

You should avoid writing stories when doing Text Completions. You should avoid introducing new, interesting ideas.

What you want for your fill-in is **complete predictability and redundancy**. There should be no surprises in the blank. Remember, there is only one right answer. **No new ideas! No interesting stories!**

Try it again with the example from earlier in the chapter:

Despite his extreme _____, he failed to secure the prestigious university's coveted diploma.

inhibition
depression
diligence
magnanimity
character

First, read **only** the sentence. Get solid on its meaning. Focus on the truth, not (yet) the lies in the answer choices.

Now write your own fill-in, using the proof in the sentence. What's the proof? Well, a dramatic action *failed to secure the prestigious university's coveted diploma*. And there's a signal to reverse course: "Despite." Write your own fill-in—here, *studying* or *hard work* would be a good choice.

Finally, compare *studying* with every answer choice:

studying *or* hard work

A ✗
B ✗
C ✓
D ✗
E ∼

The answer is **(C)**. "Diligence" is the closest match to *studying* or *hard work*. Notice that it's not a perfect match: diligence is more of a character trait, whereas studying or hard work is more of an actual activity.

But the connection is clear and close. A *diligent* person studies hard and works hard. (That's you, right? Hey, you're reading this book! "Full marks," as they say in Great Britain, and keep going!)

9

Be a little flexible as you make your match. You might not have predicted the exact contours of the right answer, but that's okay. In fact, it was better that you didn't waste time trying to make an extremely precise prediction.

On a separate note, you may have some question marks on your page because you lack some vocabulary knowledge (e.g., *refractory*). In that case, make your best guess and move on. You have limited time to complete the section, and staring at the words for longer will not suddenly make up for a lack of vocabulary.

Just be ready to pick a word you don't know or don't feel 100 percent comfortable with (maybe like *refractory*), once you've eliminated the other possibilities.

And during your preparation, keep working to fill those vocabulary gaps.

How to Write Good Fill-Ins

As you try to write good fill-ins, keep in mind the following simple equation:

Fill-in = Proof

The fill-in is really nothing more than the proof in the sentence, just restated in different words. There should be no new ideas in the fill-in.

Take a look at an example:

> In the past decade, the coffee chain has dramatically expanded all across the country, leading one commentator to describe the franchise as _____.

First, read the sentence and make sense of it, as always.

The next big step is to write the fill-in, using the proof in the sentence. Let's break that down into sub-steps. What's the proof?

The blank is about "the franchise" (that's just another term for "the coffee chain"). So look for other descriptions, especially opinionated ones, of that franchise or its actions.

The sentence tells you that the coffee chain "dramatically expanded." That's part of the proof.

But you're not done with finding the proof. Look for a signal or signals that tell you how the "dramatically expanded" idea connects with the blank. Does the blank agree or disagree with that idea?

Signals can also indicate causation or some other type of relationship. But even then, you can often get away with simply determining whether the idea you've already found ("dramatically expanded") and the blank agree or disagree.

In the previous example sentence, the words "leading" and "describe" tell you that the blank agrees with "dramatically expanded." You have enough proof at this point to write a good fill-in.

So go ahead and do so! Construct a fill-in out of the proof you have found.

Recycle words if possible. This instinct will keep you from straying too far from the given meaning of the sentence. Remember, no new ideas! Feel free to use a phrase.

Your fill-in might be this: ***having dramatically expanded***

Or you might have gone just a little further to describe the *result* of such a dramatic expansion: ***everywhere***

Notice how uninteresting these fill-ins make the sentence.

> In the past decade, the coffee chain has dramatically expanded all across the country, leading one commentator to describe the franchise as <u>having dramatically expanded</u>.

What a silly, redundant thing to say in real life! That's exactly what you want for GRE Text Completions.

Don't overthink. In real life, you could easily imagine the fill-in taking you substantially further than *having dramatically expanded*.

For instance, your prediction may add a negative spin (*having overreached*), but the GRE will make the fill-in much more boring in meaning. Assume as little as possible.

> In the past decade, the coffee chain has dramatically expanded all across the country, leading one commentator to describe the franchise as <u>everywhere</u>.

A good answer among the choices might be something like *ubiquitous*, a GRE favorite meaning "being everywhere."

Signal Words

Let's get in a little practice with signal words.

Fill in the blank with your own word or phrase:

> Despite his reputation for _____, the politician decided that in a time of crisis it was important to speak honestly and forthrightly.

Did you predict something like *not being honest*? Perfect!

Be redundant. Recycle the specific words "honest" or "forthright." And very importantly, catch the reversal and put in the *not*.

The signal word "Despite" indicates that reversal. Since the signal was negative, the correct answer needs to pivot 180 degrees **away** from "honestly and forthrightly."

> Despite his reputation for <u>not being honest</u>, the politician decided that in a time of crisis it was important to speak honestly and forthrightly.

Try another:

> For all her studying, her performance on the test was _____.

This one relies on an idiom. Did you say something like *not good* or *bad*? Good!

The idiomatic expression *for all X, Y* is at work here. *For all* here means "despite." It's another reversal signal.

Since studying usually leads to *good* performance, you want to reverse that expectation. So you need to have the sentence say that, despite her studying, her performance was **not** *good.*

> Although he has a reputation for talking too much, others at the party didn't find him to be especially _____.

Did you say something like *talkative*? Or did you go for *not talkative*? Notice that you have a bit of proof ("a reputation for talking too much" and a signal word that reverses direction: "Although."

But you also have another reversal signal—the *not* in "didn't."

As mentioned earlier, reversing yourself twice (much like turning 180 degrees twice) is like not reversing yourself at all. In your blank, you just want another word for "talking too much."

> **Although** he has a reputation for talking too much, others at the party did**n't** find him to be especially <u>talkative</u>.

Here are some common signal words, phrases, and structures, grouped into three very general categories. Pay attention to the reversals, especially when you have more than one of them.

SAME DIRECTION	OPPOSITE DIRECTION (Reversal)	CAUSAL RELATIONSHIP
; (semicolon)	Although	As
: (colon)	Belied	As a result
Also	But	Because
And	Despite	Consequently
Besides	In spite of	Hence
Furthermore	Nevertheless	Since
In addition	Not	So
In fact	On the contrary	Therefore
Just as	On the other hand	Thus
Moreover	Rather than	
Not only . . . but also	Still	
So . . . as to be	Though	
Too (= also)	Whether X or Y	
X, Y, and Z (items in a list)	Yet	

Drill: Sentence Analysis

> Analyze each sentence for the proof, then fill in the blank in your own words.

1. The camp established by the aid workers provided a _____ for the refugees, many of whom had traveled for weeks to get there.

2. While others had given only accolades, the iconoclastic critic greeted the book's publication with a lengthy _____.

3. Though many have impugned her conclusions, the studies on which she based her analysis are beyond _____.

4. The ancient poem's value was more _____ than literary; the highly literal work made no attempt at lyricism and ended by warning the reader never to lie.

5. French food could be said to be the most _____ of all cuisines, considering the high saturated fat content of the otherwise delectable *bechamels* and *remoulades*.

6. It is unfair and incorrect to _____ about an entire minority group based on the actions of a few people, whether those people are reprobates or model citizens.

7. For all the clamor about bipartisanship, in the end, the actual votes _____ to factional loyalties.

8. While digital media should theoretically last forever, in actuality, there are warehouses full of abandoned computer tape drives and other media that have since been _____ by newer technologies.

9. Chad was the most mercurial of young people, but as an adult was able to _____ his wild fluctuations in personality.

10. The _____ position he adopted on the issue belied his reputation for equivocation.

9

Answers and Explanations

1. This sentence is pretty straightforward—you have the proof that "aid workers" are providing something for "refugees," who have traveled for a long time to get there. A good fill-in would be *haven* or *sanctuary*.

2. This sentence has an opposite-direction signal: "While." You also have the proof that the critic is "iconoclastic." Since most critics gave the book "accolades"—and an "iconoclastic" critic would do the opposite—a good fill-in would be something like *condemnation*.

3. The blank is talking about "the studies." This sentence also has an opposite-direction signal: "Though." It seems that this person's conclusions aren't so great. The studies she used, though, *are* pretty great. You want to say something good about the studies, but you have *another* opposite-direction signal, "beyond." You want to say that the studies are so good that they are *beyond* something bad. This sentence would almost certainly be completed with the expression *beyond reproach*.

4. The blank is talking about the poem. You know that it is "more _____ than literary"—so it's *not* very literary. You then find out that it's "highly literal" and not even trying to be lyrical—sounds like a really bad poem! It ended by "warning the reader never to lie." Whoa—that sounds like a *terrible* poem! Maybe the kind that would appear in a children's book. A good fill-in would be *moralistic* or *didactic*.

5. The blank is talking about "French food." You might be tempted to put *delicious* in the blank, but that would be incorrectly inserting an opinion. The sentence says that French food is full of fat. That's proof that a good fill-in would be *fatty* or perhaps *unhealthy*.

6. The blank is talking about an "entire minority group." What should you *not* _____ about them? At least one part of the proof is "based on the actions of a few people." And another part is "unfair and incorrect." A good fill-in might be *make stereotypes* or *generalize*.

7. The blank is about "the actual votes" (something those votes *did*). This sentence depends on an idiom you've seen before. "For all" here means "despite." One part of the proof is "clamor about bipartisanship," and the signal "For all" tells you to reverse that idea. So the second part of the sentence should indicate that the voting was the opposite of **bi**partisan—that is, *partisan*. Since "factional loyalties" describe a partisan environment, a good fill-in would be *conformed* or *adhered*.

8. The blank needs to tell you something that happened to "abandoned computer tape drives and other media," as a result of "newer technologies." In the first part of the sentence, you have the proof "While digital media should theoretically last forever," which contains the reversal signal *while*. Also notice the adverb "theoretically," which sets up a *practically* to come. In other words, digital media does **not** last forever in practical terms. This tracks with the idea of the computer tape drives being "abandoned." A good fill-in would be *replaced*. GRE-type words that might appear here would be *supplanted* or *superseded*.

9. The blank is describing Chad, or whatever Chad was able to do to his personality fluctuations. You have a bit of dramatic proof about Chad—he was "mercurial" (moody, erratic in mood or feeling), which matches the idea of "wild fluctuations in personality." You have a reversal signal, "but," indicating that you need to go in the opposite direction. Thus, Chad was able to *hold back* or *moderate* his wild fluctuations. GRE-type words that might appear here would be *temper* or *damp*.

10. The blank describes the person's "position." You know that the person in question has a "reputation for equivocation." (*Equivocation* means "wavering in your mind or speech about something, maybe even deliberately so.") Don't miss the reversal signal "belied," which means "contradicted" or "gave a false impression of." So a good fill-in would relate to the opposite of *equivocation*—something like *firm* or *resolute*.

9

Double-Blank and Triple-Blank Text Completions

Most Text Completion questions have more than one blank. Consider the following example:

Twentieth-century America witnessed a nearly (i) _____ ascent to ever greater wealth, leaving its leaders (ii) _____ of publicly acknowledging budgetary limitations.

Blank (i)	Blank (ii)
portentous	chary
pertinacious	capable
unremitting	guilty

In the sentence, the blanks are labeled with lowercase Roman numerals.

Below the sentence, the first column contains the choices—*portentous, pertinacious,* and *unremitting*—for the first blank. The second column contains the choices—*chary, capable,* and *guilty*—for the second blank.

Your choice for the first blank is independent of your choice for the second blank. That is, if you choose *unremitting* for the first blank, that does **not** mean that you have therefore chosen *guilty* for the second blank. You must instead make a separate decision for the second blank.

This means that you cannot "cheat" off one column to make your decision for the other. More importantly: *there is no partial credit.* You must get *both* words right or you receive no credit for your response. Thus, your chance of randomly guessing the correct answer is quite low (1 in 9).

It is very difficult to get these questions right based on incomplete information. You must understand the sentences, and you must know all or most of the words.

Fortunately, the fact that you must choose each word independently is somewhat compensated for by the fact that, for each blank, there are only three options, not five (as in single-blank Text Completions).

One more pleasant feature of double-blank and triple-blank problems is that, while they may *seem* harder because they are generally longer, there are also more clues for you to find. Also, having multiple blanks means you get to choose which blank to tackle first … and some blanks are easier to solve than others!

Start with the Easier (or Easiest) Blank

Don't just try to fill in the first blank automatically. Look at all of the blanks, and figure out which one has the easiest proof. Then create a fill-in, and use that fill-in as extra proof for the harder blank(s).

Take a look at this example:

Even seasoned opera singers, who otherwise affect an unflappable air, can be (i) _____ performing in Rome, where audiences traditionally view (ii) _____ performers as a birthright, passed down from heckler to heckler over generations.

Blank #2 is easier. Why? Compare the proof for each blank:

	Proof	**Signals**
Blank #1:	*Even seasoned … otherwise … unflappable*	The signals *even* and *otherwise* express opposition. What is the opposite of *unflappable*?
Blank #2:	*heckler*	No particular signal = agreement

9

Your fill-in for #2 should probably be *heckling*. Remember to reuse the given language in the fill-in when you can.

Now you can use that fill-in as more proof. There is no reversal signal between the two blanks, meaning that the two fill-ins agree in some way. The relationship seems to be causal: the opera performers are going to react to that heckling. A likely fill-in would be *upset by* or *afraid of*.

Your paper might now look like this: **afraid of ... heckling**

Also on your paper, draw a grid so that you can do process of elimination:

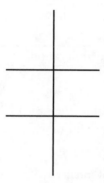

Or, if you prefer, write:

A   A

B   B

C   C

Now compare to the answer choices and mark your paper:

Blank (i)	Blank (ii)
intrepid about	extolling
daunted by	lionizing
tempered by	badgering

Here is an example of what a student might have written down for this question. This student wasn't sure about *tempered by* and didn't know exactly about *lionizing* but felt that it wasn't quite right.

afraid of ... heckling

     ✗   ✗

     ✓   ~

     ?   ✓

The student picked *daunted by* and *badgering*, which are the correct responses.

Remember, the only way to get credit for the question is to pick BOTH *daunted by* and *badgering*.

Now here's an example with three blanks:

> Perceptions of the (i) _____ role of intellectual practices within modern life underlie the famil-iar stereotypes of the educated as eggheads, ideologues, or worse. These negative characterizations may be rooted in a (ii) _____ of the aims of academia, but they are unlikely to be (iii) _____ unless teachers take efforts to address them directly.

Blank (i)	Blank (ii)	Blank (iii)
incongruous	dissemination	espoused
refractory	confounding	dispelled
salubrious	corroboration	promulgated

While this sentence has three blanks instead of two, and is made up of more than one sentence, your method is the same—start with the easiest blank. The easiest blank is often the one surrounded by the most text—that is, the one that is furthest from the other two blanks and thus has the most potential proof located near it. Here, the first blank seems promising:

> Perceptions of the (i) _____ role of intellectual practices within modern life underlie the familiar stereotypes of the educated as eggheads, ideologues, or worse.

The blank describes the "role," which underlies stereotypes about "eggheads … or worse." So the word describing the role should be related to the idea of intellectual = egghead (a mild slang term roughly equiv-alent to *nerd*). Don't ignore the phrase "within modern life." A good fill-in would be *irrelevant*. The sentence seems to be saying that people think intellectuals are eggheads because intellectual practices are not a helpful or important part of modern life.

The second sentence mirrors that idea ("These negative characterizations"). It seems clear that the speaker is trying to defend academia. A good fill-in for the second blank would be *misunderstanding* or *twisting* (you can't really be sure if the people who think intellectuals are "eggheads" are getting it wrong deliberately or not).

Finally, you have a reversal signal: "unlikely" (and another one, "unless"). Work backward on this sentence:

> If teachers DON'T address negative stereotypes directly …
>
> the stereotypes will continue …
>
> so the stereotypes are unlikely to be **eliminated** or **corrected**.

On your paper, you might have:

irrelevant   misunderstanding   eliminated

Or, if you prefer:

irrelevant	misunderstanding	eliminated
A	A	A
B	B	B
C	C	C

Consider your choices and mark your paper appropriately:

Blank (i)	Blank (ii)	Blank (iii)
incongruous	dissemination	espoused
refractory	confounding	dispelled
salubrious	corroboration	promulgated

Your notes for this question might look like this:

The correct answer is **incongruous**, **confounding**, and **dispelled**.

Finally, double-blank and triple-blank questions can sometimes have choices that are phrases rather than single words. These questions tend to be less about knowing difficult vocabulary words than about being able to work out the meaning of the sentence(s).

Try this question:

(i) _____ subject of the sermon, his words possessed a (ii) _____ quality few could fail to find utterly enchanting. It was only when his conclusion devolved into a (iii) _____ that the congregation began to fantasize about returning to the comfort of home.

Blank (i)	Blank (ii)	Blank (iii)
In spite of the insipid	euphonious	thoroughly fallacious slew of prevarications
Notwithstanding the salubrious	euphemistic	seemingly unending string of divagations
Because of the inauspicious	eulogistic	dubiously sanctified series of assignations

Attack the easiest blank first. That might be the last one, since you have the proof that the sermon's conclusion "devolved into" whatever goes in the blank and that "the congregation began to fantasize about returning to the comfort of home." Both bits of proof tell you that you want a fill-in that means something like *bunch of stupid or boring stuff.*

Now that you have mentally completed the last sentence, it might help to paraphrase it before using the information to work backward and analyze the rest of the sentence. Paraphrase: *It was only when the conclusion became stupid or boring that the people got bored.* The phrase "It was only when" serves as a reversal: before things got stupid or boring, they must have been pretty good, as you can verify from this piece of proof: "utterly enchanting."

The second blank is pretty easy: "… his words possessed a _____ quality few could fail to find utterly enchanting." That means that nearly everyone finds his words enchanting. In fact, you could recycle that word and put it in the blank—a good fill-in here would be *enchanting*.

Finally, the first blank. It's pretty hard to fill in this one without glancing at the answer choices, but at least try to figure out a general category of what you'll be looking for. There is a blank about the "subject" of the sermon, and then something nice about the words used in the sermon. Either these two things will go in the same direction or in an opposite direction.

You might have something like this on your paper:

something comparing subject w/ something; enchanting; stupid/boring stuff

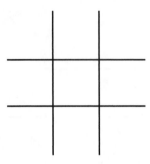

Now try the choices (in any order you prefer).

In the first blank, *In spite of the insipid* makes sense—the meaning is *In spite of the bad quality of the topic, the words of the sermon were enchanting.* In the second option, *Notwithstanding* is similar to *In spite of,* so you would expect something bad to come after, but *salubrious* means "healthy." Since the third choice begins with *Because,* you would expect something positive to come after it (*Because of some good quality of the sermon, the words were enchanting*). But *inauspicious* means "likely to be unsuccessful." Only *In spite of the insipid* works.

In the second blank, only *euphonious* works. The root *eu* means "good," but that's not too helpful here, since all three words use that root. However, *euphemistic* (substituting inoffensive words in for more explicit or hurtful ones) doesn't make sense, and *eulogistic* (full of praise, especially for a deceased person) also doesn't match the idea of *enchanting*.

Finally, the only phrase that means anything like *stupid/boring stuff* is *seemingly unending string of divagations* (*divagations* are tangents, or instances of going off topic). *Prevarications* are falsehoods, and *assignations* are romantic meet ups.

The answer is **In spite of the insipid, euphonious,** and **seemingly unending string of divagations**.

Tricky Aspects of Text Completion Sentences

Take a look at this example:

> Although Paula claimed not to be _____ that she was not selected for the scholarship, we nevertheless worried that our typically sanguine friend was not entirely _____ by the decision.

This sentence is just chock-full of switchbacks. Count the reversal signals: "Although … not … nevertheless … typically … not entirely …"

It's easy to lose your way in a thicket of reversals, especially under exam pressure. How many wrongs make a right?

When you face a situation such as this …

Break It Down

Chop up the sentence and process it in small chunks. Start with the earliest or the most concrete part of the story. Then add one chunk at a time. Change complicated reversals and other signals to simple words, such as *but* and *so*.

As you go, emotionally punctuate each part of the story. Exaggerate the switchbacks in your mental voice, as if you were telling a story you really cared about. Finally, as you think about the whole, discard unnecessary elements, so that you don't have to hold everything in your head at once.

For the previous example sentence, the breakdown might go like this:

> Our friend Paula is *typically* sanguine = optimistic ☺
> She was not selected for a scholarship ☹
> She claimed NOT to be _____
> BUT
> we still worried ☹
> that she was NOT entirely _____ by the decision.

The fill-ins should be pretty easy to generate now: *upset/saddened* ☹ for the first blank and *unaffected* for the second.

It looks like a lot of work, but your brain can generate this train of thought in seconds. Give it a try.

Other tricky aspects of the sentence yield to the same basic medicine: **break it down**.

Now break down a few more challenging sentence types.

Unfamiliar Style or Content

> That such a _____ of precedent would be countenanced was itself unprecedented in the court, a bastion of traditionalism.

The sentence starts with a *that* clause, a hallmark of a very academic writing style. If that sounds weird (and it probably does), add in *The fact* to make "The fact that such a _____ of precedent …"

Also, the content is about a legal matter. Add in the difficult vocabulary ("precedent," "countenanced," "bastion"), and it's no wonder that the sentence is forbidding.

9

Again, break it down. Swap in simpler words and phrases.

> The meaning of the sentence is something like, *The fact that such a _____ of previously established examples would be tolerated was a brand-new and surprising instance of a very traditional court going against tradition.*

A good fill-in here would be something like *rejection*.

Red Herring Clues

A red herring is something that seems to be a good clue, a nice bit of proof, but is actually only there to confuse you. Such traps occasionally appear on Text Completion questions, so be careful that all the proof you're using is *actually* proof.

(Red herring is an expression for something that seems like it's going to be important, but turns out to be just a distraction. The expression arose when criminals started rubbing herring—a type of fish—on trails to distract the hunting dogs chasing after them.)

Back to the GRE!

> By rigorously observing social behavior, anthropologists _____ strict, though implicit, codes of conduct.

Here, the word "strict" turns out to be less important to the answer than "implicit." Decoy answers might be *undermine* or *challenge* (somehow dealing with the *strict* element, but introducing too much new information in the fill-in).

The real meaning of the sentence is based on the idea that, because the behavior is implicit (hinted at or unspoken), anthropologists have to be rigorous in their observations in order to detect or decode it. A good fill-in would be something like *reveal* or *make explicit*.

Blanks in Tough Spots

> If these managers (i) _____ the purported advantages of the new deep-sea recovery methodology to be (ii) _____, then it will rapidly be judged less useful than current alternatives by the broader business community.

Some blanks are positioned in such a way that it's hard to hold the sentence in your head. The gaps occur early or in strategic places. For instance, in the sentence above, the verb of the first clause is missing.

A completed version of this sentence would read something like, "If these managers <u>find</u> the purported advantages … to be <u>lacking</u>, then …"

The main thing to remember is that, no matter how complex or awkward the sentence, you have to make sense of it. The best way to do that is to **break it down into pieces**. Start at the easiest-to-understand chunk, and work outward from there.

9

Drill: Sentence Analysis with Multiple Blanks

Analyze each sentence for the proof, then fill in the blanks in your own words. Here, you're just practicing the first two steps of the strategy. You'll practice complete problems soon.

1. The radio host claimed to have preternatural powers that allowed her to (i) _____ future events, from cataclysms and illnesses to global booms and personal (ii) _____ .

2. After Alexander Graham Bell invented the telephone, he was greeted not with (i) _____ but with a barrage of ridicule. The *London Times* called the invention the latest American "humbug," disbelieving electricians declared the machine a (ii) _____ , and prominent capitalists—always with an eye out to make a profit—all (iii) _____ to buy Graham's patent.

3. Louis Armstrong rose to (i) _____ in the 1920s as an innovative cornet and trumpet player. A(n) (ii) _____ influence in jazz, he is largely credited for shifting focus from a style based on group improvisation to one based on solo performance—such as his own distinctive, even (iii) _____ , solos.

4. For years, the idea that blind people can hear better than sighted people was considered something of an old (i) _____ . However, functional brain imaging has recently uncovered the fact that a brain region called V1, which is (ii) _____ at the back of the skull and which normally responds only to light, has been rewired in the brains of blind people and now processes auditory information in what could be termed a stunning example of the brain's (iii) _____ .

5. Throughout the history of human thought, virtually every thinker has (i) _____ of the mind as a unitary entity. (ii) _____ , in the 1960s, Roger Sperry conducted his famous studies working with epileptics who had been treated via the cutting of the *corpus callosum*, or division between the two hemispheres. During the studies, Perry was able to observe that each half of the brain could gain new information independently and that one hemisphere could be entirely unaware of what the other had learned or experienced. Truly, our brains are not unitary, but (iii) _____ .

6. The company president was not just (i) _____ but positively (ii) _____ ; his subordinates lived in perpetual fear of his reproof.

7. Marissa's date was neither (i) _____ nor (ii) _____ ; he was surly to the waiter and expatiated at great length about mechanical engineering, a topic Marissa finds quite tedious.

8. While many people think of migraines simply as bad headaches, migranes are actually neurological events that can include numbness, slurred speech, and ringing in the ears, with or without headache. Even doctors are (i) _____ to this mischaracterization, thus leading to frequent (ii) _____; these mistakes can lead to instances where both patients with migraines and patients whose disorders are confused with migraines end up getting treatment that may be ineffective or even (iii) _____.

9. We ought not (i) _____ our leaders; it is our (ii) _____ and foibles that make us human, and only by humanizing the greatest among us can we fully understand those whose achievements we admire.

10. In her later years, the artist (i) _____ the wild, chaotic imagery of her early work and instead embraced a prim, highly (ii) _____ formalism.

Answers and Explanations

1. Proof for the first blank is "preternatural powers." A good fill-in is *predict.* Proof for the second blank is "from cataclysms and illnesses to global booms." A *from … to …* structure will have to set up opposites. Furthermore, you can expect that the comparison will fit a predictable pattern. Otherwise, how could the GRE expect you to know what to put in the blanks? "Cataclysms" are big, bad things, and "illnesses" are smaller, bad things. "Global booms" are big, good things, so you're looking for a smaller, good thing. A good fill-in might be *windfalls* or *strokes of luck.*

2. For the first blank, you have an reversal ("not with _____ but with ridicule"). Thus, *praise* would be a good fill-in for the first blank. The proof about the electricians is "disbelieving," so a good fill-in for the second blank would be *hoax.* The third sentence is perhaps the trickiest. If read in isolation, the sentence would seem to indicate that "capitalists—always with an eye out to make a profit" would want to *buy* the patent. However, this item is part of a list of ways in which Graham was *ridiculed.* Thus, a correct fill-in for the third blank would indicate that the capitalists did NOT want to buy the patent. A word like *declined* would fit nicely.

3. If Armstrong "rose," then you're looking for a word describing a high position—something like *prominence* would be a good fill-in for the first blank. For the second blank, simply recycle "influence," and fill in something like *influential* (a nice GRE word might be *foundational*). For the third blank, you want something even more distinctive than "distinctive"—something like *showy, flashy,* or *ostentatious.*

4. The opposite-direction signal in the second sentence ("However"), followed by news of a recent discovery, indicates that whatever was thought "For years" has turned out to be incorrect. Thus, a good fill-in for the first blank would be *folk tale* or *urban legend.* A GRE-type word might be *canard.* The second blank should simply say something like *located.* The third blank needs to sum up the idea that part of the brain that normally only responds to light has actually been repurposed to do something else. Thus, a good fill-in would be something like *versatility* or *plasticity.*

5. The first blank should simply be a verb like *thought* or *conceived* (both words that can be followed by *of*). You learn from the first sentence that the traditional way to think of the mind is "as a unitary entity." The next sentence describes the mind acting in a very non-unitary way (a binary way, actually). So the word in the second blank should be something like *however.* Finally, the third blank simply needs to be the opposite of "unitary"—perhaps *modular* or *decentralized.*

6. The clue is that the subordinates lived in fear. You also have an important sentence pattern: "not just _____ but positively _____." This pattern indicates that the second thing should be a more extreme version of the first. Good fill-ins might be *bossy* and *domineering* or even *bossy* and *terrifying.*

7. Notice again the structure: two things are compared to two things. There must be a logical pattern. In this case, the first blank is the opposite of "surly," so *nice* would be a good fill-in. The second blank is the opposite of expatiating on a "tedious" subject, so you could go with something like *interesting.*

8. Most people make mistakes in how they think of migraines—"Even doctors." From that bit of proof, a good fill-in for the first blank would be *prone* (or something else indicating that the doctors also make this mistake). Following this idea, the second blank should say something like *misdiagnoses* (this idea is supported by the proof phrase "whose disorders are confused with migraines"). Finally, there is an important pattern in the final sentence: "that may be ineffective or even _____." The *even* indicates that you want something even worse than *ineffective.* A good fill-in would be *harmful.*

9

9. The phrase "only by humanizing the greatest among us can we fully understand those whose achievements we admire" is an important piece of proof. This strong statement gives you a very good idea of the point of the sentence. You also have a reversal signal ("not"), so a good fill-in for the first blank would be *idealize*. The second blank is matched up with "foibles," so it will probably mean something very similar, perhaps *flaws*.

10. Since the later years are being contrasted with the early years, the first blank should contain something like *cast off* or *eschewed*. In the second blank, you can simply recycle "prim" or "formalism"—she cast off her old, wild style to pursue *a prim, highly formal formalism*.

Traps to Avoid During Elimination

In this section, you're going to learn about some traps that you might see in harder Text Completion questions.

Theme Trap

Give the following problem a try:

> The event horizon (or boundary) of a black hole represents both (i)_____ and intangibility; space travelers would pass through this literal "point of no return" so (ii)_____ that the precise moment at which their fate was sealed would almost certainly not be registered.

Blank (i)	Blank (ii)
constellation	undiscernibly
irrevocability	universally
infallibility	cosmically

Which is the easier blank?

Most would agree that the second blank is easier. A good part of the proof is "the precise moment ... certainly not be registered," and the lack of any signal to the contrary tells you that the fill-in agrees with that proof. So you might fill in something like *without registering* (again, recycling language from the sentence itself).

Turning to the first blank, you can see that the *without registering* fill-in lines up with *undiscernibly*, while the first blank lines up with "point of no return." So you might fill in *no return* for the first blank.

Now you match to the answer choices. Only *undiscernibly* fits *without registering*. Only *irrevocability* fits *no return*. *Irrevocability* and *undiscernibly* are the correct responses.

A **theme trap** in a wrong answer choice shares a theme or field (such as medicine, sports, etc.) with the sentence. As a result, the choice sounds okay on its own and somehow seems to make sense in the sentence, even though it doesn't really fit the blanks.

Notice the trap language in the choices: *constellation, universally, cosmically*. These words all relate to space, but they have no actual relation to the meanings you want for your blanks. Have the mental discipline to *follow the strategy every time*, and you won't fall for traps like this!

Close But Not Close Enough Trap

Now try this problem:

> Marie was nettled by her sister's constant jocularity and preferred a(n) _____ approach to life.

miserable
indignant
waggish
staid
sycophantic

It may have been pretty straightforward for you to identify the proof ("nettled," "jocularity," "preferred") and to see that Marie is against jocularity, or joking behavior. A fill-in might be *serious*.

Now go through the answer choices. *Miserable* and *indignant* both sort of match, but they both seem a little off, too. Just because Marie doesn't like her sister's constant joking, that doesn't mean she's *miserable* or *indignant* in her outlook on life. Perhaps you don't remember what *waggish* or *staid* mean, and you don't totally remember *sycophantic* either, but you're sure it doesn't mean *serious*.

So your paper might look like this:

> serious
>
> A ~
> B ~
> C ?
> D ?
> E ✗

You can now identify another trap. You don't like *miserable* or *indignant*, but you don't know the other words, so you find yourself reluctant to choose (C) or (D). Unfortunately, you're falling into a trap . . .

The **close but not close enough trap** occurs when a wrong answer choice is "in the ballpark," but something is off in the meaning—however, the word is familiar, so it's attractive.

You might be afraid to pick a word you don't know. **Overcome this fear.** As it turns out, the correct answer is *staid*, which means "serious, sedate by temperament or habits."

You will also see **reversal traps** (you miss a reversal signal or mix up a negative). This is a matter of attention to detail in the moment.

Finally, there are **vocab traps**. *Conversant* doesn't mean "talkative" (it means "knowledgeable"), *factitious* does not mean "factual" (it means the opposite!), and *ingenuous* can look a lot like *ingenious* if you're not reading carefully. To avoid these traps, you're going to need to really know your vocab!

Text Completion Recap

Three-Step Process	1. Read only the sentence.
	2. Write down your own fill-in, using proof from the sentence.
	3. Compare to each answer choice.

Principle for Writing Fill-Ins

Fill-in = Proof	The proof determines what goes in the blank.
	Reuse material from the sentence when writing a fill-in.

9

Principle for Two or Three Blanks

Start with the easier/easiest blank. Work outward from the part of the sentence that is easiest to understand.

Things to Watch Out For

- **Double negative signals**, which create **reversal traps**
- **Unfamiliar style/content**, which can confuse you and cause you to abandon your process
- **Red herring clues**
- **Blanks in tough spots**
- **Theme traps**, where wrong answers are thematically related to the stem
- **Close but not close enough traps**, where wrong answers have the right spin (positive or negative), but are incorrect in degree or detail
- **Vocab traps**, where the GRE takes advantage of visual similarities between words to trick you into thinking one word has a similar meaning to another

Drill: Easy Questions

Here is the first of three 20-question Text Completion drills. Remember to follow the strategy! Look for the proof, write down your own fill-in on separate paper, write A B C D E or make a grid, and use process of elimination.

You won't get any more reminders after this, so it's important that you make a vow to yourself to maintain the mental discipline to use this strategy and not simply revert back to what most people do (they look at the question and pick the choice that seems best).

You will also want to make a list of vocabulary words to look up later (if you haven't been making such a list already). Even after you've done these drills, you could still spend quite a long time just learning the words in these 60 problems (and then going over the problems again—another reason to work on separate paper and not in the book).

If your current vocabulary is extremely limited, here's another idea: go through the following 20 questions looking at the answer choices only, without reading the sentences. Make flash cards for all new words (look words up on dictionary.com, m-w.com, thefreedictionary.com, etc.). Learn all of the words, *then* come back and attack these questions.

1. Although it appeared to be _____ after its stagnation and eventual cancellation in 1989, *Doctor Who* returned to the BBC in 2005, becoming the longest-running science-fiction show in history.

lackluster
ascendant
unflagging
defunct
sated

2. _____ against China's record on environmental protection has become a ubiquitous pastime at energy summits, especially among those already inclined to invective on such topics.

Inveigling
Speculating
Needling
Ranting
Lauding

9

3. In 1345, the brothers of Queen Blanche of Namur, Louis and Robert, were appointed _____ to her spouse, conveying upon them the protection of King Magnus Eriksson in exchange for their homage and fealty.

protégés
vassals
vanguards
precursors
partisans

4. Social critic Neil Postman identified what he saw as a sort of intellectual _____ when he wrote, "What Orwell feared were those who would ban books. What Huxley feared was that there would be no reason to ban a book, for there would be no one who wanted to read one."

pondering
mulishness
degeneration
cerebration
banishment

5. The doctor's presentation went into great detail about the supposed _____ of the treatment, but failed to discuss any way of obviating damage to auxiliary structures.

diagnosis
mien
prognosis
costs
benefits

6. Richardson's (i) _____ handling of the (ii) _____ scandal successfully prevented what seemed poised to become the spectacular devastation or ruination of his coalition.

Blank (i)	Blank (ii)
penitent	fretful
adroit	looming
heterogeneous	ecumenical

7. The (i) _____ forces were just barely held at bay by a loyalist battalion (ii) _____ by its allies' reinforcements.

Blank (i)	Blank (ii)
revolting	obviated

outclassed		bolstered
fascistic		sapped

8.   While it would be lovely if what he said were true, many of the shareholders are afraid he is
_____ liar, based on observations made during his long tenure at the company.

a libelous
an inveterate
a nullified
an unverified
a forfeited

9.   In determining the defendant's sentencing, the jury will take into account whether he acted
on _____ motives or, as he claims, acted primarily to shield himself and others in the
restaurant from harm.

ulterior
resolute
pathological
lucrative
violent

10.   During years of mismanagement by the Socialist Party, Burma drifted into economic _____
and isolation, a far cry from the power and influence exerted by the country at the peak of the
Toungoo Dynasty in the 16th century.

monotony
opulence
nonchalance
feebleness
recriminations

11.   As the new government revealed itself to be far more authoritarian than the people ever could
have guessed, and curfews and roadblocks threatened the _____ of citizens, the public
houses began to fill with whispers of a possible coup d'état.

insolence
epitome
belligerence
recidivism
autonomy

9

12. He is the most hubristic individual his colleagues have ever met and never passes up an opportunity for _____.

hedonism
augmentation
profit
jubilation
bombast

13. (i) _____ by circumstance, the entrepreneur once known for his overweening (ii) _____ was now seen by others as the possessor of a broken spirit and timid demeanor.

Blank (i)	Blank (ii)
Unaffected	pretension
Humbled	liberality
Exalted	wealth

14. Though she had made attempts to adopt a more (i) _____ lifestyle, she was not above indulging her proclivities toward fattening, (ii) _____ dishes.

Blank (i)	Blank (ii)
truculent	odious
salutary	sodden
frugal	unwholesome

15. The discovery that exposure to allergens through the mother's diet during the last trimester could lead to complications during the first year after birth (i) _____ the U.K. Department of Health to (ii) _____ dietary recommendations for expecting mothers.

Blank (i)	Blank (ii)
prompted	intuit
instigated	codify
lulled	officiate

16. Fearful of being seen as (i) _____, the Bieber Appreciation Society took pains to include (ii) _____ voices in its monthly newsletter.

Blank (i)	Blank (ii)
enthusiasts	conciliatory
detractors	critical
toadies	tantamount

9

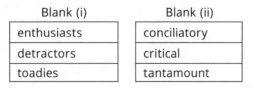

17. The fact that bringing together criminals and their victims for a moderated conversation has been shown to vastly reduce rates of (i) _____ might be explained by the fact that those who commit crimes can only do so by convincing themselves their actions have no (ii) _____.

Blank (i)	Blank (ii)
violence	inconsistencies
recidivism	aberrations
malfeasance	ramifications

18. The (i) _____ of monks and abbots in Eastern Christianity were typically of plain black modest cloth, indicating their spiritual indifference to matters of this world in favor of a commitment to a (ii) _____ mindset. In this regard, the contrast with the (iii) _____ garments of Buddhist monks is striking.

Blank (i)	Blank (ii)	Blank (iii)
vestiges	mundane	iridescent
habiliments	dogmatic	drab
paragons	transcendent	flowing

19. In many criminal trials, it emerges that the defendant (i) _____ some kind of abuse as a child. However, these biographical revelations should not have any effect on how the jury apportions (ii) _____. An excuse is not a justification, and the criminal justice system wasn't constructed to help balance the (iii) _____ of someone's life.

Blank (i)	Blank (ii)	Blank (iii)
appreciated	culpability	ledger
exploited	history	imprisonment
suffered	insanity	verdict

20. The university president argued that top universities should not (i) _____ education as an academic (ii) _____; discouraging our brightest students from pursuing teaching careers does a disservice to the next generation of students by (iii) _____ them of the opportunity to learn from the cream of the crop.

Blank (i)	Blank (ii)	Blank (iii)
disdain	recommendation	denigrating
proscribe	tome	degenerating
circumvent	discipline	divesting

Drill: Medium Questions

1. O'Neill's Irish _____ was so incomprehensible to the Royal visitors, accustomed to speaking in formal Queen's English, that they struggled to complete the negotiation.

fortitude
patois
equanimity
diffidence
consternation

2. Traditional upper class _____ such as fox hunting and cricket have largely given way to more egalitarian amusements over the course of the last century.

stereotypes
disportments
vocations
canards
professions

3. Professor Honeycutt was known as a probing questioner of her students; she always wanted to get to the _____ of any intellectual matter.

emotions
academics
pith
periphery
examination

4. Seeing its only alternative to be a (i) _____ diplomacy unbecoming of political visionaries—as members of the so-called National Liberation Organization saw themselves in those days—the militant branch veered toward a policy of (ii) _____ aggression against its perceived ethnic rivals.

Blank (i)	Blank (ii)
wheedling	supine
freewheeling	unremitting
verdant	superfluous

9

5. A (i) _____ ran through the crowd of protesters chanting slogans and threats when the queen made the sudden announcement—only a fortnight after vowing not to give in to the popular demands for her departure—that she would abdicate the throne, (ii) _____ a period of disorder and confusion.

Blank (i)	Blank (ii)
frisson	marring
murmur	precipitating
panegyric	diluting

6. After Bismarck's cunning leadership helped the Prussians overcome years of infighting, they were able to turn the aggression outward, becoming known and feared across Europe for their (i) _____.

ennui
extravagance
opulence
covetousness
truculence

7. A perfectionist in all things, Joseph expected to immediately become a (i) _____ and was downtrodden indeed when he remained (ii) _____ despite his best efforts.

Blank (i)	Blank (ii)
hack	novel
musician	inane
virtuoso	inept

8. (i) _____ is unlikely to serve someone (ii) _____ by liars and fabulists.

Blank (i)	Blank (ii)
Credulity	foresaken
Duplicity	brooked
Ingenuity	beset

9. The idea, espoused by such heavyweights as Peter Singer, that each sentient being deserves fair treatment on a par with human beings clashes with the ecological insight that _____ some members of a species is occasionally necessary to prevent the devastating effects of overpopulation.

protecting
culling
murdering
reintroducing
depleting

 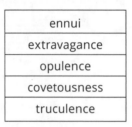

10. While she was known to all her friends as quite the (i) _____ , legendary for humorous stories from her years spent driving a taxi, her private behavior belied this (ii) _____ image.

Blank (i)	Blank (ii)
sage	belligerent
prevaricator	pedantic
raconteur	genial

11. The common opinion at the court had it that her droll utterances as often as not (i) _____ attitudes unbecoming of a lady. This reputation cost her the attentions of some gentlemen, above all thanks to their fear of being bested by her (ii) _____.

Blank (i)	Blank (ii)
eluded	subtlety
derided	doggerel
evinced	repartee

12. While courage is an important virtue to teach—and his character is indeed (i) _____—a cartoon mouse with a (ii) _____ for excessive violence is hardly an appropriate mascot for a children's charity.

Blank (i)	Blank (ii)
mettlesome	penchant
impetuous	kinship
heady	largess

13. The double-dealing ambassador's political (i) _____ and backpedaling looked all the worse when compared to the (ii) _____ straightforwardness of his Australian counterpart.

Blank (i)	Blank (ii)
plutocracy	occlusive
bugaboo	ostensible
sleight of hand	intransigent

14. The most (i) _____ puzzle was in determining how to deliver the antisense strand to the right place at the right moment, after the virus had penetrated the cell but before it had replicated and escaped to infect other cells. To accomplish this, the synthetic strand had to be potent enough to be effective and to resist rapid (ii) _____ inside the body, allowing it time to accomplish its task.

Blank (i)	Blank (ii)
recalcitrant	desiccation
pedestrian	degradation
monolithic	compunction

15. It takes only a (i) _____ of dry shrub for an errant spark to turn into a destructive (ii) _____.

Blank (i)	Blank (ii)
surfeit	conflagration
scintilla	incendiary
pallet	havoc

16. The Russo-Turkish war (i) _____ Albanians, placing before them the (ii) _____ prospect of a division of their lands among competing powers. This, above all, served to bring Albanian nationalism surging out of its former (iii) _____, culminating in a successful bid for independence only a few decades later.

Blank (i)	Blank (ii)	Blank (iii)
rankled	evanescent	latency
enervated	pernicious	insularity
debased	transient	lucidity

17. Though she acknowledges that modern farming practices are more (i) _____ than traditional agriculture, she nonetheless argues that this difference represents no real (ii) _____. Perhaps more worrying, however, is her insistence that similar claims can be advanced regarding the treatment of farmers by an often (iii) _____ social hierarchy.

Blank (i)	Blank (ii)	Blank (iii)
expensive	progress	iniquitous
efficient	disincentive	halcyon
polluting	countermand	stratified

18. The (i) _____ of the word *assassin* is (ii) _____ in philological circles, as the word comes from a sect of brutal killers believed to have smoked the drug hashish before going on a mission. The topic is equally attractive to historians, as the (iii) _____ of the sect, which dates to before the First Crusade in the 11th century, remains a mystery.

Blank (i)	Blank (ii)	Blank (iii)
introduction	notorious	provenance
derivation	unheralded	legend
circumlocution	enigmatic	bane

9

19. Statistics often need to be (i) _____ for their real meaning: in the last decade, while both the population and the amount of meat eaten annually in the nation remained (ii) _____, the growing gap between rich and poor meant that the wealthy few were eating more meat than ever, while the masses suffered from a (iii) _____ of foodstuffs of all kinds.

Blank (i)	Blank (ii)	Blank (iii)
plumbed	plastic	deceleration
calculated	static	dearth
designed	demographic	glut

20. Although Cage supported the expanded reliance on electronically produced (i) _____, most of his early music is surprisingly (ii) _____. His "Music for Marcel Duchamp," a prepared-piano work from 1947, never rises above mezzo-piano, offering instead (iii) _____ melody that maintains its softness throughout.

Blank (i)	Blank (ii)	Blank (iii)
timbre	deleterious	a noisome
murmur	auspicious	an undulating
clangor	subdued	an erstwhile

Drill: Hard Questions

1. After renouncing the significant advantages of his noble birth, he wandered from village to village as a lowly _____; this reliance on alms, he maintained along with other members of his religious order, was the life best suited to one who wished to see both the miserliness and the generosity of humanity.

abettor
mendicant
rube
anachronism
malefactor

2. The serial comma is _____ of many grammarians, who consider it an unnecessary addendum to a perfectly clear sentence structure; obviously, they're wrong, because the serial comma is critical to conveying the correct meaning.

a crotchet
an awl
an apogee
a nadir
an opus

3. In contrast to American social conventions regarding neighborly relations, in which families or individuals residing in close proximity often interact on a familiar basis, residential _____ does not necessarily imply intimacy (or even amity) among the English.

commodiousness
amiability
reciprocity
propinquity
cordiality

4. It is quite dangerous to _____ unnecessarily through the city these days, when explosions shake the buildings to their foundations without letup; it is best to conduct only essential errands, and to do so with haste.

bop
traipse
circumambulate
sidle
reconnoiter

5. The tokens given by the aristocrat, while (i) _____, still served as a reminder that the power of the Crown continued to be held in some esteem even in such (ii) _____ political times.

Blank (i)	Blank (ii)
sardonic	mercurial
nugatory	jocund
sumptuous	magisterial

6. Having built up to a (i) _____, the shelling stopped as suddenly as it had begun; gazing at the drooping barrels, one might be forgiven for thinking they were rendered (ii) _____ by the pathetic sight of their (iii) _____ targets.

Blank (i)	Blank (ii)	Blank (iii)
pique	sidereal	ethereal
crescendo	woebegone	effulgent
euphony	erroneous	haggard

7. Despite having engineered and overseen the return of several stray dioceses that had broken away under his predecessor's (i) _____, the bishop had a modest and open quality that (ii) _____ the (iii) _____ of his position.

Blank (i)	Blank (ii)	Blank (iii)
diligence	construed	tenuousness
epaulet	belied	audacity
laxity	derided	eminence

8. The (i) _____ of "surds"—irrational roots—with the Pythagoreans' faith that all phenomena in the universe could be expressed through harmonious ratios of whole numbers led the cult to (ii) _____ any mention of their existence to the uninitiated.

Blank (i)	Blank (ii)
absurdity	condone
incongruity	proscribe
imperilment	palliate

9. Architectural (i) _____ such as Koolhaas recognized Hadid's talents early and encouraged their development. By 1977, only a few years after their initial encounter, she had perfected her (ii) _____ style, inspired equally by such disparate styles as Malevich's sparse constructivism and the flowing calligraphy of her native Arabic.

Blank (i)	Blank (ii)
cognoscenti	fungible
fledglings	malleable
neophytes	heteromorphic

10. Aleister Crowley, despite being given to wildly fantastic claims—he insisted, for instance, that the founding book of his religion was dictated to him by a divine being who visited his hotel room wearing sunglasses and a trench coat—had his share of (i) _____ followers. These were likely spurred on more than dissuaded by the (ii) _____ cast on him by the popular press, whose dubbing him "the wickedest man in the world" was, to be fair, hardly (iii) _____ given the relative harmlessness of his eccentricities.

Blank (i)	Blank (ii)	Blank (iii)
sycophantic	disadvantages	glib
sordid	gauntlets	peevish
skeptical	animadversions	condign

11. The Biblical portrayal of (i) _____ times preceding the great deluge stands in stark contrast to the ancient Greek representation of the (ii) _____ past as a Golden Age from which humanity has slowly descended into godless chaos. Such observations can easily give rise to the notion that stories about the past are less faithful attempts at reconstruction than (iii) _____, expressing both our cultural fears and hopes.

Blank (i)	Blank (ii)	Blank (iii)
flagitious	proximate	allegories
dubious	antediluvian	equivocations
rustic	obscure	platitudes

12. Seeing (i) _____ as perhaps the most significant cause of preventable illness, such twelfth-century physicians as Moses Maimonides aimed the bulk of their (ii) _____ pamphlets at the prescription of medieval dietary regimens, offering advice that often appears (iii) _____ to modern sensibilities.

Blank (i)	Blank (ii)	Blank (iii)
costiveness	didactic	disingenuous
bathos	maleficent	risible
convalescence	tenable	burgeoning

13. Uncertain whether his (i) _____ attire could impress the suave, nattily dressed executive—despite her frequent affirmations of a fondness for rural life—Francis reduced himself to near (ii) _____ through new wardrobe acquisitions. If only he had known that the executive was secretly ashamed of her (iii) _____ showboating, which she only indulged to conceal her financial ruin.

Blank (i)	Blank (ii)	Blank (iii)
georgic	penury	bombastic
natty	malaise	runic
exclusive	lethargy	sartorial

14. (i) _____ is unlikely to gain a reputation for reliability; Garth's poorly disguised excuses, however, were improbably interpreted by his (ii) _____, hypochondriac employer as a sign of great foresight and (iii) _____.

Blank (i)	Blank (ii)	Blank (iii)
An embezzler	casuistic	insipidity
A malingerer	imposing	sagacity
A pilferer	trepidatious	temerity

15. History has (i) _____ the movement's leader to the extent that his quite considerable moral shortcomings—his (ii) _____ misogyny, for example—are rarely discussed and, if mentioned at all, are seen as no more than (iii) _____.

Blank (i)	Blank (ii)	Blank (iii)
lionized	risqué	malefactions
narrativized	incorrigible	peccadilloes
impugned	waggish	trespasses

16. The new film, though a chronicle of exploitation and iniquity, nevertheless is deeply concerned with notions of (i) _____, eventually showcasing the elimination of all the protagonist's abusers, granting the audience the (ii) _____ they've been awaiting for two hours. Despite the satisfying upheaval, however, the plodding plot en route to this (iii) _____ leaves much to be desired.

Blank (i)	Blank (ii)	Blank (iii)
fairness	catharsis	embellishment
slavery	relief	denouement
injustice	inconclusiveness	platitude

17. Although (i) _____ is frequently used to give otherwise insubstantial work (ii) _____ of profundity, even Wallgot's most charitable readers were known to sneer at the breadth of his references.

Blank (i)	Blank (ii)
stringency	an iota
insularity	a veneer
eclecticism	a medley

18. He rarely bothered to (i) _____ his lengthy tomes, but their surprising popularity with the public empowered him to avoid editorial complaints through (ii) _____ threats to sign a contract with a different publisher.

Blank (i)	Blank (ii)
emend	impuissant
allay	peremptory
edify	toothsome

9

19. In future discounting, subjects place a lower value on events in the distant future than on (i) _____ ones, explaining the common tendency to (ii) _____ present pleasures even at the expense of a likely (iii) _____ of future detriments.

Blank (i)	Blank (ii)	Blank (iii)
atavistic	avert	malady
remote	rescind	proliferation
proximate	protract	buttressing

20. She claims it is possible to deduce matters of fact from logic and, with just as little (i) _____, aims to derive ethical and economic truths as well. The laws of logic, in her opinion, (ii) _____ her proclamation that "existence exists," which is very much like saying that the law of thermodynamics is hot.

Blank (i)	Blank (ii)
epigram	license
warrant	occlude
fallacy	galvanize

Solutions: 20 Easy Questions

1. Defunct. The show stagnated and was canceled, so afterward it might appear to be *dead* or *gone*. *Defunct* (no longer existing) is a good match. A *lackluster* (dull) show might be canceled, but it doesn't make sense that *Doctor Who* appeared to be dull *after* it was canceled, and this would clash with the fact that the show returned in 2005 and had success. A canceled show is unlikely to appear in a positive light, such as *ascendant* (upwardly moving) or *unflagging* (not tiring; steady and unrelenting). *Sated* (fully satisfied, maybe too much) doesn't make sense in this context.

2. Ranting. *Inveighing* (expressing disapproval; railing against) would fit, but *inveigling* (winning over by flattery) is a trap. The real clues to the right answer are that this is an action done "against China's record" and "already inclined to invective" (*invective* means "insulting or harsh language"). *Speculating* is too neutral, and *lauding* (praising) is too positive. *Needling* (teasing or provoking) can be negative, but would be done to someone or to some group—not something that could be done "against China's record."

3. Vassals. The queen's brothers became something to her spouse, the king. This gave "them the protection of King Magnus Eriksson in exchange for their homage (publicly expressed respect) and fealty (loyalty)." By definition, a *vassal* is a person loyal or in service to a feudal lord. *Protégés, vanguards, precursors,* and *partisans* are all roles that people *could* serve on a king's behalf, but the sentence does not provide clues that indicate any of these meanings.

4. Degeneration. Postman's quote talks about a society in which no one wants to read books anymore. This suggests an intellectual weakening or decline (these are good suggestions for filling in the blank). *Degeneration* is a good match; its primary definition is "a decline." *Pondering* (thoughtful consideration) and *cerebration* (thinking about something) are near-synonyms that are too positively intellectual, and thus the opposite of what the blank requires. *Mulishness* (unreasonable stubbornness) and *banishment* (condemnation to exile) are unrelated to the actual proof in the sentence.

5. Benefits. The reversal signal here is "but," and the rest of the proof is that the doctor "failed to discuss any way of obviating (anticipating and preventing) damage." Thus, the doctor went into great detail about only "supposed" good things about the treatment, and only *benefits* works. *Diagnosis* (determination of disease) and *prognosis* (forecast of medical outcome; chances of recovery) both relate to the medical theme, but neither fits in the blank. *Mien* (appearance, bearing) is unrelated.

6. Adroit, looming. His handling of the scandal was successful, so *adroit* (skilled, adept) fits best. Neither *penitent* (sorry for sin) nor *heterogeneous* (mixed; composed of differing parts) "handling of the . . . scandal" is supported by proof in the sentence. The scandal seemed poised to ruin things—that is, it hadn't done so already. What makes the most sense here is that the scandal itself hadn't quite broken yet—it was only *looming* (taking shape as an impending event). Someone might be *fretful* (worried) over a scandal, but *fretful* doesn't make sense as a description of the scandal itself. There are no indications in the sentence that the scandal was *ecumenical* (worldwide in scope).

7. Revolting, bolstered. One good clue to the first blank is the word "loyalist." Those fighting the loyalists would likely be the rebels. You don't have any indication that the forces were *fascistic* (totalitarian, led by dictator). *Outclassed* (surpassed in quality) is irrelevant here, so *revolting* fits best. Don't be thrown off by the dual meaning of *revolting*—certainly *revolting* can mean "disgusting," but it can also mean engaging in a revolt, such as against a government. The loyalist battalion was helped or strengthened by "its allies' reinforcements," so only *bolstered* (supported) makes sense. *Obviated* (anticipated and made unnecessary) isn't supported by any proof in the sentence. *Sapped* (weakened, especially of energy) conflicts with the idea that allies would help the loyalists.

8. Inveterate. The "While" and the hypothetical "if what he said were true" in the first part of the sentence indicate that he is actually a liar. This is based on his long track record, so a good fill-in might be *an established* liar. *Libelous* is a trap answer—libel is lying in print for the purpose of damaging someone's reputation. *Libelous* liar would actually be redundant—and, of course, you have no indication that the lying was done in print. *Nullified* (invalidated, voided), *unverified* (unconfirmed), and *forfeited* (lost as a result of crime or fault) all don't quite work as a description of a liar; to the extent that they do, they cast doubt on his ability to lie, a doubt this sentence doesn't support. *Inveterate* (long-established and unlikely to change) is the correct answer.

9. Ulterior. There's a good structural signal here: "whether ... or." You are looking for a characterization of "motives" that would make them negative, namely the opposite of "primarily to shield himself and others in the restaurant from harm." If he truly was acting in defense of himself and others, he would likely get a lighter sentence than if he had *ulterior*, or hidden (generally selfish), motives. *Resolute* (determined; steady) is unrelated. *Pathological* (related or due to physical or mental disease; compulsive) and *lucrative* (producing large profit) introduce themes of illness and money, respectively, that are not indicated by any clues in the sentence. *Violent* is a theme trap.

10. Feebleness. You know that Burma was being mismanaged, so you want something bad (and appropriate to describe an economy). The blank and "isolation" are contrasted with "power and influence." Just as isolation and influence are (somewhat) opposite ideas, you can expect the blank to oppose power: something like *not powerful* or *not strong*. *Feebleness* (weakness) is a good match. *Monotony* (lack of variety, tedious repetition) is negative, but no proof in the sentence supports this meaning. *Opulence* (wealth, abundance) is opposite of the desired meaning. Both *nonchalance* (casual lack of concern) and *recriminations* (counteraccusations) don't make sense following "economic."

11. Autonomy. What would an authoritarian government threaten with "curfews and roadblocks"? Most likely, something like *independence. Autonomy* is more or less a synonym of *independence.* Though citizens might need to be belligerent to stage a coup, the blank describes what the citizens would lose that would **initially** cause people to just begin to utter "whispers of a possible" coup. *Belligerence* (aggressively hostile attitude) doesn't work in this context. Likewise, *insolence* (rude and disrespectful behavior) does not work in the blank. The remaining choices, *epitome* (a perfect example of something) and *recidivism* (tendency to relapse to previous behavior, often criminal), are not indicated by clues in the sentence.

12. Bombast. "Hubristic" means arrogant—a "hubristic" person would never decline an opportunity for bragging, or *bombast. Augmentation* (the action of making or becoming greater in size or amount) is not quite right; greater size or amount is not exactly indicated by the "hubristic" clue. *Hedonism* (the devotion to sensual pleasures and their pursuit) and *jubilation* (the state of rejoicing) are off topic. Finally, while an arrogant person might desire *profit*, so might anyone else. The sentence would need to include evidence more specifically about money for *profit* to be the right answer.

13. Humbled, pretension. The proof is that the entrepreneur is now "the possessor of a broken spirit and timid demeanor"—thus, he must have been the opposite of that before the change. A good fill-in for the second blank might be *confidence.* The accompanying adjective "overweening" means "conceited," or just "excessive," so the entrepreneur was previously known for his extreme confidence. So look for a negative choice for the blank. *Pretension* fits best; *liberality* (giving or spending freely; open-mindedness) is positive and not overweening, and *wealth* adds an idea that is not indicated in the sentence. Moving on to the first blank—a good fill-in might be "brought down." The only answer that is a match is *humbled. Exalted* (held in high regard; in a state of extreme happiness) is the opposite of what the blank requires, and *unaffected* is too neutral to explain the change in how the entrepreneur is seen by others.

9

14. Salutary, unwholesome. Start with the second blank. Most people would not indulge in a proclivity (inclination or predisposition) toward dishes that are *odious* (extremely unpleasant) or *sodden* (soaked); the correct word must be *unwholesome* (not conducive to health), which also agrees with the proof word "fattening." The first word should contrast with this idea because of the reversal signal word "Though." The best bet is *salutary* (conducive to health). *Truculent* (ferocious, cruel, or savage) and *frugal* (economical in the spending of money or resources) do not work.

15. Prompted, codify. A discovery that pregnancy complications are being caused and can be avoided would *prompt* action—specifically, *codifying*, or systematizing, the recommendations. For the first blank, *instigated* (urged, goaded, provoked, or incited) has a somewhat negative spin, and instigating is generally something that people do; it is odd to say that a "discovery" instigated a group of people to do something. *Lulled* (deceptively caused to feel safe) is the opposite of what the discovery of the allergen/complications link would do to the Department of Health. For the second blank, *intuit* (understand or solve by instinct) and *officiate* (act as an official in charge) are not right, though the latter represents a bit of a theme trap related to a government agency.

16. Toadies, critical. "The Bieber Appreciation Society" clearly exists to appreciate all things Bieber, but it seems that the society has become "Fearful" of being seen in a certain way. What way? Keep reading—they "took pains" to include a certain kind of voice. *Tantamount* (equivalent) doesn't make sense in the second blank, and *conciliatory* would be positive toward Bieber (so why would the Bieber Appreciation Society have trouble finding such voices?). Only *critical*, which in this context means "involving careful evaluation and judgment," works. If the society is struggling to include *critical* voices, it seems that they fear being seen as not having balanced views—that is, they fear being seen as *toadies*, making them nothing but a group of servile flatterers. There is very little danger of an appreciation society (or fan club, booster organization, or any similar group) being seen as *detractors* of their namesake. *Enthusiasts* and "Appreciation" agree in the degree of positivity, so that's not something the group would fear either.

17. Recidivism, ramifications. The people in question are already criminals, so the issue isn't one of bringing down crime or *violence* in general, but of repeat offenses, that is, *recidivism*. What meeting victims must convince the criminals of is that their actions have consequences—or *ramifications*.

18. Habiliments, transcendent, iridescent. The first blank is referring to something made of cloth, which is contrasted with the garments of "Buddhist monks." You are looking for something that means garments or clothes; *habiliments* (clothes associated with a particular profession or occasion) is the only choice that fits. The second blank is looking for a description of a spiritual reality beyond this one; only *transcendent* (above and beyond the limits of material existence) fits. *Mundane* (earthly, rather than heavenly or spiritual) agrees rather than contrasts with "matters of this world." *Dogmatic* (inclined to present opinion as unassailable truth) is unrelated. The third blank is looking for a contrast with the "plain black modest cloth" outfits of the first sentence segment; *iridescent* (colorful, lustrous, or brilliant) is the only option that directly contrasts. *Drab* actually agrees with "plain black modest cloth." *Flowing* is not necessarily the opposite of garments "of plain black modest cloth," which may or may not be *flowing*.

19. Suffered, culpability, ledger. The first blank is a good place to start. Obviously, no one *appreciates* abuse. *Exploited* is trickier, but the text never implies that the abuse is being used to exploit the system. The best choice is *suffered*. For the second blank, you only need to know what a jury does: they apportion blame, which is a synonym of *culpability*. Finally, the third blank only makes sense with *ledger* (you can't balance *imprisonment* or a *verdict*).

20. Disdain, discipline, divesting. The semicolon in this sentence indicates that the two parts of the sentence agree—the first part should mirror the meaning that "the brightest students … pursuing teaching" would be a good thing. For the first and second blanks, universities should therefore not *put down* education as an academic *area* or *pursuit*. Don't fall for trap answers; *proscribe* (ban) and *circumvent* (avoid via circuitous means) add extra meaning to the idea of *put down*. Only *disdain* fits the first blank. *Discipline* is the closest match for the second blank (*tome* means "book, especially a large, academic book"). The third blank needs something that explains the "disservice" done to future students, namely, something like *depriving* them of the chance to learn from the best. The best choice is the synonym *divesting*; don't fall for the traps of *denigrating* (defaming, belittling) and *degenerating* (deteriorating, declining). Both trap choices work with the theme, but don't fit into the blank.

Solutions: 20 Medium Questions

1. Patois. Since the negotiators find O'Neill "incomprehensible," there must be something in his speech, not the tone or content of that speech, that is confusing them. *Patois* is a regional dialect, in contrast to the official language spoken by the negotiators (Queen's English). The Royal visitors would not find any of the other characteristics—*fortitude* (courage, resilience), *equanimity* (composure, mental calmness), *diffidence* (hesitance or resistance to speak), *consternation* (amazement or dismay that leads to confusion)—"incomprehensible," nor do any of these relate to the clue about speech.

2. Disportments. Fox hunting and cricket are not professional activities for the upper class (the proof is "amusements"); they are hobbies, amusements, or diversions, that is, *disportments*. *Vocations* and *professions* both contradict the idea of these activities as "amusements." Fox hunting and cricket are not examples of *canards*, which are unfounded rumors or stories, so that choice does not fit. *Stereotypes* is a trap, since stereotypes of the upper class might have them constantly engaging in such *disportments*.

3. Pith. A "probing questioner" is looking for the central point of a matter. That it is an "intellectual matter" suggests a word other than *emotions* for the blank, as does that choice's failure to relate to the "probing questioner." *Periphery* is the opposite of central. *Examination* doesn't fit at all. *Academics* is a theme trap. The only answer that means core or central point is *pith*.

4. Wheedling, unremitting. What would seem to be unbecoming of political visionaries is to attempt to convince someone (rather than, say, commanding or dictating terms), especially in a flattering way. That's exactly what *wheedling* means. *Freewheeling* (acting without concern for rules or consequences) is not indicated by any proof in the sentence, and *verdant* (green, covered in vegetation) is totally unrelated to diplomacy. You have no indication that the aggression undertaken was *superfluous* (unnecessary); if so, why would they undertake it? A "policy of *supine* (passive; apathetic) aggression" would be contradictory. Rather, it was persistent or relentless (*unremitting*).

5. Frisson, precipitating. The protesters are getting what they want: the queen is suddenly abdicating (giving up) the throne. *Thrill* or *excitement* may work well for the first blank, and *frisson* fits. *Murmur*, while possible, doesn't capture the sense of excitement one would expect. A *panegyric* (formal speech or composition in praise of someone or something) is not something that would "run through the crowd," certainly not in praise of the very queen the crowd wishes to depose. For the second blank, one might expect a period of disorder to begin following a political upheaval; *precipitating* is the only possibility. *Marring* (damaging, disfiguring) and *diluting* (making weaker by adding other elements to it) aren't really things that could be done to "a period" of time.

9

6. Truculence The blank is referring to something that makes the Prussians feared, and something that has led to internal fighting. *Truculence*—aggression or belligerence—is the best fit here. Neither *ennui* (listlessness arising from boredom) nor *covetousness* (envious desire to possess something) are indicated by any proof in the sentence, and neither would really inspire fear. *Extravagance* and *opulence* (both mean lavishness*)* aren't especially threatening.

7. Virtuoso, inept. Since Joseph is a "perfectionist," he probably expected to become *perfect*, or at least *good*, and was disappointed when he remained something like *unskilled* or *bad*. *Virtuoso* (highly skilled, especially in music or art) and *inept* match the fill-ins well. Beware of choosing answers by comparing the options for each blank. Someone who is *inept*, particularly a writer, could be called a *hack* (a dull, unoriginal writer), but this is the opposite of what is called for in the first blank. In turn, *hack* might present a theme trap to someone mistakenly thinking of the noun definition of *novel* (book) in the second blank. For the second blank, all the options are adjectives, and *novel* (new) and *inane* (silly) don't work as contrasts to "perfectionist."

8. Credulity, beset. For the first blank, you are looking for a trait that is unhelpful in dealing with "liars and fabulists" (fabulists are just very creative liars). *Duplicity* and *ingenuity* would be actively helpful, so the answer must be *credulity* (a tendency to believe people too easily). For the second blank, you are looking for a participle describing "someone," that is, you can read it as "someone (who is) *foraken/brooked/ beset* by liars and fabulists." It wouldn't be that bad to be *forsaken* (abandoned) by liars—at least they would leave you alone. *Brooked* (tolerated) by liars doesn't make as much sense; it is the liars that would need to be tolerated by others. But someone who is *beset* (surrounded) by liars would have a problem, and would not be well served by *credulity*.

9. Culling. The discussion is about doing something to "some members of a species … to prevent the devastating effects of overpopulation." Something like *removing* or *getting rid of* would work in the blank. *Protecting* and *reintroducing* don't make sense; they are theme traps. *Depleting* can apply to a resource, but not to individuals. *Murdering* and *culling* are both types of killing, but *culling* is the better option since it is a technical term for killing individual members to avoid overpopulation. (Bonus: If you understand this sentence, you've got a handle on one of the key debates among environmentalists.)

10. Raconteur, genial. The sentence indicates that she was "legendary for humorous stories" from a certain set of life experiences. A *raconteur* is someone who tells amusing stories, but she wouldn't be "known to all her friends" as a *sage* (wise or learned person) or a *prevaricator* (someone who tells false stories) just based on that piece of evidence. In the last part of the sentence, "belied" indicates that "her private behavior" is at odds with her public reputation, but the blank refers to her image, so it agrees with the first blank. Someone who tells amusing stories would be considered *genial* (friendly and cheerful), but not *belligerent* (hostile and aggressive) or *pedantic* (overly concerned with small details or rules).

11. Evinced, repartee. The opinion about her is clearly negative, so her utterances don't *deride* (ridicule) negative utterances or *elude* (avoid) them, but rather they demonstrate (*evince*) them. One isn't likely to fear being bested by *doggerel* (triviality) or—usually—*subtlety* (if you're bested by *subtlety*, you're likely not the sort of person who notices), but clever, quick, and witty replies (*repartee*) are threatening indeed!

12. Mettlesome, penchant. You are looking for another word for courageous, but one that doesn't carry negative connotations (the "indeed" in front of the blank indicates that the spin will be the same as the spin of "virtue"). *Mettlesome* means "spirited or courageous," but *impetuous* (impulsive) and *heady* (intoxicating; exhilarating) do not match the fill-in. But the cartoon mouse seemingly engages in excessive violence, so it has a tendency toward, or a *penchant* for, violence. It does not have a *kinship* (blood relationship) or *largess* (generosity) for violence.

13. Sleight of hand, ostensible. The ambassador is "double-dealing" (duplicitous) and "backpedaling" (retreating from a position). A good fit in the first blank would be something like *deceitfulness*, so *sleight of hand* (skillful deception) works. There is no indication that the ambassador had political *plutocracy* (government by the wealthy) or political *bugaboo* (something causing fear). The "Australian counterpart" is straightforward and compares favorably with the ambassador mentioned first, so expect a positive adjective that can describe "straightforwardness" for the second blank. *Occlusive* (tending to close off) would conflict with being straightforward, and *intransigent* (uncompromising, obstinate) is too negative. Only *ostensible* (supposedly true, but not necessarily true) is neither too negative nor at odds with any proof in the sentence. *Ostensible* works in a sentence about how politicians "looked," not necessarily about how they really were.

14. Recalcitrant, degradation. The puzzle sounds quite complicated—delivering an antisense strand to the right place at just the right moment. Only *recalcitrant* (stubborn) is appropriate to describe a complicated puzzle; *pedestrian* (commonplace, uninspired) conflicts with the proof, and *monolithic* (inflexible, unchanging) is not indicated by any piece of evidence. The strand must be strong enough to resist rapid (something), "allowing it time to accomplish its task." The strand needs time to work, so it needs to resist something like *not being able to work. Dessication* (drying out) is probably bad, but there is no indication in the sentence that drying out would prevent the strand from working, and *compunction* (uneasiness due to guilt) doesn't apply to strands. However, *degradation* (deterioration, breakdown) is something the strand would have to resist in order to work on the virus.

15. Scintilla, conflagration. The signal word "only" indicates that you are looking for something that means "small amount" in the first blank. *Surfeit* (excessive amount) is an antonym, but *scintilla* (minute quantity, trace, or bit) is a perfect fit. *Pallet*, which means either "straw mattress" or "platform for storage, stacking, and moving of goods" (such as those often lifted by forklifts), doesn't follow the "only" signal, so beware of the possible straw/dry shrub theme trap. *Havoc* is destructive, but has nothing to do with fire (which is what "spark" would lead you to expect). *Incendiary* does relate to fire, but it is not quite appropriate in this spot—an *incendiary* is more of a fire-starter, like dynamite. A *conflagration* is specifically a destructive fire.

16. Rankled, pernicious, latency. The war clearly didn't weaken (*enervate*) Albanians, since it encouraged them to strive for independence. And while some features of the war might have *debased* them, the prospect of division of their lands didn't do this. However, it might have *rankled* them (angered, vexed, or caused bitterness for them). The "prospect of a division of their lands" would not be a good thing for the Albanians, so expect a negative word in the second blank. Also, the sentence indicates that "a successful bid for independence" happened a few decades later. *Pernicious* (greatly destructive, deadly, injurious, or harmful) works well, but *evanescent* (fleeting; tending to vanish like vapor) and *transient* (quickly coming into and passing out of existence; transitory) aren't negative enough and both have short-term meanings that conflict with the long time frame indicated by the proof. The Albanians' nationalism surged out—it wasn't already clear (*lucid*), and whether it was *insular* before or after doesn't seem to make much of a difference; but if it emerged out of *latency*, that would explain why it suddenly became a force that could lead to independence.

17. Efficient, progress, iniquitous. There is a difference between modern farming practices and traditional agriculture. "She nonetheless argues that this difference represents no real" *progress*, the only choice for the second blank that makes sense. *Disincentive* means "deterrent," and *countermand* as a noun means "order that revokes a previous order." *Progress* in turn provides an additional clue for the first blank: she is arguing that the difference is not really progress, even though modern farming is more (something) than traditional farming, so the blank must be something positive like *advanced*. While more advanced practices could be expensive, more expensive practices would not be thought of as progress, so *expensive* doesn't fit in this

9

context. *Polluting* is negative, so *efficient* must be the answer in blank (i). The last blank is referring to something bad about the social hierarchy and how it treats farmers. *Stratified* describes the hierarchy, but doesn't say anything negative about it (aside from the fact that it is a hierarchy!). Since *halcyon* (calm, peaceful, or tranquil) is positive, *iniquitous* (unjust) is the only fit.

18. **Derivation, notorious, provenance.** The first sentence links the word *assassin* with "hashish," so the first blank is addressing the *derivation* of the term. It says nothing about its *introduction*, since you are only told where the word originates, not how it was introduced. *Circumlocution* (roundabout or evasive speech; use of more words than necessary) represents a theme trap. Since the derivation is known, it follows that it isn't *enigmatic*; but it is *notorious* given the shadiness involved in the derivation. Nothing in the sentence indicates that the derivation is *unheralded* (unannounced, unsung). Something about the sect presents a mystery, and because the sentence discusses how it "dates to before the First Crusade in the 11th century," you can expect a word that means something like *origin* (*provenance* is a synonym). The *legend* of the sect must not be much of a mystery, given that it is summarized in this sentence. The sentence indicates nothing about the *bane* (curse, affliction) of the sect being a mystery, or even whether such a problem existed for the sect.

19. **Plumbed, static, dearth.** The "growing gap between rich and poor" and the second "while" indicate a contrast in how much meat is consumed by different groups. The "wealthy few were eating more meat than ever," so the masses must have suffered from a lack, or *dearth*, of foodstuffs. *Glut* (excessive supply) is the opposite, and *deceleration* (slowing down) could happen to the production/harvest of foodstuffs, but not to foodstuffs themselves.

The second blank is a bit trickier: the truth is that the rich are eating more meat and the poor less, but the statistics, on their face, don't make that clear. Thus, the statistics indicate that the amount of meat eaten remained the same, or was *static*. *Plastic* (artificial; flexible) has some definitions that are unrelated and others that are somewhat opposite to the fill-in. *Demographic* (related to structure of a population) is a theme trap.

Finally, consider the surprising "growing gap" and the initial piece of evidence that "Statistics ... need to be _____ for their *real* meaning" (emphasis added). Only *plumbed*, or examined closely, works in the first blank.

20. **Clangor, subdued, an undulating.** Cage's early music is "surprisingly" (something), in contrast to something "electronically produced." The reference to music is the primary proof that the first blank is something like *music* or *sound*. *Clangor* (loud racket or sustained noise) is a type of noise that could be electronically produced, and it contrasts nicely with the later clues about the earlier works having "melody" and "softness." *Timbre* (unique combination of qualities distinguishing a sound from others) is a quality of a sound, not a sound itself; this is a theme trap. *Murmur* (soft, indistinct sound) typically refers to human-generated sound, not "electronically produced," and also fails to contrast with "softness" as it should. *Clangor* serves as an additional piece of evidence for the second blank: Cage's early music is surprisingly *not clangorous*, or *soft*. *Subdued* (quiet, soft) works perfectly, while *deleterious* (harmful; unhealthy) and *auspicious* (promising or propitious) are unrelated to the sentence. If "Music for Marcel Duchamp" "never rises above" some level of volume, only *undulating* (rising or falling in pitch, volume, or cadence) works in the last blank. *Noisome* (noxious, harmful, or dangerous) and *erstwhile* (former, in the past, previous) are unrelated to the sentence. Don't be distracted by the superficial similarity between *noisome* and "noise."

Solutions: 20 Hard Questions

1. Mendicant. The proof to find is that he "wandered" and was "lowly" and lived by a "reliance on alms," which is a reliance on charity, as did the "other members of his religious order." A *mendicant* is sometimes just a beggar, but it can have a specifically religious connotation. The other choices all introduce meanings that the rest of the sentence doesn't suggest. Both *abettor* (a person who supports an action, typically wrong-doing) and *malefactor* (evildoer) introduce the unsupported idea that he was bad. *Rube* (unsophisticated or naive person) and *anachronism* (person or object out of its proper time) do not follow from the clues either.

2. Crochet. These answer choices are killer nouns! The fill-in shouldn't be too hard: something like a *peeve* or *concern*. A *crotchet* is a perverse or unfounded belief. The others are all nonsensical: an *awl* is a hole-punching tool, an *apogee* is a climax or high point, a *nadir* is a low point, and an *opus* is a musical or literary composition.

3. Propinquity. You are told that, for Americans, familiarity follows from "close proximity." The blank should be a synonym for proximity, and *propinquity* is. The other answer choices all deal with comfort or friendliness, and thus are theme traps drawing on associations with "neighborly": *commodiousness* (spacious-ness), *amiability* (friendliness), *reciprocity* (relationship with mutual exchange of favors or benefits), and *cordiality* (amity).

4. Traipse. The answer choices are all difficult; all of them mean walk or travel in some way, so nuance is key. Both *bop* (move or travel energetically) and *sidle* (walk timidly) carry a strange spin. *Circumambulate* means "walk all the way around," which would avoid the city, the explosions, and, presumably, the danger. *Circumambulate* also conflicts with "through." *Reconnoiter* (make a military observation of a place) carries an unhelpful militaristic spin. *Traipse* (walk casually or needlessly) agrees with the clue "unnecessarily" and properly contrasts with "conduct only essential errands."

5. Nugatory, mercurial. The "while" in front of the first blank suggests that the items given by the aristocrat are valuable *only* as reminders: that is, they have no real value in themselves. *Nugatory* means "of no value," while *sumptuous* (very costly, luxurious, or lavish) implies real value and also conflicts with the "tokens" clue. *Sardonic* (scornfully or derisively mocking) is unrelated. The "power of the Crown continued to be held in esteem"—you are looking not just for political conditions that are bad or dangerous, but conditions that are changeable. *Mercurial* means "frequently changeable or changing." *Jocund* (cheerful, merry) political times are not indicated by any proof. *Magisterial* (having great authority; dictatorial) is a theme trap, and it doesn't follow the signal word "even." "The Crown continued to be held in some esteem," even in political times when the esteem attributed to the Crown must have decreased.

6. Crescendo, woebegone, haggard. The shelling is building up to something like a *peak*, or *crescendo* (climax; loudest point). *Pique* (passing feeling of irritation at a perceived slight) sounds the same as *peak*, but is unrelated to the shelling. *Euphony* (pleasing sound) is positive, a meaning not indicated by this sentence. The pieces of artillery seem like they are *sad*, since that would be an apt response to a "pathetic sight." Only *woebegone*—extremely sad or full of woe—fits; *sidereal* (relating to the stars or constellations) and *erroneous* (wrong) are unrelated. Their targets aren't likely to be *effulgent* (radiant, brilliantly shining, or splendid) or *ethereal* (light, airy; heavenly, celestial) since neither of these is "pathetic." The targets are most likely *haggard*—worn out.

7. Laxity, belied, eminence. The predecessor had some quality that allowed "several stray dioceses" to break away. *Laxity* (looseness; leniency) is the only choice that works; *diligence* (perseverance; attentiveness) is the opposite of what is needed. *Epaulet* (shoulder ornament, typically worn on military uniforms) would only make sense—if at all—in an extremely metaphorical sense. The third blank refers to the (something) of the bishop's position. There is no indication of *tenuousness* (uncertainty) or *audacity* (recklessness, daring), but *eminence* (high rank, station, or status) would apply to a leader's position. You can now turn to the second blank: you don't expect someone with a position of *eminence* to be "modest and open," so his openness seems to misrepresent (*belie*) that *eminence*. *Construed* (deduced; explained) and *derided* (mocked, ridiculed) don't work.

8. Incongruity, proscribe. For the first blank, "with" is important: *absurdity* (ridiculousness) and *imperilment* (endangerment) are not things that would happen "with the Pythagoreans' faith," but "surds" do seem to have an *incongruity* (lack of agreement) with their faith in "harmonious ratios of whole numbers." For the second blank, the seriousness of the problem would seem to suggest that the Pythagoreans wouldn't want to *condone* (accept, allow) the spreading of this information; they might want to *palliate* (alleviate, diminish) the impact of the information, but forbidding, or *proscribing*, any mention of it outright fits better.

9. Cognoscenti, heteromorphic. People such as Koolhaas "recognized … and encouraged" Hadid's talents, which sounds like the work of a mentor. For the first blank, look for *someone in the know*, or *cognoscenti* (people well informed about a subject). *Fledglings* (young, immature, or inexperienced people) and *neophytes* (beginners) are the opposite. Hadid's style mixes at least two diverse inspirations, so you would not expect it to be replaceable by something else (*fungible*) or easily changeable (*malleable*), but simply to exhibit a plurality of forms: *heteromorphic*.

10. Sycophantic, animadversions, condign. Followers are rarely *skeptical*, and you have no reason to think they were particularly *sordid* (morally degraded, base, or vile), since you don't know what sorts of activities Crowley engaged in, short of making "wildly fantastic claims." But followers, especially those of clearly eccentric figures, do tend to be *sycophantic* (fawning, obsequious, or servile). The press is saying something bad about him, not casting *disadvantages* or *gauntlets* (open challenges) on him, so *animadversions* (strong criticisms) fits best. The criticism seems excessive or undeserved in light of his "relative harmlessness," so the criticism was hardly *condign* (appropriate, deserved). Neither *glib* (fluent to the point of insincerity) nor *peevish* (discontented; ill-tempered) works in this context.

11. Flagitious, antediluvian, allegories. The first blank gives you a "stark contrast" with the Greek representation of these times as a Golden Age, so it should be something bad, even starkly bad. *Dubious* (warranting uncertainty or doubt) doesn't necessarily mean bad, and *rustic* (rural; lacking refinement) isn't anywhere near as negative as *flagitious*, which means "marked by vice." The ancient Greek myths are about the distant or remote past. *Antediluvian* is the correct fit (don't be misled into thinking of *antediluvian* as a trap—it does literally mean "before the flood," and thus doesn't apply to the Greek myths, but it also means "extremely ancient," which is what you're looking for). The stories about the past—in the third blank—would be *equivocations* if each of them contained a mixed message; but instead it looks like the mix comes only if you are comparing Biblical with Greek stories. *Allegories*, or stories with a moral or political meaning, are the right contrast for "faithful attempts at reconstruction" and correctly match "expressing … fears and hopes." *Platitudes* (dull, trite statements or remarks) introduces a connotation of banality not indicated by the text.

12. Costiveness, didactic, risible. *Convalescence* (a period of recovery from illness; recuperation) might seem reasonable for the first blank, but it is a theme trap. *Convalescence* would follow an illness, not cause it. The topic is medieval medicine, with an emphasis on diet, so the correct choice is *costiveness*, which is a fancy way of describing constipation. *Bathos* (anticlimax) does not fit. The pamphlets are seemingly designed to tell people what to eat; they are educational, or *didactic*. There is no indication that the pamphlets are *maleficent* (malicious; intending or producing harm or evil) or *tenable* (able to be maintained; credible). The dietary regimens might have been *tenable*, but there is no indication that the pamphlets were, and it's worth checking the second blank against the third blank and sentence ending. Since dietary and health views are quite different today from those held by medieval doctors, "modern sensibilities" are likely to find their advice funny, or *risible*. Both *disingenuous* (insincere; hypocritical) and *burgeoning* (growing rapidly; flourishing) add meaning that isn't supported by any proof in the sentence.

13. Georgic, penury, sartorial. His attire has something to do with "rural life"; *georgic* means "agricultural or related to rural life." *Natty* means sharp or stylish and is the opposite of what is required in the first blank; Francis was uncertain about whether he could impress a "nattily dressed" person, or a person dressed in *natty* clothes. When *exclusive* is used to describe a commodity, it means "not obtainable elsewhere" and is generally used in a positive sense. Out of concern, Francis "reduced himself ... through new wardrobe acquisitions." It sounds like Francis spent a lot of money on clothes—spending a lot of money could reduce someone—especially someone with *georgic* means—to near poverty (*penury*). *Malaise* (vague, general sense of unease or mental discomfort) and *lethargy* (state of sluggishness, inactivity, laziness, or indifference) are near-synonyms, and neither follows from the proof in the sentence. The executive to whom he devoted his attentions, on the other hand, was concealing "her financial ruin." But how did she ruin herself? Given that she was nattily dressed, she probably also spent her money on clothes. *Sartorial* means "relating to clothes or style," so it fits the third blank perfectly. *Bombastic* (pompous, pretentious) and *runic* (mysterious) both add meaning that isn't indicated by any clues.

14. A malingerer, trepidatious, sagacity. The first blank options all involve some sort of unreliability, but the relevant clue is that Garth's behavior was "improbably" well-received by his boss, who is a hypochondriac. Since stealing (*embezzler* or *pilferer*) has nothing to do with health, *malingerer* (someone who fakes illness) fits best. The second blank asks for something similar to "hypochondriac." The boss may be *casuistic* (practicing clever but unsound reasoning) or *imposing* (grand and impressive in appearance), but it's only his *trepidatious* (in a state of fear that something may happen) character that ties well with hypochondria. The last blank is a word similar to "foresight"; only *sagacity* fits. *Insipidity* (boringness, dullness) and *temerity* (excessive confidence, audacity) don't agree with "foresight."

15. Lionized, incorrigible, peccadilloes. The leader's "moral shortcomings" are overlooked or ignored. This isn't because he was *impugned* (disputed; called into question), but quite the opposite: he has been *lionized* (given public attention and approval). *Narrativized* (presented in a story) is too neutral; it doesn't address the second part of the sentence. His misogyny, if it is a "considerable moral shortcoming," can't be *waggish* (humorous; mischievous) or *risqué* (indecent; sexually suggestive). Only *incorrigible* (inveterate; irredeemable) fits. Finally, his moral failures are "seen as no more than" small or insignificant sins, or *peccadilloes*, not as such larger failures as *malefactions* (crimes) or *trespasses* (sins).

16. Fairness, catharsis, denouement. There is a contrast between "exploitation and iniquity" and what the film is actually concerned with: the first blank must be the opposite of exploitation or iniquity, that is, *fairness*. *Slavery* and *injustice* are theme traps in agreement with "exploitation and iniquity"; both don't fit considering the signal words "though" and "nevertheless." The film showcases "the elimination of all the protagonist's abusers," which grants the audience something like *closure*. The audience hasn't been waiting for *inconclusiveness*. Maybe it has been waiting for *relief*, but *catharsis* is a better fit, since it refers specifically to purging of built-up emotions. Finally, the plot is building up to a resolution, or *denouement*. A *platitude* (trite saying) might leave "much to be desired," but wouldn't provide a "satisfying upheaval." There is no indication that the conclusion of the film was an *embellishment* (an untrue detail added to a story to make it more interesting).

17. Eclecticism, a veneer. You are looking for something that could make a work look less "insubstantial" and that has to do with "breadth"; *insularity* (the narrow point of view resulting from life in a closed, isolated community) and *stringency* (tightness or strictness) imply the opposite of "breadth," but *eclecticism* (drawing on a wide variety of sources) fits. *Eclecticism* doesn't give a work a little bit (*iota*) or a mixture (*medley*) of "profundity," which means "deep insight"; *eclecticism* gives a work a surface appearance (*veneer*) of profundity.

18. Emend, peremptory. For the first blank, you are looking for something the writer could do to "his lengthy tomes" that would appease editors; something like *edit*, *redact*, or *change* seems to fit, and *emend* is a synonym that often has a text as its object (as it does here). He avoids editorial complaints through threats, which are certainly not delicious (*toothsome*) and don't seem to be powerless (*impuissant*)—rather, they prevent complaints from publishers in advance; *peremptory* fits this role.

19. Proximate, protract, proliferation. The first blank asks for a contrast with "distant future"; *remote* is a synonym trap, and *proximate* fits. *Atavistic* (manifesting or reverting to ancestral characteristics) events don't make sense in context. Future discounting involves placing more of a premium on present than on future events, and pleasures are desirable while detriments are not. It follows that subjects will tend to want to promote or prolong (*protract*) present pleasures, not *avert* (avoid by turning away or aside) or *rescind* (revoke) them. This is the common tendency "even at the expense of" a rapid increase in or a large number of (*proliferation*) "future detriments." Neither *malady* (illness) nor *buttressing* (reinforcing) fits in this context.

20. Warrant, license. It is clear from "claims" and the generally derisive tone of the sentence that the author does not think it is possible to deduce matters of fact from logic (that would be pretty silly, come to think about it). Thus, the "she" who is the subject of the text has little *warrant* (justification) for doing this, and just as little *warrant* for using logic to inappropriately derive other "truths." A *fallacy* is a mistaken belief, especially one based on unsound argument—her *fallacy* is a major issue, not something to be described as "just as little." An *epigram* is a witticism or quip, an extra meaning not indicated by any proof in the text. *License* is similar to *warrant* and serves the same function in the second sentence. The "laws of logic" do not *occlude* (close, cover, or obstruct) or *galvanize* (spur to action) "her proclamation."

Sentence Equivalence

In This Chapter ...

CHAPTER 10 **Sentence Equivalence**

Sentence Equivalence questions on the GRE are very similar to single-blank Text Completion questions, with one twist.

There are *six* answer choices, and *two* of them are correct.

For example:

> The judge dismissed Steffen's lawsuit, ruling that since Steffen had been the first to _____ the contract, the company he was suing was no longer obligated to uphold the provisions of the original agreement.
>
> ☐ forswear
>
> ☐ transmute
>
> ☐ breach
>
> ☐ abrogate
>
> ☐ vituperate
>
> ☐ slake

Note that the answer choices are marked not with letters (as in, choices A–F), but with checkboxes. Throughout the exam (in math, too), the GRE uses circular radio buttons for questions with one correct answer and square checkboxes to indicate questions with more than one correct answer.

To get a Sentence Equivalence question correct, you must select **both** correct answers. There is no partial credit. In the previous question, the correct answer is **breach** and **abrogate**, which both mean "fail to do what is required by."

Take a look at what Educational Testing Service (ETS) has to say about the approach for this question type before revisiting this question.

According to ETS:

> *Like Text Completion questions, Sentence Equivalence questions test the ability to reach a conclusion about how a passage should be completed on the basis of partial information, but to a greater extent they focus on the meaning of the completed whole. Sentence Equivalence questions consist of a single sentence with just one blank, and they ask you to find two choices that both lead to a complete, coherent sentence and that produce sentences that mean the same thing.*

Success on a Sentence Equivalence question sometimes depends on hard vocabulary words in the answer choices, sometimes depends on hard vocabulary words or complex sentence construction in the sentence itself, and sometimes hinges on both of these things at once.

Although the idea of two correct answers is an interesting test-making twist, it doesn't actually make the questions any harder for you. In fact, it opens up the strategic tool of Answer Choice Analysis, which will be explained in this chapter.

Many of the skills you have already learned for Text Completion still apply here, such as looking for proof in the sentence and filling in your own word in the blank.

There are two main methods of attack for a Sentence Equivalence question, both of which will be reviewed in the pages that follow:

1. Sentence Analysis

2. Answer Choice Analysis

Sentence Analysis

Like Text Completion questions, Sentence Equivalence (SE) questions ask you to fill in a blank based on the information contained in the text around it.

As with Text Completions, it is very important to remember that the sentences are not anything like sentences pulled from a newspaper, with a few words blanked out. In such a real-life case, you might not be able to fill in the missing word. What if the sentence didn't provide any context for figuring out what word should go in the blank?

On the GRE, things have to be much more concrete. In order to construct a Sentence Equivalence question that has two objectively correct answers and four objectively incorrect answers, *the test makers have to write sentences containing definitive **proof** for what has to go in the blank.*

It's not just context or support. It's *proof*. The proof is always there.

The basic process for Sentence Equivalence is the same as it is for Text Completion. Here are the same three steps:

1. Read only the sentence.

Again, you don't want to be distracted by the answer choices. The four wrong answers are in fact called *distractors* by the test makers. Don't let the distractors do their job too early.

2. Write down your own fill-in, using proof from the sentence.

The proof you're looking for is what the sentence tells you about the blank, in such a way that the blank is fully determined. What takes away any wiggle room in the blank, pinning it like a wriggling bug to the right answer? That's the proof.

You can typically narrow down the proof to a couple of key phrases, including anything opinionated or dramatic, as well as signal words that tell you the relationship between that opinionated stuff and the blank.

When you write down your fill-in, reuse and recycle text you've just been studying in the sentence. Don't add new ideas.

3. Compare to each answer choice.

Now take your home-written fill-in out for a spin with the answer choices. You're ready to handle and dismiss those evil distractors (i.e., wrong answers).

10

In comparison with Text Completion, the wrinkle for Sentence Equivalence is that you need to find exactly *two* good answer choices out of the six. But that's not much of a wrinkle for this process.

Okay, let's try it out. Here's an example problem with some admittedly tough vocabulary:

The village's water supply had been _____ by toxic industrial by-products that had seeped into groundwater.

- [ ] adumbrated
- [ ] vitiated
- [ ] abashed
- [ ] adulterated
- [ ] truncated
- [ ] abridged

The blank is about the water supply. What do you know about that supply? You know that "toxic" substances seeped into it. If you had to pick a single word as proof, there it is: *toxic*. There is no reversal signal (like *but* or *however*) that sends you in the opposite direction.

So your fill-in could be made toxic (points for recycling *toxic*!) or something close by something like *contaminated*.

The answer is **adulterated** and **vitiated**. *Adulterated* means "contaminated," and *vitiated* means "spoiled, made defective, corrupted." (In the incorrect answers, *truncated* and *abridged* both mean roughly the same thing, "shortened." *Adumbrated* means "outlined or sketched lightly," and *abashed* means "made to feel shame.")

Try one more. Again, bring your big-kid vocabulary skills:

Unlike the more genial researchers, who often went out together after work, the _____ Dr. Spicer believed that socializing was nothing more than a distraction, and thus made few friends at the lab.

- [ ] sedulous
- [ ] baneful
- [ ] standoffish
- [ ] partisan
- [ ] glacial
- [ ] assiduous

The blank is about Dr. Spicer. A key signal is the word "Unlike," which sets up a comparison between "the more genial researchers" and "the _____ Dr. Spicer."

The rules of a comparison tell you that the blank should be something that means "*less* genial," in contrast to the "*more* genial" folks.

Your fill-in could actually be *less genial*. If it was, you get the gold star for recycling sentence material. That's the safest habit to adopt for both Sentence Equivalence and Text Completion. Once you get comfortable recycling the proof right into your fill-in, you'll find the process both easier to carry out (it's *less work* than coming up with new words!) and more effective. With recycled material in your fill-in, you'll be much less likely to infect that fill-in with the virus of any new, unsupported idea.

It's okay, though, to put down *less friendly*, simplifying from "genial" a bit. You can even write something decidedly negative like *unfriendly*.

The answer is **standoffish** and **glacial**. Both words can mean "emotionally cold and distant." (*Glacial* can also mean "slow, physically cold, or pertaining to glaciers.") Both are a good enough match to *less genial* to be the winners.

Rounding out the vocab lesson, *sedulous* and *assiduous* mean "hardworking or persistent." *Baneful* means "harmful," and *partisan* means "biased, in favor of only one's own side or party."

10

Drill: Sentence Analysis

> Analyze each sentence for the proof, then fill in the blank in your own words. (This drill is kept brief, as a similar practice set appears in the Text Completion chapter; the skill is the same for both question types.)

1. The biography was neither encomium nor condemnation, but rather a _____ look at a life, its facts verifiable and delivered without commentary.*

2. After her friends betrayed her, she vowed never to trust anyone again or maintain even the lightest of social contacts, becoming a virtual _____.

3. While several months of progress had been made on the new highway plan in the early part of the year, it was now questionable whether the plan would ever reemerge from its current state of _____, its funding held up while politicians bickered about the changing state of the economy.

4. Josh's generally lackadaisical attitude toward his work caused his boss to suspect that his "moral objection" to the task was really just a way to _____ his duties.

5. In isolation, the data may seem _____, but when the context is supplied, trends can indeed be isolated.

* In situations where *a* or *an* comes before the blank, the *a* or *an* will often be included with each answer choice rather than in the sentence itself so that some of the answer choices can begin with vowels and some with consonants.

Answers and Explanations

1. The blank describes the "biography." What you know about it is that it is neither "encomium nor condemnation." Even without knowing the word *encomium*, you could probably figure out from the "nor" that the phrase means "neither praise (the opposite of criticism) nor criticism." Thus, the biography must be neutral or in the middle. "Its facts verifiable and delivered without commentary" corroborates this. A good word to fill in the blank would be something like (an) **objective**, (a) **disinterested**, or (an) **unbiased**.

2. The blank refers to the subject of the sentence ("she"). She has "vowed never to . . . maintain even the lightest of social contacts" again, a good phrase to fill the blank would be something like "person without social contacts." A single-word fill-in could be **recluse** or **hermit**. Note that "virtual" here has nothing to do with technology. Rather, it means "nearly complete, in essence."

3. The blank describes the "highway plan." "While" is an opposite-direction signal, indicating that the fill-in should be on the opposite side of making "progress." Indeed, you are told that the project's funding is "held up" (tied up or delayed). A good fill-in would be something like **gridlock**, **deadlock**, or simply **not moving**.

4. The blank is about both "Josh" and his "duties"—more precisely, the relationship between Josh and the duties. Some relevant pieces of evidence are that the boss suspects (which has a negative connotation) that Josh's "moral objection" (the quotes in the original sentence also indicate suspicion) are motivated by something else. One more clue fills in the blank for us—the fact that Josh is "lackadaisical" (casual or lazy). A good fill-in would be **avoid** or **shirk**.

5. The blank describes the "data." You know that, with "context," trends can be found. So your blank should disagree with the notion that one can find trends in something. A good fill-in phrase might be *to lack trends*. Single-word fill-ins (adjectives) could be **random** or **chaotic**.

Answer Choice Analysis

When Educational Testing Service introduced the Sentence Equivalence format, most people's natural response was, "So we pick a pair of synonyms, right?" ETS officials insist that the two correct answers don't have to be precise synonyms:

> *Do not simply look among the answer choices for two words that mean the same thing. This can be misleading for two reasons. First, the answer choices may contain pairs of words that mean the same thing but do not fit coherently into the sentence, and thus do not constitute a correct answer. Second, the pair of words that do constitute the correct answer may not mean exactly the same thing, since all that matters is that the resultant sentences mean the same thing.*

Hmm. When the two correct answers are inserted into the sentence, the resulting sentences mean the same thing? Sounds like those words would have to be pretty close, right?

Theoretically, the GRE could give a question like this one:

Miriam broke up with John because he was _____.

- ☐ boring
- ☐ handsome
- ☐ limber
- ☐ unintelligent
- ☐ kind
- ☐ fun

Since Miriam "broke up" with John, you are looking for something bad to fill in the blank. There are only two negative answer choices: **boring** and **unintelligent**. These two words certainly are not synonyms, although each makes sense in the sentence.

Theoretically, could the GRE ask a question like this one? Yes, *theoretically*. However, there is little evidence for this degree of loose construction on the real GRE.

A question like this one, in which the correct choices really *aren't* synonyms but share some key feature, would have to have answers that fall into pretty easily distinguishable categories (e.g., something bad versus something good or at least not bad). Such questions would typically be easy to answer correctly.

What seems to be going on is that the GRE is being overly respectful of the English language. To quote the famous science-fiction writer Theodore Sturgeon, "There are no synonyms."

In other words, subtleties of meaning technically separate **any** two words you find listed in any individual entry in a thesaurus. *Deluge* and *flood* **don't** mean the exact same thing (a *deluge* is, by definition, a **severe** flood). The GRE wants to acknowledge that the two words you pick will likely differ in terms of some similar nuance.

However, unless you are trying to write some very stylish and precise prose, the difference between *deluge* and *flood* doesn't really matter. And on the GRE, that difference definitely *won't* matter.

10

On any real Sentence Equivalence problem we've seen, the two correct answers are pretty close to being 100 percent synonymous. Here's an example:

Many people at the dinner party were inordinately interested in questioning the _____ new guest, who refused to reveal his profession or even the origin of his exotic accent.

- ☐ acerbic
- ☐ mysterious
- ☐ insightful
- ☐ trenchant
- ☐ intrepid
- ☐ inscrutable

Look for the proof. The blank describes the new guest, who "refused to reveal" things about himself. If there were a word meaning "not self-revealing," you'd pick it. The word needs to be something like *secretive* or *mysterious*.

As it turns out, **mysterious** and **inscrutable** are the correct answers. *Inscrutable* means "not able to be scrutinized" and often indicates hiding emotions. It's not exactly the same thing as *mysterious*, but there's a substantial overlap in their meanings.

You've discovered that most correct answer pairs are at least as closely related as these two. For the purposes of this book, call them *near-synonyms*.

Finding Near-Synonym Pairs

Most Sentence Equivalence questions have a built-in secret strategy: Answer Choice Analysis.

As an alternative to Sentence Analysis (the three-step process that starts with the sentence), you can actually ignore the sentence completely and *start with the answer choices.*

Look for pairs of synonyms (or near-synonyms, to be precise). The right answer must be one of these pairs. And there just can't be that many reasonable pairs.

Why would we tell you to start with the answer choices? After all, we've been calling them distractors, even lies. We've told you to focus on the truth of the given sentence first, analyzing it so closely that you come up with your own fill-in-the-blank answer. And only then should you go look at the answer choices.

Well, yes. That's still good advice.

But you start every SE problem with a whole lot of possibilities: 15, to be exact. That's how many ways there are to choose a group of two words out of six choices, when order doesn't matter.

Your chances of guessing correctly *at random* are 1 in 15. That's under 7 percent. Pretty terrible chances, much worse than the 20 percent you're used to on a typical five-answer multiple-choice problem.

But on Sentence Equivalence, Answer Choice Analysis can raise those chances *dramatically.* It can get you from 1 in 15 to 1 in 3 or 1 in 2. It even sometimes gets you to 1 in 1: that is, it gets you all the way to the right answer.

10

This is why Answer Choice Analysis needs to be a real tool in your toolbox for Sentence Equivalence. Sometimes, you ought to start with the answer choices. (In the next section, we'll help you figure out when to do what.)

Let's look at some examples. Many sets of SE answer choices are "two by two"—that is, among the six choices there are two different pairs of synonyms, plus two "loose," unrelated words.

Typical two by two:

> horrible
> nice
> pleasant
> impoverished
> terrible
> dying

Horrible and *terrible* are a pair of synonyms. *Pleasant* and *nice* are a different pair of synonyms. *Impoverished* and *dying* are unrelated.

This means that there are only two real, viable answers to consider: the two different pairs of synonyms.

After Answer Choice Analysis of the set of choices above, you're down to just *two* choices! You've raised your probability of guessing right at random from under 7 percent to 50 percent.

Here is a weaker variant of a two by two:

> wicked
> healthful
> evil
> qualified
> gifted
> well-practiced

Wicked and *evil* are a pair. *Gifted* and *well-practiced* are sort of a pair—that is, *gifted* implies an ability that comes from within, whereas *well-practiced* implies an ability that comes from, obviously, practice. However, both are different paths to the same goal (being talented or skilled). They're a weak pair.

In any sentence, it should be pretty easy to tell whether *wicked/evil* or *gifted/well-practiced* is the more appropriate match. However, in the case that a set of choices provides a closely related pair and a less closely related pair, *the more closely related pair is more likely to be the answer.*

Occasionally, three words will seem to match up (a *triplet*). Usually, in this case, two are really synonyms, and the other is off in terms of spin or strength. The triplet will be false.

For instance, in the case of *excoriate*, *admonish*, and *castigate*, the real pair is *excoriate* and *castigate*—both mean "to criticize or scold very harshly," and *admonish* means "to scold mildly." (Note that if all three triplets really were synonyms, they would necessarily all be wrong as a result, since there can only be two correct answers. However, this is unlikely.)

False triplet:

> determined
> talkative
> hapless
> unsuccessful
> unlucky
> resolute

Determined and *resolute* are a pair. *Hapless, unsuccessful,* and *unlucky* seem to be a triplet. (*Talkative* is not related to the others.)

However, *hapless* really does mean *unlucky* (*hap* is actually a rarely used Old English word for "luck" or "lot"). A person can be *unsuccessful* without being *unlucky*. *Hapless* and *unlucky* are the true pair.

It is also possible to have just one pair, or three.

Only one pair:

> pale
> flexible
> hidden
> celebrated
> equitable
> fair

Equitable and *fair* are a pair. The other four words are unrelated. Answer Choice Analysis gets you all the way to the right answer!

Three pairs:

> candid
> latent
> ingenuous
> inimical
> dormant
> hostile

Candid and *ingenuous* are a pair. *Latent* and *dormant* are a pair. *Inimical* and *hostile* are a pair. Answer Choice Analysis gets you down to three choices.

That's still a huge jump in your random-guessing chances, from under 7 percent to over 33 percent.

When to Use Answer Choice Analysis

When you use Answer Choice Analysis as your main tool for Sentence Equivalence questions, you proceed to the choices first, before even reading the sentence. For instance:

Blah blah blah blah blah blah blah blah blah blah blah blah blah _____, blah blah blah blah blah blah blah blah blah.

- ☐ toadies
- ☐ aesthetes
- ☐ tyros
- ☐ lackeys
- ☐ anchorites
- ☐ novices

Go straight to the words and attempt to make pairs: *toadies* and *lackeys* are subordinates who follow without question. *Tyros* and *novices* are both beginners. *Aesthetes* love or study beauty, and *anchorites* are recluses, especially religious hermits, and thus those two words are not related.

Therefore, the answer must be *toadies/lackeys* or *tyros/novices*. The only question you need to ask at this point is, "Does the sentence call for a *suck-up* or a *beginner*?" Here is the complete problem:

It may be true that everyone likes flattery, but a good manager is not unduly persuaded by it, and thus not taken in by _____, who use wheedling and fawning to get ahead.

- ☐ toadies
- ☐ aesthetes
- ☐ tyros
- ☐ lackeys
- ☐ anchorites
- ☐ novices

There is a lot of proof (such as "flattery" and "wheedling and fawning") that the question is calling for **toadies** and **lackeys**.

Answer Choice Analysis can be very effective when you know all of the words in the choices.

However, you should recognize that most test-takers don't have strong enough vocabularies to be able to complete Answer Choice Analysis consistently, especially when the words get really tough.

Moreover, most of the time this approach does *not* get you all the way to the right answer. Most of the time, you'll still need to guess. That's unsatisfying.

So in general, Sentence Analysis probably ought to be your first line of attack. Start with the *sentence* when you see Sentence Equivalence, and follow the original three-step process.

But Answer Choice Analysis is a great backup plan.

When should you break out this backup plan?

1. When you read and reread the sentence, but you're not getting it. Maybe the topic or the structure is really confusing. Or under the pressure of time and the exam, you just can't get a handle on the original text.

2. In the middle of Sentence Analysis, you're struggling. You can't figure out how you'd fill in the blank, and you're not really sure about the proof in the sentence. As in case #1, you're rereading a lot.

In either case, you might be starting to hit a state of "semantic satiation." Have you ever repeated some word over and over, until it loses meaning and sounds like nonsense? That's semantic satiation.

Under exam pressure, even the glimmers of this state can be terrifying and lead to a downward spiral. As meaning slips from your grasp, you reread the sentence even more frantically, berating yourself for not getting it, falling even further into semantic satiation, distraction, and panic …

Stop it. Stop what you're doing. Go do some Answer Choice Analysis.

You'll make good progress toward the goal. If you come back to the sentence, you'll be refreshed and ready. If not, you'll make a good guess and move on.

In fact, as you progress through the exam, you might proactively change it up for yourself. Go ahead and decide to attack the next Sentence Equivalence with Answer Choice Analysis from the get-go. That strategic decision will reassure you. It will remind you that you're in charge of the exam. Not the other way around.

10

Drill: Answer Choice Analysis

> For each set of choices, match up the pairs. Most, but not all, sets of choices consist of two pairs of near-synonyms and two other unrelated words. A few will have one or three sets of near-synonyms.

1. verbose
   turbid
   diffident
   prolix
   self-effacing
   pious

2. amicable
   pithy
   scholarly
   arcane
   succinct
   esoteric

3. distend
   traduce
   alienate
   flatter
   slander
   complement

4. auxiliary
   cardinal
   principal
   ordinal
   collateral
   prefatory

5. hawkish
   cogent
   turgid
   eloquent
   bombastic
   intelligible

6. pellucid
    transparent
    rustic
    sedulous
    assiduous
    earthy

7. eclecticism
    aberrance
    deviation
    idiosyncrasy
    adulation
    eccentricity

8. bevy
    modicum
    paucity
    excess
    surfeit
    bunch

9. disclosure
    epitome
    scruple
    apothegm
    contumely
    maxim

10. pique
    slake
    quench
    succor
    fructify
    stimulate

10

Answers and Explanations

1. Two pairs: **Verbose** and **prolix** are a pair, each meaning "talkative." **Diffident** (lacking confidence) and **self-effacing** (putting oneself down) are a pair; they are not perfect synonyms, but they are close enough for Sentence Equivalence questions on the GRE. *Pious* and *turbid* have no relationship.

2. Two pairs: **Pithy** and **succinct** both mean "short and to the point." **Arcane** and **esoteric** both mean "obscure or specialized, known to only a few" (about information). *Amicable* and *scholarly* are not related.

3. One pair: **Traduce** and **slander** are a pair, meaning "tell malicious lies about." **Complement** and **flatter** are a TRAP—*complement* (to complete, to make up a whole with) is *not* the same word as *compliment* (to say something nice about). *Distend* and *alienate* are also unrelated.

4. Two pairs: **Auxiliary** and **collateral** mean "secondary, off to the side." **Cardinal** and **principal** (first, main) are actually synonyms with each other *and* antonyms with *auxiliary* and *collateral*. *Ordinal* and *prefatory* are not related.

5. Two pairs: **Turgid** and **bombastic** are a pair. *Bombastic* means "pompous, overinflated" and is used to describe speech. While *turgid* can simply mean "swollen," when it is applied to speech, it has the same meaning of "overinflated, showing off." **Eloquent** and **cogent** are a weak pair—*eloquent* means "beautiful and articulate" (about speech), and *cogent* means "compellingly persuasive." *Intelligible* and *hawkish* are not related.

6. Three pairs: **Pellucid** and **transparent** are a pair (see-through), as are **rustic** and **earthy** (primitive, of the earth, undeveloped) and **assiduous** and **sedulous** (hardworking).

7. Two pairs: **Aberrance** and **deviation** are a pair (being different from the normal). *Eclecticism, idiosyncrasy*, and *eccentricity* may all seem similar. However, **idiosyncrasy** and **eccentricity** (harmless personal oddness) are a true pair. *Eclecticism* (having mixed, wide-ranging tastes) is unrelated to *adulation* (excessive admiration).

8. Two or three pairs: **Bevy** and **bunch** are a pair, as are **surfeit** and **excess**. **Modicum** and **paucity** are questionable as a pair because they differ in spin—*modicum* means "a little," and *paucity* means "not enough." It's the subtle but key difference between *having a little* and *having little*.

9. One pair: **Apothegm** and **maxim** are a pair (proverb; pithy statement). *Disclosure, epitome, scruple*, and *contumely* are unrelated.

10. Two pairs: **Pique** and **stimulate** are a pair. **Slake** and **quench** (satisfy, especially of thirst) are a pair. *Succor* (provide comfort or relief) might seem related the second pair, but one *succors* a person, and one *slakes* or *quenches* a desire. *Fructify* (make productive) is unrelated.

What If I Don't Know the Words?

It almost seems as though Sentence Equivalence on the GRE was designed to prevent lucky guesses. As we noted earlier, on a typical multiple-choice question with choices A–E, a test-taker has a 1 in 5 chance of randomly guessing the correct answer. On a Sentence Equivalence, a random guess of two out of the six answers has only a 1 in 15 chance of being correct.

If you know *one* of the correct choices and randomly guess on the other, your chance of getting the question correct is 1 in 5.

Thus, it is very important that you *assiduously augment* your vocabulary.

That said, even a little Answer Choice Analysis can help you make a good guess, increasing your odds of success.

As mentioned earlier, many Sentence Equivalence questions match the two-by-two format. That is, the answer choices contain two pairs of synonyms or near-synonyms and two other loose words.

So if you can find a single pair of synonyms in the choices, there is about a 50 percent chance that that pair is correct (it is only *about* 50 percent, since not all sets of choices follow a two-by-two format). Here is an example:

- ☐ agog
- ☐ akimbo
- ☐ obeisant
- ☐ dyspeptic
- ☐ kowtowing
- ☐ crotchety

If you were able to pick out that *dyspeptic* and *crotchety* were a pair—or that *obeisant* and *kowtowing* were—then you should test that pair in the sentence and pick it if it seems to be a good match. (As will be the case in most questions, the two remaining words, *agog* and *akimbo*, have no relationship.)

If the pair that you are able to find is not a fit for the sentence, cross off both words. You now have a 1/6 chance of guessing correctly.

If you cannot find a synonym pair, you are unlikely to get the question correct. Accept that fact and don't waste time. Your strategy here is simply to make a guess and move on. Save time for questions that you will be able to answer later.

Although the GRE allows you to move around within a section and come back to questions you previously left blank or wish to reconsider, keep in mind that **if you don't know the words, you won't do any better by attempting the question twice**. You'll only waste time and lower your overall score.

If you don't know the words, **do not leave the question blank**. Make your best guess and move on. Don't waste time coming back. Spend that extra time on Reading Comprehension or other vocabulary questions that you are able to answer more effectively.

10

Why It Is Important to Learn Words in Context

Educational Testing Service tells you not only to check that the two answers you select for a question create sentences that mean the same thing, but also to make sure that each one "produces a sentence that is logically, grammatically, and stylistically coherent."

Hmm. Asking test-takers to check that the completed sentences are grammatically coherent implies that some of the choices will create sentences that are not. Here's an example:

Education advocates argued that the free school lunch program was vital to creating a school environment _____ to learning.

- [ ] conducive
- [ ] inimical
- [ ] substantial
- [ ] appropriate
- [ ] beneficial
- [ ] hostile

"Education advocates" are certainly in favor of learning; your fill-in might be something like *helpful*.

Looking at the choices, *conducive*, *appropriate*, and *beneficial* all seem to be matches.

However, if you place each word into the sentence, one choice creates an incorrect idiom. "Conducive *to*" and "beneficial *to*" work, but "appropriate *to*" is not a correct idiom—instead, you would say "appropriate *for* learning."

Thus, it is important not only to memorize dictionary definitions of words, but also to be able to use those words in context, in a grammatically correct way.

Here's another example:

He's a _____ fellow, always grandstanding and deploying his formidable lexicon for oratorical effect.

- [ ] declamatory
- [ ] grandiloquent
- [ ] didactic
- [ ] florid
- [ ] titanic
- [ ] cabalistic

The target is "he" and the clue is "grandstanding and deploying his formidable lexicon for oratorical effect." That is, he speaks in a pompous way, as though showing off his vocabulary for an audience.

The word *florid* seems appropriate—it means "flowery" and often applies to words, as in *florid poetry*. But wait! *Florid* applies to writing, speech, decor, etc.—not the people who produce those things! (Actually, you can apply *florid* to people, but in that context it means "flushed, ruddy," as in having rosy cheeks, which is not appropriate here.)

The answer is **declamatory** and **grandiloquent**, both of which describe pompous orators (that is, people who make speeches) or the speech of such people.

Memorizing that *florid* means "flowery" is better than nothing, but doesn't really tell you what kinds of things to describe with that word or how to use it metaphorically. Once again, it is important to learn words in context.

There are several ways to do this. Manhattan Prep's *GRE Vocabulary Flash Cards* provide example sentences for all 1,000 words. Many online dictionaries provide quotes from literature in which the word being defined is used in context. In some cases, it is fruitful to simply Google a word to see how different writers are using it.

Whatever your process, your goal is to be able to do two things for any given word. First, to define it in a concise and straightforward way. Second, to be able to use it in a sentence in a descriptive way (such that someone reading the sentence would understand what it meant from the context).

You want to be comfortable when seeing a word used in any legitimate way. For instance, you would understand if the word *darkness* were used metaphorically (*While she at first resisted going on antidepressants, she ultimately decided that she would do anything that might lift the darkness*) or if the word *enthusiastic* were used sarcastically (*As enthusiastic as I am about unnecessary surgery, I will have to decline your offer to appear on an extreme makeover reality show*).

To perform with excellence on the GRE, you want to know your new words inside and out. You want to be *flexible* in how you use and interpret those words. The Vocabulary unit in this book provides more guidance for formidably fortifying your lexicon.

Drill: 20 Easy Questions

1. The children's story—seemingly a simple tale of animals gathering for a picnic in the forest—took a _____ turn at the end, admonishing readers to always be honest.

   ☐ magnanimous
   ☐ beneficent
   ☐ didactic
   ☐ garrulous
   ☐ moralistic
   ☐ futile

2. Floodwaters had already breached the library's walls, but hopeful volunteers in hip boots worked tirelessly to _____ the damage.

   ☐ mitigate
   ☐ exacerbate
   ☐ abase
   ☐ bolster
   ☐ forestall
   ☐ flummox

3. The candidate campaigned on a platform of willingness to cooperate with the members of other political parties, yet many commentators were nevertheless surprised that he indeed turned out to be less _____ than his predecessor.

   ☐ irate
   ☐ divisive
   ☐ impulsive
   ☐ wily
   ☐ infuriated
   ☐ combative

4. When Sven got angry, whether it was during an argument with his family or just with a coworker, it proved almost impossible to _____ him and thereby return him to his normal demeanor.

   ☐ condemn
   ☐ pacify
   ☐ judge
   ☐ incense
   ☐ mollify
   ☐ influence

10

5. The graduate student's experiment yielded results as surprising as they were promising; her next step was to pursue additional data that would _____ her findings.

    ☐ undergird

    ☐ buttress

    ☐ gainsay

    ☐ undermine

    ☐ eschew

    ☐ lecture

6. There is no fundamental difference between a person who quietly _____ a bigoted viewpoint to a friend and one who spews chauvinist vitriol on television.

    ☐ eschews

    ☐ espouses

    ☐ professes

    ☐ denies

    ☐ reneges

    ☐ substantiates

7. A 1957 lawsuit against the U.S. Department of Agriculture regarding aerial pesticide spraying was the _____ for Rachel Carson to begin the writing of her environmentalist manifesto *Silent Spring*, though she had become concerned about and started researching the practice years earlier.

    ☐ stimulus

    ☐ conspiracy

    ☐ atrocity

    ☐ impetus

    ☐ catastrophe

    ☐ climate

8. A commentator with a more _____ worldview would not find it so easy to divide up the nation into good guys and bad guys.

    ☐ belligerent

    ☐ subtle

    ☐ philosophical

    ☐ aberrant

    ☐ peaceful

    ☐ nuanced

10

9. James Joyce's *Finnegan's Wake*, written in a stream-of-consciousness style full of convoluted puns and obscure allusions, has a deserved reputation for linguistic _____.

   - ☐ elaborateness
   - ☐ opacity
   - ☐ meaninglessness
   - ☐ informality
   - ☐ uniqueness
   - ☐ inscrutability

10. The financial situation in many European nations is _____ enough that even a small incident could lead to catastrophe.

    - ☐ drab
    - ☐ unstable
    - ☐ illegitimate
    - ☐ unsafe
    - ☐ precarious
    - ☐ churlish

11. While the argument for global warming may not be _____ by the record low temperatures reported this year, this data does not undermine the overall trend of steadily higher global temperatures.

    - ☐ bolstered
    - ☐ fortified
    - ☐ subverted
    - ☐ defined
    - ☐ supplanted
    - ☐ subordinated

12. The debate coach expected some gravitas from her team, arguing that pithy quips and gibes, while sometimes effective, had no place in a _____ argument.

    - ☐ polite
    - ☐ shallow
    - ☐ competitive
    - ☐ serious
    - ☐ cantankerous
    - ☐ substantive

13. Last year it was discovered that *South Park* writers _____ part of its *Inception* spoof from a similar *College Humor* sketch.

☐ amalgamated

☐ filched

☐ indulged

☐ combined

☐ poached

☐ assumed

14. Some critics view Abstract Expressionism, which is characterized by geometric shapes and swaths of color, as a _____ of realist painting.

☐ rejection

☐ manifestation

☐ renunciation

☐ memento

☐ commemoration

☐ vindication

15. The first spy of the nascent United States, Nathan Hale, was captured by the British when he attempted to _____ British-controlled New York City to track enemy troop movements.

☐ thwart

☐ penetrate

☐ infiltrate

☐ permeate

☐ research

☐ conquer

16. Romantic comedies of the 1950s were characterized more by sexual _____ than the straightforward vulgarity that characterizes dialogue in today's rom-coms.

☐ conversation

☐ blatancy

☐ insinuation

☐ illusion

☐ innuendo

☐ rapport

10

17. Inflation isn't dead, only _____; as the economy turns around, the purchasing power of the dollar is likely to fall again.

   - [ ] paralyzed
   - [ ] dormant
   - [ ] indigent
   - [ ] itinerant
   - [ ] problematic
   - [ ] inactive

18. Some boxers talk about trying to access their more _____ selves in order to counter the fact that civilized people generally don't punch each other in the face.

   - [ ] seething
   - [ ] barbaric
   - [ ] irate
   - [ ] insidious
   - [ ] dynamic
   - [ ] primitive

19. Many people assume that creative work is less _____ than manual labor, but they underestimate the difficulty of being entirely self-motivated (as well as writing one's own paychecks).

   - [ ] inventive
   - [ ] collaborative
   - [ ] serious
   - [ ] arduous
   - [ ] taxing
   - [ ] grave

20. The education debate is only getting more _____ as politicians demonize teachers unions and every special interest group jumps into the fray.

   - [ ] vehement
   - [ ] overt
   - [ ] heated
   - [ ] problematic
   - [ ] tired
   - [ ] unavoidable

Drill: 20 Medium Questions

1. While many individual religions insist on the primacy of their particular deity, syncretism advocates the _____ of multiple religious beliefs, attempting to reconcile even opposing principles and practices.

   ☐ exclusion
   ☐ marriage
   ☐ commingling
   ☐ division
   ☐ transgression
   ☐ schism

2. The ambassador was invested with _____ power by his government and hence was able to draft and finalize the agreement unilaterally, without first consulting with even the president.

   ☐ tertiary
   ☐ consummate
   ☐ enigmatic
   ☐ tyrannical
   ☐ complete
   ☐ dictatorial

3. Sometimes it seems that today's politicians will exploit any opportunity to _____ their views to the world, no matter how sordid or partisan.

   ☐ declaim
   ☐ invoke
   ☐ disparage
   ☐ parrot
   ☐ adduce
   ☐ trumpet

4. The many chapters of the organization decided that a mandatory national _____ would be necessary to reconcile what had become a haphazard and often chaotic set of bylaws and regulations.

   ☐ introduction
   ☐ acclamation
   ☐ intervention
   ☐ colloquium
   ☐ symposium
   ☐ mediation

10

5. Though it seems implausible that one could be a great writer without some experience of life, many famous authors have led a(n) _____ and solitary existence.

- [ ] idiosyncratic
- [ ] cloistered
- [ ] susceptible
- [ ] enigmatic
- [ ] sheltered
- [ ] cryptic

6. Though he wasn't particularly well-known as a humanitarian, his deep sense of responsibility for those who were suffering was real, and was belied by an outward appearance of _____.

- [ ] concern
- [ ] sagacity
- [ ] mirth
- [ ] felicity
- [ ] nonchalance
- [ ] indifference

7. Excessive patriotism is by definition _____, as the elevation of one country to the rank of quintessential on Earth necessarily requires some amount of demonization of other people.

- [ ] minatory
- [ ] xenophobic
- [ ] unethical
- [ ] bigoted
- [ ] nationalistic
- [ ] truculent

8. One possible explanation for the mandatory debauchery of most bachelor parties is that if the husband-to-be is able to practice _____ in those circumstances, he must be ready for marriage.

- [ ] forbearance
- [ ] gentility
- [ ] fiat
- [ ] tenacity
- [ ] temperance
- [ ] autonomy

10

9. Jon Stewart's "Rally to Restore Sanity" was purportedly organized to prove that it was possible to discuss politics humorously but civilly, without _____ those on the other side of the fence.

    ☐ bespeaking

    ☐ eulogizing

    ☐ lampooning

    ☐ vilifying

    ☐ caricaturing

    ☐ maligning

10. Though occasionally used in practice, very few forms of corporal punishment have been _____ by the military, due less to the Geneva Conventions than to the overwhelmingly negative popular response to reports of abuse.

    ☐ upbraided

    ☐ sanctioned

    ☐ endorsed

    ☐ considered

    ☐ rejected

    ☐ polarized

11. The budget debate progressed well for the first few months, in spite of all the ardent and sometimes bitter squabbling, but slowly descended into a _____ of competing interests and claims.

    ☐ quagmire

    ☐ covenant

    ☐ feud

    ☐ morass

    ☐ quarrel

    ☐ accord

12. The difference between similes and metaphors is subtle, but for the poet who takes his or her work seriously, it is absolutely _____.

    ☐ synoptic

    ☐ null

    ☐ optional

    ☐ crucial

    ☐ nominal

    ☐ requisite

10

13. It is _____ reasoning to characterize Keynesian economics as recommending that the limit on how much debt the government can incur should be perpetually raised, when Keynes states clearly that deficit spending must be done responsibly.

    - [ ] indigenous
    - [ ] corrupt
    - [ ] venial
    - [ ] fallacious
    - [ ] specious
    - [ ] axiomatic

14. In many ways, teenage rebellion can be seen as the effect of a communication gap between an older generation's calcified language and the protean _____ of the new generation.

    - [ ] patois
    - [ ] defiance
    - [ ] prolixity
    - [ ] insubordination
    - [ ] verbosity
    - [ ] jargon

15. His cantankerous reputation was cemented by years of _____ at every conceivable opportunity.

    - [ ] imputing
    - [ ] grousing
    - [ ] assaulting
    - [ ] protesting
    - [ ] convulsing
    - [ ] imbibing

16. Last St. Patrick's Day, the police were called when people in the neighborhood witnessed a small _____ in progress outside of a bar.

    - [ ] fracas
    - [ ] discourse
    - [ ] altercation
    - [ ] battle
    - [ ] colloquy
    - [ ] mutiny

17. Given her sheltered upbringing and the limited breadth of experience imposed on her by economic circumstance, her work reflected a surprisingly _____ sensibility.

   - [ ] shallow
   - [ ] eclectic
   - [ ] profound
   - [ ] multifarious
   - [ ] callow
   - [ ] facile

18. Many people expect documentary filmmakers to be dispassionate and objective, but Michael Moore has a reputation for never missing a chance to _____ against those with whom he disagrees.

   - [ ] rail
   - [ ] advertise
   - [ ] fulminate
   - [ ] inveigle
   - [ ] strain
   - [ ] aspirate

19. The movie critic was best remembered for the way he used the language of food to describe films, for example, how he praised Iñarritu's action sequences by comparing them to a _____ empanada.

   - [ ] insipid
   - [ ] spectacular
   - [ ] brilliant
   - [ ] piquant
   - [ ] zesty
   - [ ] stupefying

20. Every few years, someone manages to survive a skydive with a parachute that doesn't open, often with only a few broken bones, some _____, and a gash or two.

   - [ ] torpor
   - [ ] trauma
   - [ ] bruises
   - [ ] finesse
   - [ ] lesions
   - [ ] contusions

Drill: 20 Hard Questions

1. As official _____ from Japan to this country, he was called upon to answer questions about the Japanese government's position on various issues.

   ☐ envoy
   ☐ tyro
   ☐ emissary
   ☐ neophyte
   ☐ ascetic
   ☐ libertine

2. While the group's street protests had had an aggressive, uncompromising tenor, once admitted to the halls of power to begin formal lobbying, its leaders wisely chose to _____ the stridency of their rhetoric.

   ☐ metamorphose
   ☐ gild
   ☐ wane
   ☐ palliate
   ☐ succor
   ☐ damp

3. The women's rights movement has been mostly _____ in the Middle East, but it is likely that activists will be newly galvanized by the political upheavals currently sweeping the region.

   ☐ dogged
   ☐ quiescent
   ☐ interminable
   ☐ lissome
   ☐ abeyant
   ☐ feckless

4. Debate rages on between proponents and detractors of corporal punishment and the death penalty, though even the most ardent supporter agrees that punishments must be _____ and the justice system evenhanded and thorough.

   ☐ equitable
   ☐ clement
   ☐ delimited
   ☐ apposite
   ☐ tantamount
   ☐ merciful

5. Peer-reviewed journals are a sacred cow of most scientific rationalists, but studies have shown that the premise of impartiality is _____, as results tend to be colored by the personal proclivities and suppositions of the experimenters.

   - [ ] inane
   - [ ] prejudicial
   - [ ] fatuous
   - [ ] chimerical
   - [ ] fallible
   - [ ] vexing

6. The description of the restaurant as a garden of _____ delights is fair enough, as Chef Marcel conjures up a menu of texture and taste that calls into question one's preconceived notions of what constitutes a meal.

   - [ ] salubrious
   - [ ] epicurean
   - [ ] carnal
   - [ ] voluptuous
   - [ ] terrestrial
   - [ ] gustatory

7. Most of his books drone on and on for chapter after chapter, each one providing yet another example of his thesis, the _____ of which can be found in précis form in the tome's first few pages, and which is recapitulated from that point on.

   - [ ] gist
   - [ ] adage
   - [ ] pith
   - [ ] stub
   - [ ] nimbus
   - [ ] nut

8. In order to ascertain the efficacy of the new GRE vis-à-vis the old one, it will be necessary not only to collect, but also to _____ detailed score reports from test-takers from both groups, as only by studying the differences and similarities in results can proper inferences be drawn.

   - [ ] aggregate
   - [ ] deduce
   - [ ] collate
   - [ ] juxtapose
   - [ ] agglomerate
   - [ ] glean

10

9. In World War I, trenches were dug so that the soldiers could avoid the near constant _____ from the other side of the line of battle, but not even a trench could protect a battalion from grenades or aerial bombardment.

    - ☐ volleys
    - ☐ provocations
    - ☐ fervency
    - ☐ imprecations
    - ☐ goadings
    - ☐ salvos

10. Cary Grant's reputation as a suave and _____ ladies man extended beyond the silver screen to his real life, where he was known to never let a woman pull out her own chair, in keeping with the custom of gentlemen at that time.

    - ☐ consummate
    - ☐ genteel
    - ☐ debonair
    - ☐ waggish
    - ☐ courtly
    - ☐ cosmopolitan

11. Focusing primarily on self-awareness, empathy, and honest self-expression, the communication process known as "nonviolent communication" states that the attempt to find parity in a relationship is a fallacious principle, as any notion of fairness is entirely _____.

    - ☐ subjective
    - ☐ introverted
    - ☐ pragmatic
    - ☐ utilitarian
    - ☐ illicit
    - ☐ personal

12. Education has become a kind of albatross in American politics, in that a speech with any hint of _____ is actually more pernicious to a politician's reputation than one with numerous signs of ignorance, or even outright stupidity.

    - ☐ bromide
    - ☐ erudition
    - ☐ patrimony
    - ☐ condescension
    - ☐ cerebrality
    - ☐ bloviation

10

13. Laurent Cantet's *Time Out* tells the true story of a man so obsessed with retaining the _____ of plenitude even after he is discharged from his employment that he doesn't even tell his wife and his kids about his termination.

    ☐ corollaries

    ☐ paradigms

    ☐ semblance

    ☐ prepossessions

    ☐ veneer

    ☐ consequences

14. What people fail to remember about Don Juan is that his astronomical number of amatory adventures were due more to his _____ approach to seduction than any surfeit of charisma or skillfulness.

    ☐ sumptuous

    ☐ lurid

    ☐ covert

    ☐ indiscriminate

    ☐ blanket

    ☐ hedonistic

15. Even the most far-reaching campaign finance reform proposals will fail to _____ the influence of money, which doesn't just buy speedboats and golf weekends in the Bahamas, but directly relates to a politician's capacity to run for office.

    ☐ attenuate

    ☐ graft

    ☐ pander

    ☐ abate

    ☐ importune

    ☐ indemnify

16. In their landmark study of Victorian literature's relationship to feminism, Gilbert and Gubar _____ the many ways in which 19th-century women writers created characters that fit into archetypes of "angel" and "monster."

    ☐ interrogate

    ☐ interpolate

    ☐ debunk

    ☐ limn

    ☐ explode

    ☐ castigate

10

17. While it's inarguably prejudiced to imply that there is some kind of innate _____ in certain countries, it's more reasonable to say that certain cultures are more willing to prioritize relaxation and a sense of moderation between work and play.

    - [ ] obtundity
    - [ ] enfeeblement
    - [ ] enervation
    - [ ] languor
    - [ ] seemliness
    - [ ] lethargy

18. Autodidacts may argue that the enforced lucubration of a standard education is _____, but while some people are able to learn without outside guidance and strictures, most people learn better when accountable to others.

    - [ ] slack
    - [ ] prudent
    - [ ] lax
    - [ ] extraneous
    - [ ] unnecessary
    - [ ] sagacious

19. The best of Sigur Ros's music evokes _____ landscape, as if the music had transported one to some twilit avenue in a long since abandoned city.

    - [ ] a dusky
    - [ ] an urban
    - [ ] a crepuscular
    - [ ] a precipitous
    - [ ] an avuncular
    - [ ] a civic

20. Some historians argue that at least in so far as the broad strokes are concerned, cataclysmic events such as the Great Depression are _____, due to what some have termed "the inertia of history."

    - [ ] ineluctable
    - [ ] incontrovertible
    - [ ] interminable
    - [ ] infallible
    - [ ] inexorable
    - [ ] unspeakable

Solutions: 20 Easy Questions

1. Didactic, Moralistic. The children's story was "seemingly" simple—which means it was not actually simple. Instead, the story took some kind of "turn"—meaning that it changed in some way—and admonished "readers to always be honest." That is, it took a turn by talking about morals or prescribing correct behavior.

Magnanimous (generous) and *beneficient* (good, or doing good) are an incorrect pair. *Garrulous* (overly talkative, wordy) and *futile* (ineffective, useless) have no relationship.

2. Mitigate, Forestall. That "floodwaters had already breached the library's walls" sounds very bad—the water is already inside. The signal word "but" tells you that the sentence is going to change direction, and indeed, the volunteers are "hopeful." So you're looking for something good in the blank—although it doesn't seem like they're going to cure the problem entirely. A good fill-in would be something like *limit* or *hold back.*

Exacerbate (make more severe, aggravate), *abase* (reduce in prestige, humiliate), *bolster* (support, boost), and *flummox* (confuse) do not contain any pairs.

3. Divisive, Combative. The most important proof words here are the signal words "nevertheless surprised" and "indeed," which tell you that the candidate actually stayed true to his campaign promise. That means he acted cooperatively, which is contrasted with the actions of his predecessor. A good fill-in would be *uncooperative.*

Irate and *infuriated,* both of which mean "angry," are an incorrect pair. *Impulsive* (moved or swayed by emotional or involuntary urges) and *wily* (crafty or cunning) have no relationship.

4. Pacify, Mollify. This sentence provides the clues that when Sven "got angry," returning him "to his normal demeanor" was "almost impossible." His normal demeanor must be something like *not angry,* so you're looking for something like the verb *calm* in the blank.

Condemn (censure; sentence), *judge* (form an opinion about), *incense* (infuriate), and *influence* (determine or guide) do not contain any pairs, though *condemn* and *judge* are close.

5. Undergird, Buttress. The blank contains what the data will do to the findings. You have the clue that the results "were promising" (but "surprising," indicating some uncertainty about the apparent conclusion). The semicolon is a signal to keep going in the same direction. Thus, her next step would likely be to *verify* or *corroborate* the findings.

Gainsay (deny or prove false) and *undermine* (weaken or subvert secretly) are a pair representing the opposite, in fact, of what you want. *Eschew* (shun, avoid, or abstain from) and *lecture* (speak at length) are unrelated.

6. Espouses, Professes. This sentence originally posits that there is "no fundamental difference" between two things, but the overall point is that the two things do look different on the surface. That means you want something that does the opposite of "spews chauvinist vitriol on television," such as something that quietly *expresses* it. A good fill-in would be *communicates.*

Denies and *reneges* (renounces or denies) are an incorrect pair. *Eschews* is also pretty close to that pair. *Substantiates,* meaning "to support or verify," goes beyond *communicates* and is too positive to go with "a bigoted viewpoint."

10

7. Stimulus, Impetus. Prior to 1957, Rachel Carson was already concerned about "aerial pesticide spraying," but the lawsuit caused her to begin work on the book. A good fill-in would be *inspiration*. *Atrocity* (extremely wicked or cruel act) and *catastrophe* (disaster) have similar spins, but they are not really a pair. *Climate* (the general weather conditions in an area over a long period), which presents a theme trap, and *conspiracy* (a secret plan by two or more people to do something unlawful) have no relationship.

8. Subtle, Nuanced. In this sentence, the commentator is described as finding it easy to split people into "good … and bad" categories. This is a very simplistic way of looking at the world. Someone with a more complex worldview would be unlikely to break things down so simplistically.

Belligerent (inclined to aggressive hostility), *philosophical* (devoted to the study of knowledge; calm about difficulties or disappointments), *aberrant* (deviating from the normal or proper course, especially in behavior, or atypical), and *peaceful* (tranquil) have no relationship.

9. Opacity, Inscrutability. Joyce's book is described as "stream-of-consciousness," with "convoluted puns and obscure allusions." The adjectives "convoluted" and "obscure" are the most important parts of this sentence. They tell you that the novel is likely hard to understand. A good fill-in would be *difficulty* (specifically, of understanding).

Elaborateness (marked by complex detail; intricacy), *meaninglessness* (nonsense), *informality* (relaxed style), and *uniqueness* (the quality of being one of a kind) have no relationship. While *meaninglessness* might seem tempting, it's too extreme to be correct.

10. Unstable, Precarious. The situation in Europe is described as (something) enough that even a small incident might lead to a catastrophe. This means that everything is on the brink of disaster. You could fill in the blank with something like *shaky*.

Drab (dull, colorless, or cheerless), *illegitimate* (not authorized by the law), *unsafe* (not safe; dangerous), and *churlish* (uncivil, boorish, or vulgar) have no relationship, though all are negative.

11. Bolstered, Fortified. The second half of this sentence is not relevant to the blank. All you need to notice is the contrast between "warming" and "record low temperatures," as well as the signal word "While." Clearly, record low temperatures would not help an argument about global warming. A good fill-in would be *helped*.

Subverted (undermined, in terms of power or authority) and *subordinated* (made inferior or subservient) are an incorrect pair. *Defined* (described exactly) and *supplanted* (replaced, substituted for) have no relationship.

12. Serious, Substantive. The debate coach values "gravitas" (seriousness) and argues that "quips" (witty remarks) and "gibes" (taunts) don't belong in a certain kind of argument. *Serious* and *substantive* is the only set that works.

Polite could work, but it has no pair. *Shallow*, *competitive*, and *cantankerous* (disagreeable or difficult to deal with) have no relationship.

13. Filched, Poached. The most important word here is the adjective "similar." If both *South Park* and *College Humor* created a similar spoof, then one of them must have *stolen* the sketch from the other.

Amalgamated and *combined* are an incorrect pair. *Indulged* (allowed oneself to enjoy) and *assumed* (supposed without proof) have no relationship. *Assumed* can mean "took or began to have (power or responsibility)" or even "took on or adopted (an appearance, manner, or identity)," but you wouldn't use *assume* to mean the taking of any other kind of item, such as a comedy spoof.

10

14. Rejection, Renunciation. Abstract Expressionism is described as "characterized by geometric shapes and swaths of color." Clearly, this is very different from "realist painting." A good fill-in would thus be something like *repudiation*, which means a rejection or a refusal to deal with something.

Memento (an object serving as a reminder; souvenir) and *commemoration* (a service, celebration, etc., serving to remember a person or event) are an incorrect (and imperfect) pair. *Manifestation* (the action or fact of showing an abstract idea; symptom or sign) and *vindication* (exoneration, acquittal) have no relationship.

15. Penetrate, Infiltrate. You are told that Nathan Hale was a spy working for the "nascent (coming into being) United States" and that he was captured by the British. That means he must have been involved in some kind of espionage in "British-controlled" New York. A good fill-in would be *break into*.

Thwart (prevent [someone] from accomplishing something) and *conquer* (take control of by military force) are vaguely related, but are not quite a pair. *Permeate* (spread throughout; pervade) and *research* have no relationship.

16. Insinuation, Innuendo. The signal phrase "more by X than Y" implies some kind of contrast between the two elements. The second element here is "straightforward vulgarity." You want to contrast that with something. The adjective "sexual" may seem to confuse things; you need a word that will undercut it, such as *allusion*.

Conversation (an informal verbal exchange) and *rapport* (a harmonious relationship) are not quite a pair. *Blatancy* (obviousness) and *illusion* (something that looks or seems different from what it is) are almost opposites.

17. Dormant, Inactive. The blank is there to describe "Inflation" (in a way that contrasts with being entirely "dead"). You're told that in the future, the purchasing power of the dollar may fall, which means there will be inflation. So inflation may come back at any time. A good fill-in would be something like *dormant* (there aren't a lot of simple words that get across this meaning).

Paralyzed (unable to move or act), *indigent* (impoverished or needy), *itinerant* (traveling from place to place), and *problematic* (presenting a difficulty) have no relationship.

18. Barbaric, Primitive. Boxers are described as having to "punch each other in the face," which isn't "civilized." In order to do this, they would need to access a part of themselves that was *not so civilized* (which would work well enough as a fill-in here).

Seething and *irate* are an incorrect pair, both meaning "angry." *Insidious* (seductive but harmful; treacherous, deceitful) and *dynamic* (characterized by constant change) have no relationship.

19. Arduous, Taxing. This sentence describes "creative work" as having a particular difficulty, namely that one must be "self-motivated." Some might contrast this with "manual labor," but the author of the sentence wants to render them equivalent. Thus, a good fill-in would be *difficult*.

Serious and *grave* are an incorrect pair. Never in the sentence is it discussed whether or not creative work is more serious than manual labor. *Inventive* (able to create, design, or think originally) and *collaborative* (made or done by two or more parties working together) have no relationship.

20. Vehement, Heated. If politicians "demonize" teachers unions and other jump into the "fray," the debate will get more and more *passionately angry*, a good fill-in here.

Overt (done openly) and *unavoidable* (impossible to ignore) are not quite a pair. *Problematic* and *tired* have no relationship.

Solutions: 20 Medium Questions

1. Marriage, Commingling. This sentence begins with the signal "While," before describing religions that "insist on the primacy of their particular deity." "Syncretism" is then introduced as relating in some way to "multiple religious beliefs." Because of the opening signal, you know syncretism should be in favor of multiple religious beliefs. The fill-in is something like *inclusion* or *mixture*.

Division and *schism*, which often refer to a division within something like a religious organization, are an incorrect pair. *Exclusion* (deliberate act of omission) and *transgression* (act that violates a rule or duty; an offense) have no relationship.

2. Consummate, Complete. The blank is about the ambassador's power. You have a same-direction signal ("hence"), and an important clue is that, due to this power, he "was able to draft and finalize the agreement unilaterally" (seems like a lot of power for a diplomat). A good fill-in would be something like *a lot of* or *total*.

Tyrannical and *dictatorial* are a pair that goes too far, introducing a meaning (exercising total power, in a cruel way) that isn't supported by any proof in the sentence. *Tertiary* (third) and *enigmatic* (mysterious) have no relationship.

3. Declaim, Trumpet. The portion of this sentence after the comma is not actually relevant to the blank. All you need to determine is what most politicians do in regards to "their views." Clearly, they like to *proclaim* or *announce* those views.

Invoke and *adduce* are an incorrect pair. *Disparage* (belittle or discredit) and *parrot* (repeat mindlessly) have no relationship.

4. Colloquium, Symposium. The sentence tells you that the organization has somehow acquired a "haphazard and often chaotic set of bylaws and regulations." Thus, it is likely that they will want to get everyone together in order to reconcile all these rules. A good fill-in would be *meeting*.

Intervention and *mediation* are an incorrect pair. *Introduction* and *acclamation* (loud demonstration of approval or welcome) have no relationship.

5. Cloistered, Sheltered. The signal word "Though" tells you that you are going to contradict the first portion of this sentence, which says that writers ought to have "some experience of life." Your blank should go against that notion. Because you already have "solitary," a good fill-in word would be *protected*.

Enigmatic and *cryptic* (having hidden meaning; mysterious) are an incorrect near-pair. *Idiosyncratic* (unique to an individual; eccentric, quirky) and *susceptible* (likely to be influenced or harmed by something specific) have no relationship.

6. Nonchalance, Indifference. In this sentence, the key is the word "belied," which functions as a kind of reversal signal. *Belie* means "to misrepresent or contradict," suggesting a contrast to "his deep sense of responsibility." A good fill-in for the blank would be *not caring*.

Mirth and *felicity* are an incorrect pair, both meaning something like "happiness," though *mirth* additionally often implies laughter. *Concern* and *sagacity* (keen judgment) have no relationship.

7. Xenophobic, Bigoted. The blank here is defined by the second half of the sentence. "Patriotism" represents the "elevation of one country to the rank of quintessential on Earth," which implies that one country is the purest example among all countries on Earth. So your blank should be something that involves the "demonization of other people." A good fill-in would be *prejudiced*.

Minatory and *truculent* are not quite a pair (the former means "threatening," while the latter means "aggressively defiant"), and *unethical* and *nationalistic* have no relationship to each other. It is certainly true that excessive patriotism is *nationalistic*, but this word does not match the proof in the sentence.

8. Forbearance, Temperance. It's important to know the word "debauchery" (meaning "excessive indulgence in sensual pleasures") to solve this question. The sentence describes a husband-to-be who will *not* be engaging in debauchery at the bachelor party, so you need a word that describes someone who exhibits *self-control* or *moderation*.

Fiat (authoritative decree) and *autonomy* (the right to self-government; independence) are not quite a pair and are incorrect anyway. *Gentility* (the state of belonging to polite society; refinement of manner) and *tenacity* (the quality of being persistent or stubborn) have no relationship.

9. Vilifying, Maligning. The rally here is described as discussing politics "humorously but civilly, without" doing the thing in the blank. A good fill-in for the blank would be *abusing* or *badmouthing*.

Lampooning and *caricaturing* make an incorrect pair, both meaning "mocking or ridiculing," though *caricaturing* specifically means to do so by exaggerating particular features or traits. Though they are close to the correct meaning for your blank, the sentence mentions that the rally was "humorous." This means that *lampooning* and *caricaturing*, both of which imply a kind of humorous teasing, would be welcome at the rally, so not plausible for the blank. *Bespeaking* (suggesting; ordering or reserving something in advance) and *eulogizing* (to praise highly, especially at a memorial service) have no relationship (and the latter is the opposite of what you want here).

10. Sanctioned, Endorsed. The second half of this sentence tells you that reports of corporal punishment receive an "overwhelmingly negative popular response." This means that the military would be unlikely to *authorize* these forms of abuse.

Upbraided (criticized), *considered*, *rejected*, and *polarized* (broken up into separate groups) have no relationship.

11. Quagmire, Morass. The first part of the sentence, which describes how the budget debate "progressed well … in spite of … squabbling," is very important. If you didn't see that, you might be tempted to choose the wrong words here. However, because of the reversal signal "but," you want something that contrasts with something that progresses well. A good fill-in would be *mess* or *muddle*.

Feud and *quarrel* are an incorrect pair. While they correctly get across the negative spin you want for the blank, they don't address the idea of progressing badly, and the "but" indicates a need to contrast with a situation that was always prone to "squabbling." *Covenant* and *accord* are an incorrect pair, both indicating an agreement.

12. Crucial, Requisite. This is a tough question, because the sentence gives you only "subtle" as any kind of clue. Your blank should oppose it, but you don't want the opposite of "subtle" (which would be something like *obvious*, which clearly doesn't make any sense here). Instead, you need to think about the overall meaning of the sentence. Most likely, the point is that the difference between similes and metaphors is *important*.

Null and *nominal* are an incorrect pair, both meaning "insignificant." *Synoptic* (presenting a summary of the whole) and *optional* have no relationship.

13. Fallacious, Specious. This sentence is thick with content, and it's important that you understand all of it. You are given two statements about economics. First, that "Keynesian economics" may or may not recommend that "the limit (on government debt) should be perpetually raised." Then you are told definitively that Keynes says "deficit spending must be done responsibly." If the latter is true, then it is likely that he would *not* have made the former recommendation. So your blank should say something like *incorrect*.

Indigenous (native to or naturally occurring in a region), *corrupt, venial* (forgivable or pardonable), and *axiomatic* (self-evident or unquestionable) have no relationship. In addition, *axiomatic* is the opposite of what is needed for the blank.

14. Patois, Jargon. This sentence is describing rebellion as the effect of a communication gap, which you will need to make concrete with the blank. Something "protean" (meaning "tending to change frequently or easily") is being compared to the "older generation's calcified language." Actually, the best fill-in for your blank is simply *language*.

Defiance and *insubordination* are an incorrect pair, both meaning something like "disobedience." *Prolixity* and *verbosity* are another incorrect pair, which introduces a theme trap, as both words mean "wordiness."

15. Grousing, Protesting. "Cantankerous" means "bad-tempered and argumentative." Because there is no reversal signal here, you simply need a word that means those things. A good fill-in for the blank would be *arguing* or *complaining*.

Imputing (attributing or blaming), *assaulting* (physically attacking), *convulsing* (suffering violent involuntary contraction of the muscles), and *imbibing* (drinking) have no relationship.

16. Fracas, Altercation. In this sentence, you need to figure out what kind of thing would result in the police being called—likely, some kind of *crime* or *fight*.

Discourse and *colloquy* are an incorrect pair, both meaning "conversation." *Battle* may be close to what you want, but relates to a larger event than a bar fight. *Mutiny* (open rebellion against authorities) is not related to the others.

17. Eclectic, Multifarious. In this sentence, the word "surprisingly" is functioning as a kind of reversal signal, disagreeing with the portion before the comma. There, you learn that the woman in question had a "sheltered upbringing" and a "limited breadth of experience." Your blank should be the opposite of that. A good fill-in would be *varied* or *not limited*.

Shallow and *facile* are an incorrect pair, in that both can mean "superficial." *Profound* has the right spin, but it isn't the opposite of "limited" or "sheltered." *Callow* (immature or inexperienced) has no relationship with the other choices, and it incorrectly agrees with "limited breadth of experience."

18. Rail, Fulminate. The word "but" acts as a signal to reverse course here, taking you in the opposite direction of the adjectives initially used to define documentary filmmakers: "dispassionate" and objective." A good fill-in would be *speak out*.

Advertise (draw attention to publicly in order to promote sales), *inveigle* (win, or win over, by flattery), *strain* (make a strenuous effort), and *aspirate* (pronounce a sound in the exhalation of breath) have no relationship. Note that *inveigle* is *not* the same as *inveigh* (which does not appear as a choice but would have been a suitable correct answer, as it means "express angry disapproval"—the GRE sometimes plays on commonly confused words).

19. Piquant, Zesty. There are two important portions of this sentence to focus on. First, the word "praised," implying that the critic's review will be positive. The second part is the way he's described as using "the language of food to describe films." So you want two words that are positive and that could also be used to describe food.

10

Spectacular and *stupefying* are an incorrect pair. They are both positive, but they aren't generally used to describe food. *Insipid* (bland, tasteless, or flavorless) and *brilliant* have no relationship, and *insipid* is the opposite of what is needed in the blank.

20. Bruises, Contusions. In this sentence, a short list of possible injuries after a skydiving accident is described. Two of the items are "broken bones" and "a gash," which means your blank should be a physical injury different from those two. A good fill-in would be *bruises.*

Torpor (a state of physical inactivity; apathy, lethargy), *trauma* (physical injury; shock following a disturbing event or injury), *finesse* (skillful or adroit handling), and *lesions* (wounds, ulcers, tumors, etc.) include no synonym pairs. In addition, *finesse* is not a physical symptom, as are the other two pieces of evidence given in the sentence, while *torpor* is a physical condition but not an injury.

Solutions: 20 Hard Questions

1. Envoy, Emissary. The person in question is serving as "official" something for Japan to another country, and is "called upon to answer questions about the Japanese government's position." A good fill-in would be something like *representative* or *ambassador.*

Tyro and *neophyte* are an incorrect pair, both meaning "beginner." *Ascetic* (self-denying; austere) and *libertine* (one who is debauched or without moral restraint) are not synonyms, though both have something to do with self-control, in opposite ways.

2. Palliate, Damp. The blank is about both the leadership and the "stridency of their rhetoric"—you need the relationship between those two things. "While" is a reversal signal. In the first part of the sentence, the protests are "uncompromising." Thus, in the second part, they should be softer, more on the side of compromising. Since "stridency" means harshness and is on the same side as "uncompromising," the group thus chose to *reduce* or *tone down* the stridency.

Metamorphose, gild, wane, and *succor* do not contain any pairs. *Wane* means "decrease" and is an attractive trap answer. However, *wane* is an intransitive verb—that is, something (such as the moon) *wanes* on its own; you can't *wane* an object. Therefore, the word does not fit in this sentence. *Metamorphose* (change) could work, but it doesn't indicate the direction of the change (increase or decrease), which the blank needs to do in order to show that the leaders "wisely" chose to do something. *Gild* (cover in gold; give a deceitfully pleasing appearance to) and *succor* (aid, assist, or relieve) have no relationship.

3. Quiescent, Abeyant. The key bit of proof that you're looking for here is that "activists will be newly galvanized." Because of the reversal signal "but," you need a blank that means the opposite of "galvanized." A good fill-in word would be *dormant* (implying that the movement is quiet but could rise again).

Dogged (persistent, tenacious, or stubbornly determined), *interminable* (endless), *lissome* (flexible or easily bent), and *feckless* (ineffective, lacking in vitality) have no relationship.

4. Equitable, Apposite. The first half of this sentence sets up the topic, but the important information is in the second half. There, you're told about the "most ardent supporter [of corporal punishment]." This supporter agrees with detractors on at least one thing, for which "evenhanded and thorough" is a clue. A good fill-in for your blank would be *deserved* or *fair.*

Clement and *merciful* are an incorrect synonym pair. They both go against the spin that the blank calls for. *Delimited* (having limits established; bounded) and *tantamount* (equivalent; virtually the same as) are not related.

5. Chimerical, Fallible. The portion of this sentence after the blank tells you that "results tend to be colored by … personal proclivities and suppositions." This provides an explanation of the blank, which in turn is trying to tell you something about "impartiality." That last portion describes something the exact opposite of impartial, so a good fill-in for your blank would be *wrong* or *nonexistent*.

Inane and *fatuous* are an incorrect pair, both meaning "silly." While the "premise of impartiality" may not in fact exist, that doesn't make it silly. *Prejudicial* (harmful; detrimental) and *vexing* (irksome; irritating) have no relationship.

6. Epicurean, Gustatory. Everything in this sentence relates to food, whether it's the "texture and taste" or the "notion of what constitutes a meal." This means you need a word that relates to food. A good fill-in would be *culinary*.

Carnal (relating to physical, especially sexual, activities) and *voluptuous* (characterized by luxury or sensual pleasure) are an incorrect pair, relating to sensuality rather than merely food. *Salubrious* (promoting health or well-being) and *terrestrial* (of, on, or relating to the earth) have no relationship.

7. Gist, Pith. The verb "drone" has a very specific meaning, implying that someone is going on at length in a dull or boring way. The implication is that the point could be made more efficiently. This sentence then tells you that a "précis" (summary) can be found in "the tome's first few pages." This précis is really the book's *essence* or *thrust*, which is the kind of word you want for the blank.

Adage (a traditional expression of a common observation), *stub* (a short part left after a larger part was broken off), *nimbus* (a circle of light), and *nut*, which among its many definitions can mean "a hard problem or task," have no relationship.

8. Collate, Juxtapose. The final portion of this sentence describes "studying the differences and similarities" between two different things. This implies you'll be doing some sort of comparison, so a good fill-in word would be *compare*.

Aggregate, agglomerate, and *glean* are an incorrect triple, all meaning "gather." While gathering the data together is required in order to make a comparison, the sentence already said "not only to collect." All of these words are just fancy versions of "collect," which you don't need to repeat. *Deduce*, which means "to arrive at a conclusion logically," doesn't match any other choice. In addition, it doesn't quite fit the context: you can reason logically *about* the score reports, but you wouldn't reason the score reports themselves.

9. Volleys, Salvos. The second half of this sentence doesn't tell you anything interesting. In fact, everything you need to know comes from the few words before the blank: "trenches were dug so that soldiers could avoid" something. What would you avoid in a trench? *Bullets*, more or less, or *barrages*, if you wanted to get a little fancier.

Provocations and *goadings* are an incorrect pair, though *goad* specifically means "to provoke by prodding." *Fervency* (fervor; strong feeling of excitement) and *imprecations* (offensive words or phrases said in anger) have no relationship.

10. Genteel, Courtly. Near the beginning of the sentence, Cary Grant is described as "suave," meaning "confident and elegant." Your blank should not mean the exact same thing, or it would be redundant. Instead, you want a word that is best exemplified by someone who always pulls out a woman's chair, such as *well-mannered*.

Debonair and *cosmopolitan* are an incorrect pair. These words mean "sophisticated," but they don't necessarily imply good manners. *Consummate* (complete or perfect) and *waggish* (humorous in a playful way) have no relationship.

10

11. Subjective, Personal. The sentence states that the attempt to find "parity," or fairness, is "fallacious," or logically incorrect. How could fairness be illogical? Only if it isn't real or objectively determinable. A good fill-in would be *prejudiced* or *based on feelings*.

Pragmatic and *utilitarian* are a near-pair, meaning "practical." *Introverted* (introspective) and *illicit* (unlawful) are not related.

12. Erudition, Cerebrality. This sentence compares the blank with speeches that feature "ignorance" and "stupidity." You also want something that relates to education. A good fill-in would be *knowledge*, which is the result of education.

Bromide (commonplace or trite saying) and *bloviation* (talking at length in a pompous or boastful way) both have some relationship to speech, but they aren't a pair and neither relates to "education" or "ignorance." *Condescension* (patronizing attitude; disdain) is similar to *bloviation*, but both disagree with the proof word "actually" (it is not surprising that condescension would be resented by voters!), and neither contrasts properly with "ignorance." *Patrimony* (inheritance from a father or other male ancestor) is unrelated to everything else.

13. Semblance, Veneer. In this sentence, you're told about a man who has been fired and doesn't tell his wife and kids. This somehow relates to "plenitude," which means "the condition of being full or complete." Clearly, if you get fired and don't tell your family, it's because you want to pretend that you're still okay. A good fill-in word would be *appearance*.

Corollaries and *consequences* are an incorrect pair. *Paradigms* (things serving as an example or model) and *prepossessions* (attitudes or beliefs formed beforehand) have no relationship.

14. Indiscriminate, Blanket. The sentence tells you that Don Juan had "an astronomical number of amatory adventures," but that it was not because he had a "surfeit of charisma or skillfulness." What might explain this discrepancy? Perhaps if Don Juan weren't particularly choosy. A good fill-in for the blank would be *not choosy*.

Sumptuous and *hedonistic* are an incorrect pair, meaning "luxurious" and "devoted to luxury or pleasure," respectively. While they both describe someone like Don Juan, they don't explain how he had so many lovers. *Lurid* (gruesome, shocking) and *covert* (not openly done; veiled) have no relationship.

15. Attenuate, Abate. The sentence indicates that "Even" major campaign finance reform will "fail" to do something to "the influence of money." This money "directly relates" to a politician being able to become a politician, so the influence of money must be pretty strong. Thus, the reform proposals will fail to *lessen* or *reduce* the influence.

Graft (join or unite), *pander* (cater to the lowest or most base desires), *importune* (harass with constant demands; annoy, irritate), and *indemnify* (protect against loss or damage) have no relationship. On the GRE, the choices for a given blank will always be of the same form of speech; here, they are verbs. Don't confuse the verb *graft* with the noun *graft*, which means "acquisition of money (or other valuable) in dishonest or questionable ways" and represents a theme trap here.

10

16. Interrogate, Limn. There are no signals to reverse course in this sentence, so you simply need a word that fits the description of a book that explores the "many ways in which 19th-century women writers ..." In other words, you can just fill in the blank with *explore*. Note that *interrogate* is being used in a figurative sense here (i.e., it's not referring to a literal interrogation, as of a criminal), though the goal of both types of interrogation is to pry deeply into an issue.

Debunk and *explode* are an incorrect pair, meaning "disprove." *Interpolate* (insert between parts, pieces, or things) and *castigate* (criticize or punish severely) have no relationship. *Castigate* almost fits into a triple with the incorrect pair, but it's more of a criticism than an attempt to disprove something.

17. Languor, Lethargy. With the signal word "While," this sentence creates a contrast between a positive and negative view of the same fact. The positive view is that certain cultures prioritize "relaxation" and "moderation between work and play." The negative view of this would be something akin to *laziness*.

Enfeeblement and *enervation* are an incorrect pair, meaning "weakening" or "weakness." Though they are close to what you want, they imply a taking away of energy, which is not the same as simply being lazy or tired. *Obtundity* (lessening of intensity; dulling or deadening) and *seemliness* (the state or condition of conforming to standards of proper conduct) have no relationship.

18. Extraneous, Unnecessary. Autodidacts ("those who teach themselves") would argue against "enforced lucubration (study)" and "standard education." A good fill-in might simply be *unnecessary*.

Slack and *lax* are an incorrect pair, meaning "loose." *Prudent* and *sagacious* are an incorrect pair, meaning "wise; having good judgment."

19. Dusky, Crepuscular. The only piece of real proof in this sentence comes in the second half, a "twilit avenue in a long since abandoned city." So you want a word that implies "twilit" and "abandoned," such as *dark*.

Urban and *civic* are something of a pair here. Though they both reflect the sentence's reference to a "city," they fail to correctly reference either "twilit" or "abandoned," which are really the most descriptive terms in the original sentence. *Precipitous* (extremely steep) and *avuncular* (relating to an uncle; kind to younger people) have no relationship.

20. Ineluctable, Inexorable. The key phrase here is "the inertia of history." Inertia is resistance to change, so this phrase must mean that history is on track and can't deviate from that track. So your blank here should be something like *unchangeable*.

Incontrovertible (not able to be denied or disputed), *interminable* (endless), *infallible* (incapable of making mistakes or being wrong), and *unspeakable* (not able to be expressed in words; too horrible to express in words) have no relationship.

Essays

This Essays unit equips test-takers with guidelines, strategic tips, and handy analytical tools to compose excellent essay responses for the Issue and Argument essay questions found on the GRE.

In This Unit ...

- Chapter 11: Essays Strategy

Essays Strategy

In This Chapter ...

- Analyze an Issue

- Analyze an Argument

- GRE Issue Essay Quotes

CHAPTER 11 Essays Strategy

The first part of the exam will consist of two essays to be completed in 30 minutes each:

Analyze an Issue (30 minutes)—Discuss a general interest topic.
Analyze an Argument (30 minutes)—Analyze the argument presented.

These essay assignments can occur in either order, but the essay section will always come first. The essays do not factor into your main GRE score; they are scored on a separate 6-point scale in increments of 0.5 (0 is lowest, 6 is highest).

In a Nutshell

For those who consider themselves already very good at essay writing and have limited study time, here's the skinny:

The Issue essay is very much **like every other five-or-so paragraph academic essay** you've ever written. Some people have trouble thinking of examples for abstract topics, such as "Is justice more important in a society than compassion?" But if you feel confident about that, it's likely you won't need much preparation.

The Argument essay requires you to analyze a flawed argument. You're not being asked to bring in outside information or give your own opinion. If you've taken philosophy or logic classes, been on a debate team, or studied for GMAT Critical Reasoning or LSAT Logical Reasoning questions, you shouldn't have much trouble here. However, if none of the above applies to you, you'll probably want to read the Analyze an Argument portion of this chapter. You don't need tons of preparation, but you want to **go in with a game plan** and a box of tools, so you can calmly get to work.

When you take practice tests, **do** write the essays, even if you don't need the practice or don't care about the essay score. It's harder to write for an hour and then start answering multiple-choice questions, so you want to make sure that your practice mimics what will happen during the real test.

Write a lot. No matter what the official rules say, longer essays get higher scores.

Pay attention to the specific instructions. On the new GRE, ETS has gone out of its way to write a dozen or so different specific instructions for both Analyze an Issue and Analyze an Argument essays. In the *Official Guide to the GRE General Test*, test-takers are warned that even if they write an otherwise perfect essay, they will not score higher than a 4 without addressing the specific instructions provided in the question prompt.

You can actually read all of the essay prompts in advance at:

www.ets.org/gre/revised_general/prepare/analytical_writing/issue/pool
www.ets.org/gre/revised_general/prepare/analytical_writing/argument/pool

Certainly, don't spend the time to write practice essays for each of the prompts on these lists, but do scan through them so that you can get a sense for the types of prompts you could receive on your exam.

11

How Essays Are Used by Graduate Schools

ETS says: "Validity research has shown that the Analytical Writing essay score is correlated with academic writing more highly than is the personal statement." That is, the essay you write under controlled conditions in a testing environment is guaranteed to be your own work, whereas your actual application essays might have benefited from the assistance of others (as well as a spell-check program).

In the "Guide to the Use of Scores" that ETS offers to university admissions departments, ETS writes, "A GRE essay response should be considered a rough first draft since examinees do not have sufficient time to revise their essays during the test. Examinees also do not have dictionaries or spell-checking or grammar-checking software available to them."

It is impossible to say how much (or even whether) the essay counts in graduate school admissions: there are simply too many programs and too many schools. Some math and science programs may take little or no account of the essay, and some more writing-intensive graduate programs may consider the essays more carefully. Graduate schools may use the essays as a screening device (so a very low essay score might keep the rest of your application from being given a serious review). It's also reasonable to presume that your essays are more likely to be taken into account if your first language is not English or if you are applying from a country outside the United States.

In sum, the admissions department at the particular university to which you are applying is the best source of information about how the GRE essay will be used. If the admissions department is not forthcoming (many schools will simply say, "We look at each student's entire application holistically," or something like that), you'll just have to do your best (a good policy anyway).

Graduate schools to which you send your GRE scores will be able to read your actual essays. Don't write anything you wouldn't want the admissions committee to read (avoid writing anything offensive or anything with a very political or self-exposing slant).

The Physical Mechanics of Essay Writing

Assuming that you are taking a computer-based GRE (true in the United States and most other countries), you will be typing your essays into a text box. There is no limit to how much text you can enter, but you can only see about 10 lines of what you've written before you have to scroll. The system feels like a clunky, old-fashioned word processing program. You will have "Cut" and "Paste" buttons, as well as an "Undo" button. There is no bold, italic, or underline. There is no tab/indent. The program does not offer any type of spell-check or grammar check.

In addition to "Cut," "Paste," and "Undo," you will also have the following basic functions:

Arrow Keys move the cursor up, down, left, or right.

Enter inserts a paragraph break (no indent—simply moves down to a new line).

Page Up moves the cursor up one screen.

Page Down moves the cursor down one screen.

Backspace removes the character to the left of the cursor.

Delete removes the character to the right of the cursor.

Home moves the cursor to the beginning of the line.

End moves the cursor to the end of the line.

You will have scratch paper (the same stapled paper booklet you use for the rest of the exam) on which to plan your essay, but you can also outline in the text box (though be sure to delete any notes or outlines before submitting your essay).

Once you've completed an essay and clicked on "submit," you cannot go back. If you complete an essay before the time expires, you can go immediately to the next section, but you do *not* get to use any extra time on other sections.

There is no break after the essays; you will proceed to your first Math or Verbal section.

Essay Length

For each essay, use a five-paragraph structure as a baseline. Sometimes you'll write four paragraphs, sometimes you'll write six to seven (many high-scoring essays contain six to seven paragraphs, actually), but the basic structure is an intro and a conclusion sandwiching three or more main examples or reasons, each in its own body paragraph.

Interestingly, Manhattan Prep's analysis of published GRE essays written by actual students and given real scores shows a very strong correlation between length and score. This is also consistent with ETS's grading on other tests, such as the SAT.

Let's be very clear: **Even when ETS says that essay length doesn't matter, it does. A lot.**

To ensure your essay is long enough, you will have to brainstorm and plan your essay very efficiently (3–4 minutes for the Issue, 2–3 minutes for the Argument) so that you can get started writing as soon as possible.

Write as much as you can in the time allotted!

Spelling and Grammar

Many other GRE books have long chapters on essay writing containing exercises on how to use the semicolon and other such feats of literary mechanics (we suspect these publishers have simply recycled essay-writing chapters from other textbooks, with little concern for how the GRE essay is scored).

On the GRE, while good spelling and grammar are better than poor spelling and grammar, of course, the ideas you present (and the length of your essay) are far more important.

According to ETS, "Scorers are trained to focus on the analytical logic of the essays more than on spelling, grammar, or syntax. The mechanics of writing are weighed in their ratings only to the extent that these impede clarity of meaning." In other words, as long as the grader can understand you, he or she is not supposed to count off for minor and infrequent spelling and grammar errors.

The ETS report also says, "The ability of ESL students to write in English may be affected not only by their language capacity but also by their prior experience with the kinds of critical writing tasks in the test. Where educational systems do not stress these skills, performance may not reflect the applicant's ability to learn these skills in a graduate setting." In other words, ETS is of the opinion that students from educational systems focused more on memorization than on critical reasoning may have particular trouble writing high-scoring essays. (But don't worry. The strategies in this chapter will help!)

11

Scoring

As mentioned earlier, essays are scored from 0–6, and the essay score does not count as part of your main GRE score. According to ETS, an essay that scores a 6 addresses the specific instructions while doing the following:

- presenting an insightful position on the issue
- developing the position with compelling reasons and/or persuasive examples
- sustaining a well-focused, well-organized analysis, connecting ideas logically
- expressing ideas fluently and precisely, using effective vocabulary and sentence variety
- demonstrating facility with the conventions (i.e., grammar, usage, and mechanics) of standard written English, with possibly a few minor errors

Essays are scored by specially trained college and university faculty who will not see your name, gender, geographical location, or any other identifying information. Each of your essays will be read by two graders, giving a total of four essay scores (two for each essay). These scores are averaged, and then the averaged score is rounded up to the nearest half point. (Thus, it is possible to get a score such as 4.5.) The two graders for any one essay will always grade within 1 point of each other; if they were to grade farther apart, a third grader would be brought in to adjudicate.

It goes without saying that any evidence of cheating, which includes using anyone else's work without citation, will get your GRE score (the entire thing, not just the essays) canceled and your fee forfeited.

Analyze an Issue

For the Analyze an Issue assignment, you will be presented with a statement or a claim. Your job is to agree or disagree with the statement, and then write a compelling essay to support the position you've taken.

The topic that you are given on the real test will be chosen from a list of topics available on the ETS website:

www.ets.org/gre/revised_general/prepare/analytical_writing/issue/pool

Yes, that's right—you can view all of the possible topics ahead of time. The topic you end up writing about will be on the list at the preceding page, possibly with minor wording changes.

In the issue essay, you are generally expected to **take a side**, which means it will not be enough to simply deconstruct the particular issue. Don't just say, "It depends" (even if you're thinking that it does depend!); rather, articulate a specific point of view. When arguing one side or another of an argument, be sure to acknowledge the issue's complexity. That is, acknowledge that the other side has some merit (in a way that doesn't hurt your own argument).

That being said, it is critical that you pay attention to the specific instructions given along with the essay, which may affect how much or how little you have to write about the side of the argument you are *not* in support of. ETS lists six different possible ways you might be prompted to respond to a topic. Here they are, from page 13 of *The Official Guide for the GRE General Test*:

1. Write a response in which you discuss the extent to which you agree or disagree with the statement, and explain your reasoning for the position you take. In developing and supporting your position, you should consider ways in which the statement might or might not hold true and explain how these considerations shape your position.

2. Write a response in which you discuss the extent to which you agree or disagree with the recommendation, and explain your reasoning for the position you take. In developing and supporting your position, describe specific circumstances in which adopting the recommendation would or would not be advantageous and explain how these examples shape your position.

3. Write a response in which you discuss the extent to which you agree or disagree with the claim. In developing and supporting your position, be sure to address the most compelling reasons or examples that could be used to challenge your position.

4. Write a response in which you discuss which view more closely aligns with your own position, and explain your reasoning for the position you take. In developing and supporting your position, you should address both of the views presented above.

5. Write a response in which you discuss the extent to which you agree or disagree with the claim **AND** the reason on which that claim is based. (NOTE: For this prompt, the claim will be accompanied by a reason why the claim has been made. You'll need to give your opinion on both.)

6. Write a response in which you discuss your views on the policy above, and explain your reasoning for the position you take. In developing and supporting your position, you should consider the possible consequences of implementing the policy and explain how these consequences shape your position.

These instructions may seem quite different, but they really fall into three general categories:

1. Pick a side of the prompt and defend it, but explain when the other side might be true or more logical (#1, #2, #3, and #4 from above).

2. Pick a side of the prompt, and also make sure to discuss the reason given in defense of that prompt (#5 from above).

3. Pick a side and discuss the consequences of your opinion (#6 from above).

There is not yet enough data to determine how much weight ETS will put on these specific instructions. While they claim that an essay that fails to address the instructions will not score above a 4, the top-scoring essay examples given in *The Official Guide to the GRE General Test* do not seem to do a very good job of addressing the specific instructions. What seems most likely is that if you write an essay that intelligently supports your own position while also fairly describing and responding to the other side of an argument, you will do well whatever the specific instructions. As it turns out, because the instructions are tailored to the prompt itself, it can be difficult to write intelligently on the subject and *not* address the specific instructions.

In the end, you will *always* want to do the following, regardless of the Issue prompt you're given:

1. Take a point of view on the given issue.

2. Support your point of view using relevant and *specific* examples.

3. Acknowledge both sides of the issue and the specific instructions in the question.

Brainstorming

Spend 3–4 minutes brainstorming specific, real-world examples for each side. *Real world* means some event or phenomenon that actually occurred, whether in history, in your own life, or even in a book that you read. Why brainstorm both sides of an issue? It is often true that the side you don't believe is the easier side to write—perhaps because, when you believe something strongly, it seems obvious to you, and it's harder to come up with concrete reasons or examples. Another good reason to brainstorm both sides is …

11

You don't always have to agree.

Some people just have a habit of being agreeable. That is, some students just automatically assume they should agree with the topic. However, some GRE topics are actually phrased in a pretty extreme way, such that they would be difficult to defend.

For instance, one example from the GRE's topic pool reads, "Societies should try to save every plant and animal species, regardless of the expense to humans in effort, time, and financial well-being." While most people are in favor of saving endangered species, the phrase "regardless of the expense to humans" makes it sound as though it would be necessary to do things such as shut down an entire city in order to save a threatened form of bacteria. You're welcome to argue in favor, of course, but this is a topic it would be much easier to argue against. (An argument against this topic can still certainly be in favor of saving *some* or *most* endangered species—in fact, such a view would definitely be encouraged as part of acknowledging both sides of the issue.)

That said, here's how you get started brainstorming. Try it with this topic:

> **"The better a new idea is, the greater the opposition to that idea when it is first presented. Only later, usually once the person who had the idea is no longer around to enjoy its success, do we consider the thinker a genius."**

First, make a T-chart, like this:

By writing down "For" and "Against," you are setting yourself up to think in each direction. This is especially useful when you are trying to come up with counterexamples. The term *brainstorm* is really just suggesting that you write down one-word tags for each possible reason or example. For instance, Galileo might pop to mind, because he was persecuted for saying that the earth moved around the sun, and in fact had to spend the rest of his life under house arrest; after his death, his ideas were vindicated, and he was considered a scientific hero. On the other hand, there are plenty of geniuses who are renowned during their own lifetimes (Einstein was quite famous in his own time). Jot these down on your T-chart—Galileo on the left, and Einstein on the right.

A good way to get your brainstorming done quickly is to piggyback off examples you already have. Once you've thought of Galileo, can you think of other people like him who were persecuted for their ideas—ideas that are now considered correct? You might think of someone like Nelson Mandela, who spent 27 years in prison. But wait! He was hailed as a hero for so much of his life! He was the first democratically elected president of South Africa! This is actually a pretty good example for the other side. (This is why it's good to brainstorm both sides!)

Also on the "Against" side—once you've thought of Einstein, can you think of other famous geniuses? How about Stephen Hawking? If you run out of steam, think to yourself, "Hmm, Einstein and Stephen Hawking are both scientists. Can I think of the "Einstein" of some other field?" Perhaps someone like W. E. B. DuBois, who was considered a radical in his own time; however, after his death, his ideas were vindicated by the civil rights movement of the 1960s. Hmm, DuBois actually fits better on the "For" side. Is there someone else who was a social activist whose ideas were later vindicated? How about the early feminists, such as Elizabeth Cady Stanton and Lucretia Mott? See, you're on a roll!

Here, the example goes a little further than it needs to for the sake of demonstrating the brainstorming process. You probably could have stopped after Nelson Mandela—stop as soon as you have two to three good ideas for one side.

For	Against
Galileo	Einstein, Hawking, Mandela

Your initial thought might have been that you wanted to argue for, but you've come up with three against examples. Go with it! Your goal is to write the best essay you can as quickly and as easily as possible. You've got what you need to do that, so start writing.

You may have noticed that the previous examples were drawn from history and current events. While personal examples are allowable, they don't tend to make for the most rigorous and persuasive essays. Personal examples should be considered a backup plan for when you get stuck in your brainstorming.

Of course, you are *not* required to use example after example in your essay. You are also perfectly welcome to use well-considered reasoning. However, some topics lend themselves better to examples, while other topics lend themselves better to argumentation. Here's another example topic:

> **"Every nation should require students to study at least one foreign language from the elementary school level through the university level."**

This topic seems to lend itself better to reasoning than to concrete examples, although you might be able to come up with enough examples—the United States doesn't typically require foreign language study, and most European countries do. You could use these examples on either side; for instance, you could argue that the United States doesn't need foreign language study because, in being a world power, the United States prompts everyone else to follow its lead; or you could argue that Europeans are, by and large, much more educated than Americans, and therefore run more peaceful societies and have more appreciation for culture. Many examples are really quite flexible.

In any case, try an argument-based brainstorming. Again, make a T-chart:

For	Against

Your challenge here is to "divide up" your reasoning into discrete (that means separate!) arguments so that your essay doesn't just ramble on without structure.

You might just start with the first thing that comes to mind. For instance, people in large countries, such as the United States and China, don't seem to need foreign languages as much as people in smaller countries do. Many people in the United States and China never leave their own countries. Jot this down in the right column.

On the other hand, the world is becoming more connected. Most people who end up conducting international business, or emigrating to new lands, don't know from childhood that they're going to do so. As children, they're not in a position to decide whether to take foreign languages. It would be best to require foreign languages so that they're prepared for whatever happens in their adult lives. This would go in the left column.

11

One possible thesis might be, "While foreign language study has many benefits, both practical and intellectual, it is going too far to say that such study should be mandatory for every citizen of every nation. Other factors, such as whether the nation's primary language is already an international language, whether the nation's primary language is in danger of dying out, and whether the nation has more pressing, survival-related concerns should be taken into account." This thesis certainly isn't arguing that foreign language study is bad—it is taking a very reasonable, balanced approach.

When a topic is phrased in an extreme way ("everyone should do X"), **don't ignore practical issues**. In some nations, it would be difficult to even find foreign language teachers. Some nations barely have schools of any kind, so foreign language instruction hardly seems like a main priority. And who decides which languages are mandatory? Not all students are the same—maybe most students could be required to take foreign languages, but the few who are having trouble with basic skills that they will need for adult life ought to be waived from foreign language requirements so that they can focus on things they will really need.

Here is a sample T-chart containing some of these ideas:

For	Against
World is more int'l—students don't know what they'll need as adults, so prep them now.	Some nations need f.l. more than others.
	Some nations not practical—schools very basic, no f.l. teachers.
	Which f.l.? Who decides?
	Preserve culture, some nations' languages might die out.
	ALL PEOPLE EVERYWHERE? Some students can't, some nations must focus on survival! Too extreme.

It's totally okay to have an unbalanced T-chart. You *want* to use this to pick which side to write on. It looks like you have your answer! (Of course, there is no "right" answer to an Issue question, and your T-chart might have led you to argue in favor.)

This chart shows five arguments against. You probably won't have time to write an entire body paragraph about each one, and some ideas are really building off of other ones (for instance, it might be hard to write an entire paragraph on the idea "Who decides which foreign languages to take?"). So you want to either pick your three or so strongest arguments, or else *group* your arguments into three or so groups.

Here is what a test-taker might jot on paper next to the chart:

F.l. good but shouldn't be mandatory for all.

    I.   Diff countries, diff needs.

    II.   Some nations must focus on survival—priorities!

    III.   Not practical—some nations can't, what lang? Some want to preserve culture.

    IV.   Individual students are diff.

You also want to make sure to **acknowledge the other side** (usually in the introduction, although sometimes in the course of the body paragraphs). This is very easy to do, since you have brainstormed both sides. Just take a point or two from the side you *didn't* pick, and say something like, "While a reasonable person might think X, actually Y is more important," or "While a reasonable person might think X, this is not the case *all of the time*." For instance, on the foreign language topic:

> *While a reasonable person might suggest that because children don't know whether they'll move to other nations or engage in international business as adults, we should prepare them for such experiences now. However, children also don't know whether they'll do manual labor, become doctors, or run for president. There's no way to prepare young people for everything that might happen, so it makes sense to leave decisions about education in the hands of each nation and its school systems.*

Acknowledging the other side is a great way to fill out your introduction, or, if you have a lot to say, you can write a body paragraph of the form "objection → your response → your argument."

In other words, *anticipate counterarguments and respond to them*. This is especially important if you have decided on what you know to be an unusual viewpoint. If your argument is that governments should not provide public schools, you absolutely must address the first thing that pops into everyone's mind: "But what about children whose parents can't afford to pay private school fees?"

Briefly mention the specific instructions. While the specific instructions may ask you to add something into your essay that you wouldn't necessarily have included otherwise, there shouldn't be any need to radically change an essay from the standard format described here in order to obey the specific instructions. Generally, adding a single sentence to each paragraph, or even a few words, will suffice. For example, one set of instructions, taken from *The Official Guide for the GRE General Test*, says this:

> *Write a response in which you discuss the extent to which you agree or disagree with the statement, and explain your reasoning for the position you take. In developing and supporting your position, you should consider ways in which the statement might or might not hold true and explain how these considerations shape your position.*

Notice that the instructions don't really recommend anything that a well-written essay wouldn't do anyway. Therefore, feel free to write your outline without even worrying about the instructions, then simply check to be sure there will be space to include whatever little details the specific instructions requested (in this case, instances when the statement might or might not hold true). If you've done a good job in your brainstorming, adding sentences to address these instructions shouldn't be very difficult.

Finally, a word about your thesis or main idea. While sometimes it makes sense to simply agree or disagree with the topic, feel free to take a balanced, in-between approach. The graders enjoy nuance. Just be very clear about what you mean. Still, *in between* doesn't mean vague or wishy-washy. For instance, if you want to say that foreign language instruction should be mandatory in some countries and not others, say exactly what should be the deciding factor. A good thesis (for someone who is more on the "for" side of the foreign language topic) might be:

> *Because foreign language instruction is increasingly important in our interconnected world, it should be a priority in school curricula. However, in some nations, foreign language instruction is simply not practical or even possible. Thus, foreign language instruction should be mandatory at all levels of schooling except in nations where such a requirement is impracticable or for individual students whose learning difficulties make the requirement unreasonable.*

Note that this person isn't exactly arguing for the topic as written. But there's no question what the writer's position is. This is a detailed, balanced, and reasonable thesis.

Your thesis or main idea might be simpler, but make sure it's clear. It's fine to modify the argument, as in the previous example, to meet what it is you want to prove. A good standard to use is the **dinner table test**. Imagine yourself presenting your thesis at the dinner table. Would you really want to defend the idea that every student everywhere must study a foreign language? Even students in severely distressed nations where it might be more important to learn something else? Even students with severe learning disabilities? Literally everyone? This is starting to sound a bit ridiculous, right?

Now imagine yourself at the dinner table presenting this thesis—foreign languages should be mandatory, excepting countries where that isn't practical and individual students with learning difficulties. Now, you're still saying something someone could disagree with (you are, after all, arguing that most Americans should have been better educated!), but you sound like a pretty reasonable person starting an interesting discussion.

Now imagine that you took your thesis too far in the *other* direction—saying something no one could ever disagree with. Like, "Foreign language instruction should be made available to students who want it, when the school system has enough money and teachers to offer it." Umm ... so what? Your dinner companions are dozing off in their seats. You are boring everyone. Someone will probably shrug and change the subject. You went a little *too* far in making your main idea non-extreme. Consider these examples:

Too extreme:

> *All human beings should be forced to study a foreign language.*

> *Foreign languages should not be made mandatory for any students, because students should never have to study something they don't want to. Children should always make their own decisions.*

Too mushy:

> *Students who want to should be able to study a foreign language if it's available.*

> *Foreign languages can be valuable in certain pursuits. For example, foreign language study can help students become translators, foreign language teachers, or travel writers. (Note: Not only is this so mushy no one could argue with it, it also fails to address the question.)*

Just right:

> *Foreign languages should be mandatory for most students in nations where it is practicable to offer such instruction on a national basis.*

> *Foreign language instruction is important and should be encouraged, but for every subject one learns, there's another subject one will not have time to learn. Foreign language study should not be made mandatory, thus allowing students free choice in how to best engage and nurture their individual interests and talents.*

In sum, your thesis or main idea shouldn't be something so extreme that you can't defend it, but it also shouldn't be something so humdrum and obvious that a reasonable person couldn't take an opposite view. Don't oversimplify the topic. Pick a thesis you would use to start an interesting, intelligent discussion among reasonable people.

About timing: Note that the brainstorming and planning process above might sound as though it would take a person *much* longer than the 3–4 minutes recommended at the beginning of the chapter. Keep in mind that the sample T-charts contain a bit more information than you would need to write down, since you'll only be writing for yourself. If you write "SH" for "Stephen Hawking," you only have to remember what your abbreviation means for a couple of minutes, so feel free to be brief. You also don't have to write a separate outline—that might be more of a mental process, or you might just write "I," "II," "III" next to various arguments on the T-chart.

About brainstorming practice: Some practice with brainstorming will also speed up the process. You may find that the same examples seem to pop up for you over and over. There's nothing wrong with that! Many topics lend themselves to discussing climate change; for instance, the issue of whether technology/progress/new ideas can have a downside seems to be a common underlying theme. And, of course, write about what you know. If you were a philosophy major, or an environmental science major, etc., feel free to draw disproportionately on those types of examples.

Again, you can practice brainstorming by visiting this link and exploring the pool:

www.ets.org/gre/revised_general/prepare/analytical_writing/issue/pool

Try making T-charts, picking a side, and making a rough outline, as described, for some of the topics listed.

Don't just pick out the topics that you most want to write about! Force yourself to start at the beginning, or scroll down a bit and do the first topic you see.

When you practice brainstorming, give yourself plenty of time the first time through—maybe 10 minutes. The next time, cut it down to 8 minutes, then 6, 5, 4 … With practice, you should be able to reliably brainstorm in 3–4 minutes or even faster.

How to avoid getting stuck: As one GRE student said, lamentably: "It seems, since I graduated from college, I've forgotten everything I used to know!"

If you suffer from this problem, be assured that it is only temporary. One good suggestion is to simply jog your memory regarding what you once knew quite well—how about reading your old college papers? If you majored in a humanities field, you might have dozens of your own essays saved on your computer, ready to mine for ideas. Similarly, your old college textbooks might be fruitful (more so if you majored in history or sociology than if you majored in chemistry, though).

Also, keep in mind that you are not limited to talking about things the grader will have heard of. If you attended school in a non-English speaking country, you can still use examples from your own education.

If you still feel like you need new information to draw from, take a look at the suggestions below.

The book *The Intellectual Devotional Modern Culture: Revive Your Mind, Complete Your Education, and Converse Confidently with the Culturati*, by David S. Kidder and Noah D. Oppenheim, provides interesting single-page summaries of 365 topics from civil disobedience to Walt Disney to the European Union. There is actually an entire series of Intellectual Devotional books, so you might also check out the original book, or the American history one, as per your interests.

The website www.aldaily.com (Arts and Letters Daily) is an excellent source of articles with high intellectual content. In addition, magazines such as *The New Yorker, The Economist,* and *The Atlantic* are good sources of generally well-reasoned, in-depth articles on topics that may be of use to you in brainstorming.

Of course, it's too late for all of this once you get to the real test, so expand your reading list as soon as possible.

Okay. You've done a bunch of planning. Now on to a discussion about how to actually write this thing.

Writing the Issue Essay

Structure

Here is a basic structure for the Issue essay:

Introduction: Briefly restate the issue *with the goal of demonstrating to the grader that you understand the topic*. Do not simply repeat the prompt (the grader knows what topic you are writing about). Then define terms (if needed), acknowledge complexity, and establish your "take" or thesis on the issue.

Body: Write two to four paragraphs, each illustrating one of your main points. Keep in mind: *don't spend too much time making a single point or you will run out of time!*

Conclusion: Resummarize your position, acknowledging the other side. An exemplary conclusion adds some final extra insight—a new window to the main idea you've been discussing all along.

Aim for three substantive sentences in your conclusion, and these sentences can vary widely in length and content. A relevant quote would be a good way to fill out a conclusion.

A conclusion often ends with a final sentence that either generalizes the situation and makes it more universal or looks toward the future. For instance:

> As our world becomes more interconnected through technology and increasingly global outlooks, we must look for every possible way to prepare the next generation for a more international world— a world replete with possibilities, if we are willing to look beyond our already blurring national boundaries and engage with humanity at large.

Of course, many wind up right near the end of the 30 minutes when it comes down to writing a conclusion. So while a new insight would be nice, it may not realistically happen. Don't stress. In general, if you are running out of time or are stuck for a final concluding sentence, try something along the lines of "In order to have a better world in the future, we must do X."

Style Points

Tone: There's no specific rule against saying "I," but don't be too informal. Avoid conversational asides, and don't try to be funny. Keep the tone serious and academic.

Varied diction: Throughout the essay, you will say the same thing several times. Don't use the exact same words! That is, paraphrase yourself. If in the introduction, you wrote, "The most important virtue in a leader is a strong sense of ethics," in your conclusion, you might write, "A strong moral framework is paramount for a leader."

However, don't get excessive about it—if you're writing an essay about the environment, you're definitely going to have to use the word "environment" numerous times. It would be great if you could switch up "environment" every now and then with something like "global ecosystem," but don't get too distractingly creative (Mother Earth, Gaia, the rotating blue orb we call home).

Varied sentence structure: Aim for a mix of long and short sentences. Throw in an occasional semicolon, hyphen, colon, or rhetorical question. For example:

> Is it the case that sacrifice is the noblest of all virtues? Even a cursory analysis ought to indicate that it is not; the greatest of all virtues can hardly be said to be the one with, typically, the least utilitarian value.

Make sure you know how to correctly use any punctuation you decide to include, of course.

Vocabulary: Use GRE-type words in your writing (but only if you're sure you can use them correctly). Some good vocab words to think about are those about arguments themselves, since those will work in nearly any essay. Some examples are: *aver, extrapolate, contend, underpin, claim, hypothesize, rebuttal, postulate, propound, concur.*

Transitions: A top-scoring essay has body paragraphs that lead logically into one another. You can create this chain of logic by arranging your examples or reasons in a progressive way and by using transition phrases and similar signals. The simplest transitions involve phrases such as "On the other hand ..." or "Finally ..." A more sophisticated transition might take the following form:

The obstacles toward international cooperation include not only [the stuff I discussed in my last paragraph], but also [the stuff I'm about to discuss in this paragraph].

Transitions are usually located in the first sentence of a new body paragraph.

Million-dollar quotes: This is by no means mandatory, but it looks great if you can throw in a relevant quote you've memorized. Example:

As Winston Churchill famously said upon assuming control of Parliament and the British war effort: "I have nothing to offer but blood, toil, tears, and sweat." Similarly, great leaders are those who get in the trenches with their people.

At the end of this chapter, you'll find a sample list of quotes that are relevant to a variety of topics. If you like, memorize a few that appeal to you.

Finally, as a reminder: *length* on the GRE essay is highly correlated with scores. If you had a choice between checking your spelling and punctuation and writing another paragraph, it would probably be best to write another paragraph (provided that the paragraph contains an additional idea that contributes to the essay as a whole).

Trouble Getting Started?

Remember, you're writing on a computer. If you freeze when trying to start your introduction, write something else first! Just pick whichever example seems easiest to write and dive in! You can certainly cut and paste as needed. In the worst case, use a starter sentence to turn the engine over in your mind: "This is a dumb idea because ..." or "This is a great idea because ..." Just keep an eye on the clock and make sure you leave enough time for both an intro and a conclusion.

A Note on Proofreading

Very few test-takers will have time for significant proofreading. Keep in mind that the graders are aware of your time constraints. They are not judging your spelling or punctuation, except where it muddies your meaning. In fact, the most important part of proofreading on the GRE is to check that you responded to the specific instructions that were presented in the prompt. Beyond that, just try to put yourself in the shoes of the grader, and check that all of your points are stated clearly. Let the commas fall where they may.

Sample Essays

> **Every nation should require students to study at least one foreign language from the elementary school level through the university level.**
>
> Write a response in which you discuss the extent to which you agree or disagree with the recommendation, and explain your reasoning for the position you take. In developing and supporting your position, describe specific circumstances in which adopting the recommendation would or would not be advantageous and explain how these examples shape your position.

Foreign language study can be a valuable component of a balanced education. So, too, can poetry, economics, or public speaking. But students are individuals, and live in a wide variety of circumstances around the world. It is going too far to say that every nation should require its students to study foreign languages.

Different countries have different needs and circumstances. While many bemoan the lack of international outlook in the United States, it is reasonable to note that most Americans do just fine speaking only one language. Of course, universities, prep schools, and other institutions are still free to make foreign language instruction mandatory, as many do now. In Sweden, however, it is a sound policy to make foreign language mandatory for nearly everyone; Sweden has an excellent school system, free through the university level, and it is clear that Swedish is a minority language, and English has actually become the language of international business in Sweden and throughout Europe. Sweden currently mandates the teaching of English, as it should. If the government did not compel students to learn English, they would struggle to compete in the global job market.

While Sweden has one of the highest standards of living in the world, many nations simply have no ability to provide foreign language instruction, nor does it seem as though such instruction should be the top priority. In many countries, primary schools cost money, and many girls don't get to go to school at all, or must drop out due to lack of funds, early marriage, or their families' needing them to work. If female students in Afghanistan are to receive only a few years of education in their entire lives, it seems absurd to mandate that they learn foreign languages, as this would be a waste of their time and effort. Individual schools and teachers should be free to decide how to best use the limited time available.

Finally, not only are nations different from one another, but so are students. Many students have learning disabilities that make foreign language learning virtually impossible. Even those who don't have such disabilities have individual differences and interests that should be respected. A scientific prodigy who may go on to cure cancer or AIDS ought to be permitted to focus solely on science at least at certain levels of his or her education. For every hour spent learning a foreign language, there is an opportunity cost, something else not being mastered.

Of course, virtually everyone is in favor of a more global outlook, and virtually no one thinks that foreign language study is bad. However, making foreign language instruction mandatory in every nation, at every level of schooling, is unjustifiable. Different nations have different needs, and different individuals have their own capacities and goals. Foreign language study can truly open the world to those who partake, but there are many reasons not to mandate it.

Comments:

This is a moderately lengthy, argument-based essay that takes the somewhat obvious tack of disagreeing with an extreme topic.

The essay contains good transitions at the top of the third and fourth paragraphs, linking a discussion of Sweden to a discussion of poorer nations, and then linking differences among nations to differences among individuals. The examples progress in a logical way.

The language and ideas are clear, and the essay persuades by acknowledging common beliefs on the topic ("virtually everyone is in favor of a more global outlook, and virtually no one thinks that foreign language study is bad") and addressing those beliefs ("there are many reasons not to mandate it"). Also, the essay responds to the specific instruction to describe how the mandate would be advantageous (as in Sweden's case) or not advantageous (as in the case of the United States, learning-disabled children, etc.).

The previous essay is not perfect, but even if it had contained several typos, misspellings, or grammar errors, it would likely receive a 6.

Strong beliefs prevent people from thinking clearly about issues.

Write a response in which you discuss the extent to which you agree or disagree with the claim. In developing and supporting your position, be sure to address the most compelling reasons and/or examples that could be used to challenge your position.

The phrase "strong beliefs" may bring to mind images of heroes, people who have fought valiantly for what they knew to be right, or it may bring to mind images of tyrants, people whose beliefs were so strong (if misguided) that they were able to commit atrocities without regard for others. Whether such figures fall on the right side of history or not, strong beliefs often brook no adjustment and permit no new information to be considered. However, some beliefs are strong for good reason—who is not possessed of a strong belief that the earth is round, for instance? Strong beliefs do prevent people from thinking clearly about issues when those beliefs are based on emotion, group loyalty, or tradition; however, strong beliefs need not cloud our thinking when those beliefs are a genuine product of a logical, ongoing search for truth that is open to revision and new evidence.

Seventeenth-century Italian astronomer Galileo Galilei alleged that the earth moved around the sun, rather than the reverse; for this heliocentric theory he was tried by the Catholic Church, convicted of heresy, and placed under house arrest for the rest of his life. Leaders of the Church held the strong belief that the earth must be at the center of the universe. When presented with evidence that the orbits of the planets seemed to go every which way in this model (yet Galileo's model showed the planets moving, more sensibly, in ellipses), the Church did not admit this new evidence into its thinking. Of course, Galileo himself was possessed of strong beliefs, and although he was forced to publicly recant, he did not actually change his view. Yet Galileo's belief was not dogmatic; it was based on years of astronomical observation and careful calculations. Furthermore, Galileo, a Catholic, began with a geocentric worldview; his very heliocentric position was proof of his willingness to change his mind in the face of new evidence.

While Church leaders possessed strong beliefs that brooked no adjustment, Rene Descartes was a devout religious thinker whose strong beliefs did not cloud his thinking. The purpose of Descartes's famous "I think, therefore I exist" was to create a system of logic that would allow him to clear away that which he only thought he knew (but didn't actually know for sure) so he could logically build a case for his religious belief. Adopting a position of ultimate skepticism, Descartes asserted that all he really knew was that he existed. He then reasoned, logically, from that point. Whether one agrees with Descartes's conclusions, his "Meditations" is a masterwork of clear and rigorous thinking.

Just as Descartes was willing to toss aside all he thought he knew in pursuit of verifiable truth, thinkers on moral issues, such as slavery, have demonstrated that strong beliefs cloud our thinking if we don't admit of new evidence, but can be a force for good if we do. In the United States prior to the Civil War, pro-slavery forces argued that the great society of ancient Athens had been built on a framework of slavery. When presented with new information—such as that Greek slavery was very different from the slavery practiced in the United States or Sojourner Truth's poignant "Ain't I a Woman?" address, reprinted across the nation—most did not change their minds. Of course, some did, and the North had no shortage of outspoken abolitionists. The Civil War was a war of strong belief against strong belief; the side most willing to change its mind in the face of moral argument was, rightfully, the side that won.

All people are created equal, but all strong beliefs are not. Strong beliefs based on evidence and logic are strong beliefs that are nevertheless changeable, and need not muddy our thinking. It is dogmatism that is the enemy, not strength of conviction.

Comments:

This is a lengthy, example-based essay that gives a balanced, nuanced position on the topic. "Strong beliefs prevent people from thinking clearly about issues" is a fairly extreme statement, so a well-developed thesis here is a good strategy. The introduction is long in order to give time to develop that thesis: "Strong beliefs do prevent people from thinking clearly about issues when those beliefs are based on emotion, group loyalty, or tradition; however, strong beliefs need not cloud our thinking when those beliefs are a genuine product of a logical, ongoing search for truth that is open to revision and new evidence."

The first body paragraph is sophisticated—it actually gives two intertwined examples by showing that the Church's strong belief was indefensible, but Galileo's strong belief was justifiable.

The second body paragraph is somewhat weaker, but there is a nice transition between the two paragraphs ("While Church leaders possessed strong beliefs that brooked no adjustment, Rene Descartes ..."), and the writer balanced out an example about religious belief gone wrong with an example of religious belief the writer thinks falls on the other side of the thesis.

The third body paragraph is fine, although it doesn't seem to fit the topic as well as the first two; the writer makes no distinction between "new information" such as astronomical observation and "new information" in a moral sense. However, the slight shift in emphasis allows the writer to incorporate other examples recalled from his or her college course on pre–Civil War U.S. history.

The conclusion flows nicely from the third example (although this is not necessarily expected in an essay). It is brief and to the point and restates the thesis in different words.

Though the essay doesn't really take a side, it does make very clear what the strongest arguments both for and against the prompt are, and thus succeeds adequately in addressing the specific instructions.

The writer's language and main ideas are clear. The second and third examples are not as strong as the first, but this essay's main strengths are its well-developed main idea and sophisticated attempt to validate a two-part thesis with relevant examples.

The previous essay is also not perfect, but would likely receive a 6.

More Sample Issue Essays

For more sample Issue essays—with comments provided by the people who grade the real GRE—see *The Official Guide to the GRE General Test*— Analytical Writing section.

How to Prepare

1. Read a variety of sample essays.

2. Brainstorm examples for a large number of topics from ETS's published topic pool:

   www.ets.org/gre/revised_general/prepare/analytical_writing/issue/pool

3. Write several practice essays under timed conditions, also using topics from ETS's published topic pool. Don't select the topics you most *want* to write about—just scroll down the list and do the first topic you land on, or ask someone else to assign you a topic. Write your practice essays on a computer, using only the functions available to you on the real exam (i.e., turn off spell-check and grammar check).

4. Take a full-length Manhattan Prep GRE practice exam, and don't skip the essay section!

Analyze an Argument

The Analyze an Argument task gives you 30 minutes to plan and write a critique of an argument presented in the form of a short passage. A critique of any other argument will receive a score of zero. To score well, you need to do three things. First, analyze the line of reasoning in the argument (which will always be faulty). Then, explain the logical flaws and assumptions that underlie that reasoning. Finally, you must discuss what the author could add in order to make the conclusion of the argument more logically sound.

It is absolutely critical that you recognize that you are *not* being asked to present your own views on the subject matter of the argument. You are being asked only to discuss how well the author made his argument.

Argument Essay Ground Rules

The topic that you actually see on the real test will be chosen from a list of topics available on ETS's website:

   www.ets.org/gre/revised_general/prepare/analytical_writing/argument/pool

Yes, that's right—you can view all of the possible topics ahead of time. The topic you end up writing about will be one of the ones on the list at this page, possibly with minor wording changes.

Like the Analyze an Issue task, the Analyze an Argument essay requires you to respond to specific instructions. This change was effected in order to obviate the practice of using a pre-written response and simply swapping in words related to the specific argument presented. In *The Official Guide to the GRE General Test*, ETS lists eight possible sets of instructions that could accompany an Argument essay prompt. However, the eight of them are even less interesting than the six provided for the Issue essay! Not one of them demands anything that wouldn't be featured in any successful Argument essay on the given prompt. Here they are, from *The Official Guide to the GRE General Test*. You would be given an argument followed by one of these:

1. Write a response in which you discuss what specific evidence is needed to evaluate the argument, and explain how the evidence would weaken or strengthen the argument.

2. Write a response in which you examine the stated and/or unstated assumptions of the argument. Be sure to explain how the argument depends on these assumptions and what the implications are if the assumptions prove unwarranted.

3. Write a response in which you discuss what questions would need to be answered in order to decide whether the recommendation and the argument on which it is based are reasonable. Be sure to explain how the answers to these questions would help to evaluate the recommendation.

4. Write a response in which you discuss what questions would need to be answered in order to decide whether the advice and the argument on which it is based are reasonable. Be sure to explain how the answers to these questions would help to evaluate the advice.

5. Write a response in which you discuss what questions would need to be answered to decide whether the recommendation is likely to have the predicted result. Be sure to explain how the answers to these questions would help to evaluate the recommendation.

6. Write a response in which you discuss what questions would need to be answered in order to decide whether the prediction and the argument on which it is based are reasonable. Be sure to explain how the answers to these questions would help to evaluate the prediction.

7. Write a response in which you discuss one or more alternative explanations that could rival the proposed explanation and explain how your explanation(s) can plausibly account for the facts presented in the argument.

8. Write a response in which you discuss what questions would need to be addressed in order to decide whether the conclusion and the argument on which it is based are reasonable. Be sure to explain how the answers to the questions would help to evaluate the conclusion.

A well-written essay in which you locate logical flaws in the argument and then explain how they could be fixed will likely score highly. That said, you should, of course, read the specific instructions and make sure that they are addressed, just to be on the safe side.

The Construction of Arguments

It may be helpful to quickly diagram an argument to reveal its structure, similar to the way you take notes for Argument Structure Passages.

When you diagram, the point is to put the conclusion at the top and the supporting arguments (premises) below in a logical way—the way they are being used to support the argument. Sometimes, the diagram will look a bit strange because the argument itself is a bit strange—and therein probably lies a flaw. Feel free to note your questions in parentheses as you go.

Try one:

The town of Arcana should institute an 11 PM curfew for teenagers in order to curb crime and improve academic performance. Many crimes are being committed by young people after dark, and a curfew would both make such crimes impossible, and provide an extra legal offense with which to charge those who do break the law. Furthermore, many young people study less than one hour per night. An 11 PM curfew would improve students' grades.

11 PM curfew for teens will ↓ crime, ↑ GPA

crimes after dark (same as "11 PM"?)	teens study < 1 hr (they're going to start studying at 11 now?)
curfew → "impossible" to commit crimes	
→ extra charge	
(if it's impossible, who would we be charging?!)	

Feel free to make use of a two-column format, liberal use of arrows, etc.—whatever makes visual sense of the argument.

Once you've diagrammed (either on paper or mentally), it's time to brainstorm the flaws. How do you find them? Fortunately, most of the mistakes have been made before …

Argument Essay: Flaws to Watch Out For

The following is a list of common fallacies found in GRE arguments. After you read through the examples and try to find the flaws, practice finding some of them in real GRE arguments.

Note that the list is quite long. You don't have to "get" every one, nor do you have to memorize the list. This is just to get you thinking about some of the kinds of things to look out for. You do not need to memorize the names for the flaws, nor should you actually use the names in your essay. Just deconstruct the argument, pointing out the sorts of things detailed in this list.

In a typical GRE argument, you can expect to find one to five of these flaws. It is also possible that some GRE arguments may possess flaws not listed—as with anything, there are an infinite number of ways to mess something up.

Unjustified assumptions: The argument is based on a questionable assumption. That is, in order for the argument to be true, the author is depending on a premise that he or she didn't write down and hasn't proven. Thus, the conclusion can't be validated unless the assumption(s) can be proved to be true.

> The Urban Apartment Towers complex has seen a number of police visits to the property recently, resulting in the police breaking up loud parties held by young residents and attended by other young people. These police visits and the reputation for loud parties are hurting Urban Apartment Towers' reputation and ability to attract new residents. To reduce the number of police visits and improve profitability, Urban Apartment Towers plans to advertise its vacant apartments in a local publication for people age 50 and up.

What is this argument assuming but not proving? That *people age 50 and up are less likely to have loud parties or attract police visits.* That doesn't sound like a totally unreasonable assumption, but it is an assumption nevertheless, and it is the job of the arguer to prove it (and your job to point out that the arguer hasn't done so). Perhaps older residents would attract visits of another type (e.g., healthcare personnel) that could also impact the reputation of the complex.

Skill and will: The argument assumes that people have the ability (skill) to do something or the motivation (will) to do it, when this has not been proven to be the case. The recommendations that "Everyone should exercise two hours per day" and "Children should be offered green vegetables three times daily" run into

11

problems regarding the ability of people to exercise that much (what about people who are already ill?) and the desire of children to eat the vegetables.

The Urban Apartment Towers argument above also has both a "skill" problem and a "will" problem. Maybe over-50 people in the local area are largely on a fixed income and cannot afford to live in the Towers. And why would they want to? It's not clear that people over 50 have much motivation to live in an apartment complex where the police are always raiding loud parties.

Extreme language: The argument (usually the conclusion) uses language so extreme that the premises cannot justify the conclusion.

> People who jog more than 10 miles per week have a lower incidence of heart disease than people who exercise the same amount on stationary bicycles. Therefore, jogging is the best method of exercise for reducing heart disease.

The conclusion is the final sentence: *Jogging is the best method of exercise for reducing heart disease.* The word *best* is quite extreme! The best method ever? Better than swimming, tennis, and a million other things? Proving that jogging is better than stationary bicycling (and there are some problems with that as well) just proves that jogging is better than one thing, not the best.

Other extreme words to watch out for include the following: *only, never, always, cannot, certainly.*

Terms are too vague: Just as you are on the lookout for language that is too extreme, you're also on the lookout for language that is too vague.

The people who jog argument above has this problem. What on earth does it mean to "exercise the same amount" as someone who is jogging 10 miles? Does it mean biking for the same amount of *time* or the same *distance*? The same number of calories burned? Since it's much faster to ride 10 miles on a stationary bike than to jog 10 miles, if the arguer means that the distances are the same, then there's another reason (besides the author's conclusion) that the joggers have less heart disease: they are exercising more hours per week.

Predicting the future: There's nothing wrong with trying to predict the future, of course; it's hard to run a government (or anything) without doing so. However, whenever an argument tries to predict the future, that's your opportunity to point out that the future could actually turn out some other way. Anyone who tries to predict the future is automatically introducing a level of uncertainty into his or her argument.

> The police chief in Rand City, a major urban metropolis, has proposed cutting down on speeding by doubling the fines levied on those who are caught. Speeding has been a major problem in Rand City, where over 5,000 tickets are issued each month. Of those who are issued tickets, over 95 percent mail in the fines, while less than 1 percent contest the charges in court, thus indicating the offenders' admission of guilt. Doubling the fines for speeding will substantially reduce speeding in Rand City.

The arguer is trying to predict the future: "Doubling the fines for speeding will substantially reduce speeding." To find a weak link in this chain of events, ask yourself what could happen in between the fines doubling and people speeding less. What else could happen? What about the fines double and then people speed just the same but don't pay their tickets? What if the fines are so low already (hence the lack of motivation to contest the charges) that doubling them won't make a difference? You can think of lots of ways that the first part of the conclusion could lead to something other than the second part of the conclusion.

What's their motivation? Whenever an argument is in the form of an advertisement or company announcement, you get to ask, "What's the speaker's motivation?" Is the speaker trying to promote a medication, make a company look good, sell something, or get elected?

The police chief in Rand City argument above potentially has this problem. What motivation does the police chief have in doubling traffic fines? Probably an honest desire to reduce speeding—but maybe a desire to increase the police budget by increasing what has historically been a reliable source of funding.

The troubled analogy: There's nothing wrong with a good analogy, of course, but analogies in GRE arguments are never good. Every time you make an analogy, you're saying that something is like something else—except that it isn't *exactly* like that, or you'd just be talking about the original topic. It's your job to find and exploit the dissimilarities.

> Bowbridge University, a prestigious institution with a long history of educating great scholars and national leaders, launched a distance learning program five years ago. Bowbridge students were very happy with the flexibility afforded to them by the program; for instance, they could continue studying with professors on the Bowbridge campus while conducting research, traveling, or volunteering anywhere in the world. A study showed that the quality of education, as measured by students' grades, did not decrease. Thus, if the tuition-free Local City College implements a distance learning program, student satisfaction will increase without compromising quality of education.

Is Bowbridge Univerisity similar to Local City College? There are a lot of assumptions there. You're told that Bowbridge is prestigious, and that its students travel, volunteer, and conduct research around the world. They sound like a wealthy bunch! The students at the free Local City College? Probably not as wealthy. Maybe they don't even own computers. Do they need distance learning? It's not clear that someone who attends a "local" college would want—or have the means—to attend that college from halfway around the world.

In the end, you don't know that much about Local City College. It's not your job to prove that distance learning *won't* work there; it's your job to point out that the arguer has not established enough similarities to make a good analogy between the two institutions.

Confusing signs of a thing for the thing itself: Medical tests often report false positives, while failing to catch everyone who actually has the disease. The number of people who test positive for a disease is not identical to the number of people who have the disease.

This effect is especially acute when people have an incentive (such as money) to over-report something or an incentive (such as fear or laziness) to under-report something. For instance, reports of crimes such as littering and jaywalking are extremely low, but that doesn't mean people aren't committing those crimes all the time. Reports of whiplash from car accidents tend to be highly inflated, since victims are often in a position to gain money from insurance companies. Reports of workplace harassment may be lower than actual incidents of harassment because workers fear losing their jobs or worsening the problem.

The argument about Bowbridge University has this problem. "The quality of education, as measured by students' grades, did not decrease." Maybe professors grade online students more leniently or give them easier assignments. Grades are not the same as "quality of education."

Another common variation on this problem assumes that because a law exists, people must be following it. *A law is not the same as compliance with a law.* One GRE argument says that the city has instituted water rationing and that local businesses are doing worse, and it concludes that water rationing is hurting businesses. However, the fact that a regulation exists doesn't mean it is being followed—to establish causality, the arguer would first need to show that businesses are even obeying water rationing in the first place (if there's no enforcement, it's entirely likely that at least some businesses would simply ignore rationing).

11

Short term vs. long term: Something that's good in the short term, under certain circumstances (antibiotics, for instance), may not be good for you in the long term. Something that is a good idea in the short term (working all night to rescue people in an emergency) might not even be possible in the long term.

Similarly, something that's good or possible long term may not be good or possible short term. Eating a carrot a day may be beneficial for your eyesight over many years, but it won't help you pass your pilot's exam next week.

> A study of 120 elderly, hospital-bound patients in the United Kingdom showed that daily consumption of Nutree, a nutritional supplement containing vitamins, fiber, and sugar, increased by an average of four months the typical life expectancy for people of the same age and physical condition. Thus, anyone who wants to live longer should drink Nutree every day.

Because 120 elderly, hospital-bound patients did it, you should, too? There are several problems here. (The next three flaws are also about this argument.) First, take a look at short term/long term. People who were already elderly and living in the hospital drank a sugary beverage every day and lived four months longer. The fact that you've already calculated their life expectancy seems to imply that all of the people in the study have already died. Drinking a sugary beverage every day for a short period of time might be beneficial to some people, but what if you start drinking it when you're 25? Maybe that much sugar isn't good for you over several decades.

Sample isn't representative: If the GRE mentions a study, chances are that the sample is not representative. One in the argument pool refers to "French women in their eighties who were nursing-home residents." Wow, what a very specific group! It's your job to point out that what works for French female octogenarians might not work for non-French people, men, and people under 80.

The argument above about the 120 elderly, hospital-bound patients also has this problem.

Sample is too small: If a GRE argument mentions how many people were in a study, it's your job to say that the study should've been bigger. *A study of 120 elderly, hospital-bound patients* is a pretty small study.

No Control Group — A good study should have a control group—that is, a group of people who are as similar as possible in every way, and differ from the test group by only one variable.

You can't just give people a new medicine and measure whether their condition improves; you have to get together a big enough group of people who meet certain conditions (such as having a particular illness at a particular stage), divide the people into two groups (balanced by gender, age, and a host of other factors), and give the drug to only one group. It's important to make sure that the people receiving the drug do not just get *better*, but *better than the other group*. After all, what if it's the sort of illness that goes away on its own? Maybe some outside force (the changing seasons?) will cause improvement in both groups. It's your job to point out when a study lacks a control group, and what impact this might have on the study's findings.

"A study of 120 elderly, hospital-bound patients" makes reference to another group of people of the same age and physical condition, but does not specify whether they are hospital-bound UK residents. Where is the group of elderly, hospital-bound UK residents who did not drink Nutree over the same period of time? Maybe they would also have exceeded "the typical life expectancy for people of the same age and physical condition." Maybe the Nutree is irrelevant, and it was just being in the hospital that kept people alive that extra four months.

The ever-changing pool: Most groups of people have a rotating cast of members. If a civic club voted in favor of something yesterday and against it 20 years ago, you wouldn't automatically conclude that people in the club changed their minds over time; it's pretty likely that the club includes different people than it did back then.

> The following is a letter to the editor of a city newspaper:

> A petition is circulating in our city to oppose the building of a new sports center at State University, on land now occupied by abandoned strip malls. Just five years ago, many city residents opposed the building of the new State University dormitory complex, yet in a poll just this year, 80 percent of respondents said they thought building the dormitory complex was a good idea. If the people who currently oppose the new sports center just wait and see, they will change their minds.

Five years ago, people opposed the new dorm, and now 80 percent of respondents to a poll like the dorm. Are the poll respondents the same population as the people who opposed the project five years ago? (For instance, if the poll was conducted on or near campus, a high percentage of students being polled might skew results.)

Even if the poll were representative of the city's current residents, it's not clear that they are the same residents as five years ago. Maybe some residents disliked the college's expansion plans enough to move out of town. Maybe the new dorm allowed the college to admit significantly more students, thus merely diluting the pool of people who disliked and still dislike the dorm. Remember to look for a "survivor bias"—the people who stuck around didn't hate the dorm enough to leave.

Correlation does not equal causation: Just because two things are happening at the same time doesn't mean one causes the other.

> Researchers have noted that cats that eat Premium Cat Food have healthier coats and less shedding. While Premium Cat Food costs more, the time saved cleaning up pet hair from furniture and rugs makes Premium Cat Food a wise choice.

Two things are happening at the same time: cats are eating Premium food, and they are shedding less. Does that mean the food causes the reduced shedding?

Broadly speaking, there are two other possibilities. First, consider whether the causation could be reversed; that is, the argument states that A causes B, but perhaps B causes A. In this particular case, it's unlikely that a reduction in shedding causes the cats to eat a certain brand of cat food.

Second, a third factor could be causing both A and B. In this case, perhaps a pet owner who is willing to pay for Premium Cat Food is also willing to pay for regular grooming, or for a dietary supplement that helps create healthy skin and fur, or…let your imagine run wild! Perhaps people who pay for Premium Cat Food are also more likely to own special breeds of cats that naturally shed less. This kind of setup—a third factor that could cause both A and B—is very common when an argument makes a causation claim based solely on the fact that two things are correlated.

Nothing is quantified: Sometimes, you can get away with failing to attach numbers to things. Most people would be happy to be healthier or richer, even if you can't measure that exactly. However, quantification (expressing things as numbers) becomes important when you try to argue something like "the eventual savings will outweigh the startup costs." Be on the lookout for this type of situation—you are trying to compare two things that *can* be quantified, but aren't.

11

The Premium Cat Food argument has this problem. "Healthier coats and less shedding" sounds like a nice enough benefit without needing to have numbers attached, but you run into problems with "the time saved cleaning up pet hair from furniture and rugs makes Premium Cat Food a wise choice."

Really? To validate this claim, you would need to know 1) how much more the cat food costs than the cat food the pet owner currently buys, 2) how much time the pet owner spends cleaning up cat hair, and 3) the monetary value of the pet owner's time.

Of course, all of these factors vary from pet owner to pet owner, so even if you could get all the facts and figures, it would certainly not be true that the premium food would be a "wise choice" for everyone.

How was it before? Model Heidi Klum once responded to a fan's question about getting back into shape after pregnancy with the question, "Well, how were you before?" It's hard to judge the present or predict the future without information about the past.

> A youth group applied for and received a permit to use the city park for a Culture Festival, which took place last weekend. On Wednesday, the Environmental Club, a group of local volunteers, visited the park and picked up 435 pieces of trash. The presence of such a quantity of rubbish signals a clear lack of respect for the park. Clearly, the youth group should be denied permits to use the park for any future events.

Here, it is unclear whether the 435 pieces of trash were left by the youth group or whether they were there beforehand. Who counts trash like that anyway? (At least they're quantifying.)

Alternate cause: Just because two things happened in a certain order doesn't mean one caused the other. Could some outside force be the cause?

The 435 pieces of trash argument has this problem. Maybe the trash was left by other groups that used the park (perhaps on Monday or Tuesday before the Environmental Club arrived). There are many possible scenarios. Perhaps the trash was blown in by the wind.

Alike doesn't mean identical: People who (or things that) are alike in some ways are undoubtedly different in others.

> Cetadone, a new therapy for the treatment of addiction to the illegal drug tarocaine, has been proven effective in a study centered around Regis Hospital in the western part of the state of New Portsmouth. The study involved local tarocaine addicts who responded to a newspaper ad offering free treatment. Participants who received cetadone and counseling were 40 percent more likely to recover than were patients assigned to a control group, who received only counseling. Conventional therapies have only a 20 percent recovery rate. Therefore, the best way to reduce deaths from tarocaine overdose throughout all of New Portsmouth would be to fund cetadone therapy for all tarocaine addicts.

Are tarocaine addicts in western New Portsmouth the same as tarocaine addicts in the rest of the state? Perhaps one area is rural and one is urban or the demographics of different parts of the state vary. Furthermore, the addicts in this study seem pretty functional and motivated—they managed to successfully respond to a newspaper ad, and apparently weren't paid, so their motivation seems to have been to recover from addiction. Maybe the addicts who do well on cetadone are not the same addicts in danger of a fatal overdose.

While drug addiction may seem to be a defining feature, the only thing that you can assume is uniform about tarocaine addicts is that they are addicted to tarocaine—anything else is up to the speaker to prove.

Percents vs. real numbers (and other mathematical confusion): If David pays 28 percent of his income in taxes and Marie pays 33 percent of her income in taxes, who pays more money to the government? Without knowing how much the two people make, it's impossible to say. Don't confuse percents with actual numbers of dollars, people, etc.

The cetadone argument has big-time math issues. Certainly, 40 percent looks like a higher number than 20 percent. And there are no real numbers of people here anywhere, so you're not confusing a percent with a real number.

However, the 20 percent is an actual *recovery rate for* conventional therapies. The 40 percent is a *percent increase on an unknown figure*—the recovery rate of the control group (which received counseling—not necessarily a conventional therapy). You have no way to compare this 40 percent increase to an actual 20 percent recovery rate. For instance, what if the control group had a 50 percent recovery rate? Then the cetadone group would have a 70 percent recovery rate (1.4×50). But what if the control group had a 1 percent recovery rate? Then the cetadone group would have a 1.4 percent recovery rate, making it much less successful than conventional therapies.

In sum, if any numbers are presented in an Argument topic, see whether they are being cited in a logical way. This is the exact same reasoning about percents and percent change that you will need for the Data Interpretation part of the exam (and of course, the math on the actual Quant section is much harder than anything that would ever occur in an essay topic), so it pays in numerous ways to have a solid knowledge of percents.

Don't Forget to Strengthen the Argument: Just Flip the Flaw

Some sets of Argument essay instructions ask you to strengthen the argument. To discuss in your essay how the argument might be strengthened, just flip the flaw around. For instance:

Nothing is quantified?

This argument could be improved by quantifying X, Y, and Z . . .

Possible alternate causes?

This argument could be improved by investigating and ruling out alternate causes such as . . .

Correlation does not equal causation?

This argument could be improved by proving that X causes Y through a controlled study . . .

No control group, nonrepresentative sample, too-small sample?

This argument could possibly be validated by a new study having the following qualities . . .

Brainstorming the Argument Essay

Look back at the list of flaws, and try to find several that apply to the following argument:

Invoice Regulators, Inc. (IRI) can make your company more profitable. IRI examines our client firms' outgoing invoices and vendor receipts to help clients recoup money owed and refunds due. One client, a family firm with a 100-year history, discovered $75,000 worth of uncashed checks in an employee's desk drawer, and others have also made large gains. 80 percent of our client firms have experienced an increase in sales during the quarter our services were acquired. Hire IRI to improve your firm's profitability.

Did you make your own list of flaws? Jot some down before you keep reading.

Here's an example for this argument:

Correlation does not equal causation: So 80 percent of client firms had a sales increase around the time IRI was hired. So what? Firms often have sales increases; one thing didn't necessarily cause the other.

Alike doesn't mean identical/unjustified assumptions: The argument assumes that other businesses have outgoing invoices in the first place and that, quite frankly, the business owners are a bit incompetent. It does not seem likely that the "family firm with a 100-year history" and a drawer full of forgotten money is representative of other companies. There are **small sample/unrepresentative sample** issues here as well.

Short term vs. long term: The promise to "make your company more profitable" implies an ongoing financial improvement. The two cases cited seem temporary—the $75,000 is a one-shot deal, and the "increase in sales during the quarter" makes no mention of some improved, systemic way to enhance ongoing profitability.

Terms are too vague/nothing is quantified: Other clients have "made large gains." How large? Big enough to offset the cost (which was never mentioned) of IRI's services? What percent of clients experience the large gains?

What's their motivation? Obviously, this is an advertisement. But it doesn't hurt to point out that IRI clearly has its own financial interests in mind here.

There is also another big problem that isn't named in this chapter, but is specific to this argument:

Confusing sales with profitability: Here, the argument confuses increased profitability (which is at least temporarily achievable by cashing a drawer full of checks or chasing refunds) with sales. Perhaps IRI costs more than the sales increase and would thus hurt profitability.

Once you've identified the flaws, make a quick outline. (Don't use the names for the flaws—just write down what you're going to say.)

If you have more than four or so flaws to write about, you may wish to group any that are very similar or simply omit the weakest.

You also want to put your ideas in a logical order so that your argument is persuasive and so that you can write nice transitions from one idea to the next.

Here is one sample outline:

   the "checks in the drawer" client ≠ representative of other potential clients

      idiots!
      even if not idiots, one biz is insufficient evidence
      not all biz even have outgoing invoices

   claims of "other biz" are vague, nothing quantified
      gains big enough to outweigh costs of IRI? (what ARE costs of IRI?)

   claims of enhanced profitability even for existing clients are suspect
      sales ≠ profitability
      sales "in same quarter"—not even clear it's AFTER IRI
      even if it were, correlation ≠ causation!

   "profitability" implies ongoing

If this seems like a lot to write before even getting started typing, don't worry—we wrote more here than you would probably write, since you'll be able to skip anything you know you'll remember.

Make sure that you're not just throwing disconnected ideas on the page. Remember the **dinner table test** from the section on the Issue essay. Make sure that, in deconstructing a bad argument, you yourself are making a good argument.

The following is an argument from a "debater" perspective (this isn't something you'd actually write down, since you're about to type the real essay, but your outline should reflect a coherent argument that you've formed mentally before you begin to write):

  I.   Just because hiring IRI has been profitable for some clients doesn't mean it would be profitable for others.

  II. However, it's not even clear that IRI *has* been profitable for anyone, since we don't have any actual numbers to quantify most of the firms' gains, and we don't know what it costs to hire IRI.

  III. The claims of profitability for existing clients are also suspect because IRI has confused sales with profitability, taking credit for something that is irrelevant to IRI's services and that possibly even began before IRI was hired.

  IV. Profitability implies an ongoing financial improvement. IRI fails to define the period. A one-shot cash infusion is not the same thing as enhanced profitability.

These statements are the parts of the argument each body paragraph will make. Note how the order seems "right"—it goes from arguing that IRI won't be profit-enhancing for everyone to questioning whether it's profit enhancing for anyone at all. Statements II and III make the same point from different angles and clearly should come one after the other.

The outline/argument above leaves out the question "What's their motivation?" (the idea that, because the text is from an ad, the speaker is biased). This point seems way too obvious to write an entire paragraph about, although mentioning it would be perfectly appropriate in an introduction. Also note that the outline says, "idiots!" Feel free to write stuff like this in your own notes, but don't use that type of language on the GRE. In writing the real essay, you would say something about "a possibly incompetent employee."

Note that there is no thesis written down. The thesis for an Argument essay will pretty much always be something like, "The argument rests on questionable assumptions, suffers from vaguely defined terms, and contains numerous logical flaws that make it impossible to validate the conclusion."

About timing: On the real test, you should spend 2–3 minutes on the entire process of diagramming, brainstorming flaws, and organizing your thoughts into a coherent and persuasive outline. However, for now, it would be reasonable to take a bit more time (say, 5 or 6 minutes), knowing that with practice you'll get better and faster at spotting flaws.

A brief mention of specific instructions: While the specific instructions may ask you to add something into your essay that you wouldn't necessarily have included otherwise, there shouldn't be any need to radically change an essay from the standard format described here in order to obey the specific instructions. Generally, adding a single sentence to each paragraph, or even a few words, will suffice. For example, one set of instructions says this:

> Write a response in which you discuss what questions would need to be answered in order to decide whether the prediction and the argument on which it is based are reasonable. Be sure to explain how the answers to these questions would help to evaluate the prediction.

Notice that the instructions don't really recommend anything that a well-written essay wouldn't do anyway. Therefore, feel free to write your outline without even worrying about the instructions, then simply check to be sure that there will be space to include whatever little details the specific instructions requested (five out of eight of the specific instruction prompts involve responding to "questions that need to be answered," for example).

About brainstorming practice: Some practice with brainstorming will also speed up the process. You may find some flaws seem to occur more often than others (that's definitely true). If you find yourself brainstorming or writing three "correlation does not equal causation" essays in a row, there's nothing wrong with that. The GRE writers implant the same flaws into their argument topics over and over.

You can practice brainstorming by visiting this link and exploring the pool:

www.ets.org/gre/revised_general/prepare/analytical_writing/argument/pool

Try diagramming the argument, finding flaws, and organizing an outline, as described above, for some of the topics listed.

Don't just pick out the topics that you most want to write about! Force yourself to start at the beginning, or scroll down a bit and do the first topic you see.

Okay. You've done a bunch of preparation. Next up: how to write this thing.

Argument Essay Outline

I. Introduction: In the intro, summarize the argument at hand and give your "take." Do not repeat the argument; the grader is already very familiar with it.

> Candidates for office are often prompted to make unlikely promises to gain support. While it is clear that the people of Brownsville would like more jobs to be created, it is unlikely that the mayoral candidate's plan will bring about the intended effect.

You are then going to establish your "take" or thesis. Unlike in the Issue essay, where you were instructed to brainstorm both sides and construct a sophisticated, nuanced main idea, here your main idea is much easier. It's pretty much always going to say that the argument has some serious problems:

> While the mayor's goals may be admirable, his plan rests on a number of unjustified assumptions and fails to take into account other factors affecting job creation in a seaside resort town.

Another example of an introduction paragraph:

> A study has recorded a variety of health benefits occurring at the same time as the consumption of soy beverage by a small, homogeneous study group. While it may be the case that drinking 12 ounces of soy beverage per day slows the progress of arthritis, the study presented does not actually prove this to be the case; the study's limited sample size, lack of a control group, and confusion of reported symptoms with internal body processes all serve to seriously compromise the study's conclusion.

Notice that each of these main ideas began with acknowledging some small positive—at least the mayor's intentions are good! Soy beverage *might* still be beneficial! This is a good way to add some nuance to your main idea.

II. Body: Explain one main point in each of two to four paragraphs.

Each of the flaws you decided to write about should become the main point of a body paragraph. Or if you decide to group more than one flaw into a paragraph, make sure that the two flaws are very closely and logically related; for instance, "the sample size is too small" and "the sample is not representative" are good candidates to be grouped into a single paragraph. Generally, though, keep it to one main point per paragraph. GRE graders have given high scores to Argument essays that include as many as six body paragraphs—in such cases, many of the body paragraphs are quite short.

Arrange your main points in a logical way, and use **transitions** to segue from paragraph to paragraph. Transitions are usually located in the first sentence of a new body paragraph. For instance, if you have just written a paragraph about how a study's sample size was too small and not representative, you might begin the next paragraph with something like:

> Not only should it be apparent that a study based on a sample of 80 Korean women is not necessarily applicable to humanity at large, it is also the case that, due to the lack of a control group, we are unable to evaluate the results of the study for even this extremely limited sample.

Here, the example segues from talking about the sample's size and makeup to talking about a problem related to working even within the small and limited sample. This is a logical progression of ideas; the use of such transitions throughout an essay creates a sense of coherence and fluency.

Don't forget to **improve the argument**. There are (at least) three possible ways to arrange your argument to incorporate this component:

1. Each time you mention a flaw, follow up with how to fix it. The "improve the argument" component would therefore be part of each body paragraph.

2. Write two or more body paragraphs about the argument's flaws, and follow up with one body paragraph on how to fix those flaws.

3. Use the body paragraphs entirely to discuss the flaws, and save the discussion of how to fix those flaws for the conclusion. This may be the best plan for anyone frequently stuck for a conclusion. Keeping the "improve the argument" component brief is also a good way to keep from sounding repetitive.

Don't spend too much time making a single point or you will run out of time!

III. Conclusion: In the conclusion, resummarize your critique. The conclusion does not have to be lengthy: restate your thesis or main idea in different words, and state or restate what would need to be done to improve the argument. Ending with ideas for improvement gives a nice, positive note at the end:

> The candidate for mayor who proposed bringing a big-box home improvement store to Brownsville may have been motivated by the admirable goal of creating jobs in an economically distressed area. However, the candidate failed to take into account job loss from local hardware stores that would likely be run out of business, as well as the cost to the city of tax incentives that are likely to outweigh the store's economic boost. If we are to believe in the candidate's plan—and the candidate—further research and more rigorous quantification will be required.

Ideally, the conclusion should sum things up while offering some special perspective or insight. In any case, try to avoid having your conclusion sound repetitive. If in doubt, keep it short.

Style Points

11

Debate team persuasion tactics: It's possible to say something in a way that is not very persuasive or in a way that is. Say you are trying to argue against the school superintendent's plan for year-round school:

1. The superintendent has not proven that her plan will achieve the goal of improving academic performance. However, it may serve the function of reducing crime.

2. While the superintendent's plan may indeed reduce crime, she has not proven that her plan will achieve the stated goal of improving academic performance.

Which version sounds worse for the superintendent? The last one, right? *If you have two opposing things to say, put the one that's on your side last.* This makes the one that isn't on your side seem less important. The order should be 1) concession, then 2) your assertion.

If you have a fairly weak point, use that point's weakness to your advantage to emphasize how strong your next point is. For instance, say you were only able to come up with three flaws for a particular argument, and one of them is pretty weak, but you can't toss it out because then you wouldn't have enough to write about. Put the weakest point in the middle (if that won't disrupt the flow of the argument), and use it to underscore the final, biggest point.

For instance, say your second (weak) point is that the company president is trying to predict the future, and no one can really predict the future. Say your third (strong) point is that the company president is basing his predictions on an analogy with another company—and that company is completely different from his own company. Here's a snippet of that essay (the entire second paragraph and the beginning of the third), written in a persuasive way:

> The company president's argument is also weak because it attempts to predict the future, and to predict it absolutely. He even goes so far as to say that the company will "certainly" meet its sales target. But what if the lead salesperson gets sick, or what if a nationwide crisis suddenly causes sales to plummet? The president's conclusion is dubious because he is making an unwisely extreme assertion that simply cannot be validated.

> Even if we were to accept the presence of some uncertainty in predicting the future, the most grave flaw in the president's argument is its dependence on a highly questionable analogy . . .

The second paragraph isn't wonderful. But notice how it is set up to create a nice transition into the third, stronger paragraph. You do this all the time when you're arguing in real life: "But if that's not good enough for you, try this!"

Tone: There's no rule against saying "I," but don't be too informal. Avoid conversational asides, and don't try to be funny. Keep the tone serious and academic. When you're referring to an argument and it's not clear who's talking, you can refer to that person as "the speaker."

Varied diction: Throughout the essay, you will say the same thing several times. Don't use the exact same words. That is, paraphrase yourself. Let's say in the introduction, you wrote:

> While it is indisputable that a new train line would create some new jobs in Arrin City, the mayor's argument that the train line will improve the city's overall financial health is flawed due to a variety of counterfactors, including possible job loss in other sectors, that the mayor has neglected to take into account.

Then in your conclusion, you might write:

> The mayor's contention that a new train line would improve the city's financial health is sadly misguided; while undoubtedly there would be some benefits, such as new jobs directly serving the train line, the financial benefit of those jobs would likely be dwarfed by other financial losses sustained in the wake of the train line's implementation.

Note that "undoubtedly" has been switched in for "indisputable," and the three ideas in the sentence have been shuffled ("some new jobs, mayor is wrong, other factors" vs. "mayor is wrong, some new jobs, other factors").

However, while you do want to avoid saying "indisputable" over and over when there are so many other good words (undeniable, unquestionable, irrefutable, incontrovertible, indubitable) you could use in its place, don't worry about repeating words such as "train" and "mayor." There's absolutely nothing wrong with using the word "train" many, many times in an essay about whether a new train line should be built.

Varied sentence structure: Aim for a mix of long and short sentences. Throw in an occasional semicolon, colon, hyphen, or rhetorical question.

Vocabulary: Use GRE-type words in your writing (but only if you're sure you can use them correctly). Some good vocab words to think about are those about arguments themselves, since those will work in nearly any essay. Some examples:

> *aver, extrapolate, contend, underpin, claim, hypothesize, rebuttal, postulate, propound, concur*

Transitions: A top-scoring essay has body paragraphs that lead logically into one another. You can create this chain of logic by arranging your examples or reasons in a progressive way and by using transition phrases and similar signals. The simplest transitions involve phrases such as "On the other hand . . ." or "Finally . . ." A more sophisticated transition might take the form:

> In addition to the loss of income from tolls paid by drivers, another potential loss of income to the city is from parking fees.

Transitions are usually located in the first sentence of a new body paragraph.

Finally, as a reminder: *length* on the GRE essay is highly correlated with scores. Write as much as you can in the time allotted. If you had a choice between painstakingly checking your spelling and writing another paragraph, it would probably be best to write another paragraph.

Trouble getting started? Remember, you're writing on a computer. If you freeze when trying to start your introduction, write something else first. Just pick whichever body paragraph seems easiest to write and dive in! You can certainly cut and paste as needed. In the worst case, use a "starter" sentence to turn the engine over in your mind: "This is a dumb idea because . . ." or "This is a great idea because . . ." Just keep an eye on the clock, and make sure you leave enough time for both an intro and a conclusion.

A note on proofreading: Very few test-takers will have time for significant proofreading. Keep in mind that the graders are aware of your time constraints. They are not judging your spelling or punctuation, except where it muddies your meaning. In fact, the most important part of proofreading on the GRE is to check that you responded to the specific instructions that were presented in the prompt. Beyond that, focus on making sure your points are clear.

Sample Essays

> **Invoice Regulators, Inc. (IRI) can make your company more profitable. IRI examines our client firms' outgoing invoices and vendor receipts to help clients recoup money owed and refunds due. One client, a family firm with a 100-year history, discovered $75,000 worth of uncashed checks in an employee's desk drawer, and others have also made large gains. Eighty percent of our client firms have experienced an increase in sales during the quarter our services were acquired. Hire IRI to improve your firm's profitability.**
>
> Write a response in which you discuss what questions would need to be answered in order to decide whether the recommendation and the argument on which it is based are reasonable. Be sure to explain how the answers to these questions would help evaluate the recommendation.

One ought to consider the claims of any advertisement with skepticism, and the entreaty to acquire Invoice Regulators' services is no different. IRI offers to examine a firm's invoices and receipts, and asserts that these services will enhance profitability. The argument is dubious; it rests on a questionable analogy, suffers from a lack of quantification, confuses sales with profitability, and makes unwarranted claims of causality.

IRI's ad relates the peculiar story of a company employee who neglected to cash $75,000 in checks. We don't know anything else about this company, or whether what worked for that type of business would work for other types of businesses—some types of businesses, such as retail stores, collect money on the spot, so it is unclear whether IRI's services could enhance such firms' profitability. However, we need not even go that far—very few employees could forget $75,000 in a desk drawer, and very few firms would need outside assistance to notice that such a sum had gone missing. But are there any other businesses that have had similar lucky discoveries because of IRI's help? The argument fails to extend the analogy from this "family firm with a 100-year old history" to any other types of businesses, or even to more competently managed businesses of the same type.

One might object that IRI has made "large gains" for other clients. However, this claim is vague. What are "large gains"? What kind of companies were these, and would their results apply to other companies? This claim utterly lacks quantification, an argumentative offense made all the more egregious when we consider that "gains" are not the same as "profitability." For the gains to translate into profitability, we would need to know the cost of IRI's services and whether the gains outweigh the cost.

IRI goes on to claim that 80 percent of clients achieved an increase in sales. However, just because increased sales happened around the same time as hiring IRI does not mean that IRI is responsible for the sales. The ad never explains how reviewing invoices and receipts could have an effect on sales. Is there any evidence to directly link the increase in sales to IRI's intervention? In fact, the ad doesn't even say that the sales increase happened after IRI was hired—just "in the same quarter." Maybe the causal relationship actually runs the opposite way—perhaps it was the increased sales that gave the companies the funds to hire IRI in the first place.

IRI is soliciting new clients based on an advertisement that makes an extremely weak analogy from a single case study, fails to quantify gains made or costs incurred by clients, confuses sales and profit, and assumes a model of causality for which there is no evidence. To better evaluate IRI's argument, the reader would need to know whether IRI has helped businesses similar to her own and whether IRI's success at those companies could be reasonably predicted to be repeated, as well as the cost of IRI's services so that the two costs could be weighed. The ad would be further improved by the omission of the irrelevant claim about sales; perhaps the space could be better used to quantify other claims central to evaluating IRI's services.

Comments:

This is a fairly lengthy essay that comprehensively covers the errors made in the argument. The language is clear, and the main idea ("The argument is dubious; it rests on a questionable analogy, suffers from a lack of quantification, confuses sales with profitability, and makes unwarranted claims of causality") gives a good road map of the rest of the essay.

The transitions between paragraphs are nice, especially "One might object …" which astutely anticipates the objection that more than one company was mentioned, but then points out that the mention was so vague as to be useless.

The coverage of causality in the third body paragraph was good, especially the counterexample ("perhaps it was the increased sales that gave the companies the funds to hire IRI in the first place").

The conclusion thoroughly covers how the argument could be improved, including the omission of irrelevant claims.

Notice how each body paragraph presents at least one question that the author of the argument would need to address, as requested in the specific instructions.

This essay, while not perfect, would likely score a 6, even if it had several typos or errors.

The following appeared as a letter to the editor of National Issues magazine in the country of Ganadia.

Last month, *National Issues* ran an article about the decline—as measured by shrinking populations and the flight of young people—of small towns in Ganadia. Here in Lemmontown, a small resort town on the ocean, we are seeing just the opposite: citizens from the neighboring towns of Armontown and Gurdy City are moving here at a record rate. Furthermore, greater than ever numbers of high school graduates in Lemmontown are choosing to stay in Lemmontown, as the building of new hotels has created a significant number of jobs. All along the eastern seaboard are similar stories. Small towns in Ganadia are not in decline.

Write a response in which you discuss one or more alternative explanations that could rival the proposed explanation, and explain how your explanation(s) can plausibly account for the facts presented in the argument.

A letter to the editor of *National Issues* magazine takes issue with the magazine's claim that small towns in Ganadia are declining. It seems that the writer is from a small town that is not declining. Of course, the magazine's contention was almost certainly that small towns, on average, are declining; a single counterexample does not disprove that claim. The arguments' other flaws stem from the same central problem: Lemmontown is just one town, and not necessarily a very representative one.

11

The writer explains that Lemmontown is a resort town on the ocean. Resort towns depend on income flowing in from visitors, and the seaside (or whatever else visitors are there to see) is an asset that most towns do not have. These atypical resort assets are directly cited as the driver behind the jobs that are keeping young people in Lemmontown. Non-resort towns would not likely experience a similar effect. To set the argument on more sound footing, the writer would need to demonstrate that Lemmontown is typical of other Ganadian towns.

Of course, the writer does mention two other towns: Armontown and Gurdy City. While the writer means to cite those towns as evidence that Lemmontown is doing well, he or she inadvertently weakens the argument by giving two counterexamples: both Armontown and Gurdy City are losing residents, in accordance with the trend cited by *National Issues*. In fact, of the three towns the writer references, two of them are losing people. To strengthen the argument, the writer would have to prove that there are more Lemmontowns (so to speak) than Armontowns and Gurdy Cities, or that Armontown and Gurdy City are not small towns.

Finally, the writer points out that "all along the eastern seaboard are similar stories." This assertion is vague. Are there enough stories of non-declining small towns to outweigh accounts of declining small towns? The claim lacks quantification. Also, the eastern seaboard is not necessarily representative of the rest of Ganadia. Perhaps the seaboard is full of thriving resort towns, but the bulk of Ganadia's small towns exist in the interior and on the west coast, where conditions are worse. To validate his or her claims, the writer would need to quantify the claim that eastern seaboard success stories are more numerous than accounts of small towns in decline.

The letter to the editor takes exception to a general claim by providing a specific exception. One anecdote does not make an argument. The argument as written fails to establish that Lemmontown's happy situation is representative of Ganadian towns at large.

Comments:

This is a moderately lengthy essay that effectively takes apart the writer's attempt to use an anecdote to disprove a general trend. "The arguments' other flaws stem from the same central problem" is an apt description and ties the essay into a coherent whole.

The essay follows the structure of detailing a problem in each body paragraph and then offering suggestions for improving the argument within the same paragraph. Thus, the conclusion is fairly short, which is fine.

The language is clear, and adequate transitions between body paragraphs are provided.

Notice that each paragraph succeeds in giving an alternative explanation for a given fact, as requested in the specific instructions.

This essay, while not perfect, would likely score a 6.

More Sample Argument Essays

For more sample Argument essays—with comments provided by the people who grade the real GRE—see *The Official Guide to the GRE General Test*—Analytical Writing section.

How to Prepare

1. Read a variety of sample essays.

2. Brainstorm a large number of topics from ETS's published topic pool:

   www.ets.org/gre/revised_general/prepare/analytical_writing/argument/pool

3. Write several practice essays under timed conditions, also using topics from ETS's published topic pool. Don't select the topics you most *want* to write about—just scroll down the list and do the first topic you land on, or ask someone else to assign you a topic. Write your practice essays on a computer, using only the functions available to you on the real exam (i.e., turn off spell-check and grammar check).

4. Take a full-length Manhattan Prep GRE practice exam, and don't skip the essay section!

GRE Issue Essay Quotes

An excellent way to go above and beyond on the Issue essay is to strategically deploy a relevant quote. The following quotes by notable thinkers have been selected for brevity as well as for relevance to common GRE essay themes: just government, human virtues, altruism, the value of progress, the purpose of education, etc.

Try completing several practice essays while "cheating" off this guide; you're looking to drop one quote per essay, usually in the introduction or conclusion.

While writing practice essays, see which quotes appeal to you and seem easy to memorize. Your goal for this activity is to memorize a few of your favorite quotes such that you'll be able to make one of them fit on test day. That said, **do not stress** about having a quote—if this feels unnatural or cumbersome to you, feel free to skip it.

Albert Einstein (German-born theoretical physicist):
"Any intelligent fool can make things bigger, more complex, and more violent. It takes a touch of genius—and a lot of courage—to move in the opposite direction."
"Two things are infinite: the universe and human stupidity, and I'm not sure about the universe."

Calvin Coolidge (30th U.S. President, advocate of small government):
"The world is full of educated derelicts."
"The slogan 'Press on' has solved and always will solve the problems of the human race."

Samuel Beckett (Irish avant-garde writer, highly minimalist, known for bleak outlook):
"We lose our hair, our teeth! Our bloom, our ideals."
"What do I know of man's destiny? I could tell you more about radishes."
"Nothing happens, nobody comes, nobody goes, it's awful."
"There's man all over for you, blaming on his boots the fault of his feet."
"The tears of the world are a constant quality. For each one who begins to weep, somewhere else another stops."

Oscar Wilde (Irish writer and prominent aesthete):
"The public have an insatiable curiosity to know everything. Except what is worth knowing."
"Democracy means simply the bludgeoning of the people by the people for the people."
"Discontent is the first step in the progress of a man or a nation."

11

Camille Paglia (modern-day American author, professor, "dissident feminist"):
"Education has become a prisoner of contemporaneity. It is the past, not the dizzy present, that is the best door to the future."
"Popular culture is the new Babylon, into which so much art and intellect now flow."

Martin Luther King, Jr. (American pastor, leader in African-American civil rights movement):
"We may have all come on different ships, but we're in the same boat now."
"He who passively accepts evil is as much involved in it as he who helps to perpetrate it."
"The question is not whether we will be extremists, but what kind of extremists we will be."
"Freedom is never voluntarily given by the oppressor; it must be demanded by the oppressed."
"Everybody can be great ... because anybody can serve."
"Injustice anywhere is a threat to justice everywhere."

Voltaire (French Enlightenment writer, philosopher, advocate of civil liberties):
"As long as people believe in absurdities they will continue to commit atrocities."
"It is hard to free fools from the chains they revere."
"I disapprove of what you say, but I will defend to the death your right to say it."
"It is dangerous to be right when the government is wrong."

Julius Caesar (Roman general, statesman, author of Latin prose):
"Men willingly believe what they wish."
"As a rule, men worry more about what they can't see than about what they can."

Virgil (classical Roman poet):
"Who asks whether the enemy were defeated by strategy or valor?"
"Evil is nourished and grows by concealment."

Franz Kafka (20th-century existentialist fiction writer, author of *The Trial* and *Metamorphosis*):
"There are questions we could not get past if we were not set free from them by our very nature."

Winston Churchill (led the UK during World War II):
"I have nothing to offer but blood, toil, tears, and sweat."
"Without victory there is no survival."

Napoleon Bonaparte (French military and political leader during the French Revolution):
"Men are moved by two levers only: fear and self-interest."
"A people which is able to say everything becomes able to do everything."
"Greatness be nothing unless it be lasting."

Jean-Paul Sartre (20th-century French existentialist writer/philosopher):
"Once you hear the details of victory, it is hard to distinguish it from a defeat."
"I hate victims who respect their executioners."
"All human actions are equivalent ... and all are on principle doomed to failure."
"Hell is other people." (from the play *No Exit*)

John F. Kennedy (35th U.S. President):
"Do not pray for easy lives. Pray to be stronger men."
"Efforts and courage are not enough without purpose and direction."

Theodore Roosevelt (26th U.S. President):
"Far and away the best prize that life offers is the chance to work hard at work worth doing."

Woodrow Wilson (28th U.S. President, leading intellectual of the Progressive era):
"No nation is fit to sit in judgment upon any other nation."

Ralph Waldo Emerson (19th-century American transcendentalist author, proponent of individualism):
"It is said that the world is in a state of bankruptcy, that the world owes the world more than the world can pay."
"Can anything be so elegant as to have few wants, and to serve them one's self?"

Daniel Webster (leading American statesman during antebellum period):
"Liberty exists in proportion to wholesome restraint."
"A mass of men equals a mass of opinions."
"Whatever government is not a government of laws, is a despotism, let it be called what it may."

Tom Stoppard (20th-century playwright renowned for use of humor):
"Life is a gamble, at terrible odds—if it was a bet, you wouldn't take it."

Sinclair Lewis (20th-century American novelist, author of *Babbitt*):
"Pugnacity is a form of courage, but a very bad form."

Thomas Jefferson (3rd U.S. President, author of Declaration of Independence):
"The will of the people is the only legitimate foundation of any government, and to protect its free expression should be our first object."

Florence Nightingale (English nurse, came to prominence tending to soldiers during Crimean War):
"I think one's feelings waste themselves in words; they ought all to be distilled into actions which bring results."
"How very little can be done under the spirit of fear."
"The martyr sacrifices themselves entirely in vain. Or rather not in vain; for they make the selfish more selfish, the lazy more lazy, the narrow narrower."

Virginia Woolf (20th-century English modernist writer, author of *To the Lighthouse*):
"Really, I don't like human nature unless all candied over with art."

Socrates (ancient Greek philosopher, teacher of Plato):
"Life contains but two tragedies. One is not to get your heart's desire; the other is to get it."
"The only good is knowledge and the only evil is ignorance."
"From the deepest desires often comes the deadliest hate."
"I am not an Athenian, nor a Greek, but a citizen of the world."
"Nothing is to be preferred before justice."
"Let him that would move the world, first move himself."

11

John Locke (17th-century English philosopher influential in the Enlightenment):
"The actions of men are the best interpreters of their thoughts."

Thomas Hobbes (17th-century English philosopher):
"Leisure is the mother of Philosophy."
"The life of man: solitary, poor, nasty, brutish, and short."

Henry David Thoreau (transcendentalist writer, author of *Walden*):
"The mass of men lead lives of quiet desperation."
"Distrust any enterprise that requires new clothes."
"If you have built castles in the air, your work need not be lost; that is where they should be. Now put the foundations under them."

Immanuel Kant (18th-century German philosopher):
"Out of timber so crooked as that from which man is made nothing entirely straight can be carved."
"Live your life as though your every act were to become a universal law."

Gertrude Stein (avant-garde American writer who lived as an expatriate in France):
"Money is always there but the pockets change."

Mohandas Gandhi (political and spiritual leader of Indian Independence Movement):
"There is more to life than simply increasing its speed."
"God comes to the hungry in the form of food."
"Non-cooperation with evil is as much a duty as is cooperation with good."
"I suppose leadership at one time meant muscles; but today it means getting along with people."

William Shakespeare (16th-century poet, playwright, and actor):
"There's small choice in rotten apples." (From *The Taming of the Shrew*)
"Sweets grown common lose their dear delight." (From *Sonnet 102*)
"The worst is not, so long as we can say, 'This is the worst.'" (From *King Lear*)
"When sorrows come, they come not single spies, but in battalions." (From *Hamlet*)

UNIT FOUR

Vocabulary

This unit provides students with a comprehensive approach to learning vocabulary, as well as a number of specialized lists not found elsewhere, including idioms and metaphorical language, vocabulary particularly applicable to Reading Comprehension, and roots.

In This Unit ...

- Chapter 12: Learning Vocabulary

- Chapter 13: Idioms & Metaphorical Language

- Chapter 14: Vocabulary & Reading Comprehension

- Chapter 15: Roots List

Learning Vocabulary

In This Chapter ...

- Practical Strategies and Games for Learning Vocabulary

- Flash Card Games and Activities

- Use Roots Ahead of Time

- Using Social Media to Buttress Your Vocabulary Studies

CHAPTER 12 Learning Vocabulary

Test-takers' success on Text Completion and Sentence Equivalence is often tied to their mastery of vocabulary, but that doesn't mean you should memorize a large number of obscure words.

Many students want to know *how many* words they have to learn in order to get a high score on the GRE, but it is not so simple as that.

Imagine this: You tell us you know everyone in your university graduating class! All 2,000 people! Well, how can we test this astounding assertion? One good way would be to start by picking 10 reasonably well-known students and seeing if you know them. If you do, then we'll pick 10 very shy students, rarely seen around campus, and see if you know them, too. If you know all 20 randomly selected students, then we would be inclined to believe your assertion that you know all 2,000 people, or some number very close.

That's what the GRE is doing. They're not testing you on a couple hundred words because they want you to know those couple hundred words. They're testing you on 100+ easier words in the first Verbal section, and then if you do well, they're testing you on 100+ harder words in the second Verbal section. If you do well at all the words they hit you with, the GRE is assuming you have a much larger vocabulary than was actually tested and rewarding you for it.

It would be a truly pointless process if you could simply memorize the dictionary definitions of 1,000 vocabulary words, be tested on those words using the definitions you memorized, and then get a good GRE score and forget about those words. That's not going to happen. Students who try it end up disappointed. (We suspect that these are the same students who spent all of school asking, "Is this going to be on the test?")

Quite frankly, when you learn words for the GRE, you are trying to trick the test into thinking that, for the past 10+ years of your life, you have been the model English student who looked up all the words you didn't know in *The Scarlet Letter* and *The Great Gatsby*. It will also seem like you spent four years reading university-level material and looked things up or asked questions every time you got stumped. And then, if you've been out of school, that you've continued reading college-level material ever since.

Simulating that level of verbal knowledge (when you haven't actually been doing the things listed above) takes some work. It can be done! But it's very important to *learn*—not just memorize—vocabulary words.

Many students make the mistake of memorizing dictionary definitions of words without really understanding those definitions or being able to comfortably use those words in sentences. Memorizing by itself is not learning. It is not flexible. If you've learned *torpid*, you shouldn't be thrown off by *torpor*. If you've learned *anthropology* and *engender*, you should be able to make some reasonable assumptions about *anthropogenesis*.

You want to learn words like *traduce* and *bonhomie* in the same way you know words like *study* and *mistake*—that is, you want to barely even remember a time when you didn't know those words.

For sources of difficult material, try *The Economist* (economist.com), *Scientific American* (scientificamerican.com), *Smithsonian* (smithsonianmag.com), *Foreign* (foreignaffairs.com), *MIT Technology Review* (technologyreview.com), or any of the articles posted on aldaily.com (that's Arts and Letters Daily). Of course, these are precisely the same resources recommended for improving your reading comprehension; certainly, it is possible to do both at the same time!

If you've ever learned a foreign language, think about the words that were easiest to learn. When you're in class, most of the words you learn (*stove*, *tire*, *classroom*, *grandmother*) seem equally important. But when you are actually in a foreign country, trying to speak that language, it is *very, very easy* to learn and remember words and phrases like *bathroom* and "How much?" and "No pigs' feet, please." That is, the easiest things to learn are things that you *really wanted to know* at the time that you looked them up. It's easier to retain a new word when there's a "hole" in your knowledge that you just cannot wait to fill.

Similarly, if you are reading something interesting and come across a word you don't know, and then you look up the word and consider its usage in the sentence you were just puzzling over—well, that's almost as good as learning the word *bathroom* when you really need to use one.

Finally, don't hesitate to look up or ask someone about words you *thought* you knew but seem that to be used in novel ways. (Did you notice what just happened there? As a noun, a *novel* is a book-length work of fiction, but as an adjective, *novel* means "new, original.") How about the use of *informed by* in the sentence "Her historical analysis of family dynamics in the antebellum South is informed by an academic background in feminist theory"? Clearly, an "academic background in feminist theory" can't talk—*informed by* means "influenced by" in this context. Or the use of *qualified* in the sentence "Dr. Wong could give only qualified approval to the theory, as the available data was limited in scope." (*Qualified* here means "limited, conditional, holding back.")

If you read a definition of a word—on a flash card, in a test prep book, or anywhere else—and it doesn't make sense to you, look up the word in several online dictionaries (Dictionary.com, TheFreeDictionary.com, and m-w.com), ask someone, and/or simply Google the word to see how other people are using it.

Once you've studied the definition, read the word in context, and worked the word into conversation a few times (this may cause your friends to look at you funny, but it'll be worth it!), that word is probably yours for life.

Finally, in embarking on your vocabulary-learning journey, it is crucial to cultivate a productive attitude.

Learning 500–1,500 new words certainly seems daunting (although an assiduous approach will indubitably be conducive to a virtuosic lexical performance). Some students say, "I'm already a college graduate. Why do I have to spend months studying for this exam? That's just too much time."

Here's one way to look at it: if you do physical exercise for only one hour a week, you've almost thrown that time away, because that's not enough time to get results. But if you exercise for five hours a week, you'll end up in much better shape! That is, it's exercising *insufficiently* that is a waste of time. Learning words *shallowly* is also a waste of time.

Similarly, if you spend three weeks cramming for the GRE—memorizing words just for the GRE score, without really becoming a more verbally educated person—you probably won't improve your score that much, and it really will seem like you wasted your time, because what you're doing is really about the GRE and nothing else. But if you spend months developing a more erudite vocabulary, improving your comprehension of graduate-level articles, and becoming significantly more articulate, then you have remodeled your brain for the better. That time is not lost! Those skills will benefit you forever (i.e., in graduate school)!

Here's something to think about—the GRE test writers aren't evil. They don't want to hold you back. They want to test real skills. Sure, you might be able to game the test a little bit with tricks and quick fixes, but probably not enough to achieve your goal score.

A serious, academic approach to GRE study isn't about tricks and quick fixes. It's about applying the actual material and skills that the GRE is designed to test. And no amount of time is too much to spend on becoming a more knowledgeable person, equipped with hundreds of new words that can be assembled in infinite combinations to express your ideas for decades to come.

Practical Strategies and Games for Learning Vocabulary

How to Make and Use Flash Cards

Flash cards are a time-tested way to learn vocabulary, and we like them a lot. You can make your own, or you can use Manhattan Prep's *500 Essential Words* and *500 Advanced Words: GRE Vocabulary Flash Cards* sets. While we're big fans of our own flash cards (we made them after all!), evidence has shown that you're more likely to retain the information if you make the cards yourself.

If you decide to make your own flash cards, try to write sentences for each word, and add synonyms or extra information where appropriate. Here is a sample of one of our flash cards that you might wish to use as a model for making your own:

torpid (adj) Also *torpor* (noun)

Definition: Slow, sluggish, lazy Usage: After a massive Thanksgiving dinner, Jane felt too **torpid** to even get up off the couch. "My **torpor** is overwhelming," she said.

You can find a word's synonyms by using the "Thesaurus" tab on Dictionary.com, although make sure you click on a synonym and verify that it really is similar in meaning—many thesauruses will give more than 20 synonyms for a single word, but most of them won't be that closely related (and some will be quite obscure). Make sure to look at the etymologies of any words you don't know. This is how you learn the roots of words; such knowledge will occasionally allow you to work out the definitions of words you've never seen before!

So flash cards are pretty important, but here's what a lot of people actually *do* with flash cards:

Okay, here's my enormous stack of flash cards. How many is this? 500? Okay, let's start. *Synoptic*. Hmm, I don't know. Okay, I guess I'll just look at the answer, then. Oh, okay. Next. *Turpitude*. Hmm, I don't know. Okay, I guess I'll just look at the answer, then. Oh, okay. Next. *Platitude*. Hmm, I don't know. Okay, I guess I'll just look at the answer, then. Oh, okay. Next . . .

You see how this is getting you nowhere?

One problem with this approach is that your brain has no motivation to actually remember much, because, deep down, it knows that the information is already written on the flash card, and you'll be seeing that flash card again next time it comes up in the rotation. (You forget way more than you remember—imagine if you remembered everything you saw, did, ate, etc., in just a single day! Your brain dumps well over 99 percent of the information it is presented with. You need to give it a very good reason to do otherwise!)

The other problem with this approach is that you have no idea when you're done, and it rarely feels like you're making any progress. Instead, use this method:

1. Pull out a small stack of cards, perhaps 20.

2. Go through the stack one word at a time. When you get one right, *take it out of the stack* and lay it aside.

3. As you continue, the stack will get smaller and smaller. It will become easier and easier to remember the words that are left.

Now you're done. You did a set. Move on to another set if you like.

Because this exercise has an ending (as opposed to just cycling through your flash cards over and over again), you get to feel a sense of accomplishment when you're finished.

Depending on your timeline and goal score, you might decide to do this once or twice per day. In fact, if you are working a full-time job and have a hard time studying on weeknights, make a vow that you can do this one thing *every* day, no matter what (if you're really tired, you can make it a 12–15 card set rather than 20, but you should do at least a little vocab every single day).

Flash Card Games and Activities

One benefit of physical flash cards (as opposed to various electronic study tools) is that you can physically spread out and group your flash cards in a way that is not possible when you can only see one card at a time on a screen.

Here are some strategies that take advantage of the old-school properties of flash cards:

Whack-a-word: Whack-a-Mole is an arcade game in which you have to hit a bunch of mechanical creatures with a mallet before the time runs out. Play whack-a-word by spreading out a huge pile of flash cards on a table, bed, or floor, and then trying to remove words from the pile by defining them before looking at the back of the card. If you get a word wrong, put it aside in a "to review" pile. If you end up with words you don't know anything about, make a stack and try the technique mentioned on the previous page. Once you've learned those words better, spread them all back out and play whack-a-word one more time. Whack-a-word is also fun with a friend. Take turns defining words and removing them from the spread, working together to clear the space as quickly as possible.

Storytelling: Take a stack of about 20 cards. Shuffle, and don't look at the first card. Think of a topic for your story—something funny and interesting. It's very important that every sentence in your story *defines* the word in question. For example, if you decide to tell a story about robots and monkeys, and your first card says *captious* (tending to find fault or raise petty objections), you wouldn't want to write, "Monkeys are captious." That doesn't really help you define the word. Instead, write something like, "The monkeys were captious creatures, always arguing about some little thing or another." Now you turn to the next card, *itinerary* . . .

The Robot/Monkey War began when a monkey went on vacation and misread an item on his itinerary, causing him to accidentally invade Robot Headquarters when he really just meant to visit the Monkey Art Museum. The robots were jingoists, so patriotic toward their robot kingdom that the accidental monkey invasion was interpreted as a declaration of war. The robots considered waging a war of espionage and secretly assassinating the monkey king, but decided that they'd have better luck with direct warfare. Providentially, the monkeys discovered oil in Monkeyland and were able to sell it to buy weapons to defend themselves. One taciturn monkey finally got the courage to speak up and suggest that the monkeys engage in ninja training. A meal of sushi helped whet their appetites for the training.

You can see where this is going, and it's ridiculous—but a fun way to learn! The brain retains things much better when it *does something* with that information (such as using words in sentences) rather than merely *looking* at information.

More on Storytelling and Using Words in Sentences

You can also use storytelling as a vocabulary learning technique without involving flash cards. Use any GRE vocabulary list or source and write a story using 20 or more words—either one per sentence or as many as you can incorporate.

If you're not so big on telling stories, try writing a daily journal entry using some number of words per day.

You could even vow to work a certain number of words per day into your regular emails to unsuspecting colleagues and family members. (Use caution when dropping bombastic language on your boss, but why not try out your new lexicon on your parents? They'll probably be glad to hear from you no matter how grandiloquent you become!)

Chat with a Study Buddy

Another fun technique is to find a study partner and agree to email or text each other every day using a certain number of GRE words in your messages (three seems about right—if you make the task too daunting, it might be too hard to stick with the plan).

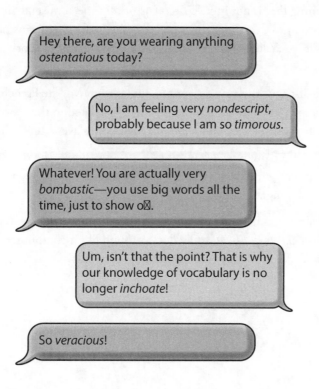

Hey there, are you wearing anything *ostentatious* today?

No, I am feeling very *nondescript*, probably because I am so *timorous*.

Whatever! You are actually very *bombastic*—you use big words all the time, just to show off.

Um, isn't that the point? That is why our knowledge of vocabulary is no longer *inchoate*!

So *veracious*!

Use Roots Ahead of Time

The Appendix of this book includes a targeted Root List. Take a good look through it.

Take judicious advantage of roots. There is no doubt that you need to know a good number of Latin and Greek roots to understand modern English academic vocabulary. Many words are easily decomposed into roots and can be understood clearly in terms of those roots.

12

Because the meaning of words may have changed quite a bit since the time of the Roman Empire, though, some words now have misleading roots or derivations. During the exam itself, you have to be very careful when you resort to root analysis to guess an unknown word's meaning. The GRE loves to use words with surprising meanings. For instance, *baleful* does not mean "full of hay bales"—it means "threatening or menacing." Although a *scribe* is a person whose job is to copy by hand, *proscribe* isn't really about writing—it means prohibit or condemn.

Still, if you learn that a word *doesn't* relate very logically to its roots, that can be helpful in itself. Many words have strange and memorable relationships with their etymological roots. For instance, the word *desultory* means "lacking in method or purpose; disappointing." That's not so interesting, but if you know that the word comes from a Latin word describing circus riders who *jumped from* horse to horse (*de* = from, *sult* = jump), then you might remember the word *desultory* better. *Proscribe*, meaning "to forbid by law or denounce," contains the root *scribe* (as in *script, scribble, scripture*, etc.) because, in ancient times, to *proscribe* was to publish a record of someone's punishment—to condemn or sentence that person publicly.

Here are a few more favorites (more information like this appears in *500 Essential Words* and *500 Advanced Words GRE Vocabulary Flash Cards* sets from Manhattan Prep):

Amortize (gradually pay off a debt, or gradually write off an asset) contains the root *mort*, meaning death. **Amortization** is when a financial obligation dies a long, slow death.

Anachronism (something that is not in its correct historical time; a mistake in chronology, such as by assigning a person or event to the wrong time period)—the prefix *ana* means "against," and *chron* means "time." This is one word you can work out entirely with a knowledge of roots: **anachronistic** means "against time."

Legerdemain (sleight-of-hand, trickery, deception) comes from Middle French, meaning "light of hand." The modern French word for hand is *main*, which is related to the root in the English *manual* (relating to hands, as in *manual labor*) and *manumit* (free from slavery, untie the hands).

Malediction (a curse) has the prefix *mal* (meaning "bad," of course). The root *dict* comes from *dicere* (to say) and also appears in *dictator, dictionary*, and *indict* (connect to a crime), as well as in **malediction**'s antonym, *benediction* (blessing).

Not all words have a cool story or a helpful derivation. For instance, *pulchritude* means "beauty." The reason that seems so weird (*You're so pulchritudinous* really doesn't sound like a compliment) is that the Latin root *pulcher*, meaning "beautiful," doesn't occur in any other English words.

So recognize that roots are just one of many helpful tools. One good way to proceed is to go through the Root List in the Appendix and just focus on roots that actually look familiar to you (and like something you'd be able to spot in the future); for instance, *circum* (meaning "around") appears in *circumference*, and it's pretty hard to miss the root in *circumnavigate, circumcise, circumambulate,* and *circumlocution.* So you might make a flash card for this and other roots that seem most useful to you.

Using Social Media to Buttress Your Vocabulary Studies

Do you spend all day on Facebook or Twitter? Developing a social network around your word network is an incredible way to make vocabulary fun and to get other people's perspective on words that are new to you. In fact, scientific studies show that having a social group related to your studies can substantially improve learning.

Supposedly, your Facebook friends are your, well … friends, right? So they should be supportive of your GRE efforts. Try announcing on Facebook that you're studying for the GRE and will be posting vocabulary words for the next few months.

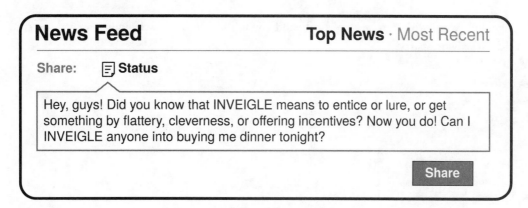

News Feed   **Top News** · Most Recent

Share: ▤ **Status**

Hey, guys! Did you know that INVEIGLE means to entice or lure, or get something by flattery, cleverness, or offering incentives? Now you do! Can I INVEIGLE anyone into buying me dinner tonight?

Share

If you post a word and its definition as your status update, it only takes one hilarious comment from a friend (some people have way too much time on their hands) to help you remember the word forever.

Manhattan Prep maintains a Facebook presence (we're "Word Beast"), and we were pleased to see that someone posted the word *deleterious* (meaning "harmful or damaging") in a status update: "Does anyone actually use that word?"

A friend wrote back:

> *Deleterious* is used quite a bit in genetics. For example, "Epigenetic silencing of transposable elements may reduce *deleterious* effects on neighboring gene expression in the genome."

The original poster replied, "I looked for examples of this word's use in a sentence. It seems that *deleterious effects* is indeed the way it is most often used."

Now that's how to learn *deleterious*!

12

You can also use Twitter as a tool for learning vocabulary. You can follow Manhattan Prep at:

http://twitter.com/manhattanprep

But don't just be a follower. Start up a Twitter account (if you haven't already), and Tweet each word you study. You can simply post words and definitions, or try using the words in sentences (or both).

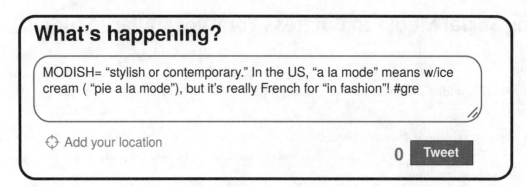

Try tagging your Tweets with #gre or #grevocab, and you'll find a lot of new friends who are also studying for the GRE. It's a word party!

Idioms & Metaphorical Language

In This Chapter ...

- List of Idioms & Metaphorical Language

CHAPTER 13 Idioms & Metaphorical Language

Although closely related, studying idioms is not the same as studying vocabulary. While difficult vocabulary words mostly appear in GRE answer choices, idioms are more often found within Reading Comprehension passages and complex Text Completion sentences. However, it should be noted that a command of vocabulary will aid understanding in these areas as well.

This chapter contains expressions that are appropriate for use in the type of writing excerpted on the GRE and that often appear in writing about culture, literature, business, science, and history.

It also contains words used metaphorically; for instance, an *albatross* is large web-footed bird, but it is also a burden or obstacle, as in the expression *an albatross around one's neck* (from "The Rime of the Ancient Mariner," in which a sailor had to wear an albatross around his neck as punishment for his sins).

This section will be extremely helpful for many non-native speakers of English. Others may simply want to look over it and see if there are any "surprises."

To increase retention of this material, try to use these expressions in your own sentences.

The idioms are followed by a 20-question drill allowing you to test your understanding of these expressions when used in complex sentences.

List of Idioms & Metaphorical Language

". . .": Quote marks can indicate 1) that the word or phrase is not to be taken literally; 2) the introduction of a new, made-up word or phrase. So some context is needed to understand the meaning. For example:

The factory employs several people who add defects and rough edges to its popular line of **"antique"** furniture. (The furniture is not really antique).

The company has sent its top people to ethics training and courses on Aristotle in an attempt to build a **"philosophically correct"** business. (The quotes tell you that the concept of *philosophical correctness* is something new—likely invented by the company itself—rather than a well-established concept or institution.)

Account for: 1) Take into consideration or make adjustments based on; 2) cause. This is not the same as *give an account of*, which just means "explain."

I **accounted for** the fact that Joe is always late by telling him to meet us at 1:30 when the event is really at 2. (Here, *accounted for* means "made adjustments to compensate for.")

I did get us the meeting, but Ellen's hard work **accounted for** the rest of our success. (Here, *accounted for* means "caused.")

A given: The use of *a given* as a noun is different from the use of *given* alone. For instance, a person's *given name* is the one *given* by his or her parents (a *first name* in the United States), and we might also say, "The truth differs from the *given* explanation." Here, *given explanation* just means "the explanation that someone gave." Simple. However, *a given* means something taken for granted, something assumed or that does not require proof. For instance:

> When planning my wedding, it was **a given** that my parents would invite anyone they wanted, since they were paying for everything.

> It's **a given** that everyone here is against human trafficking—what we disagree about is the best way to fight it.

Albatross: A constant burden or worry; an obstacle. Literally, an albatross is a bird. The expression *an albatross around one's neck* creates the silly image of a person wearing a (dead?) bird—but that certainly sounds like a constant burden or worry!

> The city has done an admirable job of rebuilding its infrastructure and marketing itself, but the crime rate continues to be an **albatross** around the city's neck in trying to attract tourists.

All but: Almost definitely. *The bill's passage is all but assured* means that the bill will almost certainly pass.

> Your objections have arrived too late; the matter is **all but** decided.

And yet: A stronger way of saying *yet*. The expression *and yet* seems ungrammatical (two conjunctions right next to each other is very strange—we don't say *and but*), but it is an idiom used for emphasis. It indicates a surprising twist, an ironic realization, etc. It is often used at the beginning of a sentence for emphasis and can even be used on its own, although this usage is casual.

> The company was lauded for its commitment to the environment. **And yet** its employees regularly fly in private jets, creating carbon footprints that would embarrass any true environmentalist.

Arms race: Competition between two countries to build up the best and largest supply of weapons. This term is often associated with the Cold War between the United States and the Soviet Union. Metaphorically, an *arms race* is a competition that implies a competitive and perhaps not entirely rational series of escalations.

> Analysts carefully watched stock prices as the two Internet giants competed in an **arms race**, expanding rapidly by buying up smaller companies with little due diligence.

Aside from: In addition to.

> **Aside from** the obvious financial benefits of investing in a socially responsible fund, you can rest assured that your money is used to maximize social good.

(Adjective) as it is, . . . : This pattern is used to contrast the part after the comma with the part before. For instance, *Charming as she is, I just don't want to be friends with her anymore.*

> **As pleased as we are** to see more minorities on the board than ever before, discrimination in hiring and promotion is still a serious problem.

As well as: Sometimes *as well as* just means "and," as in *I had ramen for lunch, as well as a hot dog.* But *as well as* can also be used to mention one thing as a way to contrast with or emphasize another.

At best: At the most, interpreted in the most favorable way. *The seminar drew 20 people at best* means that 20 or fewer people attended.

My college algebra teacher can barely factor a polynomial! He is qualified to teach elementary school math, **at best**.

At fault: Guilty.

The insurance company is investigating who is **at fault** for the collision.

At loggerheads: In conflict; at a standstill.

The strike is not likely to end soon—the transit authority and the union representatives have been **at loggerheads** for weeks.

At odds: In conflict.

The teachers union and the state government are always **at odds**.

At once: 1) Immediately; 2) at the same time.

If the hurricane comes near the coast, the governor will order us to evacuate **at once**.

The question is whether we can pursue all three plans **at once**, or if we only have the resources to try them one at a time.

Beside the point: Irrelevant, off-topic.

The better part: The largest or longest part. *The better part* does *not* have to be good! The word *better* is a bit confusing here.

For **the better part** of human history, slavery has been a reality. (The speaker is *not* saying that slavery is good. The speaker is saying that, for most of human history, slavery has existed.)

When the oil magnate died, he left **the better part** of his fortune to his third wife, and only a small sliver to his children.

Bite the hand the feeds you: This expression means exactly what it sounds like (think of a mean and not-very-smart dog). Although informal sounding, this expression has appeared in business writing.

The music industry **bites the hand that feeds it** when it penalizes consumers who share (and therefore publicize) their favorite songs with friends.

Brook: Tolerate, allow. Often used with the word *no*. You could say *The dictator will not brook dissent*, but a more common usage would be *The dictator will brook no dissent*.

(Verb) by so (verb)ing: The second verb is equivalent to or causes the first verb. He *defaults by so refusing* means "when he refuses, he is defaulting" (that is, neglecting to fulfill the duties of a contract). *By so agreeing* also occurs on its own, meaning "by agreeing to do the thing that was just mentioned."

He agreed to run as the Green Party candidate though he already holds a Democratic Party chairmanship, which he effectively **abandoned by so agreeing**.

The case at issue: The matter at hand, the thing we are discussing.

Usually, raising prices results in a drop in demand, but in **the case at issue**, the price jump convinced consumers that the product was a luxury good, thus spurring demand from those who wished to be perceived as wealthy.

Caught red-handed: Caught in the act of doing something wrong so that the person cannot deny guilt. The expression refers to having blood on one's hands.

> The company could no longer claim that the fish in the river were all dying from natural causes once it was **caught red-handed** dumping waste at the river's mouth.

Colored by: Influenced or prejudiced by.

> Her skeptical opinions regarding unbridled capitalism were **colored by** her upbringing in a factory town devastated by outsourcing.

Couldn't have come at a better time: The same as *could hardly have come at a better time*, this expression means that something happened at the best possible time, such as at a very convenient moment or just in time to prevent disaster.

Curry favor: To try to gain favor (such as preferential treatment from a boss) through flattery or servile behavior. The expression is derived from French and is not related to *curry*, the food.

Cut bait: Give up; abandon an activity. Often part of the expression *fish or cut bait*, to *cut bait* is to stop fishing.

> As much as he wanted to be an entrepreneur, after a year of struggling, he **cut bait** and asked his former boss for his old job back.

Due diligence: Research or analysis done before taking action (such as investing); care that a reasonable person would take to prevent harm to others.

> The company was expanding so rapidly that it didn't have time to do its **due diligence**; a number of unexceptional employees were hired as a result.

En masse: All together, in a group. This expression is from French and is related to the word *mass*. Like many foreign expressions, *en masse* is often written in italics.

> The protesters marched **en masse** to the palace.

Entree: Admittance, permission to enter. Most people in the United States think of an entree as the main dish of a meal, but it originally was an appetizer—a dish that leads into the main course (the word is related to *enter*). A person who wants to rise in society might seek an *entree* into a certain social group.

> For disadvantaged young people, good public schools can provide an **entree** into the middle class.

Fishy: Suspicious, unlikely, questionable, as in a *fishy* story. This expression probably arose because fish smell very bad when they start to spoil.

For all X, Y: This sentence pattern means "Despite X, actually Y"; that is, X and Y will be opposites, or one will be good and one will be bad. The word *actually* (or a similar word) often appears in this pattern, but doesn't have to.

> **For all** of its well-publicized "green" innovations, the company is one of the worst polluters in the state.

Former and latter: When two things are mentioned, the first one is the *former* and the second one is the *latter*.

> Your grades are slipping, and you've been very secretive about your behavior—it's **the latter** of these things that worries your father and me the most.

> I intend to choose a business school based on reputation and cost, the **former** more so than the **latter**.

For show: For appearances only.

The politician's speechifying in regards to eradicating poverty is all **for show**; when he actually had the chance to improve the lot of the poor, he voted against expanding the social safety net.

For years to come: Until much later. *The consequences won't affect us for years to come* means that they *will* affect us, but not for the next several years.

My parents are only in their sixties and are healthy and active, so I am hopeful that my children will get to enjoy their grandparents **for years to come**.

Full throttle: With much speed and energy. On a related note, sometimes *juice* is used to mean "energy."

The plan is to go ahead **full throttle** as soon as the money for implementation comes through.

Garden-variety: Ordinary, common.

Gloss over, paper over, whitewash: These are all expressions for covering up a problem, insult, etc., rather than addressing it or fixing it. Think of a dirty floor that you just put a pretty rug on top of instead of cleaning. Because *gloss* is slippery (think of lip gloss), *gloss over* often has the sense of trying to smoothly and quickly move on to something else.

The government had been accused of trying to **whitewash** the scandal, **glossing over** any discussion of the issue in press conference after press conference. The press secretary claimed it was a question of national security, but everyone knew that the president was simply trying to protect his reputation.

Go down the tubes: Become much worse, fail. One theory is that this expression is about the plumbing attached to toilets.

Go sour: Think of milk going bad—that's the idea behind the expression *go sour*. A relationship *goes sour* before the couple breaks up. An economy *gone sour* can't be good. This is not the same as the expression *sour grapes*, which refers to pretending something you can't have wasn't any good anyway, as in, *Her hatred of the rich is just sour grapes—if she could afford luxury, she'd take all she could get.*

Hand-wringing, wringing of hands: An excessive expression of concern, guilt, or distress.

There has been much **hand-wringing** over falling test scores, but the rising costs of a college degree are far more worrying in terms of America's continuing relevance in the global economy.

Hold the line vs. **toe the line:** *Hold the line* means "keep something the same." It is a reference to (American) football, in which you don't want the opponent to get the ball past the line of scrimmage in the middle of the field. To *toe the line* is to conform to a policy or way of thinking, or follow the rules. One theory about the origin of the expression is that, on ships, barefoot sailors were made to line up for inspection—that is, to put their toes on an actual line on the deck of the ship.

My boss doesn't want to hear original ideas at all—he just wants me to **toe the line**.

If colleges cannot **hold the line** on rising tuition costs, students will have to take on even more crippling loan burdens.

However much, as much as: Even though, no matter how much.

However much people may agree that saving money is a virtue, the majority of Americans don't have sufficient funds for any kind of emergency.

As much as I'd like to attend your wedding, I just can't afford a trip to Taiwan.

In contrast to: This phrase is important in Inference questions on Reading Comp. If a writer says *In contrast to X, Y is A,* you can draw the conclusion that *X is not A.* For instance:

> **In contrast to** our competitor's product, our product is made with organic materials. (This means that our competitor's product is *not* made with organic materials, which very well could be the answer to a question about what we can infer from the passage.)

Just cause: *Just* as an adjective means "justified, legal, fair." *Just cause* means a legally sufficient reason. In some legal codes, an employer must show *just cause* for firing an employee.

Legions or **is legion:** *Legions* are large military units, generally consisting of a few thousand soldiers. Saying that a group *is legion* is saying that it is large.

> Surely, the developers could have foreseen that **legions** of Mac users would protest when news emerged that the new version of the software would not be Mac-compatible.

> The former governor has been called a demagogue by many commentators who nevertheless must grudgingly admit that her supporters **are legion**, populating rallies in every state.

No X *or* Y vs. **No X *and* Y:** When you are talking about having two things, saying *salt and pepper* is very different from saying *salt or pepper.* However, when you are talking about a lack of two things, *and* and *or* can often be used to express the same idea. The following two sentences have the same meaning:

> Pioneer towns were characterized by little access to the outside world **and** few public institutions.

> Pioneer towns had almost no access to the outside world **or** public institutions.

Not (adjective): Of course, putting *not* before an adjective indicates the opposite. However, sometimes it indicates a softer or more polite way to say something. If someone asks if you like the meal he cooked or the outfit he is wearing, and you know him well enough to be honest, you might say, *It's not my favorite.* Sometimes we say something like *not irrelevant* instead of simply *relevant* in order to indicate that we are correcting someone else's misconception:

> Concern about foreign debt is **not misplaced**. (Here, we mean that we should be concerned! We also may be implying that others incorrectly think we should *not* be concerned.)

Not only X, but also Y (also appears as **Not only X, but Y**): This is a two-part expression, introducing the first part before adding on the second more extreme or surprising part. For instance:

> The executive was **not only** fired, **but also** indicted for fraud.

> He **not only** bought his girlfriend an iPhone for her birthday, **but also** took her entire family on a vacation to the Catskills.

Not X, let alone Y: The meaning is *Not X and definitely not this even more extreme thing, Y.* For instance:

> Our remaining funds are **not** enough to get us through the week, **let alone** pay next month's payroll. (Here, getting through the week is less expensive than next month's payroll, so if we can't afford the cheaper thing, we *definitely* can't afford the more expensive thing.)

No worse than: Equal to or better than.

> Although exotic, this illness is really **no worse than** the common flu.

On its face: At first appearance, superficially. If someone says *on its face*, you can expect that later on, the person will give the "real story." In a Reading Comprehension passage, seeing *on its face* is a good clue that the author's main idea will probably be the opposite of what *seems* true at first glance.

> **On its face,** the donation seems like a selfless act of philanthropy. However, the wealthy donor mainly made the donation for the tax benefits.

Only looks (adjective): Appears (some certain way) but isn't really.

> She **only looks** homeless—she is actually a famous and wealthy artist who lives eccentrically.

On par with: Sometimes *on a par with*, this expression comes from golf and means "about equal to" or "equivalent to."

Opening salvo: A *salvo* is a simultaneous discharge of gunfire or release of bombs. Metaphorically, an *opening salvo* is something that starts a fight.

> The introduction of Bill H.R. 2, given the inflammatory name "Repealing the Job-Killing Health Care Law Act," was seen by some as an **opening salvo** by the Republicans.

Outside of the home: Working *outside of the home* means having a regular job, such as in an office. However, working *out of your home* is actually working at home. If that's hard to understand, think of the expression *living out of your car*, which actually means living *in* your car—the idea is that you leave the car to go "out" but return back to the car as your base, just as someone who works *out of her home* leaves the home to go to meetings, for example, but uses the home as a central point.

> The study compared incomes of women who had worked **outside of the home** to incomes of women who worked **out of their homes** as freelancers or owners of small businesses.

Per se: In itself, by itself, intrinsically. From Latin, often written in italics. *Per se* is often used to indicate that while X isn't *naturally* or *the same as* Y, it still has the same effect as Y.

> The policy isn't sexist, **per se**, but it has had a disproportionate impact on women that deserves further study.

Press for: Argue in favor of. Think of *pushing people* toward what you want them to do.

> The advocates **pressed for** greater regulation of child-care providers.

Rabid: Rabies is a disease that some animals (dogs, raccoons, etc.) contract and that causes the animal to become insane and violent. Thus, we use *rabid* (having rabies) metaphorically to mean "zealous" or "excessively or angrily passionate." One symptom of rabies is *foaming at the mouth*, which is also an expression for being extremely (and violently or irrationally) angry.

> One debater called himself a "peace activist" and his opponent a "**rabid** right-wing gun nut." His opponent called himself a "champion of the American way" and his opponent a "**rabid** anti-American zealot."

Ranks of: The people in a group other than the leaders. Many people know the word *rank* as "a level or grade," as in *A general has a higher rank than a sergeant*. The other use of *ranks* is also originally related to the military: the *ranks* or sometimes the *rank and file* means "all the regular soldiers" (not the officers).

> Among the **ranks** of our alumni are two senators and many famous authors.

Reap and **sow:** These are metaphors related to farming, and specifically the idea that the seeds that you plant (or *sow*) determine what you will later harvest (or *reap*). *Sow* is pronounced the same as *so*, and the past tense is *sown*, as in *Having sown the love of knowledge in the minds of children, the teacher's influence extended well past her own lifetime*. A common expression is *You reap what you sow*.

> He worked night and day in the strange new country, never stopping to rest, for he knew he would **reap** his reward when his family greeted him as a hero for all the money he had sent back home.

Red flag: Warning sign or something alarming.

> Bernie Madoff's sustained, ultrahigh returns should have been a **red flag** for the banks with which he did business.

Red herring: Something irrelevant that distracts from the real issue. A herring is a fish. One theory for the origin of the expression is that criminals trying to escape the police would sometimes rub a smelly fish across their trail as they ran away in order to mislead the dogs used to track them down.

> When the company was robbed, police immediately suspected Johnson, who purchased a brand-new Maserati just after the crime was committed. This turned out to be a **red herring**, however, as it was Johnson's wife, who'd just come into a large inheritance, who bought the car.

Reign vs. **reins:** Reign means "rule" (noun), as in *Conditions have improved under the king's reign*. *Reins* are leather straps used by a rider to control a horse. Both words are often used metaphorically.

> People were worried when the inexperienced new CEO took the **reins** of the multinational corporation, but under her **reign**, profits soared.

(Adjective)-ridden: Dominated, burdened, or afflicted by (adjective). In a *disease-ridden slum*, it's pretty obvious that the meaning is bad, but actually, adding *-ridden* to anything makes the meaning bad. If someone said *an equality-ridden society*, that person is actually against equality! *Ridden* can also be used alone, as in *The neighborhood was ridden with crime*.

Scarcely or **scarce:** Sometimes *scarce* is used where it sounds like the adverb *scarcely* is needed. This is an idiomatic usage:

> She lived a lavish lifestyle she could **scarce** afford. (She could not afford the lifestyle.)

Save: But or except. As a verb, of course, *save* means "keep safe, store up, set aside." But as a preposition or conjunction, *save* can be used as follows:

> All of the divisions of the company are profitable **save** the movie-rental division. (This means that the movie-rental division was not profitable.)

> He would have been elected president, **save** for the scandal that derailed his campaign at the last minute. (Here, *save* means "if not.")

School of thought: A group of people with similar beliefs or perspective on things, or the beliefs themselves. If a GRE writer says *One school of thought argues X*, it is probably the case that the author is about to say the opposite (calling something a *school of thought* can emphasize that it's not the only way to think about the issue).

> One **school of thought** says that companies don't need to "give back" directly to communities, because their economic activity causes money to trickle down to everyone through taxes; a competing **school of thought** says that companies benefit from a nation's infrastructure and education system, which confers an ethical obligation to be philanthropic.

Sight vs. **site** vs. **cite:** To **sight** is to see, or discover by looking. A **site** is a location. To **cite** is to reference or give credit to.

> The sailors had nearly given up hope when they finally **sighted** land. When they reached the shore, they planted a flag on the **site** of their landing.

> A good research report **cites** relevant studies.

So much as: This phrase is used an adverbial intensifier. In *My teacher is so awful, she won't so much as answer a question*, the meaning is that, whatever the teacher will do, it is not *as much as* answering a question—it is something less than that. It can also be used as a synonym for *but rather*.

> After her husband decided to take up day trading and lost $100,000 in one day, she wouldn't **so much as** look at him.

> She's not an iconoclast **so much as** an attention-hound; she'd do anything for the spotlight.

Sound the depths: Explore, investigate, or look into something really deeply. This expression is a metaphor based on the idea of a sounding line, which is a rope with a weight on the bottom that you drop to the ocean floor to see how deep the ocean is.

> Other books have dealt with the topic in a superficial way, but this is the first book to really **sound the depths** of the response of the British lower class to the American Revolution.

Steeped in: Immersed in, saturated with. A teabag *steeps* in hot water. A person *steeped in* classic literature really knows a lot about old, famous books.

> The Met's new youth-targeted campaign seeks to answer the question of whether music lovers **steeped in** hip-hop and pop can learn to love opera.

Stem from: Be caused by. This is related to the idea of a plant's *stem*.

> The psychologist believed that his neurosis **stemmed from** events in his childhood.

Hold sway over: Have great power or influence over a person, group of people, or place.

> Repressive governments are suspicious of those who **hold sway over** the people, and often imprison or execute such people.

Table: In American English, to *table* something means to postpone discussion of it until later. (In British English, to *table* a bill is the opposite—to submit it for consideration.)

Take umbrage: Become offended.

> With 15 years of experience on all kinds of campaigns, she **took umbrage** of her sexist coworker's suggestion that she was only qualified to develop advertising for "women's products."

The very idea (or **the very notion**, etc.): This expression is used to express a strong contrast.

> The author conjures up a drifting yet haunting word picture that challenges **one's very notion** of what constitutes a story. (This means that the author's strange "word picture" story goes against the most basic things that we think must be true about stories.)

Trappings: Accessories, the characteristic items, products, etc., that come with or are associated with something. Think of the side dishes or condiments that come with a meal. The *trappings* of fame include invites to fancy parties and free items from companies.

Vanguard and **avant-garde:** The *avant-garde* (French for *in front of the guard*) were the leading soldiers at the front of an army. *Vanguard* is derived from *avant-garde* and means the same thing. Metaphorically, the *avant-garde* (noun or adjective) or vanguard (noun) are innovators, those at the forefront of any movement or those ahead of their time. Sometimes, the *avant-garde* seems a little crazy or scary at first.

While Google has won the search engine wars, in 1994 Yahoo was on the **vanguard** of search technology.

She arrived at the mixer in a dress that was a little **avant-garde** for the otherwise conservative Yale Club—she would have looked more appropriate at an art gallery or Lady Gaga concert.

Wanting: *Wanting* means lacking, insufficient, or not good enough (as in *I read the book and found it wanting*). This makes sense when you think about a person who is *left wanting*—that is, the person is *left wanting* something good. Conversely, a person who *wants for nothing* is someone who already has everything.

With a grain of salt: To take something (a statement, claim, etc.) *with a grain of salt* is to maintain a small amount of skepticism. The origin of this expression is related to an old belief that a small amount of salt could help protect against poison.

Take the consultant's advice **with a grain of salt**—the software he's recommending is produced by a company that is also a client of his.

With respect to, in some respects: These expressions are not really about giving respect. *With respect to* (or *in respect to*) just means "about." The expression *in some respects* just means "in some ways."

With respect to your request for a raise, I'm afraid no one is getting one this year.

Wreak havoc: Cause destruction. The past tense of *wreak* is *wrought*.

Unsurprisingly, a combination of heroin abuse and living on the streets can really **wreak havoc** on a person's health.

Drill: Decoding Idioms

Each of the following sentences is written in American English that is idiomatic, but still appropriate for academic writing. Pick the multiple-choice answer that best expresses the meaning of the original sentence.

Complete this quiz "open book"—feel free to go back and look up anything you want in this book and to use any online dictionary (such as dictionary.com). You will gain much more from the process of looking things up and decoding the statements than you would by merely testing yourself in the usual manner.

1. In contrast to the Swedish social welfare system, Ireland's does not provide paid paternity leave.

   (A) Ireland's social welfare system does not provide paid paternity leave and Sweden's does.

   (B) The Swedish and Irish social welfare systems are different in many ways, and Ireland's does not provide paid paternity leave.

   (C) Both the Swedish and Irish social welfare systems provide paid paternity leave.

2. He can hardly be called a liberal, for his voting record belies the beliefs he professes to hold.

   (A) He is not really a liberal because he votes in a way that goes against liberalism.

   (B) He is a very strong liberal and always supports liberal beliefs with his vote.

   (C) He is slightly liberal, and his voting record goes along with his beliefs.

3. However much the committee may be deadlocked now, the progress made to this point has been nontrivial.

   (A) The committee is now committed to one course of action and is making progress.

   (B) The committee members are fighting with one another, but have made progress on one point they were discussing.

   (C) Although it is true that the committee is stuck and not moving forward, it has already made significant progress.

4. Although the book has addressed the issue of educational equity head on, it has sidestepped the thorny question of school vouchers.

   (A) The book talked about owning stock in education, but it has talked in an indirect way about the painful issue of school vouchers.

   (B) The book talked directly about equality in education, but it avoided talking about the controversial issue of school vouchers.

   (C) The book talked in a smart way about fairness in education, but it only gave an overview of the controversial issue of school vouchers.

5. Her appointment to the office is all but assured.

   (A) She has a meeting at the office, but the time is not set.

   (B) She will almost certainly be given a new job or leadership role.

   (C) She may be promoted, but it is not likely.

6. You discount the consultant's prescription at your peril.

   (A) You put yourself in danger by dismissing the consultant's recommendations.

   (B) Paying less for the consultant's advice is not a wise idea.

   (C) You have gotten a good deal on a dangerous medicine.

7. Davis seemingly spearheaded the project and has taken credit for its success. Nonetheless, those in the know are aware of his patent appropriation of the ideas of others.

   (A) Davis seems to have led the project, and he took credit for it. However, those who know the real situation know that he openly stole other people's ideas.

   (B) Davis was the leader of the project and got the credit, and those who know about what happened know that he used the intellectual property of other people in an appropriate way.

   (C) Davis seems to have damaged the project, though he took credit for its success. However, those who know the real situation know that he used other people's ideas.

8. The experiment only looks like a success.

   (A) It is not possible to see the experiment as anything but a success.

   (B) The experiment seems successful, but we don't know for sure.

   (C) The experiment has the appearance of a success, but really is a failure.

9. On its face, the dispute is over how the groundbreaking study should be attributed when published. But in actuality, the scientists are arguing because their leader will brook no opposition to his own perspective on their findings.

   (A) The dispute is directly about who should get credit for the study. But really, the lead scientist will not "go with the flow" of opposition to his own theories.

   (B) The dispute at first seems to be about the study's attribution. But really, the lead scientist will not tolerate opposition to his own theories.

   (C) The dispute is directly about who should get credit for the study. But really, the lead scientist will not encourage opposition to his own theories.

10. We will not likely reconcile the apparent discrepancy for years to come.

   (A) It will probably take us many years to show that what looks like a contradiction really isn't.

   (B) We do not want to work out a difference of opinion in the coming years.

   (C) Over the next several years, we will probably not attempt to work out what seems like an error.

11. The dictator had tyranized his people for too long. As dissident thinkers began to sway public opinion, the country's increasingly marginalized leader reaped the bitter fruits of his cruel reign.

   (A) The dictator was disabused of his tyranny, and as rebellious thinkers began to have political power, their tyrannical leader was pushed to the margins.

   (B) The dictator had been cruel to his people, and as thinkers who disagreed with the government began to influence regular people, the regime lost influence and power.

   (C) The dictator had abused his people, and as thinkers whose ideas went against the government began to influence people, agricultural exports became bitter and expensive.

12. A variable-rate mortgage is no worse in this respect than a fixed-rate one.

   (A) There is something bad about a fixed-rate mortgage, and that same quality is better or equally bad in a variable-rate mortgage.

   (B) A variable-rate mortgage does not indicate less respect than a fixed-rate mortgage.

   (C) If you look at it a certain way, a variable-rate mortgage is the same or better than a fixed-rate one.

13. As to whether Dr. Stuttgart is a token academic on a board of otherwise mercenary executives, you need look only at the board's response to the latest crisis, when Dr. Stuttgart was at once turned to for counsel and granted discretionary power over the board's funds.

   (A) If there is a question about whether the main reason Dr. Stuttgart is on the board is so the executives who only care about money can look good, then the only way to answer that question is to look at the board's response to the latest crisis, when Dr. Stuttgart was put in charge and given power over the board's money.

   (B) If you want to know whether Dr. Stuttgart is really an academic even though he is on a board of executives who will do anything to win, then the best place to look for an answer is at the board's response to the latest crisis, when Dr. Stuttgart was asked for his advice and allowed to secretly control the board's money.

   (C) If you are questioning whether the main reason Dr. Stuttgart is on the board is so the executives who only care about money can look good, then you can easily answer that question by looking at the board's response to the latest crisis, when the board asked for Dr. Stuttgart's advice while at the same time giving him power to spend the board's money on whatever he thought was best.

13

14. The author is seemingly a garden-variety Marxist.

    (A) The author seems to be a Marxist who has a lot of diversity in his or her opinions.

    (B) The author is a Marxist who is concerned with many different Marxist issues.

    (C) It seems as though the author is a typical Marxist, but that may not really be true.

15. The windfall could hardly have come at a better time: by agreeing to a company restructuring he didn't really understand, he had just inadvertently reduced his holdings in the family business.

    (A) The disaster happened at a very bad time, because he had also just agreed to a company reorganization that he didn't understand and that improperly reduced his control over the family business.

    (B) He suddenly received some money at a very convenient time, because he had just agreed to a company reorganization that he didn't understand and thus had accidentally reduced how much of the family business he owned.

    (C) The good fortune could have happened at a better time, because he had also just agreed to a company reorganization that he didn't understand and that reduced his portion of the family business.

16. Which of the following, if true, best reconciles the apparent discrepancy?

    (A) Which of the following is true and shows that a contradiction does not really exist?

    (B) Which of the following, if it happened to be true, would show that what looks like a contradiction really isn't?

    (C) Which of the following, if it happened to be true, would help us accept a contradiction?

17. The evidence has been taken as supporting Fujimura's conclusion.

    (A) Other people have interpreted the evidence in a way that makes it seem to support Fujimura's conclusion.

    (B) The evidence definitely supports Fujimura's conclusion.

    (C) The evidence has been deeply understood by others in a way that allows them to effectively support Fujimura's conclusion.

18. Hardly an atypical example, this shifty, hedging, practically unreadable document is paradigmatic of corporate memos.

    (A) This memo switches positions often, holds back information, and is very hard to read. It is a very poor example of corporate memos.

    (B) Although this memo refuses to take a stand, tries to reduce the writer's risk, and is very hard to read, it is a poor example of corporate memos and should not be judged to be representative.

    (C) This memo is evasive or tricky, avoids taking a stand so as not to risk being wrong or offensive, and is almost unreadable. However, this is pretty standard for a corporate memo.

19. Which of the following best underscores the argument that a failure to enforce the regulation is on par with publicly condoning illegal dumping?

    (A) Which of the following most weakens the argument that a failure to enforce the regulation is just as bad as publicly tolerating illegal dumping?

    (B) Which of the following most emphasizes the argument that a failure to enforce the regulation is just as bad as publicly tolerating illegal dumping?

    (C) Which of the following most strengthens the argument that a failure to enforce the regulation is worse than publicly tolerating illegal dumping?

20. The central idea is juxtaposed with the results of a study that seemingly corroborates a long-derided school of thought.

    (A) The central idea is placed next to and contrasted with evidence that seems to support the ideas of a group of people whose ideas have been looked down on or made fun of for a long time.

    (B) The central idea is judged to be better than evidence that seems to support the ideas of a group of people whose ideas have been looked down on or made fun of for a long time.

    (C) The central idea is placed next to and contrasted with evidence that supports the ideas of a group of people whose ideas used to be looked down on or made fun of.

13

Answers and Explanations

Drill: Decoding Idioms

1. A
2. A
3. C
4. B
5. B
6. A
7. A
8. C
9. B
10. A

11. B
12. A
13. C
14. C
15. B
16. B
17. A
18. C
19. B
20. A

Vocabulary & Reading Comprehension

In This Chapter ...

- Introduction to Specialized Terms

- Vocabulary List for the GRE

CHAPTER 14 Vocabulary & Reading Comprehension

Introduction to Specialized Terms

Compared with the other Verbal question types, Reading Comprehension is less concerned with your knowledge of vocabulary. Every specialized term is defined to a sufficient degree within the passage. Moreover, even difficult "normal" words are used in context; as a result, you have an enormous leg up on knowing what the words mean.

That said, Reading Comprehension can still try to scare you off with puffed-up vocabulary and difficult idioms. For a comprehensive lesson on learning vocabulary and idoms, see our *Text Completion & Sentence Equivalence GRE Strategy Guide*. In the meantime, here is an introduction to some "10-dollar words" that have appeared in previous GRE passages.

1. Pure Jargon

Pure Jargon words are specialized terms that the passage defines on the spot, almost always within the same sentence. There is no expectation that you've ever seen these words before. For example:

> … afterward, the politician began to practice **Priusism**—a philosophy espousing the use of low-emission vehicles …
>
> … he also began to eat low-carbon vegetables, such as **aconiteotes** and **pleonasmides** …

The bolded terms are completely made up!

Pure Jargon terms can refer to particular animals, plants, minerals, or chemicals that play some kind of role (important or trivial) in the story. Or they might represent medical conditions, social movements, foreign words, and so on.

Here are some examples from published GRE passages. These words will *not* be defined here, nor should you go look them up (even if you recognize a few). After all, they will be defined in the passage!

achondrite
appendicularian
chondrule
flux (in metallurgy)
hypercholesterolemia
igneous
leitourgia
phytoplankton

Saint-Simonianism
shergottite
siderophore
zooplankton

To deal with a Pure Jargon term, first assess how important it is. If it's just a side example, ignore it. But if it seems to play a big role in the passage, then abbreviate it to a single capital letter in your notes.

For instance, in one published GRE passage, *shergottites* are very important. In fact, they present the central puzzle of the passage.

When you read that passage, you could write this: *S's* = *big puzzle*.

Notice that you can get a sequence of these Pure Jargon terms: X is used to define Y, which then is used to define Z. In the *shergottite* passage, first *igneous* is defined, then *achondrites* and *chondrules*, and finally *shergottites* are defined as a particular type of *achondrite*. There's nothing crazy here. Just keep track of the sequence!

2. Semi-Jargon

Semi-Jargon words are a bit more common than Pure Jargon. You may have heard or seen these words before. The passage may not stop to define these words, but it will give you enough within a couple of sentences to figure out a working definition.

Here are a few examples of Semi-Jargon words from published GRE passages, together with the working definition you can piece together from context:

empiricism = a philosophy of using observations to gain knowledge
isotope = some kind or version of a chemical element
lymphocyte = something from the immune system that attacks foreign stuff in the body
magistrate = some kind of public official

With Semi-Jargon words, you need to be okay with partial, incomplete definitions. It may bother you that you don't know or remember more. Relax; you can rely on the contextual meaning.

3. Glued-Together Words

Glued-Together words mean exactly what you'd guess they mean: two more common words are mashed together into one. They look fancy and imposing, but don't be intimidated. Just break them into parts.

Here are some examples from published GRE passages:

circumstellar = around a star
deradicalized = something made not radical or extreme
geochemical = having to do with geology and chemistry
historicophilosophical = both historical and philosophical
knowingness = quality of knowing something
presolar = before the sun
sociodemographic = having to do with both sociology and demography; the study of populations
spherule = tiny sphere or globule

4. Common Words Used in Fancy Ways

This isn't a big category, but it's worth watching for. You may come across a common word that momentarily confuses you, because it's used in a "literary" way—not the way you'd use it in speech.

Here are a couple of examples:

> *argue* = argue for
> *the absence of rhyme argues a subversion* ... = the absence of rhyme argues FOR a subversion ...
> *minute* = small
> *minute quantities* ... = small quantities ...

If a common word trips you up, ask yourself how else you might use it in writing.

5. Vocab You Oughta Know

These words are the most dangerous, because although the passage will still give you context, it will give you less context for them than for the Pure Jargon or Semi-Jargon words. In fact, if you aren't sure what these words mean, you might struggle briefly as you sort out the possible meanings.

However, if you know these words outright, you will move faster through passages. Moreover, these words are ones you're generally studying for the rest of the Verbal section, so you should be in good shape anyway.

Here are a few favorites (ones that have shown up in more than one published passage):

> *ephemeral* = short-lived, vanishing
> *fluctuation* = a change up and down, variation
> *ideology* = system of beliefs (also *ideological*)
> *unequivocal* = without a doubt, unambiguous (also *unequivocally*)

Vocabulary List for the GRE

Abate: Reduce or diminish.

> Her stress over spending so much money on a house **abated** when the real estate broker told her about the property's 15-year tax **abatement**.

Aberration, anomaly: Something that stands out or is abnormal. *Outlier* is similar.

> The election of a liberal candidate in the conservative county was an **aberration** (or **anomaly**), made possible only by the sudden death of the conservative candidate two days before the election.

Acclaim: Great praise or approval.

Accord, discord: Accord is agreement, and discord is disagreement.

> Our management is **in accord with** regulatory agencies; we agree that standards should be tightened.

Acquisitiveness: Desire to acquire more, especially an excessive desire.

> The firm did well in buying up its competitors as a means of growth, but its **acquisitiveness** ultimately resulted in problems related to growing too quickly.

Acreage: Land measured in acres.

> Our property is large, but much of the **acreage** is swampland not suitable for building.

Adhere to and **adherent:** To stick to (literally, such as with glue, or metaphorically, such as to a plan or belief). An adherent is a person who sticks to a belief or cause.

> The **adherents** of the plan won't admit that, in the long term, such a policy would bankrupt our state.

> Employees who do not **adhere** to the policy will be subject to disciplinary action.

Ad-lib: Make something up on the spot, give an unprepared speech; freely, as needed, according to desire.

> We have ended our policy of rationing office supplies—pens may now be given to employees **ad-lib**.

Adopt: Take and make one's own; vote to accept. You can adopt a child, of course, or a new policy. To adopt a plan implies that you didn't come up with it yourself.

Advent: Arrival.

> Before the **advent** of the internet, people often called reference librarians to look up information for them in the library's reference section.

Adverse: Unfavorable, opposed.

> The professor is **adverse** to any experiments that involve living subjects because those subjects could suffer **adverse** effects.

Agency: The ability to use power or influence.

> Some global warming deniers acknowledge that the planet is heating up, but argue that human **agency** does not affect the climate.

Aggravate: Make worse.

> Allowing your band to practice in our garage has greatly **aggravated** my headache.

Altogether: Completely, overall. *Altogether* is an adverb; it is one word. It is not the same as *all together*, as in *Let's sing all together*.

> It was an **altogether** stunning new design.

Ambivalent: Uncertain, unable to decide; wanting to do two contradictory things at once.

> The healthcare plan has been met with **ambivalence** from lawmakers who would like to pass the bill but find supporting it to be politically impossible.

Amortize: Gradually pay off a debt, or gradually write off an asset.

> A mortgage is a common form of **amortized** debt—spreading the payments out over as long as 30 years is not uncommon.

Analogous: Corresponding in a particular way, making a good *analogy*.

> Our situation is **analogous** to one in a case study I read in business school. Maybe what worked for that company will work for us.

Annex: To add on, or something that has been added on. An annex to a building is a part built later and added on, or a new building that allows an organization to expand.

Annihilate: Completely destroy.

Annul: Make void or null, cancel, abolish (usually of laws or other established rules). Most people associate this word with marriage—a marriage is annulled when a judge rules that it was invalid in the first place (because of fraud, mental incompetence, etc.), as if it never happened.

> Can we appreciate the art of a murderer? For many, the value of these paintings is **annulled** by the artist's crimes.

Anoint: The literal meaning is "rub or sprinkle oil on, especially as part of a ceremony that makes something sacred." The word is used metaphorically to refer to power or praise given to someone who is thought very highly of.

> After Principal Smitters raised test scores over 60 percent at her school, it was only a matter of time before she was **anointed** superintendant by a fawning school board.

Antithetical to: Totally opposed to; opposite.

> The crimes of our chairman are totally **antithetical** to what the Society for Ethical Leadership stands for.

Application: Act or result of applying. Of course, you can have an *application* to business school, but you can also say, *The application of pressure to the wound will help to stop the bleeding.*

Apprentice: A person who works for someone else in order to learn a trade (such as shoemaking, weaving, electrician, etc.).

Arbiter: Judge, umpire, person empowered to decide matters at hand. *Arbitration* is typically a formal process in which a professional *arbitrator* decides a matter outside of a court of law. The verb is *to arbitrate.*

> Professional mediators **arbitrate** disputes.

> The principal said, "As the final **arbiter** of what is and is not appropriate in the classroom, I demand that you take down that poster showing young people drinking alcohol."

Archaic: Characteristic of an earlier period, ancient, primitive.

> The school's **archaic** computer system predated even floppy disks—it stored records on tape drives!

> Sometimes, when you look a word up the dictionary, certain definitions are marked "**archaic**"—unless you are a Shakespeare scholar, you can safely ignore those **archaisms**.

Aristocracy: A hereditary ruling class, nobility (or a form of government ruled by these people).

Artifact: Any object made by humans, especially those from an earlier time, such as those excavated by archaeologists.

> The archaeologists dug up countless **artifacts**, from simple pottery shards and coins to complex written tablets.

> The girl's room was full of the **artifacts** of modern teenage life: Justin Bieber posters, *Twilight* books, and a laptop open to Facebook.

Ascribe to/ascription: To *ascribe* is to give credit; *ascription* is the noun form.

> He **ascribed** his good grades **to** diligent studying.

> The boy's mother was amused by the **ascription to** his imaginary friend **of** all the powers he wished he had himself—being able to fly, having dozens of friends, and never having to eat his broccoli.

Assert: Affirm, claim, state or express (that something is true).

Assimilation: The process by which a minority group adopts the customs and way of life of a larger group, or the process by which any new thing being introduced begins to "blend in." For example, *Westernization* refers to the process of *assimilation* into Western culture.

Attain: Achieve.

Attribute to: Give credit to.

Atypical: Not typical.

Backfire: To produce an unexpected and unwanted result. The literal meaning refers to an engine, gun, etc., exploding backward or discharging gases, flame, debris, etc., thus possibly causing injury.

> The company's new efficiency measures **backfired** when workers protested and staged a walkout, thus stopping production completely.

Balance: The remaining part or leftover amount. This is related to the idea of a *bank balance*—a *balance* is what you have left after deductions.

> The publishing division accounted for 25 percent of the profits, and the film division for **the balance**. This means that the film division provided 75 percent of the profits.

Baldly: Plainly, explicitly. (This word also means "losing one's hair.") To say something *baldly* is to be blunt. People are sometimes shocked or offended when things are said too bluntly or *baldly*.

> Her students were shocked when she **baldly** stated, "If you don't work harder, you will fail my class."

Balloon: Swell or puff out; increase rapidly. Also, in finance, a *balloon payment* is a single payment at the end of a loan or mortgage term that is much larger than the other payments.

> During the dot-com bubble, the university's investments **ballooned** to three times their former value.

> When he won the award, his chest **ballooned** with pride.

Befall: Happen to (used with something bad). The past tense is *befell*.

> Disaster **befell** the company once again when the CEO was thrown from a horse.

Belie: Contradict or misrepresent.

> The actress's public persona as a perky "girl next door" **belied** her private penchant for abusing her assistants and demanding that her trailer be filled with ridiculous luxury goods.

> The data **belie** the accepted theory—either we've made a mistake, or we have an amazing new discovery on our hands!

Benevolent: Expressing goodwill, helping others, or charity.

Benign: Harmless; kind or beneficent; not cancerous.

> He was relieved when the biopsy results came back informing him that the growth was **benign**.

> He's a **benign** fellow. I'm sure working with him will be perfectly pleasant, and he won't disrupt the existing team.

14

Blight: Disease that kills plants rapidly, or any cause of decay or destruction (noun); ruin or cause to wither (verb).

Many potato farmers have fallen into poverty as a result of **blight** killing their crops.

Gang violence is a **blight** on our school system, causing innocent students to fear even attending classes. In fact, violence has **blighted** our town.

Blunt: To dull, weaken, or make less effective.

The new therapy has severe side effects, but they can be **blunted** somewhat with anti-nausea medication and painkillers.

Blur: To make blurry, unclear, indistinct.

In Japan, company titles are taken very seriously and roles are sharply defined, whereas in the United States—especially in smaller firms—roles are often **blurred** as everyone is expected to pitch in on a variety of projects.

Bogus: Fake, fraudulent.

The back of this bodybuilding magazine is full of ads for **bogus** products—this one promises 22-inch biceps just from wearing magnetic armbands!

Bolster: Strengthen or support.

The general requested reinforcements to **bolster** the defensive line set up at the border.

Some people believe that self-affirmation exercises are an effective way to **bolster** self-esteem and even performance.

Broad: Wide, large; in the open (*in broad daylight*); obvious, clear; liberal, tolerant; covering a wide scope of things. (*Broad* is also a mildly derogatory term for women, in case you're confused—of course, no one would ever be called *a broad* on the GRE.)

The panel was given **broad** discretionary powers. (The panel can do whatever it wants.)

Brook: Suffer or tolerate. Often used with the word *no*. You could say, *The dictator will not brook dissent*, but a more common usage would be *The dictator will brook no dissent*.

Buffer: Something that separates two groups, people, etc., who potentially do not get along.

When the United States was controlled by England, the state of Georgia was colonized as a **buffer** between the English colonies and Spanish Florida. A breakwater of rocks would act as a **buffer**, protecting the beach from crashing waves.

Bureaucracy: Government characterized by many bureaucrats and petty administrators; excessive, seemingly meaningless requirements.

Some nations have a worse reputation for **bureaucracy** than others—in order to get a visa, he had to file papers with four different agencies, wait for hours in three different waiting rooms, and, weeks later, follow up with some petty **bureaucrat** who complained that the original application should've been filed in triplicate.

14

Bygone: Past, former; that which is in the past (usually plural, as in the expression *Let bygones be bygones*, which means to let the past go, especially by forgiving someone).

At the nursing home, people reminisced about **bygone** days all the time.

Bypass: Avoid, go around; ignore. The word can be a noun or a verb. Literally, a **bypass** is a stretch of highway that goes *around* an obstacle (such as a construction site). A synonym for *bypass* (verb) is *circumvent*, as in *to circumvent (or bypass) the normal approval process by going straight to the company president.*

Canon: Body of accepted rules, standards, or artistic works; **canonical** means authorized, recognized, or pertaining to a canon. Note that the spelling of *canon* is not the same as *cannon* (a large weapon). The *Western canon* is an expression referring to books traditionally considered necessary for a person to be educated in the culture of Europe and the Americas.

School boards often start controversies when replacing **canonical** books in the curriculum with modern literature; while many people think students should read works more relevant to their lives, others point out that *Moby Dick* is part of the **canon** for a reason.

Chancy: Risky, not having a certain outcome. This word comes from the idea of *taking a lot of chances* or depending on chance.

Channel: To direct or guide along a particular course. *Channel* can also be a noun (television channel, the channel of a river, channels of communication). As a verb, you might *channel* your energy toward productive purposes.

Check (held in check): Restrained, held back. A *check* can also be used to mean "safeguard, limitation." This is the same *check* as in *checks and balances*, which refers to an aspect of the American system of government in which the Executive, Judicial, and Legislative branches all have power over each other so no one branch can gain too much power.

Once the economy took a turn for the worse, the investors began to **hold** spending **in check**.

The situation isn't so simple—while the warlords are surely criminals of the worst degree, they are the only force **checking** the power of the dictator.

Chronological: Arranged in or relating to time order.

Joey, I'm afraid you've done the assignment incorrectly—the point of making a timeline is to put the information in **chronological** order. You've made an alphabetical-order-line instead!

Clamor: Noisy uproar or protest, as from a crowd; a loud, continuous noise. (Not the same word as *clamber*, to scramble or climb awkwardly.)

As soon as a scent of scandal emerged, the press was **clamoring** for details.

The mayor couldn't even make herself heard over the **clamor** of the protestors.

Clan: Traditional social unit or division of a tribe consisting of a number of families derived from a common ancestor. Metaphorically, a *clan* could be any group of people united by common aims, interests, etc.

Cloak: To cover or conceal. Often used as *cloaked in*. (Literally, a *cloak* is a large, loose cape, much like a winter coat without arms.)

Apple's new products are often **cloaked in** mystery before they are released; before the launch of the iPad, even tech reviewers had little idea what the new device would be.

Coalesce: Come together, unite; fuse together.

> While at first everyone on the team was jockeying for power and recognition, eventually the group **coalesced**, and everyone was happy to share credit for a job well done.

> East and West Germany **coalesced** into a single country in 1990.

Coercion: Force; use of pressure, threats, etc. to force someone to do something.

Coexistence: Existing at the same time or in the same place. *Coexistence* is often used to mean "peaceful coexistence," as in *The goal of the Camp David Accords was the coexistence of Israel and Egypt.*

Cogent: Very convincing, logical.

> Many letters to the editor are not terribly **cogent**—they depend on unspoken and unjustified assumptions.

Cognitive: Related to thinking. *Cognition* is the mental process of knowing (awareness, judgment, reasoning, etc.).

Collude: Conspire; cooperate for illegal or fraudulent purposes.

> After two competing software companies doubled their prices on the same day, leaving consumers no lower-priced alternative, the federal government investigated the companies for **collusion**.

Compliant: Obeying, submissive; following the requirements.

> Those who are not **compliant** with the regulations will be put on probation and possibly expelled.

Compound: Add interest to the principal and accrued interest; increase. When talking about substances, *compound* can also mean "mix, combine," as in *to compound two chemicals.*

> The town was greatly damaged by the hurricane—damage that was only **compounded** by the subsequent looting and even arson that took place in the chaos that followed.

> Your success in studying for the GRE can only be **compounded** by healthy sleep habits; in fact, the brain requires sleep in order to form new memories and thus solidify your knowledge.

Compromise: Reduce the quality or value of something. Of course, to *compromise* can be good in personal relationships, but often *compromise* means to give up something in a bad way, as in *to compromise one's morals.* So if we say that the hull of our boat has been *compromised*, we mean that we are going to sink!

> It is unacceptable that safety is being **compromised** in the name of profits.

Concede: Give in, admit, yield; acknowledge reluctantly; grant or give up (such as giving up land after losing a war).

> The negotiations were pointless, with each side's representatives instructed by their home countries to make no **concessions** whatsoever.

> Quebec was a French **concession** to Britain in the Treaty of Paris in 1763.

> I suppose I will have to **concede** the argument now that you've looked up evidence on Wikipedia.

Condone: Overlook, tolerate, regard as harmless.

> While underage drinking is illegal, at many universities it is tacitly **condoned** by administrations that neglect to enforce anti-drinking policies.

Confer: Consult, compare views; bestow or give.

> A Ph.D. **confers** upon a person the right to be addressed as "Doctor," as well as eligibility to pursue a tenure-track professorship.

> Excuse me for a moment so I can make a call—I can't buy this car until I **confer** with my spouse.

Consequently: As a result, therefore (don't confuse with *subsequently*, which means "afterward").

> The new medicine is not only a failure, but a dangerous one; **consequently**, drug trials were halted immediately.

Considerable: Large, significant.

Considerations: Factors to be considered in making a decision. Used in the singular, *consideration* can mean care for other people's feelings, high esteem or admiration, or a treatment or account, as in *The book began with a thorough consideration of the history of the debate.*

Consolidate: Unite, combine, solidify, make coherent.

> She **consolidated** her student loans so she would only have to make one payment per month.

> As group leader, Muriel will **consolidate** all of our research into a single report.

Contemplative: Contemplating, thoughtful, meditative.

Contend: Assert, make an argument in favor of; strive, compete, struggle. A *contention* is a claim, often a thesis or statement that will then be backed up with reasons. *Contentious* means controversial or argumentative, as in *The death penalty is a contentious issue.*

Contextualize: Place in context, such as by giving the background or circumstances.

> Virginia Woolf's feminism is hard to truly understand unless **contextualized** within the mores of the highly restrained, upper-class English society of her time.

Contract: Shrink, pull together and thus become smaller (used in this way, *contract* is the opposite of *expand*). You can also *contract* a disease or a debt, in which case *contract* means "get" or "acquire." To *contract* can also simply mean to make a contract (to *contract* an agreement).

Conventional: Traditional, customary. This could be related to morals and culture (*Her family was surprised that she had rejected the conventional wedding ceremony in favor of a bohemian ceremony on the beach*). It could be related to technology, business methods, and so on—a *conventional* oven is simply a regular oven (without certain modern enhancements).

Converge: Move toward one another or toward a common point; unite.

> I know we're driving in to the wedding from different states, but our routes ought to **converge** when each of us reaches I-95—maybe we could **converge** at a Cracker Barrel for lunch!

Conversely: In an opposite way; on the other hand.

> I am not here to argue that lack of education causes poverty. **Conversely**, I am here to argue that poverty causes lack of education.

Convoluted: Twisted; very complicated.

> Your argument is so **convoluted** that I'm not even able to understand it enough to start critiquing it.

> To get from the hotel room to the pool requires following a **convoluted** path up two staircases and down two others—to get to someplace on the same floor we started on!

Copious: Plentiful, bountiful.

> Although she took **copious** notes in class, she found that she was missing a big-picture understanding that would have tied all the information together.

Corresponding: Accompanying; having the same or almost the same relationship.

> Our profit-sharing plan means that increases in profit will be matched by **corresponding** increases in employee compensation.

Corroborate: Support, add evidence to.

> You claim that you were 30 miles away riding a roller coaster when the school was vandalized? I have a hard time believing that—is there anyone who can **corroborate** your story?

Countenance: Approve or tolerate. *Countenance* can also literally mean "face." (*Her countenance was familiar—did we know each other?*) The metaphorical meaning makes sense when you think about a similar expression: *I cannot* look you in the face *after what you did.*

> I saw you cheating off my paper, and I can't **countenance** cheating—either you turn yourself in, or I'll report you.

Counterintuitive: Against what a person would intuitively expect.

> Although it seems **counterintuitive**, for some extreme dieters, eating more can actually help them to lose weight, since the body is reassured that it is not facing a period of prolonged starvation.

Counterpoint: Contrasting item, opposite; a complement; the use of contrast or interplay in a work of art.

> The play's lighthearted, witty narrator provides a welcome **counterpoint** to the seriousness and grief expressed by the other characters.

> The spicy peppers work in **counterpoint** to an otherwise sweet dish.

Counterproductive: Defeating the purpose; preventing the intended goal.

> The candidate's attempt to win undecided voters was actually **counterproductive**—following his latest speech, his poll numbers actually went *down* 5 percent.

Credibility: Believability, trustworthiness.

> After promising to take care of a client emergency late on Friday afternoon, he lost all **credibility** when he failed to answer his phone or check his email all weekend.

Culminate: Reach the highest point or final stage.

> A Ph.D. program generally **culminates** in a written dissertation and the public defense of that dissertation.

Currency: Money; the act of being passed from person-to-person (*These old coins are no longer in currency*); general acceptance or a period of time during which something is accepted. *Cultural currency* refers to cultural knowledge that allows a person to feel "in the know."

> The call center in Mumbai trained its workers in Western slang and pop culture, giving them a **cultural currency** that, it was hoped, would help the workers relate to customers thousands of miles away.

Curtail: Cut short or reduce.

Cynical: Thinking the worst of others' motivations; bitterly pessimistic.

Debase: Degrade; lower in quality, value, rank, etc.; lower in moral quality.

> I can tell from the weight that this isn't pure gold, but rather some **debased** mixed metal.

> You have **debased** yourself by accepting bribes.

Debilitating: Weakening, disabling.

Debunk: Expose, ridicule, or disprove false or exaggerated claims.

> Galileo spent his last years under house arrest for **debunking** the widely held idea that the sun revolved around the earth.

> The show *MythBusters* **debunks** pseudoscientific claims.

Decry: Condemn openly. The *cry* in *decry* has the sense of "cry out against," as in *The activist decried the destruction of the animals' habitat.*

Deem: Judge; consider.

> "You can take the black belt exam when I **deem** you ready and not a moment before," said the karate master.

Deflect: Cause to curve; turn aside, esp. from a straight course; avoid.

> The purpose of a shield is to **deflect** arrows or bullets.

> Every time he was asked a difficult question, Senator Warrington **deflected** by changing the topic.

Delimit: Fix, mark, or define the boundaries of.

> The role of an executive coach is **delimited** by our code of conduct—we may not counsel people for psychological conditions, for instance.

Denote: Be a name or symbol for. A *denotation* is the literal meaning of a word; a *connotation* is the feeling that accompanies that word.

> There's nothing in the **denotation** of *crotchety* (grumpy, having strong and irrational preferences) that indicates any particular group of people, but because of the expression *crotchety old man*, the word **connotes**, for many people, an image of an especially unpleasant male senior citizen.

Deride: Mock, scoff at, laugh at contemptuously.

> The manager really thought that **deriding** his employees as *stupid* or *lazy* would motivate them to work harder; instead, it motivated them to hide his office supplies as an act of revenge.

14

Deterrent: Something that restrains or discourages.

Some argue that punishment should also function as a **deterrent** to crime; that is, the point is not just to punish the guilty, but to frighten other prospective criminals.

Dichotomy: Division into two parts or into two contradictory groups.

There is a **dichotomy** in the sciences between theoretical or "pure" sciences, such as physics and chemistry, and the life sciences, which often deal more with real-world considerations than with theorizing.

Disclosure: Revealing, exposing the truth; something that has been revealed. *Full disclosure* is an expression meaning telling everything. In journalism, the expression is often used when a writer reveals a personal connection to the story. For instance, a news article might read, "MSNBC may have forced the departure of popular anchor Keith Olbermann (full disclosure: this author was employed as a fact-checker for MSNBC in 2004)."

Discount: Ignore, especially to ignore information because it is considered untrustworthy; to underestimate, minimize, regard with doubt. To *discount* an idea is to *not count* it as important.

After staying up all night to finish the presentation, he was understandably unhappy that his boss **discounted** his contribution, implying that she had done most of the work herself.

Discredit: Injure the reputation of, destroy credibility of or confidence in.

The unethical consultant tried to **discredit** the work of one of his client's prospective hires because the consultant hoped to be offered the job himself.

Discrepancy: Difference or inconsistency.

When there is a **discrepancy** between a store's receipts and the amount of money in the register, the cashier's behavior is generally called into question.

Discrete: Separate, distinct, detached, existing as individual parts. This is not the same word as *discreet*, which means "subtle, secretive."

Be sure to use quotation marks and citations as appropriate in your paper in order to keep your ideas **discrete** from those of the experts you are quoting.

The advertising agency pitched us not on one campaign but on three **discrete** ideas.

Discretionary: Subject to someone's *discretion* or judgment (generally good judgment). *Discretionary funds* can be spent on anything (for instance, a budget might contain a small amount for unanticipated extras). *Begin at your discretion* means "begin whenever you think is best."

Discriminating: Judicious, discerning, having good judgment or insight. Many people automatically think of *discriminating* as bad, because they are thinking of racial discrimination. However, *discriminating* is simply telling things apart and can be an important skill—it is important to *discriminate* legitimate colleges from fraudulent diploma mills, for instance.

He is a man of **discriminating** tastes—all his suits are handmade in Italy, and I once saw him send back an entrée when he complained that black truffle oil had been substituted for white. The chef was astounded that he could tell.

You can tell a real Prada bag by the **discriminating** mark on the inside.

Disinterested: Unbiased, impartial; not taking a side. Don't confuse with *uninterested,* which means not interested, bored, apathetic.

> Let's settle this argument once and for all! We'll get a **disinterested** observer to judge who can sing the highest note!

Dismiss: Put aside or reject, especially after only a brief consideration; allow to disperse or leave; fire from a job. To *dismiss biases* (*biases* is the plural of *bias*) in science is to rule out possible prejudices that could have influenced results.

> "Before I **dismiss** the class," said the teacher, "I want to remind you of the importance of **dismissing** biases in your research by ruling out or adjusting for any unintended factors that may have led to your results."

Disparate: Distinct, different.

> He chose the college for two **disparate** reasons: the strength of the computer science program and the excellence of the hip-hop dance squad.

Dispatch: Speed, promptness (noun); send off or deal with in a speedy way (verb).

> So you want to be a bike messenger? I need messengers who approach every delivery with alacrity, care, and **dispatch**—if the customers wanted their packages to arrive slowly, they'd use the post office.

> Acting with all possible **dispatch**, emergency services **dispatched** a rescue squad to the scene.

Disperse: Scatter, spread widely, cause to vanish. *Dispersal* is the noun form.

> Because the demonstrators didn't have a permit, the police showed up with megaphones, demanding loudly that the crowd **disperse**. The eventual **dispersal** of the crowd resulted in smaller protests at various points throughout the city.

Disseminate: Scatter, spread about, broadcast.

> Nobody knows about the new company benefits; the information should be **disseminated** via email and placed in the employee handbook.

Divest: Deprive or strip of a rank, title, etc., or of clothing or gear; to sell off holdings (opposite of *invest*).

> When she found out that the most profitable stock in her portfolio was that of a company that tested products on animals, she immediately **divested** by telling her broker to sell the stock.

> Once his deception was exposed, he was **divested** of his position on the Board.

Dovetail: Join or fit together.

> When the neuroscientist married an exercise physiologist, neither thought they'd end up working together, but when Dr. Marion Ansel received a grant to study how exercise improves brain function and Dr. Jim Ansel was assigned to her team, the two found that their careers **dovetailed** nicely.

Dubious: Doubtful, questionable, suspect.

> This applicant's résumé is filled with **dubious** qualifications—this is a marketing position, but this résumé is mostly about whitewater rafting.

Echelon: A level, rank, or grade; the people at that level. A *stratum* is the same idea (*strata* is the plural, as in *rising through the upper strata/echelons of the firm*).

> Obtaining a job on Wall Street doesn't guarantee access to the upper **echelons** of executives, where multi-million-dollar bonuses are the norm.

> I'm not sure I'm cut out to analyze poetry; I find it hard to dig beyond the most accessible **echelon** of meaning.

Eclectic: Selecting the best of everything or from many diverse sources.

> **Eclectic** taste is helpful in being a DJ—crowds love to hear the latest hip-hop mixed with '80s classics and other unexpected genres of music.

Eclipse: One thing covering up another, such as the sun hiding the moon or a person losing attention to a more famous or talented person; to cover up, darken, or make less important.

> Billy Ray Cyrus, who had a hit song, "Achy Breaky Heart," in the '90s, has long since found his fame **eclipsed** by that of his daughter, Miley.

Effectively: *Effectively* can mean "in a successful manner," as in *He did the job effectively.* But it can also mean *in effect, but not officially.* For instance, when Woodrow Wilson was President of the United States, he was incapacitated by a stroke, and some people believe that Wilson's wife, Edith, *effectively* served as president. That doesn't mean she was necessarily effective. Rather, it means that she was doing the job of the president without officially being the president.

> He went on a two-week vacation without asking for time off or even telling anyone he was leaving, thus **effectively** resigning from his position.

Efficacy: The quality of being able to produce the intended effect. Don't confuse *efficacy* with *efficiency.* Something *efficacious* gets the job done; something *efficient* gets the job done without wasting time or effort. *Efficacy* is frequently used in reference to medicines.

> Extensive trials will be necessary to determine whether the drug's **efficacy** outweighs the side effects.

Egalitarian: Related to belief in the equality of all people.

> It is very rare that someone turns down an offer to be knighted by the Queen of England; however, he was **egalitarian** enough to feel uncomfortable with the entire idea of titles and royalty.

Egregious: Extraordinarily or conspicuously bad; glaring.

> Your conduct is an **egregious** violation of our Honor Code—not only did you steal your roommate's paper and turn it in as your own, but you also sold his work to a plagiarism website so other cheaters could purchase it!

Emancipate: Free from slavery or oppression. Lincoln's Emancipation Proclamation legally ended slavery in the United States. In law, to *emancipate* a minor is to declare the child (generally a teenager) no longer under the control of his or her parents.

Eminent: Prominent, distinguished, of high rank.

Emphasize: Give special force or attention to.

> In GRE Reading Comprehension passages, the purpose of a particular sentence could be to **emphasize** a point that came before.

14

Empirical: Coming from, based on, or able to be verified by experience or experimentation; not purely based on theory.

> The Ancient Greeks philosophized about the nature of matter (concluding, for instance, that everything was made of earth, water, air, and fire) without any **empirical** evidence—the very idea of conducting experiments hadn't been invented yet.

> People always knew **empirically** that when you drop something, it falls to the ground; the theory of gravity later explained why.

Emulate: Copy in an attempt to equal or be better than.

> The ardent *Star Trek* fan **emulated** Captain Kirk in every way possible—his brash and confident leadership might have gotten him somewhere, but the women he tried to impress weren't so impressed.

Enigma: Puzzle, mystery, riddle; mysterious or contradictory person.

> The enormous rock sculptures at Stonehenge are truly an **enigma**: were they created as part of a religious observance, in deference to a great ruler, or for some other reason?

Enjoy: Enjoy means to receive pleasure from, but it also means to benefit from. Thus, it is not true that only people and animals can *enjoy*. For instance:

> The college has long **enjoyed** the support of wealthy alumni.

Ensure vs. **insure:** If you buy insurance for something, you have *insured* it. If you guarantee something, you have *ensured* it.

> If you go past this security checkpoint, I cannot **ensure** your safety.

Enumerate: Count or list; specify one-by-one.

> The Bill of Rights **enumerates** the basic rights held by every citizen of the United States.

Equitable: Fair, equal, just.

> As the university president was heavily biased toward the sciences, faculty in the liberal arts felt they had to fight to get an **equitable** share of funding for their departments.

Equivalence: The state of being equal or essentially equal.

Equivocal or **equivocate:** Use unclear language to deceive or avoid committing to a position.

> Not wanting to lose supporters, the politician **equivocated** on the issue, tossing out buzzwords related to each side while also claiming more study was needed.

Erratic: Inconsistent, wandering, having no fixed course.

> When someone engages in **erratic** behavior, family members often suspect drugs or mental illness. However, sometimes the person is just building a top-secret invention in the garage!

Erroneous: Mistaken, in error.

> Hilda was completely unable to assemble her new desk chair after the instructions **erroneously** instructed her to screw the left armrest onto a small lever on the bottom of the seat.

Erstwhile: Former, previous.

A novelist and **erstwhile** insurance salesman, he told us his story of the long road to literary success, before he was able to quit his day job.

Escape velocity: The minimum velocity that an object must attain in order to completely escape a gravitational field.

Estimable: Worthy of esteem, admirable; able to be estimated.

He graduated first in his class, was editor of the Law Review, and clerked for a Supreme Court judge; his résumé is **estimable**.

Riding a roller coaster is safer than driving on the highway, but there is still an **estimable** risk.

Ethos: The character, personality, or moral values specific to a person, group, time period, etc.

At the prep school, the young man happily settled into an **ethos** of hard work and rigorous athletic competition.

Exacerbate: Make worse (more violent, severe, etc.), inflame.

Allowing your band to practice in our garage has greatly **exacerbated** my headache.

Exacting: Very severe in making demands; requiring precise attention.

The boxing coach was **exacting**, analyzing Laila's footwork down to the millimeter and forcing her to repeat movements hundreds of times until they were correct.

Execute: Put into effect, do, perform (to *execute* a process). *Execute* can also mean "enforce, make legal, carry out the terms of a legal agreement." To *execute* a will is to sign it in the presence of witnesses. To *execute* the terms of a contract is to fulfill an obligation written in the contract.

Exhaustive: Comprehensive, thorough, exhausting a topic or subject, accounting for all possibilities; draining, tending to exhaust.

The consultant's report was an **exhaustive** treatment of all possible options and their likely consequences. In fact, it was so **exhaustive** that the manager joked that he would need to hire another consultant to read the first consultant's report.

Exotic: Foreign, intriguingly unusual or strange.

Expansionist: Wanting to expand, such as by conquering other countries

Expedient: Suitable, proper; effective (sometimes while sacrificing ethics).

"I need this report by 2 PM, and I don't care what you have to do to make that happen," said the boss. "I expect you to deal with it **expediently**."

When invited to a wedding you cannot attend, it is **expedient** to send a gift.

Explicit: Direct, clear, fully revealed. *Explicit* in the context of movies, music, etc., means depicting or describing sex or nudity, but *explicit* can be used for anything (*explicit instructions* is a common phrase). The antonym of **explicit** is *implicit* or *tacit*, meaning "hinted at, implied."

The goal of my motivational talk is to make **explicit** the connection between staying in school and avoiding a life of crime.

14

Extraneous: Irrelevant; foreign, coming from without, not belonging.

This essay would be stronger if you removed **extraneous** information; this paragraph about the author's life doesn't happen to be relevant to your thesis.

Maize, which originated in the New World, is **extraneous** to Europe.

Extrapolate: Conjecture about an unknown by projecting information about something known; predict by projecting past experience. In math and science, to *extrapolate* is to infer values in an unobserved interval from values in an observed interval. For instance, from the points (1, 4) and (3, 8), you could *extrapolate* the point (5, 12) since it would be on the same line.

No, I've never been to Bryn Mawr, but I've visited several other small, private women's colleges in the Northeast, so I think I can **extrapolate**.

Facilitate: Make easier, help the progress of.

A good meeting **facilitator** lets everyone be heard while still keeping the meeting focused.

As a midwife, my goal is simply to **facilitate** a natural process.

Faction: A group (especially an exclusive group with strong beliefs, self-interest, bias, etc.) within a larger organization. This word is usually meant in a negative way (once people have joined *factions*, they are no longer willing to hear the issues and debate or compromise).

The opposition movement was once large enough to have a chance at succeeding, but it has since broken into numerous, squabbling **factions**, each too small to have much impact.

Faculty: An ability, often a mental ability. Most often used in the plural, as in *A stroke can often deprive a person of important mental faculties.* (*Faculty* can also mean the teachers or professors of an institution of learning.)

Fading: Declining.

In the face of **fading** public support for national healthcare, the senator withdrew his support for the bill.

Fashion: Manner or way.

The watchmaker works in a meticulous **fashion**, paying incredible attention to detail.

Fathom: Understand deeply.

I cannot even remotely **fathom** how you interpreted an invitation to sleep on my couch as permission to take my car on a six-hour joyride!

Finding: *The finding* (or *the findings*) refers to a discovery, report, result of an experiment, etc.

When the attorneys received the results of the DNA report, they were shocked by **the finding** that John Doe could not have committed the crime.

Fishy: Suspicious, unlikely, questionable, as in *a fishy story*. This expression probably arose because fish smell very bad when they start to spoil.

Fledgling: New or inexperienced. A fledgling is also a young bird that cannot fly yet.

The Society of Engineers is available for career day presentations in elementary schools, where we hope to encourage **fledgling** talents in the applied sciences.

Fleeting: Passing quickly, transitory.

I had assumed our summer romance would be **fleeting**, so I was very surprised when you proposed marriage!

Foreshadow: Indicate or suggest beforehand.

In the movie, the children's ghost story around the campfire **foreshadowed** the horrible things that would happen to them years later as teenagers at a motel in the middle of the woods.

Forestall: Delay, hinder, prevent by taking action beforehand.

Our research has been **forestalled** by a lack of funding; we're all just biding our time while we wait for the university to approve our grant proposal.

Glacial: Slow, cold, icy, unsympathetic. *Glacial* can also just mean "related to glaciers."

Progress happened, but at a **glacial** pace everyone found frustrating.

He had wanted to appear on the reality singing competition his whole young life, but he was not encouraged by the judges' **glacial** response to his audition.

Grade, gradation: To *grade* is to slant (the road *grades* steeply) or to blend (the dress's fabric *grades* from blue to green). A *gradation* is a progression or process taking place gradually, in stages.

The hill's **gradation** was so gradual that even those on crutches were able to enjoy the nature trail.

The marshland **grades** into the water so gradually that it is difficult to tell the land from the bay.

Graft: Join together plant parts or skin so that two living things grow together (e.g., a *skin graft* for a burn victim); the act of acquiring money or other benefits through illegal means, especially by abusing one's power.

The part of the book describing the financial crisis is good, but the "What You Can Do" section seems **grafted** on, almost as though written by a different author.

It's not cool for your boss to pressure you into buying Girl Scout cookies from his daughter. If she were selling something larger, we'd call that **graft**.

Grandstand: Perform showily in an attempt to impress onlookers.

I was really passionate about the candidate when he spoke at our school, but now that I think about it, he was just **grandstanding**. I mean, who could disagree that young people are the future? And doing a cheer for the environment doesn't actually signify a commitment to changing any public policies about it.

Guesswork: A set of guesses or estimates; work based on guesses or estimates.

Guile: Clever deceit, cunning, craftiness.

The game of poker is all about **guile**, manipulating your own body language and patterns to lead other players to erroneous conclusions about the cards you're holding.

Hallmark: A mark or indication of quality, purity, genuineness, etc.; any distinguishing characteristic (not necessarily positive).

Fast-paced rhymes, an angry tenor, and personal attacks on celebrities are **hallmarks** of Eminem's music.

Hallucination: A delusion, a false or mistaken idea; seeing, sensing, or hearing things that aren't there, such as from a mental disorder.

Handpick: To pick by hand, to personally select.

The retiring CEO **handpicked** his successor.

Hardly: Almost or probably not, or not at all. (*I can hardly see you* means "I can see you only a little bit.") But in the following sentence, *hardly* means *not*.

The news could **hardly** have come at a worse time. (The meaning is "The news came at the worst possible time.")

Hardy: Bold, brave, capable of withstanding hardship, fatigue, cold, etc.

While the entire family enjoyed the trip to South America, only the **hardier** members even attempted to hike to the top of Ecuador's tallest volcano.

Hearken or **hark:** Listen, pay attention to. The expression *hearken back* or *hark back* means to turn back to something earlier or return to a source.

The simple lifestyle and anachronistic dress of the Amish **hearken** back to an earlier era.

The nation's first change of leadership in decades is causing the people to **hearken** closely to what is happening in government.

Hedge: Avoid commitment by leaving provisions for withdrawal or changing one's mind; protect a bet by also betting on the other side.

When the professor called on him to take a stand on the issue, he **hedged** for fear of offending her: "Well, there are valid points on both sides," he said.

Hegemony: Domination, authority; influence by one country over others socially, culturally, economically, etc.

The discovery of oil by a previously poor nation disrupted the larger, richer nation's **hegemony** in the region—suddenly, the **hegemon** had a competitor.

Heterogeneous: Different in type, incongruous; composed of different types of elements. *Homogeneous* (of the same kind) is the opposite of *heterogeneous.*

Rather than build the wall with plain brick, we used a **heterogeneous** mixture of stones—they are not only different colors, but a variety of sizes as well.

Hierarchy: A ranked series; a classification of people according to rank, ability, etc.; a ruling body.

The Eco-Action Coalition was led by a strict **hierarchy**: members followed orders from district leaders, district leaders from regional leaders, and regional leaders from the national head.

Holdings: Property, such as land, capital, and stock. *The company liquidated its holdings* means that the company sold off everything. Of course, the word *hold* has many meanings. *In a holding pattern* is an expression that means "staying still, not changing."

Host: A large amount. *A host of problems* means "a lot of problems."

14

Hyperbole: Deliberate exaggeration for effect.

Oh, come on. Saying "That movie was so bad it made me puke" was surely **hyperbole**. I strongly doubt that you actually vomited during or following *The Back-Up Plan*.

Iconoclast: Attacker of cherished beliefs or institutions.

A lifelong **iconoclast**, Ayn Rand wrote a controversial book entitled *The Virtue of Selfishness*.

Imminent: Ready to occur, impending.

In the face of **imminent** war, the nation looked to its leader for reassurance.

Immunity: The state of not being susceptible to disease; exemption from a duty or liability; exemption from legal punishment. *Diplomatic immunity* is an example of *immunity* meaning "exemption from legal punishment."

Every year, New York City loses millions of dollars when United Nations diplomats don't pay their parking tickets, since the diplomats have **immunity** from U.S. laws.

Impair: Make worse, weaken.

Playing in a rock band while failing to use earplugs will almost certainly **impair** your hearing over time.

Impartial: Unbiased, fair. *Disinterested, dispassionate*, and *nonpartisan* are all related to being fair and not having a bias or personal stake.

Judge Gonzales removed himself from the case because, having a personal connection to the school where the alleged violation took place, he did not think he could be appropriately **impartial**.

Impasse: Position or road from which there is no escape; deadlock, gridlock.

If the union won't budge on its demands and the transit authority won't raise salaries, then we are at an **impasse**.

Impede: Hold back, obstruct the progress of.

I didn't realize graduate school would consist of so much group work; sadly, there's always at least one person in every group who **impedes** the group's progress more than helps it.

Impinge on: Trespass on, violate.

Civil liberties experts argued that a school system's regulation of what its students do on Facebook outside of school is an **impingement on** their right to free speech.

Implode: Burst inward; metaphorically, to collapse or break down.

The startup struggled for years before it simply **imploded**—the management team broke into factions, all the clients were scared off, and employees who hadn't been paid in weeks began taking the office computers home with them in retribution.

Imply: Hint at, suggest, "say without saying."

Impute: To credit to, to attribute to; lay blame or responsibility for.

The ineffectual CEO was nevertheless a master of public relations—he made sure that all successes were **imputed** to him, and all of the failures were **imputed** to others.

Inadvertently: Accidentally, carelessly, as a side effect.

In attempting to perfect his science project, he **inadvertently** blew a fuse and plunged his family's home into darkness.

Inasmuch: Since, because; usually *inasmuch as.*

Inasmuch as a whale is not a fish, it will not be covered in this biology course specifically about fish.

Incentive: Something that encourages greater action or effort, such as a reward.

A controversial program in a failing school system uses cash payments as an **incentive** for students to stay in school.

Incidentally: Accidentally, not intentionally. *Incidentally* can also mean *by the way* and is used to introduce information that is only slightly related. *Incidentals* can refer to expenses that are "on the side" (*The company gives us $100 a day for meals and incidentals*).

The environmental protection law was **incidentally** injurious to the rubber industry.

I think we should move forward with the new office. **Incidentally**, there's a great Mexican restaurant opening up right across the street from it!

Incinerate: Burn, reduce to ashes, cremate.

Inconsequential: Insignificant, unimportant. The sense here is that the thing is so small that it doesn't even have *consequences.*

You wrote a best-selling book and got a stellar review in the *New York Times*—whatever your cousin has to say about it is simply **inconsequential.**

Incorporate: Combine, unite; form a legal corporation; embody, give physical form to.

When a business **incorporates**, it becomes a separate legal entity; for instance, the business can be sued without personal consequences for the owners.

Local legend has it that ghosts can **incorporate** on one night of the year and walk among the living.

Indeterminate: Not fixed or determined, indefinite; vague.

The results of the drug trial were **indeterminate**; further trials will be needed to ascertain whether the drug can be released.

The lottery can have an **indeterminate** number of winners—the prize is simply divided among them.

Indicative: Indicating, suggestive of. Usually used as *indicative of.*

Your symptoms are **indicative** of the common cold.

Induce: Persuade or influence (a person to do something); bring about, cause to happen (to *induce labor* when a birth is not proceeding quickly enough).

Inert: Inactive; having little or no power to move.

All of the missiles at the military museum are **inert**—they're not going blow up.

When she saw her father's **inert** body on the floor, she thought the worst, but fortunately he was just practicing very slow yoga.

Inevitable: Not able to be avoided or escaped; certain.

Benjamin Franklin famously said that only two things in life are **inevitable**: "death and taxes."

Inexplicable: Not able to be explained.

Inextricably: In a way such that one cannot untangle or escape something. If you are *inextricably tied* to something (such as your family), then you have so many different obligations and deep relationships that you could never leave, disobey, etc.

Infer: Conclude from evidence or premises. Remember, on the GRE, *infer* means "draw a *definitely true* conclusion." It does not mean "assume"!

Inform: Inspire, animate; give substance, essence, or context to; be the characteristic quality of. *Inform* most commonly means "impart knowledge to"; thus, many students are confused when they see the word used in other ways on the GRE.

Her work as an art historian is **informed** by a background in drama; where others see a static tableau, she sees a protagonist, a conflict, a denouement.

Ingenuity: Inventive skill, imagination, cleverness, especially in design.

Ingrained: Deep-rooted, forming part of the very essence; worked into the fiber.

Religious observance had been **ingrained** in him since birth; he could not remember a time when he didn't pray five times a day.

Inherent: Existing as a permanent, essential quality; intrinsic (see the similar *intrinsic* in this list.)

New research seems to support the idea that humans have an **inherent** sense of justice—even babies become upset at puppet shows depicting unfairness.

Initial: First, at the beginning. An *initial deposit* might be the money you put down to open a new bank account.

Inordinate: Excessive, not within proper limits, unrestrained.

Students taking GRE practice tests at home often take an **inordinate** number of breaks—remember, on the real thing, you can't stop just because you're tired or hungry.

Instrumental: Serving as a means of doing something. Just as you might call a weapon an *instrument of war*, saying *He was instrumental in the restructuring* has the sense that the person was used as an *instrument* in order to get something done.

Insular: Pertaining to an island; detached, standing alone; narrow-minded (like the stereotype of people from small towns or places).

The young actress couldn't wait to escape the **insularity** of her small town, where life revolved around high school football and Taco Bell was considered exotic international cuisine.

Interplay: Interaction, reciprocal relationship or influence.

Bilingual readers will enjoy the **interplay** of English and Spanish in many of the poems in this anthology of the work of Mexican-American poets.

Intractable: Difficult to control, manage, or manipulate; hard to cure; stubborn.

> That student is positively **intractable**! Last week, we talked about the importance of staying in your seat during the lesson; this week, she not only got up mid-class, but she actually scrambled on top of a bookcase and refused to come down!

> Back injuries often result in **intractable** pain; despite treatment, patients never feel fully cured.

Intrepid: Fearless, brave, enduring in the face of adversity.

> The **intrepid** explorers volunteered for the first manned mission to Mars, despite the fact that scientists estimated the chance of success at just 40 percent.

Intrinsic: Belonging to the essential nature of a thing (see the similar *inherent* in this list).

> Despite all of the high-tech safety equipment, skydiving is an **intrinsically** dangerous proposition.

> Communication is **intrinsic to** a healthy relationship.

Inundate: Flood, cover with water, overwhelm.

> As the city was **inundated** with water, the mayor feared that many evacuees would have nowhere to go.

> I can't go out—I am **inundated** with homework!

Invaluable: Priceless; so valuable that the value cannot be measured.

Investiture: Investing; formally giving someone a right or title.

> The former dean had her academic robes dry-cleaned in preparation for her **investiture** as university president.

Involved: Complicated, intricate; confused or tangled.

> The story is quite **involved**—are you sure you have time for it?

Invulnerable: Immune to attack; not vulnerable; impossible to damage, injure, etc.

Isotope: Forms of the same chemical element, but with different numbers of neutrons in the nucleus or different atomic weights. Different isotopes of the same element have almost (but not quite!) identical properties.

Jettison: Discard, cast off; throw items overboard in order to lighten a ship in an emergency.

> We got so tired while hiking the Appalachian Trail that we **jettisoned** some of our fancy camping supplies just so we could keep going.

> Sadly, when school budgets are slashed, the first thing **jettisoned** is usually an art or music program.

Jumbo: Unusually large, supersized.

Juncture: Point in time, especially a point made critical due to a set of circumstances; the point at which two things join together.

> We are at a critical **juncture** in the history of this organization: either we can remain a nonprofit, or we can register as a political action committee and try to expand our influence.

> The little canoe started to sink when it split at the **juncture** between the old wood and the new material used to repair it.

Juxtapose: Place side-by-side (either physically or in a metaphorical way, such as to make a comparison). If a Reading Comprehension answer choice says something like, *Juxtapose two theories*, ask yourself whether the main purpose of the entire passage was to *compare* two theories. (Hint: Probably not. Usually if an author introduces two competing ideas, only one of them turns out to be the main point of the passage.)

> Making a decision between two engagement rings from two different stores was difficult, he noted; it would be much easier if he could **juxtapose** them and compare them directly.

Kinetic: Pertaining to motion.

> Marisa told her mother what she had learned in science class: a ball sitting on a table has potential energy, but a ball falling toward the ground has **kinetic** energy.

Lackluster: Not shiny; dull, mediocre; lacking brilliance or vitality.

> Many young people today are so accustomed to being praised by parents and adults that they are shocked when a **lackluster** effort in the workplace receives the indifference or mild disapproval it deserves.

Landmark: Object (such as a building) that stands out and can be used to navigate by; a very important place, event, etc.

> The Civil Rights Act of 1964 was a **landmark** in the battle for equality.

> In Lebanon, many roads are unmarked, and people navigate by **landmarks**; for instance, you might be directed to the "third house down from the water tower."

Latent: Potential; existing but not visible or active. A similar word is *dormant*.

> Certain experts believe that some people have a genetic propensity for addiction; however, if such a person never comes into contact with drugs, the propensity for addiction can remain **latent** for life.

Lateral: Sideways; related to or located at the side. A *lateral move* in a career is taking a new job at the same level.

Lax: Not strict; careless, loose, slack.

> My parents were really **lax** about homework—they never checked to see whether I did it. Sadly, this legacy of **laxity** is not serving me well while studying for the GRE.

Laypeople: Regular people, nonspecialists.

> The doctor's books were so successful because he was able to explain complicated medical concepts in colloquial language for the **layperson**.

Levy: Collect tax from or wage war on; act of collecting tax or amount owed; or the drafting of troops into military service.

> When England **levied** yet another tax on the colonists, the colonists were pushed one further step toward **levying** war. Soon, the worried British began to **levy** troops.

Liberal: Favorable to progress or reform; believing in maximum possible individual freedom; tolerant, open-minded; generous. (*Liberal* in modern American politics isn't quite the same as the dictionary definition. For instance, *liberal* Democrats tend to favor social programs that require a larger government to administer, while some conservatives say that *liberalism* means having the smallest government possible in order to maximize freedom.)

Split pea soup benefits from a **liberal** application of pepper.

Liberal reformers in Egypt pushed for freedom of speech, freedom of the press, and freedom of assembly.

Lift: Remove (such as a restriction), improve, or lighten (such as a person's mood).

If the city government **lifts** the water rationing restrictions, we'll be able to hold a car wash.

Likewise: Also, in addition to; similarly, in the same way. In conversation, *likewise* can mean "Me, too." ("Nice to meet you." "Likewise.")

Chip was baffled by all the silverware set before him, so when his host began eating salad with the smallest, leftmost fork, Chip did **likewise**.

Log: Keep a record of, write down; travel for or at a certain distance or speed; a written record.

Lawyers who bill by the hour have to be sure to **log** all the time they spend on every client's case.

You cannot get your pilot's license until you have **logged** 40 hours of flight time.

Machination or **machinations:** Crafty schemes or plots.

It's cute to think that teen idols became famous because their talent was simply so great that the music industry reached out to them, but usually any teen idol is the product of intense coaching and parental **machinations**.

Magma: Molten material (such as very hot liquid rock) beneath or within the earth's crust.

Magnate: Very important or influential person, especially in business.

Many students pursue MBAs in hopes of becoming wealthy and powerful **magnates**; some students never quite make it there, instead spending their careers staring at spreadsheets and taking orders from **magnates**.

Makeshift: Improvised, relating to a temporary substitute. The expressions *thrown together* or *slapped together* express a similar idea of a *making do* with the resources on hand. Similarly, to *jury-rig* something is to assemble it quickly with whatever materials you have available.

Lost in the woods for over 24 hours, the children were eventually found sleeping under a **makeshift** tent made from branches and old plastic bags.

Malleable: Able to be bent, shaped, or adapted. *Tractable*, *pliable*, and *plastic* can also mean physically bendable, or metaphorically bendable, as in *easily influenced or shaped by others. Mutable* means "changeable."

The more **malleable** the material, the easier it is to bend into jewelry—and the easier it is to damage that jewelry.

She is a little too **malleable**; she said she liked all the things her first boss liked, and now she says she likes all the things her new boss likes.

Manifest: Obvious, apparent, perceptible to the eye (adj) or to become obvious, apparent, perceptible to the eye (verb). Also to show, make clear, or prove (verb). As a noun, a *manifest* is a list of people or goods aboard a plane, ship, train, etc. A *manifestation* is often when something "under the surface" breaks out or becomes apparent.

Lupus is difficult to diagnose, but sometimes **manifests** as muscular weakness or joint pain.

The protest was a **manifestation** of a long-brewing discontent.

14

Mantle (of the earth): Layer of the earth between the crust and the core.

Maxim: A general truth or fundamental principle, especially expressed as a proverb or saying.

My favorite **maxim** is *Seize the day!* How much would it cost to get a tattoo with that saying? How much more for *Curiosity killed the cat?*

Max out: Take to the limit (in a good or a bad way). To *max out* your credit cards is to incur as much debt as is permitted; to *max out* your productivity is to achieve maximum productivity.

Mediated by: Brought about by means of; assisted as an intermediary. Of course, to *mediate* a dispute is to bring about a resolution, but *mediated* in science also has the idea of being in the middle. For instance, a study might show that poverty leads to inattentiveness in school. But how? Research might reveal that poverty leads to inattentiveness, *mediated by* poor nutrition. That is, poverty causes poor nutrition, which causes inattentiveness (because the kids are hungry). *Mediation* can help make sense of what seems like an indirect correlation.

Mercurial: Quickly and unpredictably changing moods; fickle, flighty.

It's tough being married to someone so **mercurial**. I do pretty much the same thing every day—some days, she thinks I'm great, and other days, the exact same behaviors make her inexplicably angry.

Militarism: Glorification of the military; government in which the military has a lot of power or in which the military is the top priority.

Mired: Stuck, entangled (in something, like a swamp or muddy area); soiled. *Morass* and *quagmire* are also words (often used metaphorically) for soft, swampy ground that a person can sink into. The Vietnam War was famously called a *quagmire.* The expression *muck and mire* means, literally, "animal waste and mud" and can be used metaphorically. To *muck up* is to mess up or get dirty, and to *muck about* or *muck around* is to waste time.

Mired in her predecessor's mess and mistakes, the new CEO found it difficult to take the company in a new direction.

The federal prosecutor spent weeks wading through the **muck and mire** of the scandal—every uncovered document showed that the corruption was deeper and worse than previously thought.

Modest: Humble; simple rather than showy; decent (especially "covering up" in terms of dress); small, limited.

The reporter was surprised that the celebrity lived in such a **modest** house, one that looked just like every other plain two-story house on the block.

Her first job out of college was a rude awakening—her **modest** salary was barely enough for rent, much less going out and having fun.

Moreover: In addition to what has been said; besides.

His actions cost us the job; **moreover**, he seriously offended our client.

Mores: Customs, manners, or morals of a particular group. Pronounce this word as two syllables (rhymes with "more ways").

A foreigner visiting a country should study the culture beforehand so as to avoid violating local cultural **mores**.

Municipal: Relating to local self-government. A *municipality* is a city, town, etc.

Narrative: Story, report, narrated account.

Nebula: A cloud of gas and dust in space. Nebulas can form star-forming regions—all the materials clump together to form larger masses, thus attracting further matter and ultimately creating stars. A *nebula* can also be a cloudy spot on a person's eye. *Nebulous* can mean cloudy, unclear.

Net: Remaining after expenses or other factors have been deducted; ultimate; to bring in as profit, or to catch as in a net.

> In one day of trading, my portfolio went up $10,000 and down $8,000, for a **net** gain of $2,000.

> All those weeks of working weekends and playing golf with the boss ought to **net** her a promotion.

Nevertheless or **nonetheless:** However, even so, despite that.

> While losing the P&G account was a serious blow, we **nevertheless** were able to achieve a new sales goal this month because of the tireless efforts of the sales team in signing three new clients.

> I really can't stand working with you. **Nonetheless**, we're stuck on this project together, and we're going to have to get along.

Nontrivial: Important or big enough to matter; opposite of trivial.

> The chief of staff told the assembled doctors, "We all make mistakes. But this mistake was **nontrivial**, and there is going to be an investigation."

Normative: Implying or attempting to establish a norm; expressing value judgments or telling people what to do (rather than merely describing that which is happening).

> The reason we are not understanding each other in this argument about grammar is that you are arguing **normatively**, telling me how people *should* talk, and I am simply reporting how people *actually* talk.

Nostalgia: Longing for the past.

> The retail store Urban Outfitters uses **nostalgia** as a marketing strategy, branding many products with cartoon characters popular 10 to 20 years ago. Sure enough, many adult women do want to buy Jem or SpongeBob T-shirts and lip balm.

Nuances: Subtle or delicate distinctions; small differences in tone, meaning, or expression. The adjective form is *nuanced*.

> Your face looks the same whether you're simply tired or whether you're actually upset with me; the **nuances** are lost on me.

> The mediator provided a **nuanced** summary of the debate, remaining accurate to the demands of both sides while minimizing differences wherever possible.

Nucleus: Structure within a cell containing the cell's hereditary material; any central or essential part; core, kernel.

> As a member of the president's cabinet, he found himself in the **nucleus** of power.

Offhand: Casual, informal; done without preparation or forethought; rude in a short way, brusque.

> I was pretty happy with my salary until my coworker Deena mentioned **offhandedly** that she was thinking about buying a house now that she made six figures.

Offset: Counteract, compensate for. *Offset* is usually a verb, but can be used as a noun: *My company provided me with an offset against moving expenses.*

> Property taxes did go up this year, but we didn't really suffer because the hit to our finances was **offset** by a reduction in fees paid to our homeowners association.

Oligarchy: Government by the few, especially by a class or a small group or clique.

Omit: Remove, delete, take out.

Operative: Operating; having influence, force, or effect; effective, key, significant. The expression *operative word* refers to the one most meaningful word within a larger phrase. An *operative* can be a worker, or a detective or spy.

> In the doctor's prescription of daily cardio exercise, the **operative word** is *daily*.

Optimal: Best, most desirable or favorable. To *optimize* is to make perfect, such as by striking just the right balance.

> Many believe that the U.S. Constitution's genius lies in its striking an **optimal** balance between freedom and order.

Oral narratives: Stories told verbally, especially by people who are not literate or whose cultures do not have writing (or didn't at the time). An *oral tradition* is a practice of passing down a culture's history verbally.

Outstrip: Surpass, exceed; be larger or better than; leave behind.

> Our sales figures this quarter have **outstripped** those of any other quarter in the company's history.

Paradigm: Model or pattern; worldview, set of shared assumptions, values, etc.

> Far from being atypically bawdy, this limerick is a **paradigm** of the form—nearly all limericks rely on off-color jokes.

Paradox: Contradiction, or seeming contradiction that is actually true.

> Kayla was always bothering the youth minister with her **paradoxes**, such as, "If God is all-powerful, can He make a burrito so big He can't eat it?"

Paragon: Model of excellence, perfect example.

> Unlike his sister, he was a **paragon** of responsibility, taking in her three children when she went to jail, and even switching jobs so he could be there to pick them up from school.

Partial: Biased, prejudiced, favoring one over others; having a special liking for something or someone (usually *partial to*); can also mean "in part."

> Although I grew up in New York, I've always been **partial** to country music.

> His lawyers are appealing on the grounds that the judge was **partial** to the plaintiff, even playing golf with the plaintiff during the trial.

Patent: Obvious, apparent, plain to see (adj); a letter from a government guaranteeing an inventor the rights to his or her invention (noun).

> Her résumé was full of **patent** lies: anyone could check to see that she had never been president of UNICEF.

Peddle: Travel around while selling; sell illegally; give out or disseminate.

> After an unsuccessful year spent **peddling** cutlery door to door, he turned to **peddling** drugs, thus landing himself in jail.

> "I don't want these people **peddling** lies to our children," said Mrs. Hoffman, protesting against candy manufacturers lobbying for more lenient advertising rules.

Penumbra: Outer part of a shadow from an eclipse; any surrounding region, fringe, periphery; any area where something only partially exists.

> The Constitution doesn't specifically mention a right to privacy, but some experts consider this to exist in the **penumbra** of the Constitution, as a guarantee of privacy is needed in order to exercise the rights that are enumerated.

> The rent in Chicago was too high, so they moved to a suburb in the **penumbra** of the city.

Per: The most common use of *per* is "for each," as in, *We will need one sandwich per child*. However, *per* may also mean "by means of" or "according to," as in *I have delivered the package per your instructions*.

Periodic: Happening at regular intervals.

Perpetuate: Make perpetual, cause to continue.

> Failing public schools in already distressed neighborhoods only **perpetuate** the cycle of poverty.

Physiological: Relating to the normal functioning of a living thing.

> A rapid heart rate is a **physiological** response to fear.

Piggyback: Depending on something bigger or more important. *Piggyback* literally refers to one person (often a child) riding on the back of another. This word can be an adverb, adjective, or noun.

> The jobs bill arrived **piggyback** on the urgent disaster relief bill—a pretty dirty trick, if you ask me.

> Maybe we can **piggyback** this smaller design project onto the bigger one and end up saving some money with our web designers.

Pilot program (or project): Program planned as a test or trial.

> Before rolling out the program nationwide, a **pilot program** was launched in just three cities.

Plutocratic: Related to government by the wealthy.

Polarized: Divided into sharply opposed groups.

> The members of the club were **polarized**; half were adamant that a bake sale would earn the most money and the other half were convinced that a car wash would be better.

Polemic: Controversial argument, especially one attacking a specific idea.

> Laura Kipnis's 2003 book *Against Love: A **Polemic*** has been called "shocking" and "scathing." Perhaps Kipnis used the word **polemic** in the title to indicate that she's making an extreme argument as a means of starting a debate. After all, who's really *against love*?

Postulate: Claim, assert; assume the truth or reality of in order to form an argument.

> Before proceeding further, let us **postulate** that men and women have some fundamental differences. If we can accept that, we can talk about what types of policies should exist to ensure workplace equality.

Pragmatic: Practical; dealing with actual facts and reality.

The congresswoman personally believed in animal rights, but she knew she had to be **pragmatic**—if she proposed animal rights legislation, she probably wouldn't get reelected.

Predatory: Living by preying on other animals; given to plundering, exploiting, or destroying others for one's own benefit.

Many check-cashing outlets are actually **predatory** lenders who charge interest rates that would be illegal in many nations.

Predisposed: Having an inclination or tendency beforehand; susceptible. A *predisposition* is an inclination or tendency.

His defense attorney argued that his abusive childhood **predisposed** him to a life of crime.

Predominant: Having the greatest importance or influence; most common, main. A design might have a *predominant color*, and a country might have a *predominant religion*.

Preempt: Prevent; take the place of, supplant; take before someone else can.

The speaker attempted to **preempt** an excessively long Q&A session by handing out a "Frequently Asked Questions" packet at the beginning of the seminar.

Premise: Proposition on which an argument is based. The functional parts of an argument other than the conclusion. Less commonly, *premise* is a verb, as in *The report is premised on (based on) this study. The premises* can also refer to a building and its surrounding land.

Prey: An animal that is hunted and eaten. *Predators* are animals that hunt and eat *prey*.

Priceless: Extremely valuable; so valuable that the worth cannot even be estimated.

Pristine: In an original, pure state; uncorrupted. A *pristine* forest has not been touched by humans. Sometimes *pristine* is just used to mean "very clean."

Progeny: Offspring, descendants.

The study showed that selective breeding could cause the **progeny** of wolves to become more like dogs in a small number of generations.

Prominent: Projecting outward, sticking out; very noticeable. A *prominent* nose might not be a desirable characteristic, according to some people, but a *prominent* citizen is generally a well-known and important person.

Pronounced: Distinct, strong, clearly indicated.

Aunt Shirley claimed we would never know that her "secret recipe" for brownies involved lots of healthy vegetables, but the brownies had a **pronounced** asparagus flavor.

Propagated: Breed, cause to multiply.

Some plants can be **propagated** from cuttings: my mother gave me a piece of her houseplant, and it grew roots after just a few days in water.

Prospective: Potential, aspiring. *Prospective students* have not yet been admitted; *prospective entrepreneurs* are people considering becoming entrepreneurs. This word is related to *prospect*, which can be both a noun (a good possibility) or a verb (to look for something good, such as to *prospect for gold*).

A committee was formed to evaluate the new plan's **prospects**. As part of their analysis, members of the committee looked at the past performance of the **prospective** leader of the new division. One member remarked that the **prospect** of opening up a completely new division was exciting, but might stretch the company too thin.

Proximity: Closeness, the state of being near.

Psyche: The spirit or soul; the mind (as discussed in psychology). Pronounce this word "SY-key."

Qualified: Modified, limited, conditional on something else. *Unqualified* can mean not limited or not restrained. If your boss gives *unqualified* approval for your plan, you can do whatever you want. *Qualified* can also mean "qualified for the job." Use context to determine which meaning is intended. A *qualified* person is suitable or well prepared for the job; a *qualified* statement or feeling is "held back or limited."

The scientist gave her **qualified** endorsement to the book, pointing out that, while it posed a credible theory, more research was still needed before the theory could be applied.

Radiometric, radioactive, carbon, or radiocarbon dating: Methods for determining the approximate age of an ancient object by measuring the amount of radioactivity it contains.

Recalcitrant: Not obedient, resisting authority, hard to manage.

The aspiring kindergarten teacher was not prepared for a roomful of 20 **recalcitrant** children who wouldn't even sit down, much less learn the words to "Holding Hands Around the World."

Recapitulate: Summarize, repeat in a concise way.

I'm sorry I had to leave your presentation to take a call. I only have a minute, but can you **recapitulate** what you're proposing?

Receptive: Capable of or ready and willing to receive, as in *receptive to a new idea*.

Reconvene: Gather, come together again (or call together again), such as for a meeting, as in *Let's break for lunch and reconvene at 1 PM*.

Redress: Compensation or relief for injury or wrongdoing (noun); correct, set right, remedy (verb).

My client was an innocent victim of medical malpractice. As would anyone who had the wrong leg amputated in surgery, he is seeking financial **redress**.

Refute: Prove to be false.

She's not a very valuable member of the debate team, actually—she loves making speeches, but she's not very good at **refuting** opponents' arguments.

Rehash: Discuss or bring up (an idea or topic) again without adding anything new.

We're not going to agree, so why **rehash** the issue?

Remedial: Providing a remedy, curative; correcting a deficient skill.

After harassment occurs in the workplace, it is important that the company take **remedial** action right away, warning or firing the offender as appropriate, and making sure the complainant's concerns are addressed.

For those who need **remedial** reading help, we offer a summer school program that aims to help students read at grade level.

Reminiscent: Looking back at the past; reminding of the past. A *reminiscent* person is remembering something; an old-fashioned object could be *reminiscent of* an earlier time.

Render: Give, submit, surrender; translate; declare formally; cause to become. To *render harmless* is to *make harmless.*

> When you **render** your past due payments, we will turn your phone back on.

> Only in her second year of Japanese, she was unable to **render** the classic poem into English.

> The judge **rendered** (submitted) a verdict that **rendered** (made) us speechless.

Repercussions: Consequences (usually negative).

> One of the worries about the financial industry is that irresponsible executives rarely suffer lasting **repercussions**.

Respectively: In the order given. This is a very useful word! The sentence "Smith and Jones wrote the books *7 Success Tips* and *Productivity Rocks*" is ambiguous—did they work together on both or did they each write one of the books? "Smith and Jones wrote the books *7 Success Tips* and *Productivity Rocks*, respectively" answers the question—Smith wrote *7 Success Tips* and Jones wrote *Productivity Rocks*. The word is typically used to match up two things to two other things, in the same order.

> His poems "An Ode to the Blossoms of Sheffield" and "An Entreaty to Ladies All Too Prim" were written in 1756 and 1758, **respectively**.

Reticent: Not talking much; private (of a person), restrained, reserved.

> She figured that, to rise to the top, it was best to be **reticent** about her personal life; as a result, her colleagues did not know whether she was in a relationship or what she liked to do outside of work.

Returns: Profits.

Revamp: Renovate, redo, revise (verb); a restructuring, upgrade, etc. (noun). Similarly, *overhaul* means to repair or investigate for repairs.

> I have my whole room decorated in *Twilight: Eclipse* paraphernalia. When *Breaking Dawn* comes out, I will surely have to **revamp** my decor.

Rife: Happening frequently, abundant, currently being reported.

> Reports of financial corruption are **rife**; there are new reports of wrongdoing in the papers every day.

Rudimentary: Elementary, relating to the basics; undeveloped, primitive.

> My knowledge of Chinese is quite **rudimentary**; I get the idea of characters, and I can order food, but I really can't read this document you've just given me.

Sanction: Permission or approval, or to give permission or approval. Alternatively, a legal action by one or more countries against another country to get it to comply (or the act of placing those *sanctions* on another country). Whoa! Yes, that's right—*sanction* can mean two different things that are basically opposites. Use context to figure it out—if it's plural (*sanctions*), it's definitely the negative meaning.

> Professional boxers may only fight in **sanctioned** matches—fighting outside the ring is prohibited.

> Canada's **sanctions** on North Korea mean that it is illegal for Canadians to do business with North Korean companies.

Satire: Literary device in which foolishness or badness is attacked through humor, irony, or making fun of something or someone.

Save: But or except. As a verb, *save* means "keep safe, store up, set aside." As a preposition or conjunction, though, *save* can be used as follows.

> All of the divisions of the company are profitable **save** the movie-rental division. (This means that the movie-rental division was not profitable.)

> He would have been elected president, **save** for the scandal that derailed his campaign at the last minute. (Here, *save* means "except.")

Scant: Not enough or barely enough. *Scanty* is used in the same way (both are adjectives).

> The new intern was **scant** help at the conference—he disappeared all day to smoke and didn't seem to realize that he was there to assist his coworkers.

> The soldiers were always on the verge of hunger, complaining about their **scanty** rations.

Scarcely: Hardly, barely, by a small margin. *Scarce* is the adjective form.

> She lived a lavish lifestyle she could **scarcely** afford.

Scrutiny: Close, careful observation.

Seemingly: Apparently, outwardly appearing to be a certain way. If an author says that something is *seemingly X*, the author is probably about to say that it is *actually Y*. The word *seemingly* means that something *seems* a certain way (but maybe isn't really).

> He's a **seemingly** honest man—I'll need to get to know him better to say for sure.

Settled: Fixed, established, concluded. Sediment can *settle* in water, people who marry can *settle down*, and a *settled judgment* is one that has been firmly decided.

Siphon: Tube for sucking liquid out of something (some people steal gasoline from other people's cars by *siphoning* it). To *siphon funds* is to steal money, perhaps in a continuous stream.

Skeptical: Doubting, especially in a scientific way (needing sufficient evidence before believing).

> Don't confuse **skeptical** and *cynical* (thinking the worst of others' motivations; bitterly pessimistic). In a GRE Reading Comprehension passage, an author might be **skeptical** (a very appropriate attitude for a scientist, for instance), but would never be *cynical*.

Sketchy: Like a sketch: incomplete, imperfect, superficial.

Skirt: Border, lie along the edge of, go around; evade.

> Melissa spent all of Thanksgiving **skirting** the issue of whom she was dating and when she might get married.

> The creek **skirts** our property on the west, so it's easy to tell where our farm ends.

Slew: A large number or quantity. *Slew* is also the past tense of *slay* (kill), so you could actually say, *She slew him with a slew of bullets.*

> As soon as we switched software packages, we encountered a whole **slew** of problems.

Slight: Small, not very important, slender or delicate; treat as though not very important; snub, ignore; a discourtesy.

> She was very sensitive, always feeling **slighted** and holding a grudge against her coworkers for a variety of **slights**, both real and imagined.

> Natalie Portman has always been **slight**, but she became even thinner to portray a ballerina in *Black Swan*.

Smelt: Fuse or melt ore in order to separate out metal.

Sparing: Holding back or being wise in the use of resources; deficient. Be *sparing* with the ketchup in order to make it last longer, but don't be *sparing* in praising your employees for a job well done.

Spate: Sudden outpouring or rush; flood.

> After a brief **spate** of post-exam partying, Lola is ready for classes to begin again.

Spearhead: Be the leader of. A *spearhead* can be the sharp head of a spear. It can also be a person at the front of a military attack or a leader of anything.

> Lisa agreed to **spearhead** the "healthy office" initiative and was instrumental in installing two treadmills and getting healthy food stocked in the vending machines.

Staggered: Starting and ending at different times, especially occurring in overlapping intervals.

> Employees who work on **staggered** schedules may only see each other for part of the day.

Static: Fixed, not moving or changing, lacking vitality. *Stasis* is the quality of being *static*.

> The anthropologist studied a society in the Amazon that had been deliberately **static** for hundreds of years—the fiercely proud people disdained change and viewed all new ideas as inferior to the way of life they had always practiced.

Stratum: One of many layers (such as in a rock formation or in the classes of a society). The plural is *strata*.

> From overhearing his rich and powerful passengers' conversations, the chauffeur grew to despise the upper **stratum** of society.

> I love this dish—it's like a lasagna, but with **strata** made of bread, eggs, and pancetta! Oh, look at the menu—it's actually called a **strata**! That makes perfect sense.

Subjective: Existing in the mind or relating to one's own thoughts, opinions, emotions, etc.; personal, individual, based on feelings.

> We can give names to colors, but we can never quite convey the **subjective** experience of them—what if my "red" is different from your "red"?

Subjugation: Conquering, domination, enslavement.

Subordinate: Having a lower order or rank, inferior, secondary.

Subset: A set that is contained within a larger set.

Subvert: Overthrow, corrupt, cause the downfall of.

Succeeding: Coming after or following. The *succeeding sentence* is the sentence that comes after.

After the sale of the company, you will receive 5 percent of the profits from the current year and 1 percent in all **succeeding** years. In 1797, George Washington was **succeeded** by John Adams as President of the United States.

Suffrage: The right to vote. *Women's suffrage* was ensured in the United States via the 19th Amendment.

Surge: Sudden, transient increase (*power surge*), heavy swelling motion like that of waves. A *surge* of troops is sending a lot of soldiers at once. A *surge* in interest is sudden.

Suppress: Prohibit, curtail, force the end of. A repressive government might *suppress* dissent against its policies.

Surpass: Transcend, exceed, go beyond, as in *It's only August, and we've already surpassed last year's sales.*

Synchronized: Happening at the same time, simultaneous, in unison.

Syntax: The rules governing grammar and how words join to make sentences (or how words and symbols join in writing computer code), the study of these rules, or any system or orderly arrangement.

Now that my linguistics class is studying **syntax**, it makes a little more sense when my computer flashes "Syntax Error" at me.

Anyone learning a language is bound to make **syntactical** mistakes—even if he or she knows the appropriate vocabulary, it is still difficult to assemble the words perfectly.

Synthesis: Combining two or more things to create a unified whole.

Table: In American English, to *table* something means to postpone discussion of it until later. (In British English, to *table* a bill is the opposite—to submit it for consideration.)

I see we're not going to agree on whether to scrap our entire curriculum and develop a new one, so let's **table** that discussion and move on to voting on the budget.

Tardy: Late, not on time.

Taxonomy: Science or technique of classification. The *taxonomic* system in biology classifies organisms by Phylum, Class, Order, Species, etc.

Temperament: Natural personality, as in *an angry temperament* or *a pleasant temperament*.

Temperance: Moderation, self-control, especially regarding alcohol or other desires or pleasures; total abstinence from alcohol. Relatedly, *temperate* means "moderate," as in a *temperate climate*.

After the end of the Civil War, economic change led to an increase in alcohol problems and the birth of the **Temperance** Movement, which ultimately led to Prohibition, the complete ban of alcohol.

Grandma is a model of **temperance**—she drinks red wine every night, but only the third of a glass that she read was the minimum amount needed to help prevent heart attacks.

Terrestrial: Relating to the earth or to land; worldly.

Mr. and Mrs. Daruza were certain they had seen a UFO, as well as aliens running around in the night. What they really saw was an especially dense flock of birds in the air and some mundane **terrestrial** animals on the ground.

Thenceforth: From that time forward.

In 1956, Grace Kelly married Rainier III, Prince of Monaco, and was **thenceforth** known as Princess Grace.

Theoretically: In theory (but not necessarily in reality). People sometimes just say *theoretically* when talking about theories, but they also often say it when they mean that something will not work in real life.

> **Theoretically**, the new process will result in reduced particle emission. (This could mean "So we will need to try it in order to find out," or it could mean "But I doubt that it will really work." We need the next sentence to know which meaning is intended.)

Thesis: Proposition supported by an argument.

Thorny: Controversial, full of difficulties. Literally, having thorns, prickly (as a rose bush).

Tides: Periodic rise and fall of the ocean about every 12 hours, caused by the attraction of the sun and moon. Metaphorically, we can say *the tides of refugees*, for instance—implying the refugees are arriving periodically, in large groups.

Token: Sign, symbol, mark, badge; souvenir, memento; sample, or person, thing, idea taken to represent an entire group. A *token* can also be a coin-like disk used as currency for subways, arcade games, etc. As an adjective, it means "not very important."

> I am starting to realize that this law firm hired me to be its **token** woman. There I am, smiling in all the ads, but I never actually get to work on important cases.

> Hollywood movies are often guilty of **tokenism**—many have exactly one black character (the "token minority"), often present only to give advice to the (usually white) main characters.

> I am giving you this "Best Friends Forever" necklace as a **token** of our friendship.

Trajectory: The curved path of an object in flight, as in *the missile's trajectory*.

Transient: Moving around, not settled; temporary, not lasting.

> In the last decade, podcasting was thought to be the "next big thing," but it turned out to be a largely **transient** phenomenon.

Transmute: Transform, change from one form to another.

Transplantation: Moving from one place to another—a *heart transplant*, for instance. We can also use the word metaphorically: a person who has just moved to a new state might refer to herself as a *transplant from Texas*.

Truce or **armistice:** Suspension of fighting for a specified period because of mutual agreement; cease-fire.

> After the earthquake, the two warring nations agreed to a **truce** and sent their soldiers to help the quake's victims.

Undergird: Strengthen, support. To *undergird* an argument is to make it stronger—the opposite of *undermine*!

Undermine: Weaken, cause to collapse by digging away at the foundation (of a building or an argument); injure or attack in a secretive or underhanded way.

Rather than searching impartially for the truth, these company "scientists" willfully ignored any evidence that **undermined** the conclusion they were being paid to produce.

You are nice to my face, but you are **undermining** me behind my back, suggesting to others in the office that I am making mistakes in my work and that you have been fixing them!

Underpin: Strengthen, corroborate, support from below.

Her argument was **underpinned** with the results of several recent studies.

Underscore: Emphasize (or, literally, to underline text).

"You're not going to mess with Joey anymore," said Joey, as his new bodyguards stepped forward threateningly, as though to **underscore** Joey's point.

Undifferentiated: Not distinguished from one another, the same.

Unfettered: Free, liberated.

Unforeseeable: Not able to be predicted.

Our company had disaster insurance and a succession plan in case something happened to the president, but we had no plans for the **unforeseeable** circumstance that our office would be completely overtaken by rats.

Unprecedented: Never before known or seen, without having happened previously.

When Nixon resigned, American bravado was at an all-time low—the resignation of a sitting president was disgraceful and **unprecedented**.

Untempered: Not toned down; not moderated, controlled, or counterbalanced. Often, *untempered by*.

The report was an **untempered** condemnation of the company's practices—the investigators didn't have a single good thing to say.

Untenable: Not defendable (as an argument), not able to be lived in (as a house).

The internet is full of **untenable** arguments that rest upon unproven assumptions.

Unwarranted: Not justified or authorized.

Utopian: Related to ideals of perfection; unrealistically idealistic.

Reducing homeless to zero is a **utopian** goal; our agency views reducing the street population by 25 percent and getting children off the streets as more practical aims.

Via: Through, by means of, by way of (by a route that goes through or touches). *Per* can also be used in this way.

We will be flying to Russia **via** Frankfurt.

Many of the students at our college got here **via** special programs that assist low-income students in preparing for college.

Wanting: Lacking, insufficient, or not good enough (as in *I read the book and found it wanting*). This makes sense when you think about the fact that people generally *want* good things, of course—so if a person is

14

left wanting, he did not get those good things. Conversely, a person who *wants for nothing* is someone who already has everything.

Warranted: Justified, authorized (*warrant* can mean "to justify or a justification," but can also mean "to vouch for or guarantee").

> The pundit's comments don't even **warrant** a response from our organization—they were mere name-calling, not suitable for public discourse.

> Your criticism of Anne is **unwarranted**—as your assistant, she has done everything you've asked her to do.

> He doesn't have his documents with him, but I'll **warrant** that he is indeed a certified forklift operator.

Whereas: While on the contrary, considering that.

> Mr. Katsoulas had always assumed his son would take over the family business, **whereas** his son had always assumed he would go away to college and never come back.

> **Whereas** squash and peppers are vegetables, a tomato is technically a fruit.

Whet: Stimulate, make keen or eager (especially of an appetite).

> Dinner will take another 20 minutes, but maybe this cheese plate can **whet** your appetite?

Wholesale: Sale of goods in quantity to resellers (opposite of *retail*). The word can also mean "extensive, in a large way."

> Neckties have an enormous markup—a tie that sells for $50 often has a **wholesale** cost of less than $5.

> The CEO's **wholesale** dismissal of a new potential product line cost him his job when the board realized that the company would have made $50 million in the first year alone.

Winnow: Sift, analyze critically, separate the useful part from the worthless part.

> We got 120 résumés for one job—it's going to take me awhile just to **winnow** this down to a reasonable stack of people to interview.

Yoke: A frame for attaching animals (such as oxen) to each other and to a plow or other equipment, or a bar across a person's shoulders to help carry buckets of water, etc. Metaphorically, a *yoke* is a burden or something that oppresses. To *yoke* is to unite together or to burden. To *throw off the yoke of oppression* is to free oneself from oppression.

> The speaker argued that humanity had traded the **yoke** of servitude to kings and tyrants for the **yoke** of consumerism, which enslaves us just as much in the end.

Roots List

In This Chapter . . .

- Roots List

CHAPTER 15 Roots List

Roots List

Many words in English, especially those that come from Latin or Greek, have more than one part. Here is the basic pattern:

Word	=	Prefix	+	Root	+	Suffix
excision	=	ex	+	cis	+	ion

The root contains the original core meaning of the word, although this meaning may have changed over time. Here, the root *cis* means "cut."

The prefix alters that meaning in some way. Here, the prefix *ex-* means "out" or "away."

Together, the prefix and the root handle most of the meaning: *ex + cis = excise*, or cut away.

Finally, the suffix determines the part of speech. The suffix *-ion* means "the action of doing X," so *excision* means "the act of cutting away."

Be careful! Many words do not break down so cleanly. Also, roots can be misleading. The original meaning of a word may have only been related in a *metaphorical* sense to the meaning of its original parts. Moreover, over time, many words drift very far from their original etymological meaning (some words transform so much that they come to mean the *opposite* of their original meaning).

Study roots, prefixes, and suffixes primarily to solidify your vocabulary. On the test, you can and should use your root knowledge to guess at the meaning of unknown words. Realize, however, that roots are most helpful *now*, while you're studying—not the day of the test. Be sure to learn the full dictionary meanings of vocabulary words.

Part I: Roots

This list includes a broad selection of roots and illustrative examples that often appear on the GRE. The examples have been chosen specifically to illustrate the root and thus to avoid meaning drift. Nearly all the roots are Latin or Greek. This list is not exhaustive; it is meant to provide a useful reference.

The definitions given for the harder words are brief. Remember to consult your dictionary for nuances.

Root	Meaning	Examples
ac **acer** **acri** **acro**	sharp *or* point *or* high	**ac**id **acr**id = sharp, bitter (of smell or taste) **acer**bity = bitterness **acri**mony = sharpness of words, behavior, or feeling **ac**me = highest point, best level **acro**phobia = "high + fear" = fear of heights **ac**umen = sharpness of intellect
ag **act**	drive *or* lead *or* do	**ag**ent, **act** dem**ag**ogue = "people + lead" = leader who appeals (falsely) to the people re**act** = do in response
alt	high	**alt**itude, **alt**imeter ex**alt**ed = "out + high" = raised high
ambul	walk	circum**ambul**ate = "around + walk" = walk around in a circle per**ambul**ator = "around + walk" = baby carriage
anim	spirit *or* breath	**anim**ate un**anim**ous = "one + spirit" = in complete agreement equ**anim**ity = "even + spirit" = calmness, balance under stress magn**anim**ity = "great + spirit" = nobility of spirit, generosity pusill**anim**ous = "tiny + spirit" = cowardly, without courage
arch	rule	an**arch**y = "not + ruler" = chaos, lack of government
aud	hear	**aud**ience, **aud**ible **aud**itory = related to hearing
bell **belli**	war	re**bell**ion **belli**cose = ready to fight, warlike **belli**gerent = "war + do" = hostile, provocative, or actually at war
cad **cid**	fall	de**cad**ent = "away + fall" = in a state of decline, often self-indulgent re**cid**ivism = "back + fall" = tendency to relapse to earlier behavior or crime

Root	Meaning	Examples
ced	go *or*	pro**ceed**, suc**ceed**, ex**ceed**, re**ced**e
cess	yield	**ced**e = yield
ceed		ante**ced**ent = "before + go" = earlier event or cause
		pre**ced**ent = "before + go" = earlier example
		cessation = end of an action
chron	time	**chron**ological, **chron**ic
		ana**chron**ism = "not + time" = something out of place in time
		dia**chron**ic = "through + time" = relating to change over time
cis	cut *or*	in**cis**ive = "into + cut" = cutting to the heart of a matter, direct
cide	kill	ex**cis**ion = "out + cut" = act of cutting out, removing
		regi**cid**e = "king + kill" = murder of a king
clud	close	in**clud**e, ex**clud**e, in**clus**ion, **claus**trophobia
clus		pre**clud**e = "before + close" = prevent, rule out beforehand
claus		oc**clud**e = "against + close" = block off or conceal
crat	rule	demo**crac**y
crac		auto**crat**ic = "self + ruler" = relating to an absolute ruler or tyrant
cred	believe	in**cred**ible, **creed**
creed		**cred**ence = acceptance, trust
		credulity = readiness to believe, gullibility
		in**cred**ulous = skeptical, unwilling to believe
dei	god	**dei**fy = "god + make" = make into a god, glorify
demo	people	**demo**cracy
dem		**demo**graphic = related to a population, or a segment of a population
		pan**dem**ic = "all + people" = something affecting everyone, usually a disease
		en**dem**ic = "in + people" = native to a population
		demagogue = "people + lead" = leader who appeals (falsely) to the people
dict	say	pre**dict**, contra**dict**, juris**dict**ion
		bene**dict**ion = "good + say" = blessing
		vale**dict**ory = "farewell + say" = expressing a farewell (often by a speech)

(Continued)

Root	Meaning	Examples
duc	lead or	pro**duc**e, ab**duc**t, con**duc**t
	pull	de**duc**e = "away + lead" = determine from general principles
		ductile = able to be led easily (people) or to be drawn out into wire (metals)
		in**duc**t = "in + lead" = admit as a member
dur, dure	hard or lasting	**dur**able, en**dur**e, en**dur**ance, **dur**ation, **dur**ing
		duress = compulsion, restraint by force
		ob**dur**ate = "against + hard" = hard of heart, stubborn
equi	equal or	**equa**tion, **equa**tor
equa	even	**equi**table = dealing fairly on all sides
		equanimity = "even + spirit" = calmness under stress, balance
		equivocate = "equal + voice" = say something open to more than one interpretation in order to mislead or to avoid commitment
		equable = uniform, steady, unchanging
fac	do or	terri**fy**, puri**fy**, paci**fy**, af**fec**t, ef**fec**t, **fac**t, arti**fic**ial
fec	make	rare**fy** = "rare + make" = make thin, pure, less dense
fic		veri**fy** = "true + make" = confirm as true
fy		sancti**fy** = "holy + make" = make holy
		dei**fy** = "god + make" = make into a god, glorify
		bene**fic**ent = "good + do" = doing good for others
		male**fic**ent = "bad + do" = doing harm or evil
		facile = easily done or understood, lacking depth or authenticity
		facilitate = to make easy, help to happen
		factitious = artificial, made-up, fake
fer	carry or	trans**fer**, of**fer**, **fer**tile, **fer**ry
	bring	proli**fer**ate = "offspring + carry" = multiply in number
		voci**fer**ous = "voice + carry" = shouting loudly and angrily
ferv	boil	**ferv**ent = zealous, intense in feeling
		ef**ferv**escent = "away + boil" = being bubbly, showing exhilaration
		per**ferv**id = "through + boil" = overexcited, overwrought
fid	trust or	**fid**elity, con**fid**ence
	faith	dif**fid**ence = "not + faith" = hesitant, lacking in self-confidence
		per**fid**ious = "detrimental + faith" = disloyal, treacherous

15

Root	Meaning	Examples
flect **flex**	bend	**flex**ible, re**flect**, de**flect**
flu **flux** **fluct**	flow *or* wave	**flu**id, **fluct**uate, in**flux** con**flu**ence = "together + flow" = a flowing together super**flu**ous = "over + flow" = unnecessary, wasteful melli**flu**ous = "honey + flow" = having a smooth flow like honey ef**flu**vium = "out + flow" = by-product, (bad) exhalation
gen	kin *or* kind *or* birth	**gen**try = upper class **gen**tility = high social status, or conduct becoming of that status hetero**gen**eous = "different + kind" = consisting of diverse parts homo**gen**eous = "same + kind" = consisting of one substance
gno	know	a**gno**stic = "not + know" = someone who isn't sure (often about God's existence) dia**gno**sis = "through + know" = identification of (medical) causes and issues pro**gno**sticate = "before + know" = predict, foretell co**gno**scente (pl. cognoscenti) = "with + know" = expert in a subject
graph **gram**	write	auto**graph,** dia**gram,** **gram**mar, **graph**ic, tele**gram** mono**graph** = "one + write" = a written report or paper on a narrow subject
grade **gress**	step *or* go	pro**gress**, re**gress**, ag**gress**ive, con**gress** retro**grade** = "backward + go" = moving backward trans**gress**ion = "across + step" = violation of a law or rule di**gress** = "away + go" = deviate from a subject
greg	flock *or* herd	ag**greg**ate = "toward + flock" = collect or add up con**greg**ate = "together + flock" = gather together e**greg**ious = "outside + flock" = conspicuously bad, flagrant **greg**arious = sociable, companionable
her **hes**	stick	ad**her**e = "to + stick" = stick to co**hes**ive = "together + stick" = sticking or fitting together
jac **ject**	throw	e**ject**, tra**ject**ory, inter**ject**, ob**ject**ion, re**ject** ab**ject** = "away + thrown" = extremely bad

(Continued)

Root	Meaning	Examples
jur	law *or*	**jur**y, **jur**isdiction
	swear	ab**jur**e = "away + swear" = renounce or reject
		ad**jur**e = "toward + swear" = command, urge
leg	word *or*	**lec**ture, mono**log**ue, chrono**log**ical, **lex**icon
lex	speak *or*	neo**log**ism = "new + word" = new word or expression
lect	read *or*	eu**log**y = speech of praise (often after death)
log	study	
locu	speak	circum**locu**tion = "around + speak" = wordiness or evasion in speech
loqu		e**locu**tion = "out + speak" = art of speaking well in public
		loquacious = very talkative
luc	light *or*	**luc**id = clear, sane, full of light
lus	shine *or*	e**luc**idate = "out + shine" = make clear, explain
	clear	trans**luc**ent = "through + shine" = permitting (some) passage of light
		pe**luc**id = "through + clear" = absolutely clear
		lack**lus**ter = dull, lacking brilliance
meter	measure	**met**ric, alti**meter**, peri**meter**
metr		metric = standard of measurement
		altimeter = "high + measure" = instrument to measure altitude (height above ground)
		perimeter = "around + measure" = distance measured around something
mit	send	dis**miss**, e**mit**, trans**mit**
miss		**miss**ive = letter, written message
		re**miss** = "back + sent" = negligent, careless, lax
morph	shape	a**morph**ous = "without + shape" = shapeless
		meta**morph**ose = "change + shape" = transform
nom	name	**nom**inate = appoint to a position
nym		pseudo**nym** = "false + name" = a fake name used by an author
path	feeling	anti**path**y = "against + feeling" = strong dislike
		pathetic = arousing pity
pel	drive *or*	ex**pel**, pro**pel**
puls	push	dis**pel** = "away + drive" = scatter, make vanish
		com**pel**ling = "together + drive" = convincing, forceful, attention-grabbing

Root	Meaning	Examples
phob	fear	acro**phob**ia = "high + fear" = fear of heights
phon	sound	mega**phon**e, tele**phon**e, **phon**ics
		homo**phon**e = "same + sound" = a word pronounced like another word
		caco**phon**ous = "bad + sound" = unpleasant sounding
		eu**phon**y = "good + sound" = pleasing sound (usually of words)
port	carry	**port**er, trans**port**ation, im**port**, ex**port**, de**port**
pos	put	im**pos**e, ex**pos**e, op**pos**e, op**pon**ent, pro**pon**ent
pon		de**pos**e = "down + put" = remove a leader, or take testimony
		superim**pos**e = "over + on + put" = place over
prob	prove *or*	**prob**e, **prov**e, im**prov**e, ap**prov**e
prov	test	**prob**ity = honesty, integrity
		re**prov**e = "back + prove" = scold, admonish, express disapproval
rog	ask	inter**rog**ation, inter**rog**atory
		pre**rog**ative = "before + ask" = special right
		ar**rog**ate = "toward + ask" = claim or take (without the right)
		ab**rog**ate = "away + ask" = abolish, nullify (a law or rule)
sanct	holy	**sanct**uary = holy place
		sanctify = "holy + make" = make holy
		sacro**sanct** = holy, untouchable
		sanctimonious = hypocritically or falsely holy
sci	know	**sci**ence
		pre**sci**ent = "before + know" = knowing ahead of time, able to predict events
		omni**sci**ence = "all + know" = state of knowing everything
scrib **script**	write	**scrib**ble, **scrib**e, **script**, pre**scrib**e
sec	cut	**sec**tion, **sec**tor, inter**sect**
sect		bi**sect** = "two + cut" = cut in half
		sect = a subdivision or segment of a group, often of a religion
sed	sit	super**sed**e = "above + sit" = replace, transcend by being better

(Continued)

Root	Meaning	Examples
sequ **secu** **sic**	follow	**sequ**ence, con**sequ**ence, con**secu**tive
		extrin**sic** = "outside + follow" = external to something's nature
		intrin**sic** = "inside + follow" = internal to something's nature
		ob**sequ**ious = "toward + follow" = overly obedient, submissive, flattering
simil **simul**	similar	as**simil**ate = "toward + similar" = make or become a similar part of something
		similitude = likeness, correspondence between two things
		simulacrum = image, semblance
son	sound	**son**ar, **son**ic
		sonorous = full of rich sound
		dis**son**ance = "apart + sound" = discord, clash of sounds
spec **spect** **spic**	look	**spec**tacle, in**spect**, retro**spect**
		circum**spect** = "around + look" = cautious, prudent
		per**spic**acious = "through + look" = able to perceive hidden truth
tain **ten** **tend**	have or hold or stretch or thin	abs**tain** = "away + hold" = refrain from
		re**tain**, con**tain**, ob**tain**, ex**tend**
		tenable = able to be held or maintained
		tenacity = courage, persistence, ability to hold fast
		dis**tend** = "away + stretch" = bloat, swell, expand
		tenuous = thin, weak
		at**ten**uate = "toward + thin" = make or become thinner or weaker
theo **the**	God	a**the**ist = "not + God" = someone who doesn't believe in God
		poly**the**ist = "many + God" = someone who believes in many gods
		apo**theo**sis = "from + God" = elevation to godlike status, or something that has that status
tract	drag or draw or pull	**tract**or, at**tract**, con**tract**, de**tract**, ex**tract**, re**tract**
		tractable = able to be led, obedient, easily managed
		abs**tract**ed = "away + drawn" = withdrawn into one's mind
trud	push or	in**trud**e, ex**trud**e
trus	thrust	unob**trus**ive = "not + against + push" = not noticeable or attention-drawing
		abs**trus**e = "away + push" = hard to comprehend

Root	Meaning	Examples
veh **vect**	carry	**veh**icle, con**vect**ion, **vect**or
		in**vect**ive = "in + carry" = bitter criticism, denunciation
		vehement = "carried (away) + mind" = passionate, nearly violent
ven **vent**	come	inter**ven**e, pre**vent**, in**vent**, e**vent**, ad**vent**ure, **vent**ure
		pro**ven**ance = "forward + come" = source, or history of ownership
		contra**ven**e = "against + come" = oppose, violate, or contradict
ver	true	**ver**ify = "true + make" = confirm as true
		veracity = truthfulness or truth
		a**ver** = "toward + true" = assert, declare
vert **vers**	turn	re**vert**, extro**vert**, intro**vert**, ad**vers**e, inad**vert**ent, a**vers**ion, a**vert**, in**vert**
		versatile = able to adapt easily, ready for many uses
		di**vert** = "away + turn" = turn aside or distract
		contro**vert** = "against + turn" = dispute in argument, engage in contro**vers**y
voc	voice *or* call	**voc**al, in**voc**ation
		equi**voc**ate = "equal + voice" = say something open to more than one interpretation in order to mislead or to avoid commitment
		vociferous = "voice + carry" = shouting loudly and angrily
vol	will	bene**vol**ence = "good + will" = kindness, readiness to do good for others
		male**vol**ent = "bad + will" = wishing harm, ready to do evil
		voluntary = done of one's own free will

Part II: Prefixes

You must be even more careful with prefixes than with roots. Certain prefixes have relatively stable meanings (e.g., *bene-* pretty much always means "good"), but other prefixes, especially short ones that correspond to prepositions, can take on a variety of different meanings. The sense of the whole word is often unpredictable. Take a simple word: *describe* = "from + write." It is not obvious how the particular meaning of *describe* originates from the combination of the prefix *de-* and the root *scrib*.

Even if the meanings of the prefix and the root remain stable, the word itself may still take an unpredictable turn. For instance, *polygraph* = "many + write." How we would work out from the roots that a *polygraph* is a lie-detector test (which writes down lots of physiological data at once) is anyone's guess. Do not simply rely on knowing the prefix and the root separately—always learn the modern English meaning of the word itself.

15

Most of the examples in the following list can also be found in the roots list so that you can see both the root and the prefix in action and reinforce the word in your memory.

Prefix	Meaning	Examples
a- **an-** **ana-**	not *or* without	**a**theist = "not + God" = someone who doesn't believe in God
		agnostic = "not + know" = someone who isn't sure (often about God's existence)
		anarchy = "not + ruler" = chaos, lack of government
		anachronism = "not + time" = something out of place in time
		amorphous = "without + shape" = shapeless
ab- **abs-**	away from	**ab**normal, **ab**sent, **ab**duct
		abstain = "away + hold" = refrain from
		abstracted = "away + drawn" = withdrawn into one's mind
		abjure = "away + swear" = renounce or reject
		abject = "away + thrown" = in a low, hopeless, depressed condition
		abrogate = "away + propose law" = abolish, nullify (a law or rule)
		abstruse = "away + push" = hard to comprehend
		abstemious = "away + liquor" = moderate in appetite or drinking
ad- **(can drop *d* and double next letter)** **ac-, ag-, as- at-, etc.**	to *or* toward	**ad**here = "to + stick" = stick to
		adjure = "toward + swear" = command, urge
		accrete = "toward + grow" = grow or pile up bit by bit
		aggregate = "toward + flock" = collect together
		assimilate = "toward + similar" = make or become a similar part of something
		arrogate = "toward + ask" = claim or take (without the right)
		attenuate = "toward + thin" = make or become thinner or weaker
ante-	before	**ante**cedent = "before + go" = earlier event or cause
		antediluvian = "before + flood" = ancient, primitive
anti- **ant-**	against *or* opposite	**anti**biotic = "against + life" = chemical that kills bacteria
		antipathy = "against + feeling" = strong dislike
		antagonism = "against + struggle" = opposition, active hostility
auto-	self	**auto**graph = "self + write" = sign one's own name
		autocratic = "self + ruler" = like an absolute ruler or tyrant
		autonomous = "self + law" = independent, self-contained

15

Prefix	Meaning	Examples
be-	thoroughly *or* affect with	**be**grudge = "thoroughly + complain" = give unwillingly
		beguile = "affect with + trick" = deceive, divert in an attractive way
		benighted = "thoroughly + night" = unenlightened, in figurative darkness
		beseech = "thoroughly + seek" = beg, implore
		besiege = "thoroughly + blockade" = surround, press upon
		besmirch = "affect with + dirt" = make dirty
bene- **ben-**	good	**bene**diction = "good + say" = blessing
		beneficent = "good + do" = doing good for others
		benevolence = "good + will" = kindness, readiness to do good for others
		benign = "good + birth" = favorable, gentle, harmless
bi-	two	**bi**sect = "two + cut" = cut in half
		bifurcate = "two + fork" = split into two branches
caco-	bad	**caco**phonous = "bad + sound" = unpleasant sounding
circum-	around	**circum**ambulate = "around + walk" = walk around in a circle
		circumlocution = "around + speak" = wordiness or evasion in speech
		circumspect = "around + look" = cautious, prudent
con- **com-** **co-**	with *or* together	**con**tract, **con**tain, **con**duct
		con**greg**ate = "together + flock" = gather together
		cohesive = "together + stick" = sticking or fitting together
		compelling = "together + drive" = convincing, forceful, attention-grabbing
		confluence = "together + flow" = a flowing together
		cognoscente (pl. cognoscenti) = "with + know" = expert in a subject
contra- **contro-** **counter-**	against	**contra**dict
		contraband = "against + command" = illegal goods
		countervail = "against + worth" = compensate for, counteract, oppose
		contravene = "against + come" = oppose, violate, contradict
		controvert = "against + turn" = dispute in argument, engage in controversy

(Continued)

 413

Prefix	Meaning	Examples
de-	from *or*	**de**fame, **de**odorize, **de**flect, **de**tract
	away *or*	**de**duce = "away + lead" = determine from general principles
	down	**de**cadent = "away + fall" = in a state of decline, often self-indulgent
		derivative = "away + stream" = originating from something else, lacking originality
		depose = "down + put" = remove a leader, or take testimony
di-	two *or*	**dia**meter, **dia**gonal
dia-	through *or*	**di**chotomy = division into two opposing parts
	across *or*	**dia**gnosis = "through + know" = identification of (medical) causes and issues
	between	
		diachronic = "through + time" = relating to change over time
dis-	away *or*	**dis**allow, **dis**respect, **dis**miss, **dis**illusion, **di**vide
dys-	not *or*	**dis**pel = "away + drive" = scatter, make vanish
di-	bad	**di**vert = "away + turn" = turn aside or distract
		dissonance = "bad + sound" = discord, clash of sounds
		distend = "away + stretch" = bloat, swell, expand
		diffidence = "not + faith" = hesitant, lacking in self-confidence
		digress = "away + go" = deviate from subject
		dystopia = "bad + utopia" = future/imaginary world
duo-	two	**duo**poly = "two + sell" = condition in which there are only two sellers
en-	in	**en**demic = "in + people" = native to a population
eu-	good	**eu**logize = "good + speak" = praise highly (often after death)
		euphony = "good + sound" = pleasing sound (usually of words)
ex-	out *or*	**e**mit, **ex**pel, **ex**ceed, **ex**it, **e**ject, **ex**port
e-	away *or*	**ex**alted = "out + high" = raised high
ef-	from	**ex**cision = "out + cut" = act of cutting out, removing
		elocution = "out + speak" = art of speaking well in public
		egregious = "outside + flock" = conspicuously bad, flagrant
		elucidate = "out + shine" = make clear, explain
		effluvium = "out + flow" = by-product, exhalation (often bad)

15

Prefix	Meaning	Examples
exter- extra- extr-	outside of	**exter**ior, **extr**eme **extra**curricular = "outside + course" = an activity pursued at school outside of normal course studies **extr**insic = "outside + follow" = external to something's nature
hetero-	other or different	**hetero**geneous = "different + kind" = consisting of diverse parts
homo-	same	**homo**phone = "same + sound" = a word pronounced like another word **homo**geneous = "same + kind" = consisting of one substance
hyper-	above or over	**hyper**sensitive, **hyper**active **hyper**bole = "above + throw" = exaggeration
hypo-	below or under	**hypo**allergenic **hypo**thesis = "under + thesis" = tentative assumption to explore **hypo**dermic = "under + skin" = injected beneath the skin
in- im-	in or into or on	**in**spect, **im**port, **in**ject **in**cisive = "into + cut" = cutting to the heart of a matter, direct **in**duct = "in + lead" = admit as a member
in- im-	not	**in**credible, **im**possible, **im**penetrable, **in**evitable
infra-	below	**infra**red, **infra**structure
inter- intro-	between	**inter**national, **inter**vene, **inter**ject, **intro**spect, **intro**vert, **intro**duce **inter**polate = "inside + polish" = fill in missing pieces, words, or data
intra- intr-	within or into	**intra**muscular, **intra**mural **intr**insic = "inside + follow" = internal to something's nature
magn-	big or great	**magn**ificent **magn**animity = "great + spirit" = nobility of spirit
mal- male-	bad	**mal**adjusted **male**volent = "bad + will" = wishing harm, ready to do evil **male**ficent = "bad + do" = doing harm or evil **mal**adroit = "bad + adroit (skillful)" = lacking skill
mega- megalo-	big or great or million	**mega**phone **megalo**mania = "great + mad" = insane belief that one is all-powerful

(Continued)

Prefix	Meaning	Examples
meta-	beyond or change	**meta**morphose = "change + shape" = transform
micro-	small	**micro**scope, **micro**processor
mis-	bad or hate	**mis**apply, **mis**take, **mis**interpret
		misanthropy = "hate + human" = hatred of humankind
		misogyny = "hate + women" = hatred of women
mono-	one	**mono**culture
		monograph = "one + write" = a written report or paper on a narrow subject
		monopoly = "one + sell" = condition in which there is only one seller
multi-	many	**multi**ple, **multi**national
		multifarious = "many + places" = diverse, varied
neo-	new	**neo**logism = "new + word" = new word or expression
		neophyte = "new + planted" = beginner, novice
non-	not	**non**sensical, **non**profit
		nondescript = "not + described" = lacking distinctive qualities
		nonpareil = "not + equal" = without equal
ob- (can drop *b* and double next letter) **oc-**, etc.	in front of or against or toward	**ob**jection
		obdurate = "against + hard" = hard of heart, stubborn
		occlude = "against + close" = block off or conceal
		obsequious = "toward + follow" = overly obedient, submissive, flattering
omni-	all	**omni**present, **omni**potent
		omniscience = "all + know" = state of knowing everything
pan-	all	**pan**demic = "all + people" = something affecting everyone, usually a disease
para-	beside	**para**llel, **para**phrase
per-	through or detrimental to	**per**mit
		perspicacious = "through + look" = able to perceive hidden truth
		perambulate = "through + walk" = walk through, inspect
		pellucid = "through + clear" = absolutely clear
		perfervid = "through + boil" = overexcited, overwrought
		perfidious = "detrimental + faith" = disloyal, treacherous

15

Prefix	Meaning	Examples
peri-	around	**peri**meter
		peripheral = "around + carry" = on the outskirts, not central
		peripatetic = "around + walk" = moving or walking from place to place
poly-	many	**poly**technical, **poly**gon
		polytheist = "many + god" = someone who believes in many gods
		polyglot = "many + tongue" = someone who speaks many languages
pre-	before	**pre**cede
		precedent = "before + go" = earlier example
		prerogative = "before + ask" = special right
		preclude = "before + close" = prevent, rule out beforehand
		prescient = "before + know" = knowing ahead of time, able to predict events
pro-	forward *or* before *or* for	**pro**ponent
		prognosticate = "before + know" = predict, foretell
		provenance = "before + come" = source, or history of ownership
re-	back *or* again	**re**do, **re**state, **re**flect, **re**tract, **re**ject, **re**cede
		remiss = "back + sent" = negligent, careless, lax
		recidivism = "back + fall" = tendency to relapse to earlier behavior or crime
retro-	backward	**retro**active, **retro**spect
		retrograde = "backward + go" = moving backward
sub-	below *or* under	**sub**standard, **sub**marine
		subordinate = "below + order" = in a lower rank, controlled by higher ranks
		subliminal = "below + threshold" = below the level of consciousness
super-	above *or* over	**super**natural, **super**ior
		superfluous = "over + flow" = unnecessary, wasteful
		superficial = on the surface
		superimpose = "over + on + put" = place over
		supersede = "above + sit" = replace, transcend by being better

(Continued)

15

Ⓜ 417

Prefix	Meaning	Examples
syn-	together *or* with	**syn**thesis = "together + thesis" = combination of ideas
		syncretism = "together + Cretan cities" = fusion of ideas and practices
		synoptic = "together + eye" = taking a comprehensive view
trans- **tra-**	across *or* beyond *or* through	**trans**fer, **tra**jectory, **trans**mit, **trans**portation
		transgression = "across + step" = violation of a law or rule
		translucent = "through + shine" = permitting (some) passage of light
un-	not	**un**happy
		unobtrusive = "not + against + push" = not noticeable or attention-drawing
uni-	one	**uni**form, **uni**cycle
un-		**un**animous = "one + spirit" = in complete agreement

Part III: Suffixes

Fortunately, suffixes are much more stable in meaning than roots or prefixes, meaning you know most of them already—just by speaking and reading in English! However, it is still worth looking over this list, in particular to examine how suffixes often change one part of speech into another.

Suffix	Description	Part of Speech	Made From	Examples
-able **-ible**	able to be X	adjective	verb	think**able**, desir**able**, inconceiv**able**, frang**ible**, feas**ible**
-al **-ial** **-ile**	relating to X	adjective	noun *or* verb	trivi**al**, critic**al**, lab**ile**, duct**ile**, versat**ile**
-ance **-ancy** **-ence** **-ency**	state *or* process of doing X *or* being X	noun (abstract)	verb *or* adjective	intellig**ence**, flipp**ancy**, decad**ence**, exorbit**ance**, despond**ency**
-ant **-ent**	doing X	adjective *or* noun	verb	accord**ant**, account**ant**, cogniz**ant**, differ**ent**, intransig**ent**, ferv**ent**
-ar **-ary**	related to X	adjective	noun	sol**ar**, stell**ar**, pol**ar**

Suffix	Descriptiom	Part of Speech	Made From	Examples
-ate (usually pronounced like *ate*) **-ite**	do X	verb	root	interrog**ate**, prevaric**ate**, mut**ate**, ign**ite**, exped**ite**
-ate (usually pronounced like *it*) **-ite**	formed by doing X *or* related to doing X	noun *or* adjective	verb	aggreg**ate**, insubordin**ate**, perquis**ite**, requis**ite**
-dom	state of being X *or* condition related to X	noun (abstract)	noun *or* adjective	free**dom**, fief**dom**, wis**dom**
-er **-or**	doer of X	noun (person)	verb	speak**er**, runn**er**, wander**er**
-fic	making into X *or* causing X	adjective	noun *or* adjective	horri**fic**, beati**fic**, proli**fic**, sopori**fic**
-fy **-ify**	make into X cause X	verb	noun *or* adjective	mag**nify**, de**ify**, indem**nify**, oss**ify**, re**ify**
-ful	filled with X	adjective	noun	bounti**ful**, beauti**ful**, plenti**ful**, fret**ful**, art**ful**
-ic **-iac**	relating to X	adjective *or* noun	noun *or* verb	man**ic**, man**iac**, asept**ic**, bombast**ic**
-ification	process of making into X	noun (action)	noun *or* adjective	desert**ification**, ram**ification**, beaut**ification**, ed**ification**
-ine	relating to X	adjective	noun *or* verb	saturn**ine**, mar**ine**, sal**ine**, clandest**ine**
-ish	similar to X	adjective	noun *or* adjective	redd**ish**, mul**ish**, fiend**ish**, lout**ish**
-ism	system *or* characteristic of X	noun (abstract)	noun *or* adjective *or* verb	capital**ism**, social**ism**, commun**ism**, stoic**ism**, anachron**ism**, euphem**ism**

(Continued)

Suffix	Descriptiom	Part of Speech	Made From	Examples
-ist -istic	characteristic of X or a person who espouses X	adjective or noun	noun or adjective	capital**ist**, social**ist**, commun**ist**, anachron**istic**, euphem**istic**
-ite	native or adherent of X	noun	noun or adjective	anchor**ite**, Ludd**ite**, sybar**ite**
-ity -ty	state or quality of being X or doing X	noun (abstract)	adjective or verb	polar**ity**, certain**ty**, convex**ity**, perplex**ity**
-ive -ative	tending toward the action of X	adjective	verb or noun	exclus**ive**, act**ive**, cohes**ive**, authorit**ative**, evas**ive**
-ize -ise	make into X	verb	adjective or noun	eulog**ize**, polar**ize**, scrutin**ize**, lion**ize**, advert**ise**, improv**ise**
-ization -isation	process of making into X	noun (action)	adjective	character**ization**, polar**ization**, lion**ization**, improv**isation**
-less	without X	adjective	noun	harm**less**, guile**less**, feck**less**
-ment	state or result of doing X	noun	verb	develop**ment**, judg**ment**, punish**ment**
-ory	characteristic of doing X or a place for doing X	adjective or noun	verb	refract**ory**, sav**ory**, deposit**ory**, compuls**ory**, mandat**ory**
-ous -ious -ose	characteristic of being X or doing X	adjective	verb or noun	carnivor**ous**, dev**ious**, numer**ous**, melliflu**ous**, mendac**ious**, verb**ose**
-tion -ation -ion	process or result of doing X	noun (action)	verb	pollu**tion**, cre**ation**, destruc**tion**
-tude	state or quality of being X	noun (abstract)	adjective	soli**tude**, vicissi**tude**, pulchri**tude**, desue**tude**

15

Acknowledgments

As with most accomplishments, there were many people involved in the creation of the book you are holding. First and foremost is Zeke Vanderhoek, the founder of Manhattan Prep. Zeke was a lone tutor in New York when he started the company in 2000. Now, 18 years later, the company has instructors and offices nationwide and contributes to the studies and successes of thousands of GRE, GMAT, LSAT, and SAT students each year.

Our Manhattan Prep Strategy Guides are based on the continuing experiences of our instructors and students. We are particularly indebted to our instructors Stacey Koprince, Dave Mahler, Liz Ghini Moliski, Emily Meredith Sledge, and Tommy Wallach for their hard work on this edition. Dan McNaney and Cathy Huang provided their design expertise to make the books as user-friendly as possible, and Liz Krisher made sure all the moving pieces came together at just the right time. Beyond providing additions and edits for this book, Chris Ryan and Noah Teitelbaum continue to be the driving force behind all of our curriculum efforts. Their leadership is invaluable. Finally, thank you to all of the Manhattan Prep students who have provided input and feedback over the years. This book wouldn't be half of what it is without your voice.